WOMEN

AND THE

FIGHT TO

BUILD A

JUST

ECONOMY

FAIR SHAKE

Naomi Cahn,
June Carbone,
and
Nancy Levit

SIMON & SCHUSTER
New York   London   Toronto   Sydney   New Delhi

1230 Avenue of the Americas
New York, NY 10020

First Simon & Schuster hardcover edition May 2024

SIMON & SCHUSTER and colophon are registered
trademarks of Simon & Schuster, LLC

Simon & Schuster: Celebrating 100 Years of Publishing in 2024

For information about special discounts for bulk purchases,
please contact Simon & Schuster Special Sales at
1-866-506-1949 or business@simonandschuster.com.

The Simon & Schuster Speakers Bureau can bring authors to
your live event. For more information or to book an event, contact
the Simon & Schuster Speakers Bureau at 1-866-248-3049
or visit our website at www.simonspeakers.com.

Interior design by Lewelin Polanco

Manufactured in the United States of America

1 3 5 7 9 10 8 6 4 2

Library of Congress Cataloging-in-Publication Data
has been applied for.

ISBN 978-1-9821-1512-8
ISBN 978-1-9821-1514-2 (ebook)

To our families.

NRC, JRC, NEL

Contents

FAIR SHAKE

Introduction

A. J. Vandermeyden had every reason to believe she would succeed at Tesla. She was passionate about Tesla's mission: the effort to disrupt the automobile industry by producing an emission-free electric car that could be sold on a mass-market basis to the world. She was so inspired by Tesla CEO Elon Musk's transformative vision that, in 2013, the then 30-year-old Vandermeyden parked herself on a bench outside Tesla's main headquarters in Palo Alto, California—and waited. When she saw someone sporting a Tesla T-shirt, she introduced herself and delivered her "please hire me" speech to him. Against all odds, it worked. She started at Tesla a few weeks later as a Headquarters Product Specialist in the Inside Sales department.

Once at Tesla, she earned her promotions the way the men did—by hustling. She had an undergraduate degree from UCLA in the biological sciences, experience in pharmaceutical sales, and no background whatsoever in automobile production. She got steady promotions, and when the head of an automotive manufacturing unit learned she had worked for twenty-six hours straight on a project, he wanted her commitment and drive on his team. She had landed a dream job as a manufacturing engineer.

The General Assembly Department that Vandermeyden joined produced Tesla's world-changing cars. The atmosphere was intense. "Tesla is one of the most innovative companies in the world," one employee wrote in a blogpost, but that same employee also explained that it is often like "working for a company of the future under working conditions of the past." Not only was the pressure unrelenting, but Vandermeyden also maintained that she was subject to "pervasive harassment." It wasn't unusual for her to be the only woman in meetings with forty to fifty men. When Vandermeyden became a manufacturing engineer and was on the factory floor, the men greeted her with catcalls, whistling, and inappropriate name-calling.

But in the end it took more than sexism to do her in. It was her commitment to the mission. She discovered inadequacies in Tesla's quality testing of cars that others had missed. She even suggested a way to fix the problem. That's when her career appears to have collided with the unspoken rules of the "winner take all" (WTA) economy. In the complaint she subsequently filed against Tesla, she charged that the automaker had retaliated against her for complaints about discrimination and the company's quality-testing flaws.

The WTA economy reserves a disproportionate share of institutional power and rewards for those at the top. Elon Musk could be the poster child for this new economy. The not-so-secret key to his success, after all, has been the audaciousness of his goals and his drive to do whatever is necessary to achieve them. The WTA economy rewards Musk's outsized ambitions—and his ability to impose them on his workers. Under Musk, Tesla reached a trillion-dollar valuation (that for a time made Musk the richest man in the world) not just by designing an innovative car but also by setting seemingly impossible production goals and ultimately producing more cars in a shorter period than industry analysts thought possible. Musk admitted that the company was able to do so by allowing quality issues to remain during the production ramp-up. A profile of Musk and his methods noted that "[t]hose who do not wish to toil under such conditions know where to find the door." In the WTA economy, Musk, who like Vandermeyden had no previous experience with automobiles, could create a new company; channel his personal ambitions through it; run roughshod over workers, labor laws, and securities regulations; and emerge victorious so long as he delivered what Wall Street valued.

After three years at Tesla, Vandermeyden decided that she had had enough and she sued Tesla in the fall of 2016, claiming sex discrimination, sexual harassment, and retaliation for her whistle-blowing about the car-testing inadequacies. According to Tesla, the company investigated Vandermeyden's claims. A spokesperson said, "After we carefully considered the facts on multiple occasions and were absolutely convinced that Ms. Vandermeyden's claims were illegitimate, we had no choice but to end her employment at Tesla." Ultimately, after Tesla insisted on arbitration—ensuring that Vandermeyden would never have a chance to present her case in court or to the public—the parties dismissed the case, reportedly because of a confidential settlement.

This book started with a question: Why, in an era of supposed gender equality, have women stalled in the American workplace? The more we dug into the issue, the more we discovered stories about women like Vandermeyden: talented, driven women who compete on the same terms as men but still do not succeed on the same terms as men.

The three of us are law professors. If you combine all our efforts, we have been studying women, employment, and the family for over a hundred years. Among us, we have written more than twenty books. And yet, while working in our respective positions at universities across the country, we discovered something we did not expect to find. Despite the tremendous gains of the women's movement over the past half-century, the gap between men's and women's economic performance in the United States is *not* closing.

The statistics that shocked us most—and that persuaded us to write this book—involved the gap between male and female wages.

When we started our research more than six years ago, the overall figures showed that women were, ever so slowly, gaining on men and the wage gap was narrowing. This seemed like promising news, except that after the mid-1990s the only reason women appeared to be gaining ground on men had nothing to do with women's progress; it was

almost entirely due to the fact that wages for blue-collar men were falling dramatically during that same period. Then when we looked at the
numbers for college graduates, we found that the gender gap in wages
was *increasing*. At first, we struggled to believe our own findings. We
were so used to hearing that women had become the better-educated
sex and that education was the key to advancement. And that *used to be
true*; in the 1970s and '80s, women's wages were gaining on men's, and
those gains were associated with more education. By 2000, women had
become the better-educated sex, earning more bachelor's and master's
degrees than men, and since 2006, more doctorate degrees. Yet, it was in
these groups—the ranks of college graduates as a group and the highest
earners among college graduates, in particular—where gender disparities had grown at the fastest rate. In 2019, a Goldman Sachs study received a lot of press for its claim that if present trends continued, women
would not catch up with men in terms of wages for another hundred or
so years. By the time we finished the book, we realized that if *present
trends continue*, women would *never* catch up; indeed, the most recent
reports bear out those predictions: they show the gender wage gap, as
a whole between men and women, increased between 2019 and 2022.

We considered the conventional explanations for women's lack of
progress—explanations we have written about for our entire careers. The
time-honored answer to why gender inequality exists is women's family
responsibilities. That the reason for women's dropout rates during the
COVID-19 pandemic or women's failure to achieve pay parity with men
is that women succumb to their "natural" instincts to stay home with
their babies. This conventional answer explains today's disparities in the
same terms as those of yore: women, by nature, simply make different
choices than men. They care more about being home with their children
than men do. They turn down opportunities for overtime because childcare costs more than any gains in pay. And when couples realize that
fathers and mothers cannot both work sixty-hour weeks, women are still
the more likely parent to call it quits on the partnership track.

The role of family responsibilities has always explained a significant part of the wage gap, and it continues to do so today. The gender pay gap for women ages 25 to 34 is smaller than for women from 35 to 54—the peak childrearing years, when mothers make different career choices than fathers to accommodate their family responsibilities. Women make up 87 percent of registered nurses, but while they earn the same base pay as male nurses, they still earn less overall than the men, particularly the male nurses who are willing to work shifts with irregular hours that pay more or who take advantage of tighter job markets by switching jobs or bargaining for higher pay. The only hope for progress, in accordance with this analysis, would involve persuading women to be greedier. Women's futures would depend on their ability to "lean in" and to find the right househusbands to care for their children—or (as many successful professional women are doing) choose not to have children at all.

The problem with this line of thinking—of focusing on women's choices to assume family responsibilities and not to lean in—is that these factors have always held women back; they don't explain why the gendered pay gap for college graduates—the group with the greatest access to quality childcare—increased after the early nineties or why Black women, who have long managed to a greater degree than white women to juggle work and family obligations, remain among one of the most disadvantaged groups in society. The United States has lagged behind much of the rest of the developed world in its provision for childcare, paid family leave, and universal pre-K education ever since President Richard Nixon vetoed a comprehensive early childhood bill *in 1971*. The lack of childcare did not get distinctively worse after the nineties, particularly for the upper-middle-class women whose incomes have most lagged behind those of comparably educated men. Indeed, the gender wage gap, which did not change during the COVID-19 pandemic, when many women left the job market as schools closed and childcare became harder to find, increased with the recovery. And it increased despite the facts that college graduate women led the movement back into the post-pandemic labor market and that many low-income jobs disproportionately staffed by women were back up to pre-pandemic levels. Yes, childcare explains a large part of the wage gap, but it explains very little of what changed after 1990. And it cannot explain what happened to Vandermeyden, a woman without children, who was known for her willingness to put in long hours.

The second conventional explanation for women's lack of progress is women's occupational choices. This account states that women are drawn to careers that simply don't pay well: creative fields like publishing, "passion" jobs like teaching, and those in the nonprofit sector or care work like nursing. Here, the answers are closer to the mark. For most people, men and women alike, wages had been stagnating since the 1970s. But for the top 1 percent, they had been increasing steadily, and during the 1990s, annual wages for the top 1 percent grew nine times more than for the bottom 90 percent. Wage growth in selected parts of the economy occurred along with the increases at the top; tech, finance, the C-suite, and the top ranks of many professions enjoyed staggering wage gains while the mid-level ranks of most occupations, even well-paying ones, did not.

All the highest-paying sectors are male dominated, and the fact that women are more likely to be schoolteachers than computer scientists does explain a substantial part of the gender gap. Still, women's greater inclination to enroll in nursing school rather than in engineering, which has long been true, is not the whole story. Instead, it's helpful to consider why the disparities between men's and women's occupational choices increased just as the wage disparities skyrocketed. For example, we were surprised to learn that the percentage of female teachers has been increasing since the 1980s and reached 77 percent in 2018 (the same percentage as a century ago). In the early nineties, teachers' salaries started to fall behind those of other workers with comparable education and skills. It didn't take long before the men left the field. We were also surprised to discover that the percentage of women in computer science peaked in the early eighties, then fell during tech's incredible boom years. In finance, women won hard-fought gains through the nineties and increased their percentage of MBAs up to a quarter of the total by 2000, only to see their representation on Wall Street fall just as Wall Street salaries began to soar. And for those women who stuck it out, the gender gaps in wages stayed high; six of the top seven categories with the largest disparities in what men and women are paid involve finance, and the largest entry-level pay gaps are in tech. It turns out that the parts of the economy that most pride themselves on being a meritocracy have starker differences between men and women than anywhere else.

We came to realize that something more than women's initial choices are at play. After all, women's representation in the high-powered Fortune 500 CEO positions remains at a miniscule number—just over 10 percent—despite the fact that women's numbers have risen steadily to 48 percent of entry-level management candidates. In our field, where women often constitute half our law school classes, and where they start out getting paid only slightly less than men, they are vastly underrepresented in the most highly paid law firm positions. In 2005, 8 percent of law firms reported that their highest-paid attorney was a woman. In 2023, that number fell: only 2 percent of law firms said that their highest-paid attorney was a woman. While the percentage of women in such positions grew over the last fifteen years (16 percent in 2006, up to 22 percent in 2020), the larger percentage of women making it into the top legal ranks did nothing to offset the increasing gap in salaries. Since the recovery from the financial crisis, women have been making modest gains, but that's not the point. In male-dominated occupations where men earn the most, women are at a disadvantage. The female-dominated occupations have lost ground to the male-dominated occupations. And many are being forced out altogether: women like Vandermeyden who enter tech are twice as likely to leave as their male counterparts. The different occupational choices theory does not explain why.

That led to a third explanation: women's failure "to lean in," to take risks, to do what it takes to succeed. Almost everywhere we looked, however, and in almost every story we will tell in this book, we saw stories like Vandermeyden's. Women who *did* lean in—by working long hours, questioning their bosses, insisting on raises, or objecting to sexual harassment—found that leaning in might mean getting booted out. The more prosaic stories involve the women who found they did not get the same raises as the men and complained; retaliation often followed. The more striking examples come from industries like finance, where the ability to break legal or ethical rules and get away with it can be handsomely rewarded. Women are substantially less likely than men to engage in financial misconduct, and they cause their employers smaller dollar losses when they do. Yet, they are also substantially more likely to be fired for misconduct and substantially less likely to be rehired. Leaning in takes a number of different forms, and many prove disastrous for women workers.

The "lean in" thesis also overlooks some of the women who are most likely to stand up for themselves. Today, the biggest beneficiaries of the union movement are women, especially women of color and those from other underrepresented groups. Unions have "leaned in," standing up for their workers' rights, producing smaller gender disparities than other workplaces, and winning benefits such as health insurance; 72 percent of Black women union members have health insurance in contrast with less than 50 percent of nonunion Black women workers. Women in nonunion workplaces, on the other hand, not only earn less than union members but also have less control over their working conditions. Yet, the war against unions has taken its toll, and there are fewer union jobs available than there once were, despite the renewed energy that has gone into organizing teachers, Walmart employees, and other workers stuck in low-wage jobs that remain disproportionately female. Throughout the economy, those who lean in, especially on behalf of marginalized workers, become targets. The story of unions is a prime example of the threats, intimidation, and legal changes that suppress collective activities.

All this suggests that the most conventional explanations of all—misogyny, discrimination, and sexual harassment—do provide part of the explanation. Feminist scholars document the catcalls, mansplaining, insults, and harassment (sexual and otherwise) that continue to demean many working women. Outright misogyny has increased online and in the political sphere. Still, we found virtually no evidence that these factors explain the changing employment picture since the nineties. Indeed, women are no longer excluded from workplaces on a wholesale basis. Some CEOs have lost their jobs because of inappropriate sexual behavior, and courts are holding companies themselves liable for failing to investigate claims of sexual harassment. These successes, no matter how scattered, are positive signs.

Ultimately, what we learned in considering cases like Vandermeyden's is that something quite different was going on from the conventional explanations. Instead, we discovered that the new "winner take all" (WTA) approach to business—rooted in the Reagan-era tax breaks and deregulation of the 1980s that gained ground in the 1990s—is to blame for undermining women's prospects for achieving equality in our lifetimes.

What do we mean by WTA? The classic economic meaning of the term "winner take all" is a system that provides a disproportionately high payoff for a single dominant player. Michael Jordan in his prime, for example, could single-handedly determine the outcome of a game to a greater degree than the number two basketball player of his era. It should not therefore be surprising he was also the first NBA player to sign a contract for more than $20 million. In business, "winning" may similarly mean dominating an entire economic sector. When Microsoft, for example, beat out Apple, making Windows the dominant desktop operating system of its time, the payoff for the company in 2000 was a market valuation of $500 billion, compared to $4.8 billion for Apple.

We are using the term "WTA economy" in a somewhat different way. We see the critical shift in the new economy as the ability of those at the top to take a much larger share of institutional resources for themselves. This new economy crosses job sectors, and it explains the patterns that had stumped us.

A little history is helpful here. Looking back, we found, to our surprise, that the company man of the fifties could have been a woman. That is, the traits that characterized the best of corporate America in that era—an emphasis on cooperation, loyalty, and consensus-based decision-making—are traits traditionally coded as feminine. Collective action, in the form of employer-union compacts, reached its height in the 1950s. Even the Black–white wage gap started to decrease, and the 1950s set the stage for the civil rights activism and reforms of the 1960s. Relative economic equality characterized the period, with CEO salaries pegged at roughly twenty times ordinary worker salaries.

In contrast, the winner-take-all era starts with the increase in CEO compensation, which rose a whopping 514 percent from 1990 to 2020. Successful CEOs in turn began to reward their top lieutenants, managers, and key employees with bonuses and stock options that could make those who succeeded very wealthy—and substantially better paid than other company employees. These bonuses, which are typically tied to short-term reductionist metrics, such as sales or earnings, or the production of Teslas, profoundly changed corporate cultures. The transformation in executive compensation brought back the late nineteenth-century robber baron mindset of no-holds-barred competition, individualism at the expense of institutions and community, and a zero-sum worldview in which those who "win" by any means necessary become the toast of the town, while those who lose, perhaps because they are too ethical to do what it takes, are relegated to a back office cubicle—if they keep their jobs at all.

This means that workplaces where there are increased rewards for those at the top are the same workplaces that pit employees against each other, allowing those calling the shots to engineer results that may not be in the collective interests of the workers themselves, the long-term health of the company, or the social order. Tesla, for example, is distinctive in the way that CEO Elon Musk—a brilliant, driven, and unforgiving boss who boasts of working 120 hours a week—demands the impossible and expects to get it. Around the time of Vandermeyden's lawsuit, another employee wrote a blogpost noting that, at one point, six of the eight people on the anonymous employee's team were on medical leave because of work-related injuries, and the writer knew of others who were scared to report they were hurting. Musk has been termed "a savior and a despot." In one case, he fired a young engineer on the spot, simply because he asked the wrong question. *Wired* magazine's article on the Tesla plant was titled, "Dr. Elon & Mr. Musk: Inside Tesla's Production Hell." Musk's personality and business practices aren't incidental to his success; they are essential to it.

Practices like these are linked to increasing gender disparities. CEOs like Musk, who dangle the promise of outsized rewards for those who meet the announced targets and dismiss those who question his methods, keep everyone insecure. Gender theorists describe the resulting workplaces as "masculinity contest cultures." This is a "zero-sum game," the scholars explain, in which "men compete at work for dominance by showing no weakness, demonstrating a single-minded focus on professional success, displaying physical endurance and strength, and engaging in cut-throat competition." Amping up production schedules becomes what a real leader does: ignore product quality issues or employee well-being and become the subordinate managers' version of "showing no weakness" in the dedication to the competition. Masculinity contest cultures "tend to have toxic leaders who abuse and bully others to protect their own egos." The resulting work environments are associated with little work or family support from the leaders; the very idea of a "work–life balance" is inconsistent with a workplace that makes winning the competition to be top dog in the next bonus cycle the primary source of status. Such environments have also been shown to produce "sexist climates where women experience either hostility or patronizing behavior" and much higher incidences of sexual harassment, racial harassment, social humiliation and physical intimidation." Inside such organizations, both female and male employees experience "higher rates of burnout and turnover; and higher rates of illness and depression." While these workplaces offer opportunity—Vandermeyden became a Tesla engineer with no engineering training and no experience in the auto industry—they can also be perilous. If you fail to outshine the employee next to you or, worse, you point out quality issues that could slow down production, you may find yourself out of a job.

One would think that, if everyone is worse off, including the long-term health of many companies, such a system would self-destruct. But that's not what is happening. These environments allow those at the top to insist on objectives that will benefit them at the expense of best practices, simple morality, and often the rule of law itself. They face little legal accountability because there are fewer external constraints than a generation ago. Musk and Tesla, for example, have repeatedly faced new allegations: of sexual harassment and racial discrimination, of securities violations, of worker safety issues, of repeated labor violations, and of efforts to cover up the violations. In 2018, the Securities and Exchange Commission charged Musk himself with securities fraud—charges that were settled when he agreed, without admitting wrongdoing, to step down as Tesla's chair and to pay a $20 million penalty (with Tesla paying another $20 million). The settlement appears to have simply empowered Musk, who retained control of Tesla, to move on to a new round of ventures and SEC charges. When Musk took over Twitter in late 2022, the *New York Times* summarized the situation as "Two Weeks of Chaos." But Musk is still winning, at least against the state: in February 2023, a jury deliberated for just two hours before clearing Musk of securities fraud charges. While the primary limit on companies like Tesla is its stock performance, that metric too often rewards these tactics.

Competition in the business world used to be about one company showing up another company. Today, corporate competition has become about what Walmart's founder Sam Walton used to call "beating yesterday," which means meeting short-term targets, such as Tesla's efforts to boost production. The stock market rewards making these "numbers"—and modern executives' longevity and bonuses—depend on it. This incentive has changed the terms of competition, shifting the competition from *outside* the company to *within* the company. Winning now means besting the worker in the next cubicle and winning the bigger bonus. Yes, some women like Vandermeyden make the teams when they outperform the men around them. But in a *Game of Thrones*–like environment, outsiders such as Vandermeyden who are without powerful protectors are also the most expendable. To make matters worse, the production of predominantly male winners validates the conclusion that women don't have what it takes to make it into the most exclusive "bros' clubs," and that men deserve the power, wealth, and glory that come with the intensely competitive territory.

Putting these pieces together helps explain why women have lost ground, but the explanation only deepens the mystery. In this competition, zero sum (if one person wins another must inevitably lose) becomes negative sum (we are all worse off), as workers see each other as the enemy and form tactical alliances to outflank their rivals. By the end of the early chapters in this book, the picture of why women lose in such environments comes into focus; but it takes until the end of the book to understand why the system has endured for so long and what can be done about it.

In *Fair Shake*, we meet women working in lower-level retail jobs and in the various echelons of banking and Silicon Valley. We'll meet engineers, office assistants, clerks, and gig workers from all backgrounds, from all walks of life, and with all pay grades. Although these women might appear to have little in common on the surface, their stories play out along familiar lines. In our efforts to capture what today's workplaces are like for women, we turned first to the legal complaints brought by women against their companies. The complaints, which are generally a matter of public record, provide information (like pay scales) that are not otherwise available, and they detail the stories of women who feel wronged by their workplaces and choose to fight back. The complaints, of course, provide only one side of the case, and they are often greeted by blanket denials. Defendants may also introduce additional facts, attack the plaintiffs, or dispute the legal conclusions. In most of the cases we discuss, there have not been any findings of fact by a court or jury. Cases often end in settlements, which at the very least means that the company was willing to pay the plaintiff to go away. In these cases, companies typically insist on nondisclosure agreements, which prevent plaintiffs from talking about cases and which prevent further inquiry. If cases instead result in dismissal, the outcomes are more likely to be based on the legal insufficiency of the claims rather than a finding that the facts are not true (our discussion of the Betty Dukes case in Chapter 1 is a prime example).

The women do not necessarily win, but in our experience as litigators, the specific facts in complaints are typically true and represent the experiences of other women who do not sue. We have generally confirmed that the nature of allegations in the complaints is consistent with public reports about the individual workplaces and their environments. And perhaps the most important evidence we have found are the statistical studies that show that the allegations in these complaints correspond to the experiences documented in the numbers. We are satisfied that the claims discussed illustrate the nature of modern discriminatory workplaces and the patterns we identify, which help explain why women are losing so much ground in today's workforce.

The key to understanding the importance of these stories is to recognize that women are trapped in what we call a reinforcing "Triple Bind." Their stories show the mechanics of how this Triple Bind works, and how it's the result of a WTA system that disregards the well-being of the many in favor of enrichment of the few.

In the first leg of the Triple Bind, we show how *if women don't compete on the same terms as the men in the WTA workplace, they lose.* Vandermeyden may have thought the job was about making cars, but the real terms for advancement were more about outflanking those around her to get the next promotion. In the first three chapters, we tell similar stories that explain why Walmart became the subject of the largest sex discrimination suit in the country, principally because of policies that disadvantaged women and suppressed wages. We also show how Jack Welch—CEO of General Electric—remade corporate America and how, even after the financial crisis of 2009, the clash between ethics and profit on Wall Street is a game women disproportionately lose.

In the second leg of the Triple Bind, *if women do try to compete on the same terms as the men, they lose because they are disproportionately punished for their sharp elbows or perceived misdeeds.* In this section, we tell the stories of Ellen Pao, a venture capitalist who electrified Silicon Valley by demonstrating the double standard women face, and Misha Patel Terrazas, who tried to thread the ethical needle at Wells Fargo, only to find that when a bank caught up in scandal needed a scapegoat, she was a more convenient one.

In the third leg of the Triple Bind, *when women see that they can't win on the same terms as men, they take themselves out of the game—if they haven't been pushed out already.* Vandermeyden, who fought so hard to land her dream job, reported violations and was pushed out. Here, we also look at how the failure to develop a childcare infrastructure is as much a product of the WTA economy as are Wall Street bonuses. We also show how the gig economy draws on women in need of part-time employment—often to compensate for a substandard childcare system—while sometimes risking their physical safety and almost always ensuring their economic marginalization.

We end the book by highlighting recent challenges to the WTA economy. We look at teachers who marshaled public support against the financial assault on public schools, and the heroes of the #MeToo movement who have summoned the courage to spotlight sexual harassment. We look at lawyers bringing cases on behalf of women who might have lost in the past because they were not "perfect" and unblemished plaintiffs. We analyze how masculinity contests, which involve mismanaging risks, are starting to face limits both from regulators and from internal pressures. The women who we profile prove that the solution to the destructive WTA culture that dominates our country is to create a powerful countermovement in which we come together to call out those in power and hold them to account. We argue that precisely because women can't win the winner-take-all game that has emerged over the last half-century, they are in a unique position to showcase the bankrupt values of that system—and lead the fight for a different set of values.

Elon Musk, after all, prevails in part because the glorification of his successes as a billionaire and a visionary emboldens him to act. Recognizing the bankruptcy of this system—and the threat it poses to all of us—creates a foundation for a new set of values that prioritize collaboration, inclusion, and productivity, rather than negative-sum competitions. Management gurus stress that such approaches are associated with better results, greater long-term stability, and rewards for the many, not just the favored few. In this future, the celebration of rule-breaking will be replaced with ethics and the rule of law.

Despite the grim statistics, the women leading the fight give us hope that change is possible and that a more equitable future awaits. Getting there requires challenging the entire WTA economy and creating a new system—one that gives every worker a fair shake.

PART 1

When Women Don't Compete on the Same Terms as Men, They Lose

In the first part of this book, we look at how women lose at the first step of the Triple Bind. While these women work hard, they often don't recognize the unwritten rules that lead to success in the hyper-competitive WTA workplace.

Chapter 1 starts with a story about a company that could be said to have written the rules of the new WTA economy: Walmart, a company whose management ethos actually predated the new economy. Sam Walton created an organizational structure that turned out to prize the traits associated with competition, amorality, and self-interest, and he used them to suppress labor costs. He then carefully cultivated an hourly labor force that exemplified the traits associated with warmth, community pride, and neighborliness, and he persuaded those workers that company identification was an adequate substitute for decent pay and benefits.

In the sixties, when Sam Walton founded his first Walmart stores, these qualities were thought to reflect intrinsic differences between men and women. By the time the sex discrimination case against Walmart profiled in Chapter 1, the largest sex discrimination class action in history, made it to the Supreme Court in 2011, the qualities Sam Walton had identified with men in the sixties—competition, amorality, and self-interest—had the traits that corporate America celebrated. These qualities became the distinguishing characteristics of success in the new economy and the key to magnification of gender disparities in both the managerial and the hourly employees' ranks. Walmart, acclaimed for its management success and vilified for its labor abuses, demonstrates the links between the growing disparities at the top and bottom of the economy and the little studied ways in which gender characteristics explain both.

Chapter 2 looks at a different sector—women in executive positions—and finds the same story. Chapter 2 focuses on an executive who worked for Jack Welch, the legendary CEO who remade General Electric (GE) from a managerial-era company that promoted cooperation, teamwork, and long-term corporate health to a dynamic exemplar of "quarterly capitalism," a system that prized the quarterly earnings reports that boosted share price gains and pitted executives against each other in the competition for outsized bonuses. For decades, Welch was a guru, a success story in every management playbook. We show how his most noted innovations—modern executive compensation, instability in the managerial ranks, and a "beat yesterday" mindset—could have simply been copied from Sam Walton. The new GE, which bit the dust not long after Welch departed, taught that winning was what mattered, even if it meant fudging the numbers and leaving someone else to hold the bag. In the WTA world, the competition that mattered became the one against the executive in the next cubicle, and in such competitions, loyalty to the women in the office, particularly ethical women, became a liability.

In Chapter 3, we explore the bros' clubs on Wall Street and analyze how deregulation has affected the competition within financial services firms. Congressional representatives in the New Deal era had championed the need to make the financial markets safe for "widows and orphans," and New Deal reforms had eliminated fraud that had fueled financial crises for a half-century. The federal reforms, together with the partnership structure of investment banking, had effectively kept Wall Street traders—the bad boys of every era—in check. The new era of deregulation handed the keys to Wall Street back to the traders, bringing a return to Wall Street's wild rides and celebrating those who most callously brag about "ripping their clients off." In environments that have been compared to high school locker rooms, women are often the victims of masculinity contests with managers who blithely overlook sexual harassment and sex discrimination when their star performers drive financial gains. Although women manage risks well—indeed, often better than men because they are less likely to be motivated by locker room one-upmanship, they are often kept out of the most lucrative parts of finance, particularly the parts that reward breaking legal or ethical rules and getting away with it. Women have nonetheless succeeded in important ways in finance in the roles that are less likely to risk a prison sentence or crash the global economy.

The patterns in finance, in business, and at Walmart are the same patterns: hyper-competition, elevation of individual interests over company interests, focus on short-term gains, and a playing field that is far from level. In this world, men and women end up with different pay, working conditions, and promotional opportunities—but not for the reasons that most people think.

CHAPTER 1

The Hidden Rules:
Wal-Mart Stores, Inc. v. Dukes

In many ways, Betty Dukes was the kind of worker Walmart—the world's largest private employer—had always sought to attract: someone looking for an entry-level job and willing to work hard for low pay. She was 44 years old with twenty years of experience in retail, but she had had a difficult life, and she came to Walmart because it was one of the few jobs open to her. She was born in Tallulah, Louisiana, in 1950, one of twelve children. Dukes had dropped out of high school and cycled through jobs, drinking hard during the bad times. She had minor brushes with the law and reached a point where she didn't think there was much left for her. She told a local newspaper, "Life had lost all its flavor, all its purpose and meaning."

Then she found God. And when she did, she became an ordained Baptist minister, volunteered as an assistant minister at her church, and became a community leader. She started school again and even made the honor role. Walmart was hiring at a relatively new store not far from where she lived, and what Dukes most needed was employment. So, she accepted a job there, starting as a part-time cashier earning $5.50 an hour (a little more than California's minimum wage of $4.25). She was certain if she kept focused and worked hard, she could work her way up what she thought of as the Walmart "ladder."

Dukes liked what she saw at Walmart. She felt that the company reflected her Christian values. The store's founder, Sam Walton, known to his employees as Mr. Sam, had died two years before Dukes's first day on the job in 1994, but his Bible-based corporate messages were still drilled into Walmart workers: this was a company that was pro-family and built on Christian principles of community, looking out for others, and taking care of customers. These were Dukes's principles, too. And in her early years on the job, Dukes quickly moved up through the Walmart ranks. By her fifth month, she had been promoted to a full-time cashier. By her ninth month, she had received a merit raise because of her excellent customer service. By 1997, she had become a customer-services manager, which despite its name was an hourly *non*-management position that still didn't offer her access to benefits.

Dukes, who kept her customers happy and was well liked by her co-workers, pressed her supervisors to consider her for the training necessary for hourly workers to move into management roles. She heard nothing, but then saw the men working next to her getting higher pay and being chosen for the management training she had been pushing for, while she was overlooked. When she complained to her supervisors, Dukes was told, "People like you don't get promoted." Since Dukes was Black and her supervisor proudly described himself as "a redneck," she assumed his comment was racially motivated. She complained again. But while she waited for a response, she was reprimanded for asking a colleague to ring up a one-cent transaction on the register to make change (a common practice). After that, she was informed she was being demoted to the position of cashier. Her efforts to speak up on her own behalf had backfired.

Initially, Dukes hesitated to challenge Walmart. As she later explained, "I was from a poor family, my education was limited, and I knew I had to support myself. I felt that I should just be grateful for the job I had and not rock the boat." It was the demotion that persuaded Dukes to fight back. She saw herself and her family as more deeply rooted in Pittsburg, a city where Walmart had only recently opened the store where Dukes worked, than Walmart, and given her role as a community leader, she felt that the demotion was an insult "not only to her but also to the town." Dukes's initial legal claim, which she filed without a lawyer, alleged racial discrimination. To the extent she thought she had suffered from discrimination, Dukes assumed it was because of a racially biased culture at the store.

At the same time, a legal team made up of prominent discrimination lawyers was putting together a much larger lawsuit accusing Walmart of sex discrimination. Lawyers on the team included Stephen Tinkler, who had already successfully brought sex abuse claims against the Catholic Church, as well as sexual harassment cases against Walmart; Joe Sellers, a veteran civil rights attorney in Washington, D.C.; Brad Seligman, a founder of the public interest Impact Fund who later became a California judge; and Guy Saperstein, Seligman's law partner. It was a high-powered group prepared to marshal the resources necessary to confront one of the biggest companies in America.

Dukes learned about the lawyers' efforts and met with them. Up to this point, she had little idea that there was such a thing as sex discrimination. Indeed, she initially assumed that "sex discrimination" had something to do with sex, "like Bill Clinton or Anita Hill," as she later explained. She soon discovered that not only does federal law prohibit treating women differently from men but also that her experience at Walmart wasn't at all unique. The numbers and the stories from Walmart women had already persuaded the lawyers that the company was engaging in systematic sex discrimination: they showed a remarkably consistent national pattern of favoring men over women. Even at the dawn of the twenty-first century, Walmart management had not seen the need to change its practices.

Thus, Dukes may well have experienced sex discrimination in the direct way most people would think; but what really prevented her from getting ahead was a set of *unwritten* rules, deliberately hidden from her view.

For Sam Walton, Walmart's larger-than-life founder, women workers had always been part of his business strategy. A former JCPenney employee, Walton opened his first store in the forties and his first official Wal-Mart (as it was then called) store in Rogers, Arkansas, in 1962. From the outset, Walton's business model was based on keeping his prices—and expenses—low, thereby undercutting his competitors and increasing his sales volume. In order to pull this off, Walton needed workers who were prepared to work for very low wages. In the forties and fifties, the farms of rural Arkansas were mechanizing, freeing women who had helped out on the farm to leave the home in search of income. The women of the Ozarks needed jobs, and they were happy to work for Sam Walton.

There's no doubt that in many ways, Walton bettered the lives of his rural female employees. He gave them jobs they needed when few other opportunities were available—and the women enjoyed the work of serving their friends and neighbors at the store. They also identified with the distinctive company culture Walton had created, a culture reinforced by daily meetings, promotional videos, and a concept Walton called "servant leadership," which echoed Christian notions of service. At the time Walton started out in business, minimum wage rules, which had first passed in the New Deal era, did not apply to retail clerks, and sex discrimination laws did not exist. Walton saw his women employees as doing what women had always done: welcoming their neighbors, making the stores attractive places to visit, emphasizing the stores' community ties. Walton thought of management, on the other hand, as "the exclusive province of men"; he explained that the retailers of the era did not believe that women were suitable for anything but "clerk jobs." The managers had the tough jobs, critical to a low-cost operation. They had to do whatever needed to be done. That meant filling in when other employees were unavailable, making the hours long and unpredictable. And it could mean doing everything from unloading trucks to mopping floors. Walton didn't think women could do either the literal or the metaphorical heavy lifting. At the time Wal-Mart began, managers were overwhelmingly male in most stores. Indeed, the want ads of the era separated "help wanted male" from "help wanted female," and managerial positions overall were much more likely to be listed in the male column.

As Walmart expanded its stores across the country, low-rung female workers remained essential to Walton's low-cost business model. Although Walmart also cut costs, creating more efficient supply chains, at the bedrock of Walton's success was always his ability to design workplaces that kept *labor* costs to a minimum. He liked to brag, "We're going to be successful, but the basis is a very low-wage, low-benefit model of employment."

Walton sought to grow his Ozarks-based operation in an era during which the federal government had expanded labor protections and, seemingly even worse from Walmart's perspective, expanded them to women. Congress passed the Equal Pay Act in 1963, the same year that John F. Kennedy's administration delivered on a campaign promise to women to finally push through legislation that extended the minimum wage to retail employees at large companies, effectively doubling the wage for (majority female) clerks. Walton evaded the new law by dividing his stores into different companies, keeping each under the $1 million in sales that would subject the company to the wage and hour requirements. The Labor Department ultimately prevailed in an action against Walton in the seventies, obtaining a ruling that subjected the entire operation to federal labor regulations. After that, he resorted to subterfuge: to find a way to pay his employees less than the law required and keep out the regulators and the unions that would make the practices visible.

By the time Dukes went to work for Walmart in the nineties, the retail empire had perfected the methods necessary to keep wages low and, moreover, export a pre–New Deal system of labor relations to the rest of the country. Its store managers and assistant managers—who held the positions to which Dukes aspired—were the "shock troops" in this system, according to labor historian Nelson Lichtenstein. Walmart had engineered low-price products through top-down supply chain management micromanaged from the corporate headquarters in Bentonville, Arkansas. It had pioneered the use of bar codes as part of its data-driven supply system. It also carefully planned its store expansions to minimize the costs of delivery from its supply centers, and it so relentlessly monitored the relationship between its warehouses and its stores that it dictated uniform national temperatures in company refrigerators. In contrast, it produced a national low-wage system by giving its managers unbridled discretion with respect to personnel decisions—and only personnel decisions.

Walmart decentralized personnel matters—and still produced uniformly low labor costs—by building the right incentives into its compensation system. Around the time of the *Dukes* litigation, the base pay for a Walmart manager was about $60,000 a year, but according to another lawsuit, managers could triple that amount in bonuses if they "hit their numbers." The managers "are relentlessly and mercilessly graded on their capacity to hold labor costs below a fixed ratio of the sales generated by their store in any given week," Nelson Lichtenstein explained. Supervisors who succeeded in keeping down such costs received higher compensation, no questions asked. Should their labor costs rise beyond the limits set by the Walmart's home office computers in Bentonville, Arkansas, "the hours worked by associates are slashed, wages are then frozen, and the regional vice president tells the store manager to relinquish his keys and find another job." Even in periods in which Walmart did well, 10 to 15 percent of store managers were demoted each year.

Successful managers, in turn, were routinely moved to new stores, often on short notice and hundreds of miles away. As Walmart expanded nationally, it required its management candidates to agree in writing to accept moves as a condition of admittance to the training program; but Walton conceded in his 1992 autobiography that the practice discouraged women from applying and he confessed that he had "seen the light on the opportunities we missed out on with women." Still, the Supreme Court's opinion in *Dukes*, written in 2011 by Justice Antonin Scalia, described the willingness to move as a condition of admission to the company's management training program. While the company eventually dropped it as a company-wide requirement, some managers continued to ask management trainees for such agreements, formally or informally. By moving successful managers to new stores, Walmart created a system for controlling labor practices in all the stores, without the need to dictate the practices from Bentonville.

The store managers' and assistant managers' roles were also critical to Walmart's operation because they kept labor costs low by minimizing personnel. Dukes thought of Walmart as offering a career ladder, but in fact Walmart had fewer managerial positions than did other stores, and the managers oversaw a huge hourly worker force. This meant there were relatively few opportunities for advancement. Instead, Walmart used its salaried supervisors, who did not have to be paid overtime, to compensate for the company's chronic understaffing. Assistant managers reportedly worked "a minimum of forty-eight hours a week, but more likely fifty-five and sixty, eating on the fly and never quite sure when they'll leave for the evening." And that doesn't include the Christmas season, when the pressures ratcheted up even more.

Within this system, hourly workers like Betty Dukes not only didn't get the promotions they deserved; they often didn't receive the compensation to which they were entitled under federal law for the work they had performed. Some managers, trying to reconcile chronic understaffing with Walmart's policy against ever paying overtime, pressured workers to clock out and then go back to work or to continue working through their breaks or lunch hour. As the *New York Times* reported, the company's "intense focus on cost cutting had created an unofficial policy that encouraged managers to request or require off-the-clock work and avoid paying overtime." Less scrupulous managers simply "adjusted" the time cards of workers who reported more than forty hours in a week, unilaterally adding rest breaks or increasing meal periods. This is also why most workers, like Dukes, start part-time; part-time workers enjoy fewer legally mandated protections. Walmart, in turn, accepted notoriously high turnover rates—about double that of competitor Costco—as the norm. Walmart just replaced the employees who left with new workers it could pay less. Workers who stepped out of line in any way, including by complaining about their pay or working conditions, often had their hours cut or, like Dukes, were accused of wrongdoing and demoted, if not fired. While these abuses were not targeted at women, they contributed to the concentration of women in the lowest-paid Walmart positions, partly because women had fewer alternatives in the job market than did men, and partly because they were more willing than men to take the part-time jobs Walmart offered, given their customary family responsibilities. Meanwhile, Walmart's loyal female employees often made so little that they had to rely on food stamps to get by. Out of the goodness of their hearts, Walmart stores have even held canned food drives—*for their own employees.*

A lightbulb went on for us when we realized that the managerial system *Dukes* challenged as discriminatory worked, from start to finish, to facilitate circumvention of the labor laws and shortchange Walmart workers without anyone in Bentonville being held accountable. In 2018, a report titled "Grand Theft Paycheck," showed that Walmart was in fact *the number one company in the country* for the fines and settlements it had paid out for wage theft (wage and hour violations). Walmart wasn't only looking for managers who were the best of its hourly employees; it was also apparently looking for managers who would do anything to lower their sales costs, regardless of the law or the impact on the employees under them.

This certainly would explain why Walmart didn't post its managerial openings for Dukes to see and why Walmart never considered Betty Dukes to be management material. When Dukes was told, "People like you don't become managers," this was an entirely accurate statement.

Betty Dukes would never have been chosen as a manager, even if Walmart did not intentionally discriminate against women, because she had the wrong qualities. Her most admirable qualities—her devotion to her customers, concern for others, and identification with her community—were traits that would have suggested to the higher-ups that she cared about something more than her paycheck or the bottom line of cutting costs; that she might not be willing to do whatever it took to produce the results Walmart valued. These we believe were among the unwritten rules, the invisible qualifications that Dukes never knew about or understood: that she just might not be ruthless enough to compete in a high-stakes bonus system.

When Dukes started at Walmart, she had fully bought into Mr. Sam's credo of "servant leadership." Now that she had the lawyers on her side, she started to see how what was happening to her at Walmart fit into a pattern. With Dukes's help, the lawyers began to build a careful case against Walmart. To prepare their fight against Walmart, the lawyers reviewed 1.3 million documents and interviewed hundreds of women across the country. They were stunned by what they found. Women at Walmart made up about 65 percent of the hourly sales employees, yet they constituted only 33 percent of the supervisory ranks at Walmart, and only 14 percent of the store managers. By contrast, in the retail industry as a whole at the time of the suit, women constituted on average a full 50 percent of the supervisory ranks. The lawyers decided to move forward with a class action, which would allow them to name one or two Walmart employees as representatives of a larger group of women claiming discrimination. The lawyers just had to decide who would be the person named in the legal documents to lead the case.

As the lawyers sifted through the stories of the women, they tried to evaluate leadership—who had a compelling story and who would be committed to changing the company structure, rather than settle for a quick payout. The lawyers chose Dukes as one of the named plaintiffs in their nationwide class action suit because she was "an everywoman kind of figure." Her motives for bringing the case would be hard to question: "She spoke with a passion that was infectious. She was devoted to the women at the company, was devoted to other workers, and was well regarded by other workers." She was willing to speak not just for herself, but for all the women who had been mistreated by Walmart. With 1.6 million plaintiffs in the class, it was the largest employment discrimination class action suit in U.S. history, alleging that Walmart discriminated against women in pay and in denial of promotional opportunities, and retaliated against women who complained.

The lawsuit began in June 2001 in the U.S. District Court in San Francisco. At a press conference given the day the suit was filed in court, Dukes spoke to reporters directly, saying: "There's a great divide between the women and the men at Wal-Mart. . . . [T]oday I'm speaking out and I hope the women in my store and everywhere else will have the courage and no longer accept the treatment that we've been subjected to."

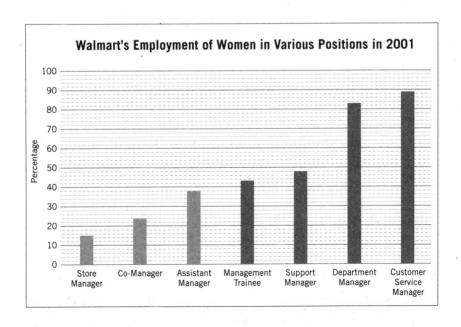

The case Dukes and her lawyers presented in court rested in large part on the statistical picture they developed. First, they showed that women made less money. On average, full-time female hourly employees earned $1,150 less per year than their male counterparts. The big differences, though, came in the supervisory ranks, where—even when they moved up the ranks—female store managers earned an average of $16,400 less than men. Women made up roughly two-thirds of the hourly workers at Walmart, the lowest paid group in the store. Yet only one-third of the managers were women, and these women tended to be concentrated in lower-level and lower-paying positions than the men. Second, the plaintiffs, current and former female Walmart employees from stores across the country, also claimed that the company systematically discriminated against women when awarding promotions. They maintained that Walmart had a "uniform 'corporate culture'" in which managers' biases against women ran rampant.

The plaintiffs presented numerous stories to support their claims. A woman who filed one of the earliest charges was a cashier in a Texas Walmart store. She learned that the man who worked next to her had gotten a pay raise, a substantial one. When she complained to the store manager, the manager told her that the male cashier "had a family to raise." She responded that she was a single working mom and she also had a family to raise. The manager told her to "draw up a budget of what you need." When she did that, she received about a quarter of the pay raise the male cashier had received. When she raised the issue again, the manager told her, "You're lucky you have a job." Another manager told a female employee in South Carolina that men would always be paid more than women because "God made Adam first." Yet another manager explained, "Men need to be paid more than women because they have families to support." Other managers simply said, "Retail is for housewives who just need to earn extra money." According to a Utah store manager, supervisory positions were "tough," and may not be "appropriate" for a woman. A store manager in Texas stated that women have to be "bitches" to survive in Walmart management. "Women will never make as much money as men," insisted a South Carolina department head.

The lawyers found evidence that Walmart had been aware of the gender imbalance in promotions for years but remained "singularly uninterested in why so few women are promoted or whether its pay practices disadvantage its female employees." Indeed, Walmart had created a task force that documented the gender disparities and then disbanded the group when it didn't like the results. In short, the lawyers presented a classic case of unequal treatment, showing statistical differences in the treatment of men and women, and included enough biased statements to support their claim that the disparities resulted from arbitrary rejection of otherwise qualified women. In addition, they had evidence that Walmart knew about these inequities and did nothing to change them.

Walmart's transformation from a small regional operation to a national behemoth occurred largely in the eighties. Lichtenstein, who has written extensively about Walmart, concludes that its growth during this period "was nurtured by the Reaganite transformation of the business environment that relieved labor-intensive employers of hundreds of billions of dollars in annual labor costs." As Walmart continued to expand, its labor suppression model set the norm for other companies. It turned the kind of low-wage, bottom-rung, woman-powered business model it had pioneered in Arkansas into an American norm. That effort required political lobbying that froze the minimum wage at the level of the mid-sixties, effectively reducing its value in inflation-adjusted dollars. It meant using business clout to gut wage and hour enforcement. By 2018, 303 of the Fortune 500 companies had been found to have committed wage theft—that is, they paid their employees less than the actual amount to which they were legally entitled. And while wage theft impacts workers broadly, it disproportionately affects low-wage workers, many of whom already are struggling to make ends meet. Wage theft also disproportionately impacts women, people of color, and immigrant workers because they are more likely than other workers to be in low-wage jobs. Finally, these stolen wages hurt local economies and tax revenue. And, although women made up less than half the labor force, they still accounted for almost 70 percent of low-wage jobs that paid under $10 per hour in America. Meanwhile, most women who started in low-level positions were stuck there without opportunities for advancement.

The one force that might have been powerful enough to have defeated Walton's remaking of the retail marketplace was unionization, but that, too, fell victim to the forces creating a winner-take-all economy. In the middle of the twentieth century, unionization had allowed individual employees to band together, giving more power to workers to negotiate for better working conditions. Mr. Sam hated unions, and he liked to complain that he didn't need someone to "tell me how to take care of my people." John Tate, the lawyer who headed Walmart's union-busting efforts, declared in 2004: "Labor unions are nothing but blood-sucking parasites living off the productive labor of people who work for a living." These executives equated unions with government interference in their company and their community.

This position is not surprising. Of course, Walmart discouraged unions. Union representatives would insist that Walmart obey the law, pay legally mandated overtime, and equalize men and women's pay and promotion opportunities. Unionization would also limit Walmart's ability to undercut its competitors who pay fairer wages—or to discriminate against women and minorities. Studies show that the gender wage gap is lowest in unionized workplaces. Union membership increases the wages of both men and women compared to nonunion workers, but the bonus is larger for women, especially for minority women. Unionized women are more likely to get paid leave and have stronger employment protections against sex discrimination and harassment. If an employer is exploiting workers, the union can bring an action, which gives workers an enforcement mechanism. Unions also increase transparency, encouraging wage standardization so that the workers performing the same jobs receive the same pay, and they create grievance procedures that allow union representatives to police any violations of the labor and anti-discrimination laws. In addition, unions give workers the power to speak up. "Hidden" practices like wage theft that disproportionately affect women more than men—and minority and immigrant women most of all—are much harder to pull off in a more transparent, unionized workplace. Declines in union membership are correlated with increasing income inequality.

Fighting unionization, which had never taken hold in Arkansas, was a large part of Walmart's business model. To date, it has proved to be an unequal fight. Walton fought unions and labor regulation in his stores throughout the 1960s and '70s, but it wasn't until the election of Ronald Reagan in 1980 that he found a kindred spirit in the Oval Office. During the Reagan era, a coalition of business leaders backed Reagan as the administration supported the business leaders' political agenda. Together with corporate lobbying efforts and individual donors, the coalition made a successful anti-union campaign a centerpiece of the right, criticizing unions for interfering with the free market economy, driving up wages and driving down profits, and hamstringing managers. The group succeeded in enacting anti-union (euphemistically called "right to work") laws in a number of states and in gutting labor enforcement. The Bush administration even placed one of the lawyers who represented Walmart during the *Dukes* litigation in charge of the Labor Department's fair labor standards enforcement efforts in 2005. Making an all-out effort to prevent collective bargaining is simply another cost of doing business the Walmart way.

This same coalition also began a concerted campaign to stack the courts with pro-business appointees, ensuring that when complaints about labor practices came before the judicial system, employers like Walmart would not have to face accountability for their actions. Empirical studies show that the Roberts Court, starting with Chief Justice

Roberts's appointment to the Supreme Court in 2005, "is significantly more likely to favor business" than "any Court era in the last 100 years" and that the Court's pro-business tilt has increased over time, reaching all-time highs in 2020. Moreover, law professor Elizabeth Pollman adds that it is not just that businesses have become more likely to win before the Court but also that "the Court has often expanded corporate rights while narrowing corporate liability or access to justice against corporate defendants." The Court has produced partisan decisions that undercut unions and make it harder to bring class actions to challenge sex discrimination or the type of wage and hour violations common at Walmart and at other low-wage workplaces. The Supreme Court's longstanding attack on workers' rights has had a disproportionate effect on women's position in the workplace.

Although Sam Walton was long dead by the time the *Dukes* litigation started, he and other like-minded executives effectively brought about the end of the post–New Deal era in corporate America. The changes not only allowed Walmart to thrive, they also undercut smaller stores that had been mainstays of small-town America and opened the door to a new generation of retailers like Amazon, which ruthlessly suppress unionization and rely on low wages. The effort to keep out unions has become so pervasive that, in almost 40 percent of union elections, employers have been charged with federal labor law violations, including coercion and firings.

Still, history-making fights like the one Betty Dukes led at Walmart, which expose the statistics on how Walmart treated women and lead to more investigations about abusive labor practices, fuel unionization efforts. In 2022, Gallup recorded the highest level of approval of labor unions—71 percent—since 1965. And the unionization victory in 2022 at an Amazon distribution center was hailed as a potential signal that it might be time to start trying to unionize Walmart workers again. Given entrenched industry and judicial opposition, however, unions have not yet been able to reverse the decline in membership, although collective responses including not only membership drives but also strikes, protests, and boycotts are an important counter to the inability to win systematic redress in the courts. In the long run, only the combination of tighter labor markets that create incentives for employers to invest more in workers and more stringent enforcement of existing worker protections can raise the status of the nation's low-wage workforce.

Walmart led in creating a new chapter in the history of American business—where a few at the top were once again free to disproportionately benefit from the labor of the many at the bottom. It also set the stage for what would happen to Dukes's case in the Supreme Court.

In late 2010, nine years after Dukes began the suit, the Supreme Court agreed to hear Walmart's appeal as *Wal-Mart v. Dukes.* Throughout the long years of the case, Dukes had continued to work at Walmart, no longer as a customer service manager, or even as a cashier, but demoted to the role of greeter, generally considered one of the worst jobs at the store. But Dukes kept fighting because she knew she wasn't alone.

Dukes's fierce advocacy for her fellow female workers turned out to be in vain, at least before the Supreme Court. On June 20, 2011, the Court ruled 5–4 in Walmart's favor, saying the 1.6 million plaintiffs did not have enough in common to constitute a "class." The Supreme Court rejected the plaintiffs' proposed class on the ground that it was *too big* to have enough common questions of law and fact. Fundamentally, the majority of the Court did not accept the argument that the statistics the plaintiffs presented, showing overwhelming gender differences, should be seen as the result of company-wide national policies.

Class actions have historically been critical in spotlighting companies that treat women badly. As in the Walmart case, statistics showing a company-wide pattern of gender disparities are often more convincing than a collection of individual cases. For example, in a 2004 case that settled during the *Dukes* litigation, retailer Abercrombie & Fitch agreed to pay $40 million in damages for race and sex discrimination; increase diversity in hiring, promotion, and marketing materials; and hire recruiters to improve the company's diversity efforts. As the Abercrombie case shows, class action suits can not only address the injustices done to individual employees but also compel reform of company-wide policies that can perpetuate discriminatory practices.

Justice Antonin Scalia's opinion in the *Dukes* case, however, was part of a series of ideologically driven decisions that have made such cases harder to bring. In her dissent, Justice Ruth Bader Ginsburg emphasized, "The practice of delegating to supervisors large discretion to make personnel decisions, uncontrolled by formal standards, has long been known to have the potential to produce disparate effects" for women and minorities; and prior cases, with a similar showing of the "disparate impact" of discretionary policies, had justified class treatment. She added that the factual record in the case established that Walmart had maintained a "carefully constructed . . . corporate culture," through the use of "frequent meetings to reinforce the common way of thinking, regular transfers of managers between stores to ensure uniformity throughout the company, monitoring of stores 'on a close and constant basis,' and 'Wal-Mart TV,' 'broadcas[t] . . . into all stores.'" Justice Scalia, as part of the majority's effort to cut back on the scope of large class actions, reached the opposite conclusion. He insisted that Dukes's lawyers had shown only a general corporate policy "of *allowing discretion* by local supervisors over employment matters" and concluded that "is just the opposite of a uniform employment practice that would provide the commonality needed for a class action; it is a policy *against having* uniform employment practices." Thus as long as Bentonville's fingerprints weren't on the individual decisions, the fact that Walmart produced a remarkably uniform pattern of gender disparities throughout the country was not subject to scrutiny. And that, of course, was the seeming point of Walmart's employee system, which entrusted its managers with almost unlimited discretion over promotions, pay, and working conditions. Managers given this unfettered autonomy, coupled with a carefully structured bonus system that incentivized wage suppression, could exploit workers without repercussions for the larger company. The Supreme Court ensured that the secrets of how this discretion was exercised would remain in the shadows.

Walmart had won. Dukes, and the 1.6 million other women who were part of the case, could not pursue their class action litigation showing that sex discrimination was built into Walmart's national model. The ruling left open the possibility that women like Dukes could still fight Walmart in *individual* lawsuits, but sex discrimination suits are expensive, and it is difficult, if not impossible, for one person to challenge Walmart's national policies. What *Walmart v. Dukes* did was to signal to big businesses that the Supreme Court was prepared to give them preference, while restricting the access of individuals with limited means to the courts. It also meant that Walmart did not have to pay what might have amounted to "billions of dollars in damages" or to reform the nationwide system that Dukes fought.

After the decision, the Senate Judiciary Committee invited Betty Dukes to appear. She testified that because of the Supreme Court's ruling, many women were going to give up. "Our fight is not over," Dukes insisted. "The Supreme Court did not rule on the merits of our case. But, there is no doubt in my mind, that the Supreme Court has made it much easier for companies like Wal-Mart to avoid accountability for their unlawful and discriminatory behavior."

She was right: few women joined the smaller spinoff cases against regional managers, and these cases have not succeeded in challenging Walmart's system-wide policies. Although some of the women have received confidential settlements, and new sex discrimination cases are springing up, legal action has produced no systemic changes at Walmart.

Dukes finally retired at the age of 66. She passed away a year later, in 2017. In its obituary, the *New York Times* lionized her as someone who had "helped draw attention to the working conditions of low-paid workers in so-called big box stores that dominate the retail landscape." Despite the mighty forces in her path, Dukes had indeed fought. After the court case failed, she continued to advocate for workers' rights, starting her own foundation to tell her story and to help other women and marginalized workers. *Ms.* magazine had named her Woman of the Year in 2004; and in 2012, the American Federation of Teachers awarded her its Women's Rights Award.

Since Dukes's days at the store, Walmart, spurred on by tighter labor markets and the need to attract and retain workers, has raised its entry-level wages, and the number of female managers at company stores has slowly increased. It now issues an annual Culture, Diversity, Equity and Inclusion Report. Walmart's CEO, Doug McMillon (who assumed the position in 2014), even called for a bump in the federal minimum wage—something Walmart fought for decades. Particularly in the aftermath of the coronavirus pandemic, however, Walmart has accelerated automation and the move to online operations. Retail jobs, of the kind that Dukes worked throughout her life, are not just bad and gendered; they are also disappearing, reducing the jobs that women like Betty Dukes will be able to get in the future.

––––––––––––

Betty Dukes's dream of "moving up the ladder" remained unrealized in her lifetime, and yet what she wanted was what so many want from our workplaces, something that once was considered the norm for white males in the postwar economy: you get a job, you work hard, you stay loyal, you acquire work-specific skills—and in return, the employer invests in you, you're in line for promotions, you get regular raises, you enjoy job security. The problem was that Dukes was never going to get what she wanted by following what she thought were the rules of looking out for her customers and her fellow employees. Walmart had been playing a rigged game all along, and the way to win was by showing that she could more effectively exploit those under her than other managerial candidates.

In the meantime, Walton's selection for bottom-line–oriented managers presaged what would happen to women in management—and workers everywhere—throughout the country. The design of the culture at Walmart is one we will see time and again in this book: the use of high-stakes bonuses that pits workers against each other, keeping everyone insecure and giving management the ability to produce its bottom-line metrics. Such environments then choose for a group of men (and a few women) who reproduce stereotypically masculine traits: competitiveness, amorality, ruthlessness.

Because the managers are motivated by the high-stakes bonus pay, they are willing to work long and unpredictable hours, and they fight to thrive in a system where promotions are tied to personalized networks, with managers using taps on the shoulder to choose new candidates who have the same qualities they see in themselves—candidates who already understand the unwritten rules of the game. These high-stakes bonuses and selection practices seed a willingness to ignore the law (and ethical norms), and that in turn becomes a sought-after trait in management in these systems. Whether these techniques appear in law firms, tech, finance, or even in education, they are all sources of women's disadvantages in our current economy.

The system endures because it pays off so handsomely for those at the top. Thanks to his ability to increase his power and impunity, Sam Walton became the richest man in America. Today, the Walton family's collective fortune makes it the richest family in the United States, and the richest nonroyal family in the world. Walton, and the Walton family, used his riches to entrench the system he created, undermining the labor protections that had produced a much greater degree of shared prosperity in the middle of the twentieth century.

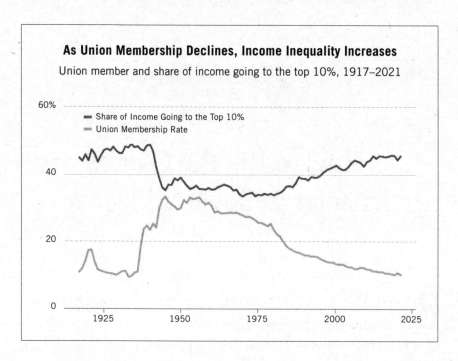

As Union Membership Declines, Income Inequality Increases

Union member and share of income going to the top 10%, 1917–2021

What we came to realize was that the discrimination against women was the symptom. The cause was a rigged system that let a very small number of people at the top benefit. Now that we've seen how that system looks at the bottom of the ladder, we turn to look at the top and see if it's any different.

CHAPTER 2

How to Rig the Game: Schaefer v. General Electric

B etty Dukes was an hourly worker at Walmart; Lorene Schaefer was the consummate professional at General Electric. Schaefer graduated from law school in 1989 in the top 10 percent of her class. Soon after that, she landed a job with a large national law firm—and gave birth to twins. Within a few years, she became part of the legal team at General Electric, joining GE Aircraft Engines as counsel in the company's Litigation Department. Like many women with children, she chose to go "in-house," exchanging the law-firm environment where firms charge by the hour for a corporate environment where efficiency means a more regular schedule. Once at GE, Schaefer eventually succeeded in getting the taps on the shoulder—the informal invitations to move up the corporate ladder—that had eluded Betty Dukes. She also did everything she could to remain competitive in-house; for example, even after the birth of her third child, she switched cities every few years to take advantage of new opportunities. She received superb performance reviews as part of GE's competitive bonus system and stock options GE executives coveted as signs of their progress. Finally, she reached a position in the upper management ranks: General Counsel of GE Transportation. And then, after thirteen years of success with the company, she hit a glass ceiling: she was never promoted to the Senior Executive Band compensation rank, unlike many of the men who had served at the same levels she held, and without warning, she was pushed out of the General Counsel position she had worked so hard to attain.

In the last chapter, we saw how Sam Walton's Walmart business model was forged in a post–World War II era. During this time of relative stability for the American economy, women entering the workforce had fairly low expectations for how far they would be able to advance. This was a cultural norm that Walton was able to exploit by offering his female employees low wages, then nickel-and-diming them using wage theft practices.

GE in the 1990s, in contrast, was an exciting place for an ambitious woman. Although women's roles at GE had once been limited to the secretarial pool, when Schaefer came on board at the company, there were women lawyers and executives, starting in entry-level positions and working their way up into the management ranks. Under CEO Jack Welch's leadership, the company was routinely rated as one of the most admired and successful in the United States, if not in the world. Schaefer had joined the company believing it offered immediate responsibility and opportunities for promotion. In fact, though, the management system that GE put in place could have been modeled on Sam Walton's—a system that used high-stakes bonuses and executive insecurity to implement hidden objectives. These hidden objectives were simple but pernicious: make the powerful look good by hitting the right earnings numbers and make everyone else feel insecure. By the time Schaefer was pushed out in 2007, GE had become a competitive WTA workplace with results for women executives not so different from the negative consequences women had experienced trying to crack the managerial code at Walmart.

Jack Welch, GE's legendary CEO, began his career in business during the 1960s, a time when revolution was in the air and when women's expectations for their own employment were starting to change. From his earliest days at General Electric, Welch sought to shake things up. The son of Irish Catholic working-class parents in Massachusetts, he went to the University of Massachusetts, a land-grant public university, just as the college dream was becoming more accessible for working-class families in the United States. He did well and went on to the University of Illinois, where he got a PhD in chemical engineering in 1960. That same year, he joined GE as a junior chemical engineer. That first job almost became his last at GE. A year after he arrived, feeling "underpaid and undervalued," he threatened to quit. His main objection was that he was getting only a standard bonus when he felt he deserved more. But that wasn't how GE operated during that time.

In mid-century America, GE management, like most of corporate America, believed that individual monetary incentives undermined teamwork. Instead, CEOs prioritized steady growth that benefited shareholders, managers, and employees alike. Welch, disgruntled about the size of his bonus in this system that cared about building a company rather than individual advancement, was on the verge of taking another job when a supervisor talked him out of it—and tripled his raise. In 1968, Welch became the vice president and head of GE's plastics division, a major role—plastics were hot in the sixties. By 1971, he had been appointed vice president of GE's metallurgical and chemical divisions, as well. Major companies offered career ladders for the talented, and Welch climbed each rung as he reached it: senior vice president, vice chairman, and eventually, chairman and CEO. By 1981, Welch was the company's youngest CEO in history, at the age of 46.

Welch assumed the helm at GE amid the worst recession since the Great Depression. The United States, which emerged from World War II as the world's dominant industrial power, now faced increasing competition from abroad, and the Federal Reserve Board's efforts to fight the stagflation of the 1970s had sent the country into a deep economic nosedive. Reg Jones, GE's CEO, knew that GE was in trouble, and he picked Welch as his successor to shake things up.

The early 1980s were a significant time in the history of American corporate management. A group of academics and ambitious corporate executives like Welch bristled at what they saw as the bloated, inefficient, and insular bureaucracies around them. They were ready for new ideas that would disrupt corporate America's status quo and open the door to an energetic and talented new generation. What took place was an unprecedented shift in corporate values—a shift crucial to grasping why women are still sidelined in our present-day workplaces. To understand what happened, we need to go back to GE's heyday.

In the era following World War II, corporate executives fit a certain mold: white males who believed that as long as they were loyal to the company, the company would be loyal to them. GE was a major player in this world. Founded by Thomas Edison in 1889, GE dominated the market for heavy electrical equipment, but its prestige came from having some of the best research labs in the world. The GE of this era prized collaboration. A young man was taught, "To get ahead, he must co-operate with the others—but co-operate *better* than they do." GE considered the "acid test" for true cooperation to be loyalty—reciprocal loyalty between superiors and subordinates. The best of GE executives rose through the ranks and did not seek better opportunities elsewhere. GE, in turn, rewarded loyalty; competent employees enjoyed regular wage increases and lifelong tenure.

GE's attitudes in this era were typical of corporate America. The men (and they were all men outside of the secretarial pool, and they were predominantly white) who rose through the corporate ranks often joined a management training program shortly after they graduated from college, and they proved their worth over the course of a lifetime with the same company. These executives "belonged" to companies they saw as giving meaning to their lives; they came to think of themselves as "an IBM man, a Corning Glass man, or a Sears man." They had been shaped by the Great Depression and World War II to look out for one another. They even looked alike, as the overwhelmingly white male executive corps donned their gray flannel suits, white shirts, and skinny ties, and trudged off to work. Fitting in involved buzz cuts and a home in the right suburb, with overlapping hobbies: golf, tennis, bowling, fishing, or hunting, depending on the region. Not only were these men trained to work together on the job, but they also had the same interests, which created camaraderie and the ability to do business both inside the office and outside, on the golf course.

In his book *The New Industrial State*, written in 1967, the twentieth-century economist John Kenneth Galbraith praised this "technocratic" system for its scientific management that valued expertise and saw the best decisions as emerging from consultation and collaboration. The goal was to forge a single group personality greater than the sum of its parts. Galbraith observed that, in corporate America generally, individuals were expected to live up to a high level of personal honesty, and they benefited as part of a group, rather than as individuals competing against each other for promotions or bonuses. Pay levels did not vary with firm profits, and the CEO's income, which was not that much higher than that of other senior management officials, paled in comparison with the compensation levels of CEOs today. In the 1950s and '60s, the ratio of CEO to worker pay was about 20 to 1. (Today it's a mind-blowing 399 to 1.) Bonuses back then were equally modest. Instead, the executives of the era gained status through their identification with the firm, and they saw their individual opportunities for advancement as intrinsically linked to the company's prominence. Modern management theorists argue that this holistic concept of loyalty to the institution provides a better motivator than monetary rewards, and makes it easier to coordinate management efforts than more competitive management systems. High marginal income tax rates also supported this system; after all, what was the point of earning vastly more than everyone else if the government was going to take most of it in taxes?

Critics, on the other hand, lampooned the omnipresent "organization man," and they faulted him for his obsession with "fitting in" and his failure to take risks that might endanger his sinecure or the company's fortunes. The mid-century journalist William Whyte was one of these critics. In 1956, he published a book of interviews with CEOs of some of the biggest companies of his time. In *The Organization Man*, he argued that without outsized compensation, getting to the top just wasn't worth it: "Why knock yourself out" he asked, when the "extra salary won't bring home much more actual pay?" Whyte marveled at how the college graduate of the times would take a job at a company like GE over a competitive sales job at a smaller firm that promised twice as much. The men whom Whyte scorned viewed their relationship with their companies "to be for keeps." They knew their bosses were looking for a "practical, team-player fellow" with "human understanding," rather than creativity and brilliance. Whyte detested this world, which placed so much emphasis on community over individualism and careful testing of initiatives over risk-taking. He disliked that the average 1950s executive preferred the "good, equable life" over working too hard. He suggested that values like security, loyalty, and reciprocity only produced laziness. The solution, he believed, was to place more emphasis on wealth, innovation, and personal ambition.

Galbraith and Whyte disagreed about what part of this corporate system constituted virtue and what part presented weakness, but they largely agreed that the white male executive of the postwar era was defined by his sense of community, collaboration, and conscientiousness. Reading Galbraith and Whyte today, it's hard not to be struck by their descriptions of the company man's traits, which sound remarkably similar to those used to define traditionally "feminine" qualities. After all, today it is women who are supposed to be the ones who prize cooperation over competition, concern for colleagues over greed, and virtue and integrity over personal advancement.

Jack Welch was firmly in the Whyte/reformer camp. Once Welch became CEO, he set out to remake GE, getting rid of not only the bureaucracy and the inefficiency but also many of the employees. As he explained in his autobiography, business is a competition that allows for no illusions or sentimentality. Winning the competition "had, both morally and practically, to come first." Indeed, during his first few years as CEO, Welch eliminated 100,000 of GE's 384,000 jobs, earning him the sobriquet Neutron Jack, "the guy who eliminat[ed] the people but left the buildings standing." He brushed off criticism about his ruthlessness in closing plants and laying off workers, later writing that "I've never seen a business ruined because it reduced its costs too much, too fast." The days of corporate loyalty to workers were gone.

Welch also remade the terms of executive compensation. In the new system, top executive pay increasingly took the form of stock options, while share-price increases would enrich both shareholders and the top executives holding these options—often at the expense of other corporate stakeholders, such as line workers or customers. With this shift, the CEO's principal objective changed from long-term corporate growth to short-term maximization of share price. Selling off or dismantling a plant with high costs could immediately boost earnings—even if that plant had the potential to be a profit center down the road. The same went for cutting basic research and development—investments that paid off only in the long term. Welch accordingly cut such expenditures as aggressively as he closed plants and laid off employees, and he personally reaped the benefits. GE no longer ran innovative plastics labs unless they contributed immediately to the bottom line.

Welch mastered the new system. Over the course of his tenure at GE, Welch's annual income rose from $4 million to $16 million. By 1999, Welch's unexercised stock options—the more lucrative component of his pay—were valued at more than $260 million. During the eighteen-year bull market that characterized most of Welch's tenure, GE's revenue grew 385 percent, while the company's stock value rose 4,000 percent. Welch had figured out a way to beat earning expectations *every quarter*. Even if it was only by a penny or two, he went on to do this virtually every reporting period over his two-decade tenure. In the process, Welch helped to usher in one of the most significant transformations in corporate American history. The CEO focus shifted, with almost laser-like intensity, from safe, long-term planning to whatever produced a short-term increase in share price.

The Welch playbook required a management team that could implement a system benefiting the few at the top at the expense of everyone else. Shutting plants, closing plastics labs, and laying off long-time employees can be painful. Welch needed subordinates who shared his vision of winning, a group of "new boys" who could be promoted to outflank the "old boys" of the GE technocracy. To do this, he created a new management-evaluation system. Dubbed "rank and yank" (a term Welch hated), the system involved regular performance evaluations that ranked employees on a forced curve. Welch handsomely rewarded those at the top while identifying a bottom group at risk of dismissal. The favored group, perhaps 20 percent, would receive outsized bonuses and be groomed for promotion. As CEO, he increased the number of employees receiving stock options from 500 to 15,000 (5 percent of GE's total workforce). "What a kick," Welch wrote, describing his enjoyment at getting a weekly printout of the names of the employees getting the performance-based options. No more standard bonuses for teams who worked together and "collaborated better than others."

The bottom group, perhaps 10 percent of the company, would be told their performance was inadequate and that they would be let go if their performance did not improve. Many left—or were fired—after receiving such evaluations. Every year, Welch reevaluated the remaining employees against each other, identifying a new group of stars and a new bottom 10 percent. These changes—the increases in executive compensation tied to quarterly earnings and the adoption of more competitive evaluation systems—worked together to change the nature of executive advancement at GE.

With large bonuses for the select winners, Welch believed he could produce any results management sought to emphasize, whether defined in terms of subjective evaluations like "teamwork" or reductionist ones tied to easily measured factors such as sales, unit profitability, or quarterly earnings. In implementing this new system, Welch became the darling of corporate reformers seeking to update an outmoded system. Economists and business school professors, starting with economist Milton Friedman in the sixties, had been pushing corporate America to focus more on the bottom line that benefited shareholders and less on such frivolous matters as saving the environment. Welch's new system spread throughout corporate America. It wasn't just about firing people; it was also about plant closings, the wholesale elimination of divisions, and the sale of businesses: "By not hesitating to get rid of slower performing operations, Mr. Welch engaged in what the economic philosopher Joseph Schumpeter called capitalism's 'creative destruction.'" Jeff Skilling at Enron—a company that crashed and burned, with Skilling going to jail for fraud—was the foremost among Welch's disciples, but at one time, more than half of all publicly traded companies adopted rank-and-yank style systems. Welch's way of doing business became *the* way for many other companies.

So, what did all this mean for women? By the time Lorene Schaefer, the ambitious young lawyer, came to work for Welch in the 1990s, the last decade of his tenure, the technocratic ideal—which rested on the notion that the organization is more than the sum of its parts, and its strength lay in its ability to weave disparate types of expertise into group-based decision-making—was gone. So, too, was the ethos that those inside looked out for their own, and the conviction that corporate interests lined up with societal interests. It had been replaced by what some call "meritocracy" or "hyper-competition." We think it can better be understood as "masculinity contest cultures"—or perhaps more accurately, a kind of ruthless tournament culture like the one depicted on the TV show *Game of Thrones*. In this new world, women were welcome to enter the game. Some, like Schaefer, appeared to prosper. But the closer they got to the top, the more likely they were to encounter stabs in the back they had not anticipated. In the new order, professional competence became less important than the right alliances.

This is exactly what happened to Schaefer. In 2005, after steadily moving up the corporate ladder, Schaefer made the most important move of her corporate career: leaving Atlanta to become the general counsel for GE Transportation in Erie, Pennsylvania. Another woman, Charlotte Begley, the CEO of GE Transportation, had recruited her for the position, but Begley soon left and a new CEO, John Dineen, replaced her.

Dineen decided to hire his own general counsel (GC). Despite her consistent track record of success and a recent "commercial excellence award" from the company, Schaefer learned that she was being demoted to a smaller role.

Schaefer learned about her demotion from Greg Capito, the Senior Human Resources Manager for GE Transportation. Capito told her that a committee of seven men including Dineen had already met and decided her fate. The only reason Capito gave Schaefer for her demotion was that Dineen wanted to replace her with a "big time GC." Capito acknowledged that "this [demotion] probably came as a surprise."

After the demotion, Schaefer decided to leave GE, but she was too good a lawyer to slink away. Her research indicated she was not the only woman GE had treated badly. In the Welch era, there had been no women in the company's top thirty-one corporate officer positions. Welch's successor, Jeffrey Immelt, did somewhat better during his first year, but Schaefer found that women had made no further gains in upper management from 2002 to 2007. She also discovered that GE had six other divisional general counsels in positions comparable to hers: five men and one woman. Company policy indicated that GCs should be appointed at the senior executive band level, a prominent rung in GE's executive classification system and one that typically came with higher pay and better opportunities for advancement than Schaefer's classification. All five of the men, but neither Schaefer nor the other woman, were members of the senior executive band. Even worse, all five of the men were paid more than the two women.

Schaefer hired her own lawyers, and in 2007, she filed a $500 million class action lawsuit on behalf of "a class of more than 1000 similarly situated women at GE, alleging that GE has engaged in systematic, company-wide discriminatory treatment of its female Executive Band employees and female attorneys." Unlike Betty Dukes at Walmart, Schaefer wasn't certain that other women would sign on. In an interview with the *New York Times*, she commented, "The women at GE are scared to death, so this is the loneliest thing I've ever done." Schaefer's complaint stated that she had "hit the glass ceiling that so many GE women face." After her lawsuit withstood the company's initial efforts to dismiss it, GE settled. Schaefer expressed pride at the time at the outcome of the suit, saying that the "results of the settlement will benefit women at the company." In a joint statement, the company thanked her for her "valuable services and dedicated professionalism" during her employment with GE and affirmed its commitment to promoting women in its executive ranks. Like most such settlements, however, this one swore Schaefer to secrecy about the details and left the GE executives involved in the case free to pursue their careers without accountability for their actions.

Why did Dineen demote Schaefer? The nondisclosure agreement was designed to make sure we don't find out, but here's our best guess. CEOs like Dineen ordinarily value GCs who are competent and efficient, and who have the judgment to resolve disputes before they get out of hand and the experience to anticipate complications. They act as experts who steer the CEO in the right legal direction, and they advise against decisions that could result in a lawsuit. Given the promotions and bonuses Schaefer received at GE, and the awards she received for her leadership of the legal team, she seemed to possess these traits in abundance. So, what was Dineen looking for?

The clue in the complaint is that Dineen wanted a "big time GC." We talked to GE experts who suggested we consider what was going on in the company during that time. During the same year Schaefer was demoted, 2007, the first of the Securities and Exchange Commission (SEC) investigations into Welch-era accounting fraud were in full swing. An important Welch move had been the expansion of GE Capital, an opaque, highly leveraged hedge fund that, at its height, produced almost 60 percent of GE's profits. GE Capital was routinely the most profitable part of the Welch empire, and if Welch had trouble meeting earnings forecasts, he "could always tweak the earnings by turning to GE Capital" to engineer the right numbers. As one CNN reporter explained, GE Capital "pours wealth into the corporate coffers by doing just about everything you can do with money except print it."

An important target of the SEC inquiries involved GE Transportation's locomotive deals. GE Capital had arranged the financing, falsely representing the timing of the transactions to game the quarterly earnings reports that had been so important to GE's success, by "report[ing] end-of-year sales of locomotives that had not yet occurred in order to accelerate more than $370 million in revenue." According to *New York Times* business reporter David Gelles, who wrote a book about Jack Welch entitled *The Man Who Broke Capitalism*, "rather than actually selling the trains to railroad operators, GE had entrusted them to other financial institutions." The result boosted GE's quarterly earnings report. Wall Street rewards such reports (and higher stock prices lead to more valuable executive stock options) even though a company loses money on the arrangements that accelerate the earnings reports—but such maneuvers constitute securities fraud. The subsequent SEC investigation went on for four years, from 2005 to 2009, with GE spending $200 million to fight it, and ultimately paying a relatively minor $50 million penalty.

Neither Dineen nor Schaefer had been in the division when the misdeeds occurred, but GE Transportation had been a major player in the scam, and Dineen undoubtedly had reason to fear he would lose key employees. GE Transportation made railroad (RR) equipment and was part of a small, insular market; there were only a handful of buyers and sellers in the entire country, a small group who all knew each other. Firing GE's players in these markets would be the equivalent of decapitating the entire group. While executives like Dineen and Schaefer would switch jobs every couple of years, the top RR guys stayed put, as their personal connections in the industry were invaluable. GCs ordinarily oversee personal matters of this kind, and GE's regulatory filings indicate that it had taken disciplinary actions, including firing those engaged in "intentional misconduct" as part of the locomotive scam—right around the time when Schaefer was pushed out as General Counsel. Our best guess is that what John Dineen wanted from a "big time GC" was someone who could protect the people Dineen thought critical to GE Transportation.

Dineen had taken charge of a unit that was being hammered by investigations. Dineen needed a subordinate who would make *him* look good in the company's internal competitions. Plus, in a politicized system of decision-making, a GC who ranked below other GCs (perhaps because she was a woman) couldn't provide the edge needed to outmaneuver other divisions. What Schaefer likely did not understand until it was too late was that Dineen didn't want a better lawyer in any technical sense, he wanted a better corporate in-fighter. In short, he wanted his own man, a "big time GC," who could protect him by asserting dominance in GE internal wars.

Though Jack Welch's innovations transformed corporate America, they didn't always improve corporate performance. Quite the contrary, his highly touted proteges mostly failed at other companies. And Harvard Business School Professor Michael Jensen, who came up with the idea of pay for performance that Jack Welch implemented, renounced his own creation once he saw what the Welch system had wrought. In his mea culpa, Jensen stated the obvious: if you pay people in terms of whether they meet arbitrary targets like quarterly earnings, they will learn to game those targets. In short, they lie. And those lies, Jensen concluded, destroy the value of the companies. Once the financial crisis of 2009 revealed the lies on which Welch's success had been based, GE never recovered.

The system of high-stakes bonus pay that makes internal competition (outfox the employees in the next cubicle) more important than external competition (outperform other companies) has outlasted Jack Welch. It endures because tying top executive pay to share price has proved an effective way to boost executive compensation and a means to allow CEOs to create whatever incentives they deem appropriate. While most companies abandoned the rank-and-yank system in its pure form, incentive pay has become almost universal. And although most companies do not follow GE and Walmart's example, and fire their bottom performers every year, the reciprocal loyalty that once tied workers to companies for entire careers is largely gone. In 1990, more than a third of the private workforce had access to a defined benefit plan that would pay a guaranteed amount when they retired, giving workers an incentive to stay with their companies. Today, that is true for only 15 percent of private-sector workers. Pensions, like workers, are portable, and the worker—not the company—bears the risk that the stock market will tank and the money will not be there for their retirement. The result rewards the alpha males William Whyte lauded—the aggressive, risk-taking narcissists who are attracted to what has been called the corporate "tournament"—and shortchanges women (and many men) who would have thrived in the win-win atmosphere prevalent in the middle of the twentieth century.

Women are at a greater disadvantage in the WTA environment for three reasons: they are less likely to put maximizing their next bonus over their families, their co-workers, and simple decency; they are more likely to be repelled by those who thrive in such environments; and they are more likely to find, as Schaefer did, that in tournament-like environments that in-group favoritism increases.

First, changing to a system of bonus pay has been shown to increase gender disparities; indeed, differences in incentive awards (as opposed to base pay) account for 93 percent of the gender disparities in executive pay. A 2018 study tracking 11,000 employees in a broader range of occupations found that women's bonuses averaged only 69 percent of men's bonuses. While the stakes are lower outside the C-suite, a shift to supposedly merit-based variable pay has similarly been found to increase gender differences in many professions, from teachers to nurses, to start-up founders.

A factor in the gender disparities is the changing relationship between long hours and high pay. Sociologists find that it's "only in the last two decades that salaried employees have earned more by working long hours." Before the WTA economy took hold, people who worked more than fifty hours a week "were paid *15 percent less* per hour on an hourly basis than those who worked traditional full-time schedules." Today, working long hours brings a premium. Those who work fifty hours or more a week make up to 8 percent more an hour than those working more standard hours. Yet those working longer hours are not necessarily more productive. Studies show that working more than fifty hours per week leads to a sharp decline in productivity: "After 55 hours, productivity drops so much that putting in any more hours would be pointless." Instead, overwork and busyness have themselves become measures of status, and performing overwork has become the expectation in many industries and across the globe. Incentive pay fuels the effect. "The reward to become the winner is a lot higher now than in the past. You have to stick out among workers, and one way is by your hours."

Incentive pay, even in more routine positions, then disadvantages those who care less about money as an end in itself, increasing pay disparities for reasons long associated with the gender pay gap. A major factor is that women are more willing to trade shorter, more predictable or part-time hours for less pay. Before the COVID pandemic, for example, male and female nurses differed little in base pay. Instead, male nurses made more because they worked longer hours, thus earning more overtime, and they were more willing to take jobs in more urban than rural settings. Since the pandemic, the demand for nurses has surged and the gender pay gap has almost doubled. Male nurses today earn more because they are more willing to opt for higher-paying emergency duties, more likely to negotiate with their employers, and more willing to change jobs for better pay.

Second, competitive pay that pits workers against each other makes the disparities worse, as it changes the nature of the people attracted to such jobs in the first place. University of Chicago economists, for example, found that men were almost twice as likely as women to apply for a job "if its salary potential was described as being highly dependent on competition with other employees." Women's applications do not fall to the same degree, however, where the competition involves teams— as opposed to individuals—competing against each other or where the competition is one to cure cancer rather than to win the biggest bonus. The issue is not competition per se—almost all the women we describe in this book thrived in competitive environments; rather, women are less likely than men to be drawn to competitions that require succeeding at the expense of their co-workers or being subject to ruthless co-workers' efforts to outmaneuver them. Indeed, women may have particularly good reasons to be wary of such environments, given that the people— male and female—drawn to such highly competitive environments are more likely to have unrealistically high opinions of themselves (including outright narcissism), a large degree of self-confidence (many would say overconfidence), and a greater willingness to take risks and cut ethical corners. These are traits that describe a distinct subset of the general population that is also more likely to be male. As law professor Donald Langevoort observes, "[T]raits such as over-optimism, an inflated sense of self-efficacy and a deep capacity for ethical self-deception are *favored* in corporate promotion tournaments. . . . [T]hey are survival traits, not weaknesses." When Jack Welch described how he reached down into the lower ranks and promoted those with "confidence to spare," he was describing the hubris that has become the hallmark of our new winner-take-all system.

Finally, negative-sum competitions—whereby one employee can win only if another loses—increase distrust and promote in-group favoritism. Research has shown that, across different types of organizations, 60 percent of male managers are uncomfortable mentoring women. Managers in intensely competitive environments, particularly those characterized by masculinity-contest cultures, are more likely to view subordinates as "tools to be exploited to achieve the appearance of the leader's success"; such environments are also more likely to reward ethically dubious or opportunistic behavior. Multiple studies suggest that women are perceived as more ethical than men, "are more likely than men to support ethical business practices," and are more likely to be penalized for violating ethical standards. Studies also show that even in conventional workplaces, such as management positions in retail chains, women receive lower rankings for "potential"—a trait often mistakenly associated with hubris and more commonly ascribed to men than women. Compounding women's disadvantages, men can more easily schmooze with more powerful men in ways that are less accessible to women, and "in fact, social bonding among men may account for more than a third of the gender gap in promotions."

Highly competitive workplaces where managers are pitted against other managers may compound all these factors, as managers may feel the stakes are higher and it is more important to promote subordinates who have "what it takes" to succeed—and to advance the managers' objectives even when they conflict with the best interests of the institution. In such environments, being perceived as more ethical can be a liability. Johanna Harris, a mediator and employee relations consultant, explains further that perhaps the most important factor in women's lack of advancement is trust; to establish trust, the manager must be able to predict the employee's behavior, and many male managers have trouble evaluating and understanding women. This ability to trust a female subordinate's behavior—and to accurately judge her "potential"—is that much more critical in environments where what the supervisor wants is not traditional workplace outcomes, such as Schaefer's legal expertise, but rather the ability to break the rules (preferably without being asked) and get away with it, if that's necessary to outflank workplace competitors. If women are unwilling to act unethically, or if women are less likely to get away with it, as we argue is true in the second leg of the Triple Bind, then women may be outright liabilities in environments that reward ethically dubious behavior.

Women are thus multiply disadvantaged—given their lack of the clout that comes from personal networks, their difficulty achieving the dominance that arises from displays of hubris, and the perception of their being too ethical to stray. When the stakes increase, as they appear to have done at GE Transportation at the height of the securities investigation, an ambitious executive like Dineen may have felt Schaefer as a GC was a risk he couldn't afford because of—not in spite of—her consummate professionalism.

Schaefer's experiences, from her steady ascent up the corporate ladder to her unexpected exit in 2007, and the treatment that ultimately led her to file suit, are indicative of women's experiences in the "new boys' clubs" of the American workplace. Women are welcome to join the entry-level ranks. They often get promotions and appear to prosper. Yet, the number of women in the top corporate ranks at the largest companies has remained miniscule. The record high, set in 2023, was just over 10 percent. And the pipeline is leaky; in 2018, the *New York Times* reported that women and men in business start out equal with respect to jobs and pay. But then the women disappear as they move up the corporate ranks. Women are 30 percent less likely than men to be promoted to manager; just over one-fifth of senior vice presidents are women; and few of them are in positions "related to generating revenue, which generally lead to C-level jobs." And of the women who make it to the senior vice president level, only a small percentage handle the type of responsibilities that would put them in line for promotion to the top jobs. Even when they get to the C-suite, women are most likely to become CEOs of nonprofits or of failing companies that are more likely to derail a career than advance it.

Yet, when women get the chance, they outperform men. Over the ten-year period from 2013 to 2023, the 41 female CEOs at Fortune 500 companies substantially outperformed the 459 male CEOs, producing returns of 384 percent, compared with 261 percent for the male-led

Are Women Better?

Of the S&P 500 companies, there are **459 male** CEOs and **41 female** CEOs.
Women-led companies have significantly outperformed.

companies. A larger study of almost 22,000 companies reported that businesses with more equal gender leadership have a "15 percent boost to profitability."

So, if women outperform the men, and Welch-inspired practices hurt company performances, how can the system be changed? The most promising movements combine calls for management reform with pressure for greater diversity. Critics have condemned the myopic focus on quarterly earnings, and even the corporate community has changed its tune. The Business Roundtable, an association of CEOs with a board that includes the heads of companies ranging from Apple to General Motors to PayPal, has issued a statement on long-term value creation; it points out that pressures, often concerning expectations about short-term earnings, could undercut long-term company growth and value. Even conservative Republican senator Marco Rubio issued a report critiquing the focus on short-term earnings, explaining that companies are "eating themselves—they're committing suicide," he said. "That's impacting industries and having a long-term impact on our national security."

Influenced by the studies showing better performance at more diverse firms, investment funds such as BlackRock have been making diversity a consideration in channeling investments, treating it both as an important societal objective and as a marker of good management practices. This is what we call "the instrumental case for diversity"— the argument that women (and often minorities) are the canaries in the coal mine for unethical or counterproductive practices, and therefore, that better diversity is aligned with better management. Diversity within this movement is both a metric and a tool, signaling problems or serving as a sign of change. As part of these diversity efforts, some countries have mandated greater gender diversity on corporate boards. So have several American states, with some mandating reporting on diversity or even quotas. And the Nasdaq exchange has endorsed the efforts to diversify boards as an important step toward greater transparency, better corporate performance, and less fraud.

We doubt that simply adding women will reform corporate America, eliminating fraud and increasing performance, but we are confident that companies that manage genuine diversity need to have greater transparency and trust to make diversity work. And those qualities turn out also to be good for business—at least if the focus extends beyond the next quarter. And there are ways to change the focus of corporate America, as we discuss in this book's Conclusion.

Jack Welch died in March 2020 at the age of 84. At the time of his death, he was reputedly worth at least 750 million dollars. His obituaries noted the bankruptcy of his management theories and the negative consequences for GE. Welch had turned a manufacturing giant—one of the biggest and most prosperous in the American economy—into an investment bank. By 2022, even that business had been dismembered;

the iconic, century-old company for all practical purposes is gone. Yet, Welch was never held accountable for the consequences of the practices he implemented while head of GE.

And Lorene Schaefer? After obtaining her settlement against GE, she put her experiences to good use. She founded her own law firm, Schaefer & Associates, a boutique firm focused on mediation that conducts internal inquiries into alleged workplace misconduct, investigating complaints and resolving disputes for major corporations. Her career, however, no longer depends on climbing a corporate ladder where the ambitious casually jettison others. With her own firm, she can mentor rising women and prepare them to succeed.

CHAPTER 3

Counting on Wall Street: Messina v. Bank of America Corp.

In May 2016, a news report caught our attention. The story, which focused on a lawsuit by Megan Messina against Bank of America, brought together charges of sex discrimination and efforts to cover up wrongdoing, a pattern we increasingly find in modern sex discrimination cases, from Tesla to dental offices.

Messina, a top female banker, was suing Bank of America (BOA) for "unlawful discrimination," accusing the company of being a "bros' club" and favoring its male employees over women. Further, she claimed that BOA had punished her when she complained about "questionable activity" at the institution, leading to her being put on leave and effectively ending her career at the company.

By the time Messina filed suit, she was a Wall Street veteran. She was a 42-year-old single mother, who had navigated her career while being the primary caregiver, sole custodian, and financial supporter of her three children ages 11, 9, and 6. She had graduated from Marymount College with a BA in sociology and history in the mid-nineties, and started work in the financial services industry at the investment bank Paine Webber soon afterward. She moved to Salomon Smith Barney in 1998; at the time she started at Salomon Smith Barney, the investment bank was still reeling from sexual harassment allegations that had made national headlines two years earlier. She established her financial career as the firm was being absorbed into Citigroup and as Ivy League graduates were flooding into Wall Street. In September 2007, she moved to Bank of America, escaping the fallout at Citi as it became the epicenter of the Wall Street–triggered financial crisis that plunged the nation into a steep recession in 2008.

By 2009, Messina wasn't only surviving but thriving. Bank of America had acquired Merrill Lynch to kickstart its entry into investment banking, and Messina joined those efforts. Messina's previous roles had placed her in a fortuitous position for this moment post-crash. A specialized type of securities that bundled mortgages and then resold them (CDOs, short for collateralized debt obligations) had just blown up the global economy. In their heyday, CDOs were so lucrative that women were frozen out of the deals. Instead, women like Messina were shunted into a similar security that bundled much safer corporate loans (CLOs, or collateralized loan obligations). In the aftermath of the financial crisis, CDOs were toast, but CLOs (thought of as their "little sisters") boomed, becoming the best-performing asset class of 2009. Messina built up this business at Bank of America. In 2011, she was promoted to managing director and then, in 2015, became co-head of Global Structured Credit Products and Credit Asset Financing. A trader, David Trepanier, was also promoted and made co-head of the same unit. *GlobalCapital*, which styles itself as the "foremost information source of the international capital markets," announced the two new co-heads with the headline, "BAML Reshuffles NY Structured Credit with New Co-Heads."

Throughout her time at Bank of America, Messina's legal complaint stated, she had worked for many managers, all of them men. She "consistently received stellar performance reviews concerning her diligence, competence, exceptional management skills, and ability to enhance the profitability of the business and services that she managed." The year of her 2015 promotion, however, she began to report to Frank Kotsen, Head of Global Credit and Special Situations. From their first conversation, her complaint alleges, it was clear that Messina was wading into choppy waters. During that meeting, Kotsen told her, "I don't understand what you do." Messina told him about the "value add" she brought to his group thanks to her understanding of CLOs, as well as her ability to cross-sell Bank of America's other products. She had a significant network of customer contacts who valued her expertise and who provided a solid base for future sales. As she spoke, Kotsen "exhibited visible boredom and was blatantly not engaged." Instead, he seemed more interested in Messina's appearance. Twice, he stopped Messina to ask: "Have you colored your hair?" and "Have your eyes always been that blue?"

Things, she maintained, got worse from there. Messina was the only female managing director reporting to Kotsen, and he continued to make it clear to her that "she was NOT welcome within his subordinate 'bros' club' of all-male sycophants." He excluded Messina from email groups, meetings, after-work dinners, and gatherings with others in their cohort. He even left Messina out of get-togethers with *her own clients* while including her male colleagues. According to the lawsuit, Kotsen treated Messina "more like a summer intern than an accomplished, experienced, and successful Managing Director at one of the world's largest banks, where her role was responsible for annually generating hundreds of millions of dollars in revenues."

Messina's description of how Kotsen treated her was demeaning but not surprising. Messina's lawsuit is one of many claiming bias on Wall Street against female bankers. In fact, only four days after Messina filed her suit, the *Wall Street Journal* ran an article with the title: "Women in Elite Jobs Face Stubborn Pay Gap." It found that five of the ten major occupations in which the pay gap for women was highest were in finance.

Messina's conviction that Kotsen's ill-treatment of her was discriminatory grew as she watched how he treated the co-head of her division, David Trepanier. While Kotsen excluded Messina from important meetings, he met regularly with Trepanier, often for long chats, as frequently as three times a day. Over the course of that year, Messina reached out to her boss on at least a monthly basis to better explain to him how she could grow Bank of America's business and in the hope of establishing a rapport with him. In response, she maintained, Kotsen either ignored her or "blew her off." Finally, in December 2015, Kotsen invited Messina to his office to discuss her annual bonus for the 2015 calendar year. It was the second and only other time Messina had met with Kotsen. As he glanced at Messina's peer reviews, he told her, "I've never seen better peer reviews (360s) such as yours. Are these real?" He also reluctantly told her that according to client surveys and informal customer feedback, she had outperformed her co-head, Trepanier.

Yet, Messina reported in her complaint, Kotsen ignored or belittled Messina's contributions while he rewarded Trepanier's. In the suit, Messina's lawyers included a chart that she presented as summarizing the imbalances at Bank of America between Messina and her "similarly situated male peers" over a period of three years. The chart, complete with names and compensation, set out the claimed gendered disparities in pay at Bank of America, and dramatically contrasted the company's differential treatment of Trepanier and Messina. In 2015, according to the chart, Kotsen gave Trepanier a bonus that was nearly $4 million more than Messina's—"an astonishing difference of 360%." Trepanier was awarded this compensation, Messina maintained, even while he was engaging in multiple instances of improper trading behaviors. The complaint also specifically alleges that Kotsen knew of and "supported and promoted Trepanier" in improper behavior.

Not only was Messina's 2015 bonus the lowest of all Kotsen subordinates by a significant margin, but it was also "grotesquely and disparately lower than many of Trepanier's reports, traders—who are less senior, less qualified, men." Messina's complaint suggests two possible explanations: blatant gender discrimination or extraordinary rewards for Trepanier's actions.

One of the first things Messina had done as head of the CLO business was to develop transactions guidelines, vetted by Bank of America's legal counsel. When she and Trepanier became co-heads of the Global Structured Credit Products division, she suggested that Trepanier, too, set up CLO transaction guidelines to govern his part of the business. His reported response was to scoff, insisting, "Without guidelines, there are no boundaries, which is how we like it." Given the nature of her own professional responsibilities, the complaint alleges Messina was "concerned about being a Co-Head to a business that did not firmly abide by regulatory guidelines and procedures, especially where the other Co-Head was cavalier about securities laws and regulations." Her complaint indicates that she was more concerned than he was about what might happen if their unit violated the law—or even if it simply acquired a reputation for a flippant disregard of legal requirements.

Elsewhere in the complaint, Messina accused Trepanier of using information about her customers' interests in purchasing securities to buy them up for Bank of America instead of for the customers, which presented a clear conflict of interest. When Messina accused him of acting improperly, Trepanier responded by telling her that he "did not care what she thought." But Messina cared; this involved her customers—the ones whose business she had cultivated and grown for Bank of America. Messina prided herself on her high customer reviews, reviews that were higher than Trepanier's. The complaint alleged that the unethical behavior was part of a pattern: Trepanier was also alleged to have conducted an auction in a way that violated industry standards, exploited conflicts of interest in ways that disadvantaged bank customers, and generated complaints from important bank clients.

The complaint describes Messina becoming increasingly concerned, and then frustrated, at what she saw as the unethical behavior and its rewards. After the December meeting with Kotsen, in which he questioned whether her customer reviews were real, Messina had reached her limit. In accordance with Bank of America procedures, she decided to report both the discriminatory behavior *and* Trepanier's improper conduct to the higher-ups. In the coming weeks, she repeatedly met with Kotsen's manager, James DeMare, as well as the HR representative for her

business, Ava Mehta, to discuss Kotsen's biased behavior toward her and
the disparities in pay between her and her male peers. She also discussed
the trading behavior she had witnessed. The complaint describes that
when Messina recounted several instances of what she maintained was
Trepanier's improper behavior, DeMare's response was "Really?" and that
"there was no follow-up and no eagerness to solve the problem."

Not only did the complaint allege that Bank of America failed to investigate any of Messina's complaints or take any actions to address her
concerns, but also that her employers responded by putting *her* on administrative leave. As a potential explanation for her employer's action,
Messina's complaint says that it occurred to her that DeMare's compensation was "directly correlated" to the profit flowing from Trepanier's
trading activities. When it became clear that her employer would not
remedy the situation, Messina sued, citing Title VII's prohibition of sex
discrimination and the whistle-blower protections in Dodd-Frank, the
financial reform act passed in the wake of the 2008 financial crisis.

Her 2016 complaint was hard-hitting. She coupled her sex discrimination claim with whistle-blower allegations about Trepanier's trading
behavior. The 2010 Dodd-Frank Act was designed to prevent the highly
risky activities that resulted in the 2008 financial crisis. It had restricted
those activities like the ones in which Trepanier was allegedly engaged,
and similar dealings were already the subject of a government investigation against Bank of America in North Carolina, where Bank of
America had its headquarters. Messina's lawyers also detailed examples
of other women at Bank of America who had suffered from similarly
discriminatory behavior. Those allegations and her reference to a Bank
of America's "bros' club" generated headlines.

Messina filed her complaint in May 2016, and by September, she had
reached a settlement—which certainly seems to be a short time period
for a case of this nature. Given the speed of the settlement, it is likely
that the charges stung, and that Bank of America was willing to rush a
settlement to avoid further publicity. As with many such settlements,
Bank of America publicly denied the allegations without providing

details, and the parties signed a nondisclosure clause that prevents further discussion of the case. We can assume only that the settlement was somewhere between the $500,000 severance package Bank of America offered her before she sued and the more than $14 million that Messina claimed as back pay and lost bonus damages in her complaint.

Messina is not the only woman who has filed suit against her Wall Street employer for equal pay, appropriate standards of performance review, and fair access to promotional opportunities. Women have historically faced an uphill battle as they fight to keep a toehold in finance, let alone break into its upper ranks. Over the course of the 1990s, women brought a series of lawsuits to claim equal status and opportunities for advancement, starting with brokerage firms.

Perhaps the most notorious was the one brought against Smith Barney in 1996 that revealed the firm's Garden City (New York) office had a raucously decorated party room, known as "the boom boom room," where clients were entertained and women who entered risked sexual assault. Suits against Merrill Lynch and Morgan Stanley quickly followed.

In the case against Merrill Lynch, broker Teresa Contardo claimed sex discrimination and sexual harassment, including pornographic pictures left on her desk, being groped at office gatherings, exotic dancers visiting the office, and phallic birthday cakes. Contardo tried to ignore the harassment and, despite the odds, became one of the top producers in Boston. But what she found worse than the "locker room atmosphere" was being relentlessly excluded from information and meetings, and being assigned low-paying accounts—what she referred to as "crumbs from the table." In a bench trial, the judge determined that the discrimination "was relatively covert, and habitual, even mindless, rather than pre-meditated, though no less detrimental from the plaintiff's point of view, or illegal from this court's point of view," and awarded Contardo $250,000.

The judge's comment that the discrimination was mindless points to the nature of the trading culture, and indeed any corporate atmosphere that is fueled by competition and testosterone. In the nineties, at least some of the sexual harassment was intended to drive women out—to say, "You don't belong here." Now, when women are present and treated as one of the boys, low-level harassment—condoms on pizzas in place of pepperoni—is an extension of frat-boy culture. It *is* mindless, but it's part of the testing process: if you can't take it, you don't belong on the trading floor.

These lawsuits brought attention to women's challenges in breaking into Wall Street and what they experienced once they had gotten in the door. HR departments took claims of physical assault and egregious harassment more seriously going forward. However, though women no longer had to worry about being assaulted in boom boom rooms, 60 percent of women financial advisors working today still report facing sexual harassment in the workplace.

Moreover, winning promotions to supervisory positions, as Messina did, does not appear to provide much protection. Researchers have found that women supervisors are more likely to experience sexual harassment than are women in other positions. Indeed, rising in a competitive institution may make them targets. If Kotsen did not see Messina as an ally, he could easily have seen her as a threat, and therefore not a candidate for membership in the type of bros' networks integral to succeeding at Bank of America. Harassment cases are neither isolated instances nor relics of the past, though today, powerful men on Wall Street quickly settle the cases that threaten to embarrass them.

While Wall Street culture has always faced challenges for women, the return of the business cycle, with economy-wide booms and busts, has made it harder for women who gain a toehold in finance to stay there. By the late 1980s, the proportion of female stock analysts at brokerage firms had risen from 5 percent in the 1970s to 20 percent. That number took a nosedive after the financial downturn at the end of the decade, though. Women's gains resumed in the 1990s, as they sought to join men in the most lucrative jobs available to new college grads, and as the investment banking and brokerage firms, stung by discrimination claims, promised to do better. Over the course of the next two decades, Wall Street, the financial sector, and the American economy would weather the dot.com bust, the Enron and World.com scandals, the housing boom, and a new financial crisis—and as they did, the percentage of women in finance continued to fall. "Catalyst [a nonprofit that works with businesses to build inclusivity] blogged in 2010 that the number of women between the ages of 20 and 35 in the brokerage and asset management industries dropped more than 15% from 2000 to 2010, while the number of comparable men rose." The percentages were worse at the higher levels. "Women in financial services comprise . . . only 16% of senior executives and none of the CEOs"—at least until Jane Fraser was appointed CEO of Citibank in 2021. Although women are in the game at the lower levels of financial organizations, they have had a harder time gaining effective leadership roles.

This is a problem because, when we look at gender gaps in all occupations, the top job categories are all in finance. An analysis of personal financial advisors, for example, showed that at the time covered by the complaint, women earned 58.4 cents on the dollar compared to men; other surveys found similar gaps among insurance agents, security sales agents, financial managers, and clerks. Moreover, as compensation within the financial sector soared, the representation of women declined. Despite increasing numbers of female MBAs into the 2000s, their numbers on Wall Street dropped after 2000, and didn't begin to recover until after 2013. The rise of finance as a more dominant part of the economy—and women's declining fortunes within it—account for a large part of the increase in the gender wage gap for college graduates since the mid-nineties. This affects not just the ability of women to profit from the high salaries in finance but also women's access to the sector that is pulling the levers of power throughout the economy.

Taken as a whole, it's clear that the world of finance is one of the principal factors in women's loss of economic clout since the 1990s. Between 1982 and the financial crash that began in 2007, wages in the financial sector doubled while they grew only modestly in other industries. They jumped even more at the top, becoming higher than in any other profession. And while wages plummeted in the immediate wake of the financial crisis, Wall Street compensation (including the bonuses Messina's complaint details) rebounded earlier than the rest of the economy. Looking at *Forbes*'s annual list of the four hundred richest Americans, "for almost one in four, finance—especially hedge funds and private equity—was the source of wealth, while 15 percent came from technology-based companies."

The conventional explanations of why women don't thrive in finance are the same explanations with which we started this book. Women are said to make different choices: they are less greedy, less drawn to jobs that involve risk, and less willing to put in long hours because of family responsibilities. Yet, finance has had no difficulty in attracting women. Indeed, in 2021, women made up 52 percent of those taking entry-level jobs in the financial services. Instead, McKinsey consultants found that the industry has a "leaky pipeline," with the representation of women falling in every tier beyond entry level, with a particularly steep decline for minority women: "from entry level to the C-suite, the representation of women of color falls by 80 percent." The question, therefore, is not why women aren't attracted to finance; it's *why they don't stay.*

To fully understand the fate of Messina, and of women like her on Wall Street, we need to look at the forces that *enabled* the dynamics she experienced and how the nature of competition within the industry undervalues the customer service on which Messina prided herself.

To comprehend who ends up in corner offices, we need to go back to the dismantling of the protections that effectively eliminated financial crises for a remarkable half-century following the Great Depression. After the financial excesses of the 1920s led to the stock market crash of 1929, the wolves of Wall Street were brought to heel by the New Deal government of Franklin D. Roosevelt. The predatory bankers and brokers who had blown up the economy were forced to reform. The Securities Acts of the early 1930s led to the creation of the Securities and Exchange Commission, an independent government agency that regulates the securities industry, maintaining fairness and protecting investors (and where author Naomi Cahn briefly worked). Meanwhile, the Federal Deposit Insurance Corporation insured bank deposits and tightly regulated the safety and soundness of commercial banks, while the Glass-Steagall Act, passed in 1933, mandated the separation of commercial banks from the riskier business of investment banking. In addition, the New York Stock Exchange had a longstanding rule requiring that investment banks trading directly on the exchange be held in partnership form; this meant that the partners' own money was on the line if the firm failed or faced liability from lawsuits or fines. Thus, taking risks meant risking their own money. Post–New Deal, the wolves of Wall Street had been firmly put in their pen.

Investment banking in this era was a fairly sedate and clubby enterprise. The investment banks were often family owned (three brothers started Salomon Brothers, and Billy Salomon, the son of one of the founders, was a driving force behind the firm into the seventies), and they tended to be identifiably WASP-ish like Morgan Stanley or identifiably Jewish like Goldman Sachs. Merrill Lynch, Pierce, Fenner & Smith, engaged in brokering the securities that investment banks originated, was once considered the "Catholic firm" of Wall Street. These family-owned enterprises were run by men who made sure that an errant trader did not tarnish the family name and fortune. The ethnically identified companies also took care of their own; Merrill Lynch employees, for example, referred to "Mother Merrill," a "family firm where you put in your time, got paid, and maybe hired an employee's son." While financial firms like Merrill Lynch managed other people's money, the postwar era reforms dampened the ability and incentive to make money through illicit or reckless means. The major financial firms prided themselves on customer care and prudent risk management. As one banker explained, investment banks were "united by joint ownership of the risks and the rewards, with each business run by a partner whose money was invested in his and his friends' businesses."

Unlike the relatively staid investment bankers of Wall Street, traders have long held a very different reputation. Known for their cocksure arrogance, willingness to take great risks, and contempt for rules that might constrain them, these traders live for the highs of the stock exchange and the fast-paced excitement of the market. For a trader, limits are there to be tested, deceit is simply another weapon in your arsenal, and delight in fleecing your less sophisticated customers is part of the game. It was men like these who had helped lead to the nation's economic downfall in 1929, but during the era of post–New Deal regulation, traders who wanted to defraud a long-time customer had to think twice before acting on that instinct. To do so would be to risk the partners' money, reputation, and wrath. They knew that their success was measured by the firm's survival, and that if they fell out of line, they would be held accountable. The traders' excesses were kept in check by formal regulation, but also by a kind of social control that prioritized the long-term success of an institution over the short-term success of an individual.

The financial deregulation that empowered and unleashed the traders took place in a series of steps that started in 1970. This was the year that the New York Stock Exchange relaxed the rule that member firms be owned by their members. Once the rule came to an end, investment banking opened up, facing greater competition (and, many argue, becoming more meritocratic). In increasing numbers in the 1980s, the investment banking and brokerage firms "went public"—that is, they switched from partnership to corporate form, limiting the liability of their owners. During the same period, the customer-based brokerage and underwriting services that had historically provided much of the revenue for firms like Merrill Lynch and Salomon Brothers became less lucrative, while new opportunities for the firms to trade on their own accounts (and risk the company's own money) increased. By the 1990s, as law professor and former investment banker Frank Partnoy explained, firms realized that they could profit from making financial instruments increasingly complex, and they would benefit "as more parties used financial engineering to manipulate earnings and to avoid regulation." As corporate executives prospered by producing the right numbers, the financiers who helped them gained in importance and collected increasingly high bonuses for doing so.

Throughout the 1980s and '90s, therefore, just as women were gaining a foothold for careers on Wall Street, the firms they went to work for were given a newfound opportunity to profit from the activities of their traders. The Wall Street wolves—who had been waiting for their next opportunity to get rich at someone else's expense—were newly liberated. These men, and they were mostly men, were more than prepared to outfox the market for long enough to bring in millions (with their supervisors either looking the other way or ignorant of the full scope of their activities until it was too late). This increase in risky behavior has been well documented. Michael Lewis's 1989 book, *Liar's Poker*, captured the new Wall Street culture and the celebration of what he called the "big swinging dick." The well-paid class of traders, hired right out of Ivy League colleges, acted "more like students in a junior high school." Firms like Salomon created complex, opaque financial products—and profited from them at the expense of their customers. Indeed, the traders bragged about "blowing up a client"—that is, persuading the client to buy a product certain to decline in value and to force the client out of the market. "Winning"—and the size of the bonus at the end of the year—was what mattered. The big investment banks rewarded, and indeed often glorified, traders who betrayed the trust of their customers. The traders who had been kept in check ever since the New Deal were effectively given back the keys to the market.

These newly public investment banks led the way into a new

financial model—one that has a predictable cycle. Over time, what
had been relatively small, storied institutions took on greater risk,
made individual bankers extraordinarily rich, and helped fuel greater
financial instability in the markets. When a downturn hit, as it did
after the savings and loan crisis of the late eighties, the dot.com bust
of the early 2000s, and the financial crisis of 2008, the Securities and
Exchange Commission and the banking agencies intervened. The
firms sometimes paid fines, some traders lost their jobs, and some
banks—including the storied Salomon Brothers—were forced out of
existence as separate entities, after the government agencies or white
knights like Warren Buffett prevented their collapse long enough to
allow them to be sold to someone else. The reorganized units would
then be acquired by larger banks, and with the economic recovery, the
traders would be back in charge.

Contributing to this growing unaccountability in finance was the
fact that the rules holding the commercial banks in check were easing.
In 1999, Congress repealed Glass-Steagall, the New Deal–era federal law
that mandated the separation of commercial and investment banking.
That meant that the big commercial banks, like Bank of America and
Citigroup, were now free to acquire the old investment banks like Salomon Brothers or Merrill Lynch. And, as the commercial banks grew, they
became "too big to fail."

With the increasing consolidation of the industry, individual bankers were no longer closely supervised. Their status in the bank came
from the size of their bonus; as a former Wall Street bond trader wrote,
a banker got paid "by growing your particular business. That's where
your bonus came from." An employee's incentive was not to make "sure
the larger bank made sustainable profits," but instead "to push the limits
of every risk and grab as much cheap funding as possible." As the financial crisis loomed, one Goldman Sachs trader even bragged in an email
that he was fully prepared to unload toxic mortgage-backed securities
on random "widows and orphans that I ran into at the airport." Then,
in 2008, the markets crashed dramatically, and even the too-big-to-fail

institutions threatened to go belly up. Wall Street's traders, addicted to the excitement that comes from taking risks and having the impunity to exploit the less sophisticated in today's economy—public pension funds and German banks, rather than individual widows and orphans—crashed and burned our economy, depriving 10 million people of their homes in the process. Rather than facing penalties for their recklessness, of course, the firms were again absorbed by the too-big-to-fail banks.

By the time the events in Megan Messina's complaint took place in 2015, one might have hoped that the Dodd-Frank financial reforms, passed in the wake of the 2008 financial crisis, had tamped down the traders' activities a bit. While it's true that tightened regulations and a deep recession limited the opportunities for traders to trigger another global crisis, at the same time the intense pressure for greater revenues and bigger bonuses remained. In fact, post-2008, Wall Street simply reshuffled its playing cards, adjusted to a few more regulations, and then the traders resumed the hunt for customers to fleece as though nothing much had changed.

When Bank of America appointed Messina and Trepanier as co-heads of the same division, it invited a clash of cultures—and an opportunity to exploit intrinsic conflicts of interest. Messina's boss, Frank Kotsen, and her co-director, David Trepanier, were traders. In the description Messina's lawyers painted in her suit, both men embodied the risk-hungry, no-holds-barred trader mentality that had dominated Wall Street since the 1980s and '90s. Trepanier made his money trading on the bank's account; that meant he sought to buy low and sell high, with the bank reaping the profits (and losses) from his transactions. Messina, in contrast, created new securities for customers who paid her fees for doing so. The work she did was therefore intrinsically safer for the bank, and it depended on customer satisfaction. Yet, financial-sector bonus systems do not necessarily take either risk to the bank or customer loyalty into account. Instead, short-term revenue generation—or the boss's subjective evaluation of bankers—is what gets the most attention.

When Bank of America made Messina and Trepanier co-heads of the same division, it thus set them up in what turned out to be a competition Messina could not win.

Seen in this context, Messina's fall seems not only unsurprising but also inevitable. Research shows that workplaces emphasizing masculinity contests, with their high-stakes bonus cultures and internal competition, also select for abusive managers who are more eager to demonstrate their own success than to encourage workplace harmony or productivity. Such managers play favorites: they identify with the workers who have the same traits they see in themselves, and they "are likely to promote exclusion and harassment toward historically disadvantaged groups," including men who are not traditionally masculine or who won't play the same games. The companies overlook the negative side of these characteristics, which include higher turnover, lower employee morale, and a greater incidence of sex discrimination, sexual and racial harassment, and bullying. In certain cases, these managers may drive out the women just to show that they can.

Like Betty Dukes and Lorene Schaefer from Chapters 1 and 2 of this book, Megan Messina had fallen victim to the first rule of the Triple Bind: if women don't compete on the same terms as men, they lose. Even by excelling at her job, as reported by those both within and outside the company, Messina was doomed to lose. She worked with people who seemed to accord little value to adherence to rules and she faced unprofessional treatment perhaps simply because she was a woman. People like Dukes, Messina, and Schaefer who believe in the importance of basic principles of fairness and the rule of law are always going to be at a disadvantage under such conditions. And Wall Street has not been kind to those who try to change the rules of the game; some of the most prominent women forced out of finance have been those who tried to challenge these practices.

Which brings us back to the conventional explanation of why

women don't do well on Wall Street: they do not have the same taste for risk as do men. A variety of studies have debunked the idea that women, simply because they are women, cannot deal with risk; indeed, the women drawn to finance have in fact proved quite good at managing risk. And it's not that women aren't as good as men at making money. In fact, women, if anything, do a little better when they run financial firms. A 2014 report, for example, found that women-owned or managed hedge funds outperformed industry benchmarks during the turbulent years of the financial crisis. Meredith Jones, director at Rothstein Kass, the firm that conducted the study, observed, "Our research shows that . . . [w]omen simply perceive risk differently than men and tend to manage their portfolios accordingly. This results in less performance slippage, a diminished tendency to sell at the bottom, and a more consistent application of their strategies." In short, the research found women in finance to be more astute risk-takers, with more patient and disciplined temperaments better suited to calculated decisions. Those findings are echoed in other research, which similarly finds that women may "trade less overconfident[ly] and focus more on risk management." Such traits certainly pay off in the CLO market: women like Messina overseeing CLO portfolios consistently outperform the men.

Indeed, financial journalist Michael Lewis has suggested that women might be the key to finally taming Wall Street. In a 2014 *Bloomberg* article entitled "Eight Things I Wish for Wall Street," Lewis argued that:

> Men are more prone to financial risk-taking and over-confidence. . . . Trading is a bit like pornography: Women may like it, but they don't like it nearly as much as men, and they certainly don't like it in ways that create difficulties for society. Put them in charge of all financial decision-making and the decisions will be more boring, but more sociable.

While we might have phrased things in less stark terms than Lewis, we think he captures an important truth: the dopamine-fueled highs that drive gambling and the overconfidence needed to believe that you will win at an intrinsically risky game feed on each other and are a critical cause of Wall Street's excesses. When trading becomes not just a job but also a masculinity contest—one in which men establish their cred with other men by competing to take the biggest risks or land the biggest bonuses—they egg each other on. During financial upturns, this atmosphere, if not tightly regulated, feeds on itself. And the more that markets are driven, as Alan Greenspan once said by "irrational exuberance," the more they devalue the greater restraint identified with women. In such environments, women-run firms, which compete with the big boys without any need for chest-thumping masculinity displays, have a decided advantage: they can more prudently manage risk precisely because their business decisions aren't based on proving their identity to others.

Women have also been less inclined to participate in Wall Street's glee in exploiting more vulnerable customers. Sallie Krawcheck, after being pushed out of both Citibank and Bank of America for sticking up for her customers, looked back in 2016 and emphasized that she did not share the guys' club worldview that prevails in finance. She speculated that the differences just might be rooted in gender, with women "more focused on relationships and long-term outcomes than the men." Yet this isn't necessarily a difference between men and women; consider the financial world of the fifties, sixties, and early seventies, where there was a corporate culture very similar to the supposedly "female" outlook. The largely male world of that era also valued relationships and long-term outcomes. While the financial firms of the postwar era did not hire many women, neither did they put traders like Kotsen in charge. A more sober financial system might reward traits, like communication and carefully calculated risk-taking, that are associated with women *and* would perform better for the country as a whole.

So, how do we address these problems in finance? We could focus on taming the Wall Street roller-coaster ride, not just for the benefit of women but also for the economy. The New Deal regulations worked; there were no fraud-fueled financial crises between the Great Depression and the deregulatory era that took hold in the eighties. And numerous studies have found that the rise of finance has produced not only greater financial instability but also lower overall productivity in the economy as a whole. The reasons for this are deeply rooted in the emphasis on short-term thinking; producing immediate gains overshadows longer-term investments. The failure of Silicon Valley Bank in early 2023 illustrates these problems. The bank, threatened by interest-rate risks, "took steps to maintain short-term profits rather than effectively manage the underlying balance sheet risks," producing the bank's failure.

Going forward, we see two causes for optimism. First, over the last three years, the "share of women grew by 40 percent at the senior-vice-president (SVP) level and 50 percent at the C-suite level"; while 64 percent of C-suite executives in the financial services industry are still white males, the trends are in the right direction. The second is that in today's financial crisis, unlike the one that triggered the 2008 Great Recession, financial regulators have launched criminal investigations. SEC Chair Gary Gensler emphasized that, particularly in "times of increased volatility and uncertainty," the SEC is "focused on monitoring for market stability and identifying and prosecuting any form of misconduct that might threaten investors, capital formation, or the markets more broadly." We are convinced that true accountability and the progress of women in finance are deeply interrelated.

PART 2

When Women Play by the Same Rules as Men, They Lose

In the first part of this book, we looked at what happens to women who are trapped in the first tier of the Triple Bind. These are women who strive to succeed in the hyper-competitive WTA workplace, but who lose because they don't see the invisible rules that the men play by. In this second part, we look at women who find themselves trapped in the second tier of the Triple Bind—the classic double bind. These are the women who try to play by the same rules as the men—and still lose.

In this part, we move into the heart of the new economy, tech and finance, where sharp elbows are honored—unless women wield them. We begin in Chapter 4 with a celebrated case from the heart of Silicon Valley. Ellen Pao sued the storied venture capital firm Kleiner Perkins, claiming that the firm had different rules for men and women with regard to pay, promotions, and, most of all, group loyalty. Her lawsuit galvanized the women of Silicon Valley, as it opened an early window into Silicon Valley's bro culture. Pao's story shows how tech innovation depends on the informal personal ties of a culture that bets enormous sums of money on brash young men (and an occasional woman), and then goads them into producing overnight successes. The very qualities Silicon Valley celebrates—the informality, the youth, the risk-taking, and the in-formed hunches of an insular group—guarantee that women will be judged differently, if they survive the bro parties that treat even the most talented women as marks rather than players.

In Chapter 5, we return to the banking sector and witness what happened in the aftermath of the financial crisis when financial services companies such as Wells Fargo shifted from the heady days of mortgage-backed derivatives to the more prosaic world of community banking. The stakes were lower, but the game re-mained the same: how to engineer the numbers that fueled Wall Street excitement and yielded ever-larger bonuses for those in a position to cash in. This time, however, women played a far more influential role, as they had long staffed the positions that attended to customer services. But when scandals focused new scrutiny on Wells Fargo, women bore the disproportionate share of the blame, since women in finance are more likely to be fired and less likely to be rehired for doing the same thing as the men.

CHAPTER 4

Sharp Elbows:
Pao v. Kleiner Perkins

Ellen Pao is a woman who always tried to play the same game as the men. She had been a high achiever from an early age. The child of Chinese immigrants, Ellen grew up with a father who was a PhD in mechanical and aeronautical engineering and who went on to teach at NYU, while her mother was an engineer, one of the first women to receive a PhD in computer science from the University of Pennsylvania. Pao learned to code at the age of 12; in high school and college, she was a straight-A student who developed a habit of sleeping only a few hours a night to give her an edge in her studies. She arrived in Silicon Valley in 1998, as an eager young engineer, entering "an army of earnest engineers who valued nonstop work and saw limitless opportunities for revolutionizing the world." She paid her dues at a series of tech businesses, including a number of startups. Raised to think that she could overcome anything by working twice as hard as those around her, she had "faith in the system," as she later wrote in her 2017 memoir, *Reset*.

When, in 2005, she first laid eyes on the chief-of-staff job description at Kleiner Perkins Caufield and Byers—one of the three most powerful venture capital firms in Silicon Valley—she felt like she was reading her own résumé. As she later described, the requirements for the role at Kleiner were: "an engineering degree (only in computer science or electrical engineering), a law degree and a business degree (only from top schools), management-consulting experience (only at Booz Allen or Bain), start up experience (only at a top start up), enterprise-software-company experience (only at a big established player known for training employees) . . . oh, and fluency in Mandarin." Pao had an electrical engineering degree from Princeton, law *and* business degrees from Harvard, and all the relevant experience and language ability. The recruiter who interviewed her agreed, Pao reports; he "acted as if he'd found a needle in a haystack."

The recruiter immediately introduced her to John Doerr, a legend in venture capital (VC) circles who had contributed to the rise of Amazon and Google. Doerr not only offered her the job, he also launched a campaign to get her to accept. Still, she hesitated. She had loved working in startups, where she felt she had the opportunity to "build something amazing." What's more, she was concerned that she would not fit into VC's culture. Raising money from university endowments, pension funds, and wealthy individuals (including their own partners), VC firms provide the so-called adult supervision, the management experience, and the funding that guide entrepreneurial success. In return, they take an equity stake as part owners of the companies they fund. She thought of VC firms as more of a "poker-and-scotch" environment, whereas by her own description, Pao preferred a board game and a can of soda. She was also worried that this would be a step down in her career, given that she was already head of business development at another company. But Doerr, a consummate salesman, sweetened the deal, telling her that she would be in a position to become a venture capitalist herself—and, if after a year, she still didn't like the job, Kleiner Perkins would get her into one of their hottest startups. Pao ultimately accepted.

When she came on board at Kleiner, she was put in charge of managing Doerr's projects and initiatives, and of identifying new investments to fund. Doerr mentored and encouraged Pao, declaring he had been looking for a "'Tiger Mom–raised' woman" for her role—suggesting he had hired her because he felt she was tough enough to survive in Kleiner's highly competitive environment. From day one, Pao was determined to live up to Doerr's expectations for her. She saw him as a father figure, and she was prepared to play by whatever rules of the game he laid out for her. She had no qualms about working seventy- or eighty-hour weeks. She learned everything she could about the field. She found she had a knack for identifying, nurturing, and supporting startup founders, and a love for understanding new technologies. This role allowed her to meet people with innovative ideas—ones who had the potential to change the world (and make a lot of money in the process). She was promoted to junior partner, and began pulling off multimillion-dollar deals. But despite her qualifications, not to mention her talent, determination, and drive, Pao soon hit a wall at Kleiner.

As she recounts in her memoir, she found herself unable to advance in promotion or pay, often blocked from being able to do her job. When Pao pitched Twitter to her bosses as an investment opportunity in 2007, at the dawn of the social media era, senior partner Matt Murphy told her that Twitter's founding team simply "wasn't business minded." Whenever Pao brought up the opportunity again, insisting Twitter was special, she was rebuffed. Three and a half years later, when a male partner suggested the firm invest in Twitter, Kleiner leapt on it. But by then, Twitter's price had gone up substantially and it was already on a clear path to global success. Nonetheless, the male partner was hailed as a genius and Pao was excluded from the later Twitter investment meetings. Over the years, Pao says she recommended a number of startups that Kleiner passed on when she proposed them but that later went on to become household names. Pao received no compensation or credit for these proposed investment decisions.

Pao became convinced that she was caught in a competition game that was stacked against her—and against the other women in the firm. Venture capital firms pitted partners like Pao against each other. Each firm has a pot of money to invest; the goal of each partner is to invest as large a share of that money as possible in the most promising of startups, gambling that at least one will make it big. Pao explained that this meant, "the more I invest, the less money for you, my partner, to make your investments." Given that many partners were eyeing the same startups, a senior partner with more clout in the firm might poach a junior partner's proposed investments. The art of making the deal, therefore, was not just spotting a promising startup but also locking in Kleiner's funding for the venture before another partner could horn in on the investment. Being too territorial, however, risked being labeled not a team player. And Pao noted that having "sharp elbows" was an epithet hurled only at women; "[j]unior men could sometimes even take ventures from senior partners." The most successful partners had to wield sharp elbows, but the female partners who engaged in the same behavior as the men were met with raised eyebrows and suspicion.

While the firm claimed to prize initiative and drive, Pao's performance reviews dinged her for "pushing too hard to establish herself instead of being collaborative," being too territorial and untrustworthy, pursuing her own agenda, and not being "a team player." This double standard was also reflected in her pay. Pao made a base salary at Kleiner of $400,000, and up to $560,000 with bonuses. Her male peers, who started when she did and were promoted ahead of her, made five times that amount. Pao received conflicting messages, she later told the *New York Times*: "You talk too much/not enough. You're too data-oriented/ you don't bring enough information. There was no consistency, and it was just baffling to me. How do I improve?" Ultimately, after trying various internal routes, she filed a formal complaint that she gave to the managing partners, describing not just what was happening to her but also to other women at the firm. When it produced no changes, she decided to sue.

Pao worked at Kleiner at the nadir of women's inclusion in Silicon Valley's venture capital firms. Clearly, she was not alone in finding the VC world difficult to crack. As Margaret O'Mara, who wrote *The Code: Silicon Valley and the Remaking of America*, explained, Silicon Valley had its own "code" for business success, and it involved, as a reviewer later explained, "casual misogyny." The code grew out of the Valley's informal venture capital culture, which over the course of the last half-century, moved innovation out of the universities and large corporations, which had dominated the early days of the information age, and into high-risk startups, populated by the young, the ambitious, and the driven. The venture capital model depended on the willingness of a small group of funders to take risks on those they saw as replicating the qualities they admired in themselves, which often meant men hiring other men. And VC's influence grew during that last half-century, setting the terms for its own success, but also remaking the foundation of technological innovation.

In the middle of the twentieth century, innovation had typically occurred in government-sponsored university research labs or private prestige centers, such as AT&T's Bell Labs. Large companies, funded by military and aerospace contracts, implemented the new technologies. In the early days, the computer industry, dominated by big companies like IBM, hired large numbers of male and female coders. The men of that era were seen more as "nerds," rather than the "bros" who would later dominate Silicon Valley startups. The women were often shunted into data entry, processing the data cards on which large mainframe computers depended. Still, male and female interest in the field rose together, with both increasing in lockstep.

Kleiner Perkins helped change the government-funded/large-business innovation model. As one of the first venture capital firms in Silicon Valley, it marshaled private funding to invest in the best early-stage tech companies. The venture capitalists, the seasoned repeat players in the business, did not just provide funding, they also set the tone for the budding corporate culture. They guided the young entrepreneurs, embedded them in the Valley's "personal, tightly networked" culture, helped them to generate favorable publicity, and oversaw their progress to an IPO (an initial public offering of company shares on the stock market) or sale to a larger company. While most startups failed, the right VC backing could increase the odds of success. Amazon founder

Jeff Bezos, for example, who enjoyed better offers from other venture capitalists, accepted Kleiner's funding offer in 1996 because "having John Doerr behind amazon.com would impress Wall Street."

Venture capital firms like Kleiner, with their billions to invest, encouraged its VCs to spot promising entrepreneurs and fund them. They backed people they got to know—men "alike in age, education and temperament." But they also were comfortable making decisions based on impulse: one engineer described how, over twenty minutes at lunch, he got a commitment for $2.5 million on the basis of a business plan written on the back of an envelope. He reported in wonder, "They believe in me. In Boston, you couldn't do that." The VC model helped jump-start tech innovation. And the model prided itself on its lack of bureaucracy, its lack of rules.

John Doerr, who went on to be Pao's boss, joined the Kleiner firm in 1980, after working as an engineer at Intel. Born in St. Louis, Missouri, he had earned a master's degree in electrical engineering from Rice University and an MBA from Harvard. Driven and competitive, he was once described in a *New Yorker* profile as "a highly caffeinated Clark Kent." Doerr was willing to take massive risks, and he had a nose for success. He became known as a kingmaker, the "wizard behind the curtain" who picked entrepreneurs and put them on the path to success.

Doerr's most striking risks—and his greatest influence—came with the dot.com boom of the nineties. The race was on to fund commercialization of the internet. Tens of billions of dollars flooded into the industry, reaching a height in 2000 of more than $100 billion, a dollar amount that would not be seen again until 2018. It was a decade in which, in Doerr's words, "we witnessed (and benefited from) the largest legal creation of wealth on the planet." So much money flooded into the market that it altered the balance between the VCs and the entrepreneurs; the VCs, accustomed to setting the terms for the startups, found the tables turned on them. In histories of this era, Doerr's backing of Jim Clark, the founder of Netscape, in the mid-nineties proved to be a turning point. Clark, a driven man with a hot temper, viewed the VCs as velociraptors—"financial predators that bought entrepreneurs' ideas on the cheap and kept most of the rewards." He demanded a bigger cut, and Doerr, who had known Clark for years (and whose trusted associates raved about Netscape), gave it to him because he believed in Clark.

The *New York Times* hailed Netscape's IPO in August 1995 as the "best opening day in Wall Street history" for a stock issuance of its size. Netscape's success on Clark's terms "shifted the balance of power in Silicon Valley." It also touched off the era of the hyper-valued firms that cashed in with IPOs before they had cleared a cent in profits.

These deals—deals on terms that entrepreneurs demanded and deals that poured millions into untested, rapidly growing startups—altered the culture of Silicon Valley. Emily Chang, author of *Brotopia: Breaking Up the Boys' Club of Silicon Valley*, describes this period as the one that cemented the rise of the "bros." The founders came to display a "volatile mix of entitlement, hubris, and risk-taking," as the firms overwhelmingly chose to fund a certain kind of man, often without any real business experience, who could stride into a room and confidently promise to create a unicorn—a billion-dollar company. Although women by that time were gaining entry into VC firms, the ideal founder was already typecast. The VCs, the supposed adults in the room, were handing the keys to the family car to untested adolescents.

The new bros of Silicon Valley created an even less hospitable climate for women than the earlier nerd-engineering culture, and when the bros crashed and burned with the dot.com bust of 2000, they took a disproportionate share of women with them. In 1999, at the height of the boom, women constituted 10 percent of venture capital partners; by 2014, that number had fallen to 6 percent. The number of VC firms also fell by half in the years after the dot.com crash. When the firms began to rebuild with the recovery, following the 2009 financial crisis, they disproportionately hired the winners of the dot.com era—and in the dot.com era, the percentage of women founders was even smaller than the percentage of women in VC firms.

At the time of Pao's trial, the percentage of VC funding going to female founders had never exceeded 3 percent of the VC total. To explain this discrepancy, at Pao's trial John Doerr testified that "it's the experience—entrepreneurial experience or considerable operating experience at a company—that counts." The problem, for women, as Doerr argued, is that women have had a hard time getting the funding that would allow them to become tech entrepreneurs in the first place. In short, women had trouble gaining entry to the VC pipeline, even in the best of circumstances—but was Doerr's assessment the whole story? Pao's experience—and the growing literature that her trial sparked—outlines a more complex set of factors than Doerr presented. For one thing, women got the message to not even join VC firms. Consider what happened at a Harvard Business School extracurricular event during that time, during which a female student asked a VC capital firm partner for guidance about entering the field: "'Don't,' he laughed, according to several students present. Male partners did not want them there, he continued, and he was doing them a favor by warning them." For another, when venture capital firms began to rebuild as the economy recovered from the 2009 financial crisis, a new group of aggressive Ivy League men, who a few years earlier would have gone to Wall Street, elbowed them out of the way. Facebook's IPO in 2012—that is, the initial public offering of Facebook stock under the leadership of then 28-year-old Mark Zuckerberg—garnered well over a hundred billion dollars, and remade Silicon Valley's reputation as the place to make a quick fortune. "Now you had the frat boys coming in, and that changed the culture," Pao wrote. "It was just a different vibe. People were talking more about the cool things they had done than the products they were building." Pao points out that at Kleiner, "managing partners were always competing for more—more board seats, more houses, more land, and, always, more jets." The venture capitalists' new culture, in turn, influenced the founders and the culture of the startups they ran; and Pao claims, they once again "tended to make investments in new firms started by people they knew, or by people who were like them."

Pao won her entry into Kleiner Perkins the same way the men did: Doerr had a model in mind and Pao fit it perfectly. Doerr recognized that Kleiner needed more diversity—he is far from a villain in this story. Doerr saw Pao as the woman to do it: she was driven, she was smart, she had startup experience—and she spoke Mandarin. During his earliest meetings with Pao, he made it clear to her that Kleiner was one of the few VC firms with women on its staff, and that he wanted to bring in more, that diversity was important to him. In the early 2000s, he had begun to see a fundamental flaw in the tight-knit Silicon Valley tech and VC networks he himself had done so much to establish: they were excluding women and people of color. So, beginning in the 2000s, he began consciously to hire from outside the white male pool in an attempt to shake things up. When he brought in Pao, she was, in many ways, his mea culpa. And he didn't simply leave her to her own devices. He nurtured and mentored her. In her first five years at Kleiner, she and Doerr formed a relationship she described, according to Kleiner's trial brief, as "positive, supportive, and like that of a father and daughter."

Doerr likely hoped that he could bring Pao into the mix, tell her to do what he did, and she would succeed. The problem was, he hadn't taken into account the second tier of the Triple Bind: that when women try to compete on the same terms as men, they lose. The problem for Pao was that traits that had worked so well for Doerr didn't work so well for her. As we've seen in prior chapters, hyper-competitive environments are much tougher on women than they are on men—and VC firms are among the most competitive out there.

Within the tight personal networks of Silicon Valley, the opportunity to spot and then land the unicorns meant being part of the "new boys' club" at Kleiner, and that club excluded Pao from the start. As she writes in her memoir, "You can't always get ahead by working hard if you're not part of the 'in' crowd," and the in-crowd at Kleiner was exclusively male. In VC, Pao writes, "a ton of power is concentrated in just a few people, who all know one another. White men dominate the field, creating a boys'-club environment." Pao, for instance, described the exclusion of women from an all-male ski trip and a dinner with former vice president Al Gore, because the men planned to show porn films on the plane ride. Women were told their presence would "kill the buzz." A big part of the VC job is about being in the know, not just about the technology but also about the people critical to success in the Valley. This, according to Pao, made it tough for the women to succeed, since they were excluded from these opportunities to network. In her complaint, Pao alleges that Kleiner even allowed male junior partners to add "multiple Boards of Director positions and investment sponsor-ships" each year while women were limited to one. For budding VCs, in-vestment sponsorship—becoming the investor who provides the funds and oversees the startup's development—and serving on that company's board is a critical source of influence and networking inside and out-side the VC firm. Since there were very few senior women at the firm, Kleiner's limits put the women at an additional disadvantage. The limits on multiple directorships and investment sponsorships, coupled with the exclusion from networking opportunities and the absence of senior women mentors, amounted to a triple handicap for junior women.

But to see a crystal-clear example of how Pao was treated measur-ably differently from the male partners at the firm, we only have to look at the trajectory of Ajit Nazre, another junior partner in the firm. This was the man with whom Pao had a brief consensual affair soon after she arrived at the firm. Pao describes Nazre as making the first move, hitting on Pao while on a work trip to Germany and continuing to chase her on their return. Initially, she says that she held him at arm's length, but he continued to pursue Pao, telling her that he was separated from his wife, that they were getting a divorce, and that he wanted to be with her. In her memoir, Pao describes herself as working long hours, lonely and open to the idea of a relationship with someone at the firm. The two began seeing one another. "It felt good to have an ally, because the workplace invited so much competition," Pao wrote. But the relation-ship did not last long. When Pao learned that Nazre had lied about his separation from his wife, she ended things immediately.

After that, according to Pao, Nazre began to retaliate against her. He became increasingly hostile to her, excluding her from meetings, leaving her off emails, and blocking her work. Pao tried to extend an olive branch, in the interests of smoothing over their working relationship, but to no avail. By the middle of 2007, she was so frustrated with Nazre's behavior she sent an email to her boss, John Doerr, telling him she wanted to leave Kleiner. Doerr persuaded her to stay, promising that he would give her more opportunities to invest. He even offered to fire Nazre, although Nazre's boss persuaded him that Nazre should stay—and Pao said she could work with him.

Soon after, Nazre was promoted to senior partner, which meant he was now in a position of power over Pao, while she remained at the junior level. Between 2007 and 2009, Pao made several complaints, both verbal and written, about Nazre, who had begun giving her negative reviews. After one of these complaints, the firm asked her to move her office to the back of their building, so that Nazre could move to a bigger one across the hall. When she pointed out that she didn't think moving her away from the corridors of power would fix the problem, it was suggested that Pao, a fluent Mandarin speaker, "transfer to the China office." More pointedly, she was simply told to "Stop talking about it [the situation with Nazre]." When, in 2009, Pao asked for compensation in line with her value, Doerr, who had once championed her at the firm, "told her to stop complaining" about it. Pao, rather than Nazre, had become "the problem."

Eventually, Pao confided in another female partner, Trae Vassallo, about her experiences. This is how she learned that Nazre had hit on Vassallo as well, showing up at Vassallo's hotel room wearing only a bathrobe and carrying a glass of wine. Vassallo sent him packing, but when she raised the issue with another partner, he joked "that she should be 'flattered.'" After learning that Nazre's behavior was not an isolated event, Pao sent an email to Kleiner's Chief Operating Officer (COO) and managing partners, laying out her concerns about Nazre and the culture at the firm, hoping to reach a solution. Vassallo made a similar complaint. Nazre was put on leave, but he continued to come into the office meetings. Pao soon learned Nazre was negotiating for a massive severance package. Two months later, he left the firm with what Pao assumes was a multimillion-dollar buyout. When the COO asked how much Pao wanted to "quietly leave," she responded. "I want no less than what Ajit [Nazre] gets." Pao's golden parachute failed to appear, and instead a number of partners, particularly Nazre's allies, continued to give her negative reviews. Kleiner tried again to persuade her to quietly leave.

The difference in treatment between Pao and Nazre appears stark; after all, they were both parties to the affair. Both were assets to the organization. Both were highly ambitious. But whereas Nazre got promoted—and, Pao speculated, received a handsome buyout when the firm received complaints that he was hitting on female partners and subordinates, and then retaliating against them—Pao faced retaliation and discrimination. Office romances are dicey in most organizations; they have always been particularly difficult for women to navigate. If the couple become allies within the organization, the woman risks resentment for sleeping her way to greater influence. If the breakup takes place publicly, particularly with charges of betrayal or misconduct, colleagues are asked to take sides. In the "he said, she said" aftermath of their affair, Nazre won the game of office politics. He had a stronger network of allies within Kleiner, and Pao, already isolated as one of relatively few women in the firm, became further disliked.

When Ellen Pao filed her sex discrimination suit in 2012, it was the first of its kind in Silicon Valley. In it, she accused her employer, Kleiner Perkins, of discriminating against her and other female employees because of their gender. The lawsuit described her struggles to be taken seriously at the firm, the hostility she faced after she ended the affair with Nazre, the retaliation she endured when she complained about Nazre's behavior, and how Kleiner had failed in its obligation to take steps to prevent retaliation and discrimination. Soon after her complaint was filed, Pao was told to leave Kleiner. She amended her complaint to include retaliatory firing.

The suit rocked the industry. Women reached out to Pao, telling her that they understood, that they had been through similar experiences. Yahoo's former president Sue Decker wrote an op-ed calling the case "a watershed moment" for women, not just in tech but also across the economy. Facebook COO Sheryl Sandberg gave a *Bloomberg TV* interview during which she admitted she had experienced much of what Pao described in her complaint.

The trial lasted five weeks and garnered massive public attention, with the story appearing on the front page of the *New York Times*. Law professor Joan Williams described it as "a gender bias training for the nation." On the stand, Pao claimed that she was held back from senior partnership because of her sex; Kleiner insisted it was because she had underperformed. It was convenient that the firm could also portray Pao as someone who had had a consensual affair with the man she later accused of harassing her.

For us, one of the most telling moments of the trial came when Pao's attorney played an audio clip of Doerr saying, in a 2008 meeting of the National Venture Capital Association, that successful entrepreneurs were likely to be "very clearly male nerds who had no social or sex lives" and who were dropouts of Harvard or Stanford. "When I see that pattern coming in . . . it's very easy to decide to invest," Doerr said. Doerr's comments described the heady environment of Silicon Valley as a "young man's game" that worships the victors of the entrepreneurial tournament without too much thought given to the stereotypically masculine nature of the entire enterprise. Doerr further emphasized that, in deciding what startups to fund, the entrepreneur mattered more than the technology. Doerr earmarked individuals for success, surrounding them with support and money, getting their names in the media and on the rosters at all the big tech conferences. It follows that in a male-driven industry, where men define the rules and the terms, men would be the ones to rise to the top—and that Kleiner's standards for success at the firm would be cast in such terms.

It was easy in Silicon Valley's insular world for this male dominance to become a self-fulfilling prophecy, even as Doerr, one of the creators of the system, sought to change it. In 2010, business school professors Emilio J. Castilla and Stephen Benard published a study called "The Paradox of Meritocracy in Organizations" that demonstrated the challenges women face. They found that where institutional cultures thought of themselves as meritocratic, the managers "show greater bias in favor of men over equally performing women." The researchers conducted a variety of experiments presenting participants with similar profiles of men and women and asked them to award bonuses. The researchers found that telling participants that their company valued merit-based decisions increased the likelihood of their giving higher bonuses to the men. The paradox is that when evaluators are told they should operate in a meritocratic system (as opposed to one that involves lockstep promotions or group rewards), the evaluators "believe they are more impartial, and thus (unknowingly) give themselves permission to act on their biases." The biases may involve not just the evaluators' personal biases; they also include the stereotypes associated with success in the field. In the study, both the men and the women asked to make meritocratic judgments favored men.

A different study, published in 2021, and co-authored by one of the experts who had testified for Kleiner, found that women were underrepresented in the venture capital world compared to other business fields—including investment bankers. One potential explanation is the same one Doerr acknowledged: "homophily," in which venture capitalists tend to hire, as well as invest in, people with whom they share similarities, including gender and ethnicity as well as school and work backgrounds.

Paul Gompers, the expert who testified for Kleiner, co-authored a study in 2014 that further explained why women lose in male-dominated cultures. His data showed that women venture capitalists in fact produced lower returns than the men. He and his co-authors concluded, however, that the gender differences in investment outcomes "are not due to female investors being less skilled but rather largely attributable to female investors receiving less benefit from the track records of their colleagues." The researchers explain that in the tight-knit venture capital networks, women VCs obtain less benefit from their firm's mentorship than the men do, and this support is critical to success. However, the researchers observed that "[p]erformance differences disappear in older, larger firms and firms with other female investors." In short, the more established fields—including the more established VC firms—have more senior women and more formal mentoring systems, eliminating the differences between men's and women's performance. The authors emphasize that research on performance differences in the workplace routinely finds that "women tend to perform better in firms that have more formal processes, greater structure, and higher bureaucratization." Even in venture capital, mature firms can and do produce more equal results. And once they do, they fund more women founders—changing the character of tech.

What would "bureaucratization" have meant for Pao? Kleiner, after all, was a large, mature firm, and she did get mentoring and feedback (however contradictory it was at the time). An institution with more "bureaucracy" might well have had more formal mentoring policies and 360 reviews that emphasized the importance of considering bottom-up, as well as top-down, perspectives. But then the firm's business model would have to change, asking how Kleiner as a whole could maximize the value of its investments rather than rewarding the partners who most effectively elbowed others out of the way. A company with more established criteria and processes for advancement is less likely to tolerate sharp elbows from anyone.

If Kleiner were run like a large New York bank, however, it might also have had had policies against sexual harassment—or office romances; witnesses testified during Pao's trial about Kleiner's lack of formal HR policies. Pao, the rule follower, might then have said no to Nazre. Or, if she said yes, and Kleiner followed its own rules, it would have fired both of them. Large institutions have policies against fraternization to prevent precisely the kind of backbiting that occurred at Kleiner. Such policies tend to reduce the overall incidence of sexual harassment, but they can also be administered in a way that disproportionately disadvantages women.

The larger challenge in women's fight in tech is the effort to crack "the code." Silicon Valley has long prided itself on the effort to create something new overnight, in defiance of the traditional rules. Tech culture then crowns the successful as products of level playing fields and treats the winners as deserving their yachts and mansions. In this environment, the underlying stereotypes see toe-stepping leaders as men, entrepreneurial wizards combining tech genius and hubris, and HR departments as bureaucracies to be circumvented so as to stack the deck against women—even women as talented and often more disciplined than the men.

Ultimately, in the face of these obstacles, Ellen Pao lost her case, with the jury clearing her employer of any wrongdoing. Although after the final vote some jurors expressed sympathy for her position, the problem may well have been that the discrimination she suffered simply wasn't "dramatic" enough. Sarah Lacy, the founder and editor-in-chief of the tech website *Pando*, put it bluntly. She noted that if Pao had a case, "then so did every woman in America." Law professor Deborah Rhode explained: "The sort of evidence you're seeing in the Ellen Pao case is very typical of what's out there in Silicon Valley. There are no smoking guns; much of it is . . . small incidents that viewed individually may seem trivial, but when viewed cumulatively point to a practice of insensitivity and devaluation that can get in the way of work performance." One of the jurors who believed that Pao was a victim of unequal treatment commented that the male junior partners at Kleiner "had those same character flaws that Ellen was cited with," but they were promoted anyway. Sharp elbows pay off only if they get you into the club. Pao had tried to compete on the same terms as the men around her, and she had lost.

Ellen Pao, unlike many of the women in our book, refused the earlier settlements offered her, which would have come with nondisclosure agreements, and so she is free to speak about her experience. As a result of her visibility, women unified around her. After she lost her case, the hashtag #ThankYouEllenPao trended on Twitter. Journalists began referring to the "Pao effect," by which they meant that in the wake of Pao's case, more women felt empowered to speak out. She published her memoir, *Reset*, and perhaps most impactfully, inspired a group of Silicon Valley investors and executives to conduct a survey of senior-level women that focused on gender and Silicon Valley. They called their 2015 report "The Elephant in the Valley" and it confirmed that Pao's experiences were, in fact, typical. Eighty-four percent of the participants had been told they were "too aggressive," 64 percent said that they had been excluded from important events because of their gender, and 60 percent reported unwanted sexual advances in the workplace. Most of the advances came from a superior; a third of the women said that they'd been worried about their personal safety. Almost 40 percent said that they didn't report the incidents because they feared retaliation. After the revelations in the wake of #MeToo in 2017, Melinda Gates, the co-chair of the Bill & Melinda Gates Foundation, commented to the *New Yorker* that "[m]en who demean, degrade or disrespect women have been able to operate with such impunity—not just in Hollywood, but in tech, venture capital, and other spaces where their influence and investment can make or break a career. The asymmetry of power is ripe for abuse."

———————————

Ellen Pao's case had a number of lasting effects on tech. Her trial, the study she sponsored, the media attention, and the reports of other women's experiences created a new form of pattern recognition: double standards, harassment, discrimination, and barriers that derail careers of women across tech. Recognition of the pattern is the first step in fighting it. Lasting changes, though, require more women in tech—especially among startup founders and the VCs who fund them.

Permanent change is challenging in an industry subject to booms, which tend to attract the men with the sharpest elbows, and busts, which disproportionately cull women. The most recent developments, though, give some cause for optimism: VC firms have started to promote more women into partnership. When venture capital funding, fueled by low interest rates and the Trump tax cuts, reached an all-time high in 2018, surpassing those of the dot.com era, the tech industry renewed its commitment to hire more diverse VCs and to fund more diverse enterprises. As a result, both the percentage of female and diverse VCs, and the funding of diverse startups has grown since Pao's trial. The *New York Times* reported that, in 2021, women made up 15 percent of general partners at venture capital firms, with the number of angel investors funding early-stage startups growing to 1,000. At under 20 percent, however, the number of women VC partners remains anemic compared to other industries.

To compensate, women increasingly are carving out their own space in the field, setting up their own VC firms to fund women-led and driven products. When female venture capitalists make the decisions, they are twice as likely to invest in founding teams that are female. Pao herself has started Project Include, a nonprofit with the mission to give everyone a fair shot at succeeding in tech. Project Include provides a series of recommendations on how companies can ensure norms of diversity and inclusion from the hiring process to onboarding and training to developing appropriate codes of conduct. Pao is also an active presence on X (formerly Twitter), cheering on other women who have encountered discrimination, who are fighting to remake Silicon Valley, and who need a supportive presence on their side.

The most lasting changes may occur, however, if women founders emerge as survivors of the next downturn. Over the last decade, the number of women founders has steadily increased, though the percentage of funding all-female teams receive is not much different from what it was at the time of the *Pao* trial. Instead, women have discovered the most important key to getting VC attention may be having a man beside them.

All-women teams received 2.4 percent of all funding in 2021, a boom year—a figure that dropped to 2.1 percent of funding in 2022, when total funding fell precipitously. Industry analysts observe that "[w]hen the economy tanks, discrimination feels justified." Women-run firms are seen as riskier, and the appetite for risk declines during downturns. Mixed teams, with both male and female founders, have fared better. They received 17.2 percent of VC funds in 2022, an increase from 15 percent in 2021. Overall, firms with at least one female founder constituted a fourth of the total, a steady increase over the last decade. This means that while the barriers to women in tech have not disappeared, women are at least making it onto the ladder that leads to the top ranks of tech.

The most interesting question is whether the female founders will thrive during the harder times facing the tech industry, and the initial news is promising. Startups that included female founders fared better than male-only startups during the downturn. For one thing, their "burn rate"—that is, the rate at which they use up cash and need new rounds of funding—was lower, with female-founded companies using 25 percent less capital per month than the overall market; that's an important metric in a period when new funding has become harder to come by. In addition, the goal for all startups is "exit"—that is, either to launch an IPO in which they go public and sell their shares on the stock market or to negotiate a purchase by a larger company. From 2021 to 2022, the number of exits dropped precipitously, but again female-founded firms did better, jumping from 9.5 percent of exits in 2021 to 18.2 percent in 2022. Overall, female founders continue to take less time to exit, a sign of greater success, than other firms. Perhaps in the

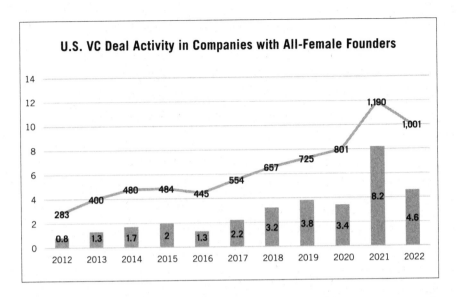

U.S. VC Deal Activity in Companies with All-Female Founders

future, male founders will need female partners to convince VCs that they are worth the risk.

In commenting on Pao's case in *Fortune* magazine, law professor Anita Hill, who had done so much to bring the issue of workplace sexual harassment to the forefront during her testimony at Clarence Thomas's 1991 Supreme Court hearing, observed that: "Hearing the ruminations on Ellen Pao's failed gender discrimination suit against her former employer Kleiner Perkins Caulfield and Byers, the famous words of Justice Louis Brandeis come to mind: 'Sunlight is said to be the best of disinfectants.' In Pao's case, the sunlight is beginning to do its work." Pao's sharp elbows, which Kleiner failed to appreciate, have made her a symbol of women's fight to become part of tech.

CHAPTER 5

Women Make the Best Scapegoats: Terrazas v. Wells Fargo

Misha Patel Terrazas, who had spent seventeen years working at Wells Fargo, was fired in March 2017. Starting out as a teller in 2000, she had risen through the ranks to Area President in the Desert Mountain region, helping to turn around one of the bank's poorest-performing sales regions. A woman of East Indian descent who was born in England, she prided herself on her work ethic, attention to detail, and drive to succeed. As a manager, Terrazas was often the only woman, the only person of color, *and* the only person under 40 at managerial meetings. She was also rated in the 90th percentile in performance at Wells Fargo, had received a perfect score of 5.0 from the eight employees she directly supervised, and had a near-perfect score of 4.68 from the 800 employees she indirectly supervised. Terrazas loved the banking business, and she assumed that she had a bright future with one of the largest banks in the country. She was wrong.

At the time of Terrazas's dismissal, Wells Fargo was in the midst of a full-blown crisis. The scandal broke in 2013, when the *L.A. Times* published an article claiming Wells Fargo employees had opened accounts that its customers didn't need, often without their authorization or knowledge. Over time, it became clear that millions of such accounts had been opened as part of a company-wide push to show sales and growth, increasing value for its shareholders. In September 2016, bank regulators imposed $35 million in penalties, the beginning of a series of regulatory actions that would be taken against Wells Fargo. Congressional hearings followed, and there was a widespread call for the heads of top executives.

Terrazas attracted media attention at precisely the wrong time—the moment at which executives at Wells Fargo were trying to persuade the press they were cracking down. A November 2016 *Wall Street Journal* article named Terrazas as the architect of a "double pack" strategy of opening a second account for each customer. She was further described as someone who trained managers to help them "overcome customer objections" to additional accounts. In response to the publicity about these sales tactics, in February 2017, Wells Fargo fired four senior-level managers—three women and one man—and the next month, it was Terrazas's turn, along with another woman and a man.

When we interviewed Terrazas for this book, she maintained that much of the media story was wrong. She had not designed the double-pack strategy; her boss had done so. And her training program did not produce the abuses. In fact, she had designed the program to correct the opening of additional accounts without the customers' knowledge or consent. Her training program was designed to show employees how to persuade customers *to agree* to second accounts by better understanding how such additional accounts could serve customer needs. The bank, however, didn't seem to care about the underlying facts. It forbade Terrazas from speaking to the press to set the record straight and then fired her, she believes because of the bad publicity.

After she was fired, Terrazas filed suit, alleging discrimination on the basis of sex and race. Terrazas believed that she had been unfairly targeted for dismissal. She became a convenient scapegoat for a company-wide policy in which, as she described in her complaint, "corporate forced aggressive sales goals upon the regional presidents." She also claimed that the men who served next to her, and who had worse records of ethical abuses than she did, had kept their jobs. Her suit was one of a number that alleged (in the words of another lawsuit) that "WELLS FARGO perpetuated a cynical and gendered double standard in which it held a female employee to a ridiculously high level of scrutiny while turning a blind eye to the illicit actions of its male employees because of the immense profits they generated."

We decided to take a closer look at the Wells Fargo story and at this "gendered double standard" to see what we could learn about the reasons financial institutions like Wells Fargo, with a track record of unscrupulous activities, were more likely to fire women. Women are less likely to commit misconduct, and they cause their employers smaller losses when they do. Yet they are more likely to be fired and less likely to be rehired than men who commit the same misconduct. And Wells Fargo's record for gender disparities in terminations is one of the worst in the financial industry.

In the prior chapter, we told the story of Ellen Pao, a woman caught in a classic workplace double bind, unable to get away with playing by the same rules as the boys in the club, accused of having "sharp elbows" and "not being a team player." For us, Pao's story demonstrates the well-documented fact that ambitious, so-called aggressive women have a tough time getting ahead because they are perceived as operating outside traditional gender roles—and can get held back or punished as a result. Pao's biggest sin appeared to be that no one liked her—in a firm where "no one much liked each other." Terrazas's story is, in at least this sense, quite different. She *was* well liked. The fact that the eight hundred employees under her gave her high marks is telling.

Terrazas was also successful in doing exactly what Wells Fargo wanted: creating growth for the company. Instead, she was facing something known as "plausible deniability." This is when senior officials in an organization claim to be ignorant of what is going on further down the food chain. Here's a classic explanation of the phenomenon from corporate law scholar Donald Langevoort: "the supervisor may communicate that there are certain things she wants to hear and certain things she does not." Critically, the supervisor may take pains to ensure that "subordinates . . . keep negative information from her in order to preserve the ability to deny responsibility should problems later be uncovered." High-stakes bonus systems make this relatively easy to do. When executives want to preserve plausible deniability, they may tie bonuses to goals or quotas, put pressure on their subordinates to meet the metrics, and look the other way from how their subordinates produce the desired numbers.

Plausible deniability is a factor in almost every chapter of this book. Walmart, which micromanaged its supply chain while delegating wholesale responsibility for personnel matters to its store managers, created a system in which the top executives in Bentonville could plausibly claim deniability for the wage-suppression practices it incentivized. Jack Welch, in implementing the modern system of executive compensation at GE, liked to brag about how much freedom he gave his managers—so long as the managers "made their numbers." Plausible deniability was widespread during the 2008 financial crisis, and those who complained about the pressure to generate more untrustworthy mortgages and the securities based on them—or acted as whistle-blowers to the unethical behavior—often lost their jobs. Wells Fargo bought into this system of plausible deniability. In 2016, Wells Fargo's CEO John Stumpf testified that the company was attentive to ethics, but also acknowledged that he cared about "outcomes, not process." Within such a system, when misconduct surfaced, senior executives claimed to be shocked that gambling went on in Casablanca. They then appear to have fired the convenient scapegoats to make it seem as if the problems were being addressed, while those persons responsible for the unethical behavior evaded accountability for the policies they tacitly allowed—or actively encouraged. Terrazas was one of these scapegoats for Wells Fargo. The question we explore in this chapter is why women are more likely than men to be the scapegoats for misconduct that the top brass wants, encourages, and benefits from.

Among large banks, Wells Fargo was almost alone in emerging from the financial crisis with a reputation for low volatility, good returns, and solid management. Founded in 1852 by Henry Wells and William Fargo to offer banking and express services, Wells Fargo's distinctive approach to banking came from its merger with Norwest in 1998. Norwest CEO Richard Kovacevich kept the Wells Fargo name and its folksy stagecoach icon, taking over the combined institution and pushing it in a new direction. Born in Washington State to a Yugoslavian immigrant family, Kovacevich considered himself an innovator. He began his career at Citicorp, moving to Norwest, where he became head of its retail banking group. Kovacevich viewed banks not as places providing *services* to customers but, rather, as places to *sell* products to customers. For him, branches were "stores" and bankers were "salespeople." Their "job was to 'cross-sell,' which meant getting 'customers'—not 'clients,' but 'customers'—to buy as many products as possible." Selling customers multiple "financial instruments—A.T.M. cards, checking accounts, credit cards, loans . . . 'was his business model,' says a former Norwest executive. 'It was a religion. It very much was the culture.'" As CEO at Norwest before the merger with Wells Fargo, Kovacevich launched an effort in the 1990s to get customers to buy eight products from the bank: checking accounts, savings accounts, direct deposit accounts, credit cards, investment accounts, mortgages, and so on. "The reason for eight? 'It rhymes with GREAT!' he said."

Under Kovacevich's leadership, Wells Fargo reached new heights. Shareholders loved the spectacular sales figures, and the bank's stock price soared. In 2005, Kovacevich stepped down and John Stumpf took over as chairman and CEO. Like his predecessor, Stumpf saw cross-selling—getting customers to open as many accounts with Wells Fargo as possible—as the secret to the bank's success. While other financial institutions cratered during the 2009 crisis, Wells Fargo seemed to emerge unscathed. *Fortune* magazine praised Wells Fargo for "a history of avoiding the rest of the industry's dumbest mistakes," and *American Banker* magazine called Wells Fargo "the big bank least tarnished by the scandals and reputational crises." It came out of the crisis as the third largest bank in the country, and in 2013, Stumpf was named "Banker of the Year."

The bank's reputation took a serious hit, when, in 2016, the entire country learned that Wells Fargo, like so many other American banks, had indeed played its part in the downfall of the economy. Like other mortgage lenders in the lead-up to the financial crisis, it had accepted inflated estimates of borrowers' incomes and then treated the inflated numbers as true. Borrowers lost their homes when they were granted mortgages they could never afford to pay. In 2016, the bank was forced to pay the federal government $1.2 billion for lying about the quality of its mortgage loans in the run-up to the financial crisis, and in 2018, in a different suit, the Department of Justice announced that Wells Fargo had agreed to pay an additional $2 billion settlement for disguising its mortgage-loan quality during the same period. Wells Fargo has continued to face new charges, with Senator Elizabeth Warren even pressing to dismantle it. She wrote a letter to the chairman and board of governors of the Federal Reserve System, noting Wells Fargo's "repeated, ongoing, and inexcusable failure . . . to eliminate abusive and unlawful practices that have cost consumers hundreds of millions of dollars," calling Wells Fargo "ungovernable," and asking the Fed to revoke Wells Fargo's status as a federal holding company and to require it "to separate its consumer-facing banking arm from the rest of its financial activities."

For Wells Fargo, however, there was an even more damaging scandal: the revelation that it had put so much pressure on its employees to meet production quotas that they responded by opening fake accounts without their customers' knowledge. As we've seen, the heart of the Wells Fargo sales culture, from its merger with Norwest in 1998 forward, was its sales metrics: how many new accounts were opened, how many mortgages were granted, how many insurance policies (needed or not) were issued. Everyone's success, from CEO Stumpf to line workers like those who served under Terrazas, depended on these numbers.

It's important to note that cross-selling—the practice at the center of the fake-accounts scandal—is not necessarily illegal. There is nothing that prevents a bank, working with a customer who opens a checking account, from offering that customer a bank-issued credit card or other financial products, such as pet insurance; it can often be useful to customers to have all their financial products under one institution. One reason banks value the practice is that customer accounts become "stickier"; customers with multiple accounts are less likely to switch to another bank that offers better terms or less expensive products. At the same time, customers can feel pressured into buying products they will not use, and the items they do want might be better and cheaper elsewhere. It thus sets up conflicts of interest, with bankers trying to sell products regardless of customers' interests or needs. Sallie Krawcheck, then the most powerful woman in banking, was pushed out at Bank of America in 2011, when she publicly objected that she "didn't even like the term cross-selling, saying it sounds like something we do to rather than for you."

What set Wells Fargo apart from the other banks pushing cross-selling, however, was the unrelenting pressure it put on employees to meet production quotas. Particularly in the aftermath of the financial crisis, this system of pressuring employees to cross-sell to meet production quotas became the key to Wells Fargo's success. Branch offices are expensive to operate; the number of branches of all banks in the country peaked in 2009, and declined by 25 percent thereafter. Wells Fargo in contrast made them central to its business strategy, and in 2021, it had more branches than any of the other leading banks. Branch offices were the point of customer contact, and Wells Fargo used the branches to increase the number of products each customer would be encouraged to purchase. Carrie Tolstedt, head of Wells Fargo's community banking efforts, oversaw the project. Described as the "Most Powerful

Woman in Banking," Tolstedt understood that sales metrics were what Wall Street rewarded, and she pushed her far-flung division to increase those sales. For instance, when one of her managers proposed a plan to increase sales by 4 percent, she insisted, in a response email marked "high importance," that "front end guidance was a minimum of 10%," and that the growth rate instead needed to be "between 10% and 15%."

Former CEO Richard Kovacevich had instituted the rule of "eight is great," but now employees reported that the quotas were much higher—increasing to as many as twenty products a day. Employees were "coached" until they met their numbers. They ended up begging family members and friends to open accounts to meet their quotas. Some cracked under the pressure; others dissolved into tears. According to an NPR report from 2016, they were quite simply "miserable."

Given such unrealistic targets, many Well Fargo employees found that the easiest way to meet those targets was by cheating the system. And cheat the system they did. In the period between 2011 and 2015, Wells Fargo staff members "applied for 565,000 credit cards that may not have been authorized by customers." In addition to credit card applications, staff members opened accounts and then closed them, reopening similar accounts for the same people, often without their knowledge. Customers complained that they were getting calls from collection agencies for accounts they were unaware they had opened. Clearly this wasn't just a few "bad apples." In fact, in the period between 2011 and 2015, 193,000 nonemployee accounts were opened with the only email domain name listing for these accounts as @wellsfargo.com. By the time the various investigations were complete, Wells Fargo had been found to have opened 3.5 million potentially unauthorized accounts.

These aggressive sales goals came from the top Wells Fargo management, and they were then administered by the regional president to whom Terrazas reported. A 2017 independent Wells Fargo investigation found that "[i]n many instances, community bank leadership recognized that their plans were unattainable—they were commonly referred to as 50/50 plans, meaning that there was an expectation that only half the regions would be able to meet them." Terrazas described how expectations about the number of new accounts employees were expected to open rose from nine a day to twenty-two a day over the last few years she was at Wells Fargo. Terrazas said she complained; she thought the goals were crazy, but her complaints made no difference.

The training program that led to Terrazas's downfall had been a response to the unrelenting pressure and the new scrutiny that Wells Fargo was initiating. The dual-pack strategy of opening at least two accounts for every customer, which her boss had long emphasized, was part of the systemwide pressure to open more accounts. Terrazas's training program, which she had been asked to conduct, was designed to help employees encourage customers to open additional accounts that might be useful, without the need to fake accounts. The success of her training program—in tailoring sales tactics to customer interests *and* in increasing sales—made her a visible part of Wells Fargo's sales culture. Additionally, Terrazas describes herself as a tough manger, a "rule follower," who sanctioned subordinates when she became aware of unethical practices. Terrazas dealt with a high-pressure environment by attempting to thread the needle between management demands and customer needs.

When she was fired, employees she trained responded with disbelief. "You were the one teaching us the right way to do this," they told her.

The larger picture, though, was a Wells Fargo culture that treated employees and customers as a means to boost the metrics that made the bank appear successful and that padded executive bonuses. While the scandal broke with an article in the *Los Angeles Times* in 2013, for example, Wells Fargo did not give supervisors tools that would have allowed them to identify problem accounts until 2015. Even then, it did not really clean house. Terrazas told us that there had never been a serious investigation; if there had been, she maintained, the investigators would have found that she had "higher performance evaluations than her Arizona Area President peers"; unlike some of them, she had never been disciplined previously, and she had fewer problem accounts. Instead,

Wells Fargo fired those who had been named in the press, while retaining men with worse records, who had committed more egregious acts of misconduct but who had not been associated with adverse publicity. When Wells Fargo told Terrazas that she was being let go, they said the region she oversaw had an unusually high level of suspicious accounts. Yet, others at Wells Fargo informed her she had fewer problem accounts than white male managers in her region who were not fired. Terrazas told us that in some of the worst cases, upper management would have had a hard time firing the male intermediate managers because upper management knew of the misconduct.

This all fits the larger pattern of plausible deniability. Wells Fargo ran a decentralized system that set ambitious goals but lacked oversight; it did not inquire too closely into what its productive employees did or how its managers encouraged the employees to obtain their results. Indeed, in 2019, three years after the fake accounts scandal went public, the *New York Times* reported that nothing had changed at the bank: "Wells Fargo workers say they remain under heavy pressure to squeeze extra money out of customers. Some have witnessed colleagues bending or breaking internal rules to meet ambitious performance goals." Even after the scandal, employees still feared retaliation for speaking out.

Misha Patel Terrazas's experience in being punished for conduct tolerated in male employees is not an outlier in banking, or in the broader WTA economy. In 2021, a team of finance professors led by Harvard's Mark Egan published a paper called "When Harry Fired Sally." They looked at financial advisors at forty-four firms in the period between 2005 and 2015—the heyday of banking meltdowns—and found that women were punished more severely than their male counterparts. Once the Wells Fargo scandal broke, they went back and ran the numbers specifically for the bank: Wells Fargo fired more women than men found guilty of misconduct; its record for gender disparities in terminating financial advisors for misconduct was an industry worst.

While misconduct benefits executives whose compensation increases in lockstep with gains in share price, lower-level employees, especially women, pay a disproportionate price for unethical behavior. Egan and his co-authors speculated that their "evidence suggests that the gap arises because of in-group tolerance by managers, who are more forgiving of missteps among members of their own gender/ethnic group." Strikingly, they found no gender gap at firms that had an equal representation of male and female executives/owners, and they also found the gap is roughly twice as large at financial advisory firms that have a history of sexual harassment. Minority men face a similar punishment gap, underscoring the role of in-group preferences in perpetuating the system.

Wells Fargo had all the preexisting problems that Egan's study outlines: it had a higher incidence of discrimination and harassment arbitrations than comparable banks. It's also interesting to note that the punishment gap is not based on cost to the bank from the misconduct; the average settlement for men was $228,593, more than double the average women's settlement. And in a subsequent investigation, *The Intercept* found Wells Fargo often held on to male brokers who had bent the rules repeatedly for years, whereas women brokers resigned or were dismissed after only one or two allegations. At Wells Fargo, 72 percent of women had an "employment separation," while only 42 percent of the men with similar records of misconduct resigned or were fired. When the women did leave Wells Fargo or were pushed out, they also fared much worse professionally than the men who also left or were fired. For her part, Terrazas had a terrible time finding another job. Today, she runs her own company—in a different industry.

And what about the women who *didn't* commit infractions? *The Intercept* found that during the same decade of the study, women had "fewer customer disputes, lower settlement costs, and fewer tangles with regulators, on average, making them less of a risk to Wells Fargo than the firm's men." And yet these factors did not convert into promotions or pay raises for the women in a system in which sales metrics were the only thing that counted.

Mark Egan and his co-authors document a dramatic case of unequal treatment. Their empirical study, however, cannot answer the question of *why* the gender disparities exist. Their discussion of "in-group favoritism" is a statistical conclusion—it means that male-run companies fired more women than men committing misconduct, and that female-run companies did not. The following possible reasons present different ways of understanding what happened to Terrazas, and other women like her.

First is the conventional account. Women generally commit less misconduct than men; indeed, Egan's research shows that prior misconduct is the best predictor, and gender is second best. Women who commit misconduct therefore defy gender expectations and may be treated more harshly because of it.

The conventional account, however, does not explain why high-pressure environments like that of Wells Fargo produce greater gender disparities than other male-run firms—both environments can be expected to punish women who commit misconduct more than men. Instead, according to both feminists and corporate theorists, the decision-making within high-stakes bonus systems becomes more politicized; managers ask what's in it for them, not what's good for the company or for their employees. They protect their allies and distrust others. These environments produce abusive managers, who identify with workers who have the same traits they see in themselves and who exploit others' weaknesses. In short, these managers, to a greater degree than managers in less competitive environments, play favorites and do so to women's disadvantage. In addition, in workplaces where no person's status is secure, all managers may be threatened by those who challenge them—whether the challenge involves calling attention to fake accounts or claims of sex discrimination. In such environments, it may be easier to fire employees than to address their grievances.

In another Wells Fargo case, Raena Krestovnikov, a mortgage consultant, alleged that she was fired for a minor offense after she complained that the women in her unit received less favorable treatment than the men. Her supervisor told her, after she aired her concerns to a senior manager, that "she had a target on her back." She was fired not long afterward. By firing employees for misconduct, even for minor offenses, a bank can show that it's taking its compliance responsibilities seriously. Moreover, a worker fired for misconduct will find it that much harder to win a case of sex discrimination or retaliation. But selectively choosing who to fire is precisely where a culture of favoritism and deceit has its most pernicious effects. Mark Egan's study, while it examined only confirmed cases of misconduct, could not distinguish between cases where the misconduct was the real reason for the termination and where it was a pretext for something else.

Finally, Egan's other work suggests that the companies with higher percentages of employees with misconduct records may be selecting for those traits. A Wells Fargo affiliate, Wells Fargo Advisors Financial Network, LLC, ranked third on the list, with over 15 percent of its advisors having misconduct records. The study observes that although "advisers face consequences for misconduct, the majority of advisers remain in the industry following misconduct"; indeed, "[m]ore than 50% remain with the same firm after a year." In short, some firms are actively selecting employees who commit certain types of misconduct, and managers may be protecting some, but not all, the employees found guilty of violations. While this study did not discuss gender, its results suggest that in-group favoritism may thus be about protecting certain types of men—the ones who commit *more* of a certain kind of misconduct—as much, if not more, than it is about punishing women. It is entirely possible, for example, that women-run firms do not discriminate in terminating men and women for misconduct because they do not tolerate it from *anyone*.

These explanations are neither exhaustive nor mutually exclusive, and they all describe forms of in-group favoritism. However, they provide answers beyond merely gender bias or stereotyping. Instead, they show how high-pressure business cultures that tolerate unethical behavior may create traps for women. If employees are expected to do whatever they need to do to perform, but are on their own if they cross the line, women are more likely to lose. The attitude inside Wells Fargo, according to lawyer Jonathan Delshad, who represented a former Wells Fargo employee, was "Do what you have to do, but don't get caught." Women who did "whatever they needed to do to perform" were at even greater risk than the men in that their careers would not fare well if they did.

So, what does all this mean for women in the workplace in the broader sense? It tells us that women will have a better chance of competing on a level playing field, in a system where the rules matter and the same rules apply to everyone. Yet, changing institutional cultures— especially those based exclusively on sales metrics—is difficult. Among large banks, Wells Fargo was unusual in the strength of its corporate culture as it groomed executives from within; CEO Stumpf, Community Banking head Tolstedt, and almost all the senior executives around them rose through the company's ranks. That contributed to the number of women like Tolstedt in the bank's top ranks, but it also made the bank's corporate culture harder to dislodge. Cross-selling became central to its operations in the nineties, and reports of fake accounts surfaced at Wells Fargo as early as the early 2000s, but the bank dismissed them as isolated incidents. The abusive practices did not receive public attention until nearly ten years later, when the *Los Angeles Times* focused the spotlight on the Southern California region. Even then, the scale of the scandal, which produced 3.5 million fake accounts, did not become apparent until after federal authorities prompted a fuller reckoning in 2016. Wells Fargo then not only cashiered Stumpf and Tolstedt, it also forced out its next two CEOs—Tim Sloan, Stumpf's Chief Operating Officer, and an acting CEO, who had been general counsel— when they failed to contain the mounting scandals. In 2019, the bank finally brought in an outside CEO with a mandate to clean house. Charles Scharf, Wells Fargo's first CEO from outside the company since the merger with Norwest in the nineties, brought in new management people who had not been raised in the company's high-pressure sales culture. In 2020, the Justice Department announced that Wells Fargo had agreed to pay $3 billion to resolve its potential criminal and civil liability stemming from its actions in providing "millions of accounts or products to customers under false pretenses or without consent" from the period from 2002 to 2016. In 2021, Wells Fargo eliminated more than 19,000 positions, and in September 2021, the Office of the Comptroller of the Currency (OCC) imposed another $250 million in fines, finding that Wells Fargo had violated a 2018 consent decree addressing its mortgage practices. In December of 2022 the Consumer Financial Protection Bureau (CFPB) ordered Wells Fargo to pay an additional $3.7 billion for more than a decade's worth of unlawful practices, including surprise overdraft fees, improper home foreclosures, and wrongful repossession of cars—to 16 million consumer accounts. The CFPB's actions went well beyond the issue of unauthorized accounts to address the unscrupulous practices that cross-selling facilitated. CFPB director Rohit Chopra commented that "in the CFPB's 11 years of existence, Wells Fargo has consistently been one of the most problematic repeat offenders of the banks and credit unions we supervise."

Corporate reformers have emphasized the importance of "clawbacks"—that is, recouping the high compensation paid to CEOs who benefit from allowing corporate misdeeds to flourish. Stumpf is unusual in that, unlike most of the CEOs in this book whom we profile, he has had to face real consequences. He was not only fired, at age 67, but he also was banned from the industry for life and subject to a $28 million clawback and a $17.5 million fine. Carrie Tolstedt, who became the focus of federal enforcement efforts once Stumpf settled, was also fired and ordered to pay $17 million in fines; she pled guilty to a criminal charge of obstructing a bank examination in 2023. Stumpf's settlement, in the meantime, still left him a very rich man. Over his last ten years at Wells Fargo, Stumpf reportedly earned "$192 million, including salary, bonuses, stock incentives, and other compensation." In 2020, his net worth was still estimated at $50 million.

The solution to the gender-punishment gap—where women who

try to compete on the same terms as men face much harsher penalties—requires not just ending the gender inequities but also ceasing the underlying misconduct and the culture in which plausible deniability flourishes. If we want real change in WTA workplaces, therefore, we will need to permanently strengthen the crackdown on shady practices that make some people very rich at the expense of others. The asset cap that the Federal Reserve imposed on Wells Fargo in 2018 is an unprecedented action, not just because it limited Wells Fargo's ability to grow but also because banking regulators have never been particularly aggressive in protecting consumers—the banks' safety and soundness has always been the regulators' paramount concern. Elizabeth Warren responded to the financial crisis by spearheading the creation of a consumer protection agency, the Consumer Financial Protection Bureau, charged with policing the type of unscrupulous practices Wells Fargo pionecred. While the agency has aggressively challenged Wells Fargo's practices, it has been hamstrung by legal challenges to its authority. Effective consumer protection (and eliminating the temptation to rig the numbers that influence share price) can only come with overlapping sources of protection that address discrimination, workplace conditions, consumer interests, and the omnipresent threat of retaliation.

As the Wells Fargo story shows us, the other game-changers will be investigative journalism and collective action, in tandem with legal enforcement. At Wells Fargo, three groups were particularly effective in bringing the scandal to light. The first group was made up of workers who complained—even as they risked being fired for doing so. These workers were supported by others, such as the Committee for Better Banks, a "coalition of bank workers, community and consumer advocacy groups, and labor organizations" that has worked tirelessly to end unreasonable sales goals and other unfair working conditions for front-line bank workers, and supported Wells Fargo employees protesting the treatment of customers. The second group was made up of people with overlapping responsibility for enforcement efforts at the federal, state, and local levels. In Wells Fargo's case, the city attorney in Los Angeles brought an initial civil suit accusing the bank of misconduct—triggering much greater scrutiny. Congressional hearings later helped trigger John Stumpf's resignation, and continuing federal pressure ultimately forced the bank to bring in new management. The third group was made up of investigative journalists who took the workers' complaints and reported them to a wider audience. The *Los Angeles Times*, for example, broke this story in 2013 in a way that focused pressure on the company. This combination of forces—united action to itemize complaints, investigative journalism to publicize them, and enforcement efforts to address them—act together not just to expose practices but also to keep the pressure on until the practices change.

And some solutions are simply good practice for all companies. If Wells Fargo really wanted to stop the practices that resulted in fraud, there are easy ways to do so that don't involve disproportionately firing women. They could have prioritized customer satisfaction rather than artificial sales metrics and emphasized fraud detection and prevention. They could have strengthened their underwriting and review procedures. They could have stopped the pressure that is designed only to increase shareholder value. And they could have refused to tolerate repeated misconduct from either men *or* women. Misha Patel Terrazas tried to implement such practices, but in an atmosphere in which it was every man for himself, when the scandal broke she was one of the many women left out of the solutions.

PART 3

When Women See What the New Rules Are, They Refuse to Play the Game

We've seen in Part 1 that when women play by different rules from men, they lose. In Part 2, we've seen that even when women play by the same rules as men, they still lose.

Part 3 covers the third leg of the Triple Bind, explaining why women get out of the game. The conventional explanation is that women aren't as competitive as men. They avoid the rush that comes with a healthy rivalry or the stress that comes with office politics. And ultimately, when push comes to shove, they'd rather stay home with their children than compete in the workforce.

But that's not the full story.

Instead, powerful institutional factors make high-stakes jobs less attractive for women and push out many women who would make effective leaders. Women who work at these institutions either learn that they must pay a much higher price than men to stay in the game or they decide they are unwilling to do the unscrupulous things necessary to win. The third leg of the Triple Bind thus explains that when women see what the terms of competition are, some take *themselves* out of the running.

CHAPTER 6

Tech Pushes Women Out: Women v. Uber

When Ingrid Avendaño went to work for Uber Technologies in February 2014, she believed she had landed her dream job—just like A. J. Vandermeyden. Still in her early twenties, Avendaño was excited about her first full-time engineering position after interning at two tech firms. At Uber, she was responsible for debugging and developing software, but the role meant much more to her than that. It offered exactly the kind of experience a budding Silicon Valley software engineer like Avendaño craved: the ability to get in on the ground floor of a company seeking to revolutionize an industry. Only five years old, Uber was still a relative newcomer to the tech world, albeit one that had already radically changed the way riders hail and pay for transportation services.

Avendaño, a first-generation American who was born in Venezuela and grew up in Minnesota, hadn't planned on a career in tech. Originally enrolled as an art major, she got into the field after someone at college bet her twenty dollars that she couldn't learn to code. After enrolling in the coding course at the University of Pittsburgh, she discovered that she loved coding and the problem-solving it involved, even if she was the only woman in the class. Avendaño talked to the computer science department about changing majors, but the faculty actively discouraged her from joining the department; they made it clear they expected her to fail. Serendipitously, she ran into an administrator for the electrical engineering (EE) program, who convinced Avendaño to switch to EE instead.

Computer coding culture was established in the late twentieth century, and the years when it began to take off on college campuses foreshadowed what would later happen in the field. As computer programming became an increasingly desirable skill, universities couldn't find enough professors to staff the courses, so they developed "hurdles . . . [p]unishing workloads and classes that covered the material at a lightning pace" to discourage anyone who wasn't a quick study. Those students most likely to make it through the computer science curriculum "were those who had already been exposed to coding—young men, mostly." Once students enter college, introductory computer science classes set the stage for a later major in the area. And even when their abilities are comparable, women typically have less confidence in their coding skills than do men. Avendaño, however, demonstrated the qualities prized in tech: when the computer science department erected barriers to her entry, she found her way into engineering, and once she was in the field, she discovered she had something traditional engineering students lacked: an eye for design.

Still, her decision proved costly. She lost her scholarships when she changed majors, and she couldn't qualify for an engineering scholarship because she had no prior engineering experience. An internship with a tech company helped to pay the bills, but the University of Pittsburgh slashed her financial aid because of the money she was earning as an intern. As a result, she ended up quitting college before graduation because she had run out of money. Fortuitously, a three-month programming bootcamp allowed her to break into an industry desperate for coders. With bootcamp and two internships under her belt, Avendaño interviewed at Uber and got the job.

At the time, Uber seemed open to a diverse group of engineers. Indeed, when Avendaño started, 20 percent of the engineers at Uber were women, and she was given the opportunity to mentor other women. She gushed on her Twitter page when she was able to hire an engineering intern, Ana Medina, exclaiming "Words can't describe how super excited I am!!—#latinacoders."

She hadn't been at Uber long before it became clear to Avendaño that competition among co-workers, not creating community, was the priority. Like all new employees during that time, she was asked to embrace the company's fourteen core values: these values included being "obsessed" with the customer, making bold bets, not being afraid of "toe-stepping," and "always be hustlin'." According to Avendaño, the problem was that those getting their toes stepped on were mostly women. From the outset, she ran into problems regarding her compensation. The starting salary she was offered was $100,000 per year, plus an additional $30,000 in incentive stock grants. She soon learned, however, that this package was substantially less than that being offered to whites and to males with similar experience. When she tried to negotiate for better pay, she was immediately told that if she persisted, her job offer would be rescinded. Indeed, Avendaño learned that the company had rescinded offers to women who tried to bargain for bigger compensation packages, but she didn't know of that happening to men. After she complained, Uber responded by ordering employees not to discuss their salaries with new applicants.

Her claims are not unusual. Women in tech receive lower salary offers than men for the same job, at the same company, 63 percent of the time. In other industries, gender differences in pay tend to be smallest in entry-level positions and grow over time. But in a field like tech, which prizes youth and faces intense competition to land the top computer science grads, women under 25 earn 29 percent less than men the same age. Banning employees from discussing their salaries, as Uber tried to do, cloaked the fact that they were systematically paying their female employees less—and the fact that it might have violated the law is something that rarely deterred Uber.

But wage inequality and a lack of compliance with basic HR policies weren't the only issues at Uber. According to Avendaño, frequent sexual innuendos and related offensive behaviors were omnipresent—and this started at the top and worked its way down through the ranks. During Avendaño's first year at Uber, company founder and CEO Travis Kalanick sent an email to the entire company with a subject line that read: "URGENT, URGENT—READ THIS NOW OR ELSE!!!!!!" and also noted, "You better read this or I'll kick your ass." Initially prepared the previous year in conjunction with a company trip to Miami, the email set out rules for having sex with co-workers at that year's company retreat, with Kalanick noting that he "will be celibate on this trip. #CEOLife #FML." And the email also made light of drug use and excessive drinking. Finally, it urged the employees to: "Have a great fucking time."

During that same period, Avendaño attended a recruiting event at the University of California, Berkeley, with a male co-worker. In front of the Berkeley students and his female colleagues, the Uber engineer made repeated belittling comments, announcing that "Uber is the type of company where women can sleep their way to the top." When Avendaño reported the behavior to HR, she was told, "dismissively," that this was a "first offense," and nothing further happened. A few months later, her complaint reports that the same employee started spreading rumors about her, insisting that Avendaño had gotten her job only because "she had slept with someone at the company."

Once again, Avendaño reported her co-worker's behavior to HR, and this time her complaints eventually led to his dismissal. But the other engineers took notice, and Avendaño reported that her problems multiplied. Her fellow engineers started to retaliate, ignoring her, denying her credit for work she had done, and isolating her within the company. She reported her experiences to her manager, to no avail. Avendaño began to experience panic attacks that ultimately required hospitalization and outpatient therapy. Meanwhile, the sexual harassment continued unabated. At a company event in Las Vegas, a drunk senior engineer touched her thigh and said she was "so cute." He told her he wanted to take her home. Other engineers commented on her figure, used the company Listserv to set up outings to a strip club, and made demeaning remarks to other employees in the office. The sexual harassment from other engineers continued, and it didn't help that Uber maintained an open beer keg, 24/7. Employees sometimes got drunk at office events, and they got so drunk at Uber's social events that they passed out; many women reported feeling unsafe because of the high levels of alcohol consumption.

Then, in 2015, Avendaño was put on a work schedule that required her to be on call twenty-four hours a day to respond to software glitches that might arise—for three consecutive months. During this period, she worked fifteen or more hours a day. She didn't know anyone else who was put on call for such a long period, yet she was denied a promotion she had been promised, and she received only minimal pay increases—all, she believed, in retaliation for her complaints. At the end of the year, she checked herself into the hospital for burnout, exhaustion, depression, and anxiety—in large part because of the continuing discrimination and harassment she experienced. Yet, despite informing her manager about her hospitalization, she was paged 142 times about technical problems with the Uber app while she was hospitalized.

On her return to work, Avendaño experienced continuing retaliation and harassment that did little to improve her mental health. The intern (and now engineer) she had recruited, Ana Medina, was going through similar problems. Medina joined Uber at the age of 22. She wasn't prepared for the constant access to alcohol and the never-ending sexual advances, often from inebriated team members. She also found it hard to deal with the endless need to prove herself because she was Latinx, with people questioning her technical capabilities. Like Avendaño, she eventually realized that she had had enough of the abuse.

For both women, February 2017 was a turning point. This was the month their former Uber colleague, Susan Fowler, published a blogpost about her experiences at the company, entitled "Reflecting on

One Very, Very Strange Year at Uber." A 26-year-old engineer who had recently left the company after a year on the job, Fowler had decided to "out" Uber for its frat-boy culture of backstabbing competition, as well as regular sexual harassment. In her blogpost, she described being propositioned by her manager her first day on the job. She reported the incident to HR and, as with Avendaño, was told it was an innocent first offense. As Fowler met other women in the company, however, she realized that many of them had the same experiences—with the exact same manager. When she confronted HR, the human resource officials simply denied it. Fowler had caught them in a blatant lie and felt there was nothing she could do. When Fowler tried to transfer out from under a manager making personal advances, he blocked her. Keeping women on his team made him look good. Fowler decided to leave and blow the whistle on her former employer.

After her blogpost, investigations into the misconduct began. Eventually, an outside law firm identified 215 complaints of workplace violations, 47 involving sexual harassment, 54 alleging discrimination, and others pertaining to "bullying, retaliation, physical security and nonsexual forms of harassment." Twenty employees, including senior executives, were fired. Yet, many of the managers and employees who had mistreated Avendaño remained at the company.

After three years at the company, Avendaño resigned in June 2017, the same month the findings of the investigations became public, and Kalanick was forced to resign as CEO (though he hung on through the end of 2019 on Uber's Board of Directors). Fowler's blog, posted four months before Avendaño's departure, had struck a chord. Women in Silicon Valley who assumed they were the only ones dealing with sexually harassing and demeaning environments understood that they were not the outliers. Women began to stand up, to make sure it didn't happen to other women, speaking to the press and bringing their own lawsuits.

The following May, Avendaño filed her lawsuit, claiming sexual harassment and that Uber's human resources department failed to act on her complaints. Further, she maintained that despite receiving praise for her work, once she complained about harassment, she was denied promotions and pay increases, and she was saddled with twenty-four-hour shifts in retaliation. "This culture was perpetuated and condoned by numerous managers, including high level company leaders," she stated. Avendaño sought compensation for lost wages, earnings, and company stock, but she also wanted her position back, with "appropriate seniority and compensation." Her co-worker Medina joined in a lawsuit with other Latinx engineers suing Uber for sex and racial discrimination, emphasizing the disparities in pay, promotions, and treatment. These suits sought to bar such practices in the future.

Avendaño and Medina are just two of the many women driven out of workplaces in the WTA economy—women who are prepared to work as hard as their male counterparts, put in the late nights, and devote themselves to the missions and goals of their companies, but who run afoul of toxic work environments that threaten their very sanity. By the time Avendaño left Uber in June 2017, the percentage of women engineers at the company had dropped from 20 percent to 7 percent. She wrote in 2018, "It genuinely feels like I'm recovering from an abusive relationship." After moving to Netflix in 2018, she reflected, "Now that I had a job where people are treated decently, I'm shocked that I put up with so much bad and didn't leave my awful job sooner . . . but then I remember it was because I had golden handcuffs, drank the Kool-Aid, and worked in a culture of fear." Being at Uber shook her to the core. The "recovery process is awful," she wrote. It "takes over a year to heal from being undervalued, spoken down to, gaslighted, dismissed, working insane hours, harassed, treated like I only got hired for (1) diversity quota or (2) must have slept with someone for my job."

Avendaño is not alone in her portrayal of the company. When the *New York Times* interviewed more than thirty current and former Uber employees in 2017, they described a "Hobbesian environment at the company, in which workers are sometimes pitted against one another

and where a blind eye is turned to infractions from top performers."
As we've seen in prior chapters, these kinds of hyper-competitive
workplaces are brutal for most workers, but they tend to be hardest on
women.

Silicon Valley has even documented the situation. Surveys like the
2015 "Elephant in the Valley" report and the 2018 report on women
in tech by Indeed found that almost half of the women who enter the
tech field leave—double of the percentage of the men—citing lack of
career growth and poor management as the most common reasons for
quitting. Unlike women in other industries, women in tech rarely leave
for family reasons, and they generally report that they like the work
and can deal with the hours. Instead, as a study by the Center for Talent Innovation found, when women drop out of tech, it is because of
"workplace conditions, a lack of access to key creative roles, and a sense
of feeling stalled in one's career. Studies show that women who work in
tech are interrupted in meetings more often than men. They are evalu-
ated on their personality in ways that men are not." And, as we learned
in Ellen Pao's case, if they are startup founders, they are less likely to
get funding from venture capitalists, who, studies show, find pitches
delivered by men—especially handsome men—more persuasive. These
negative perceptions of the workplace environment, the disparities in
treatment between men and women, and the lack of opportunities contribute to the women's decisions to head to other lines of work—and
this exodus is estimated to cost the tech industry $16 billion a year. In
other words, what seems like the ultimate level playing field—tech is a
comparatively new industry, with high salaries, low bureaucracy, and
room for growth—has turned out to be a sloping and bumpy surface for
a game in which not entirely sober young men set the terms of competition. Silicon Valley is as likely to push aspiring young women down a
chute out to get them out of the industry as it is to provide a ladder for
them to climb toward a promising career.

Although it's common knowledge that tech is one of the most challenging industries for women in America—again, Emily Chang wrote an entire book titled *Brotopia*—what's less well known is that it hasn't always been this way. Back in the seventies, when the phrase "Silicon Valley" was first coined, women joined men in moving into the growing computer science field. Over the course of that decade, men with degrees in computer and information sciences rose from 1 to 3 percent of all undergraduate degrees, and the number of women rose alongside them, from .5 to 2 percent of all college graduates.

In those days, the techies coming out of university computer science departments were more likely to work for large companies, like IBM in New York, Hewlett-Packard in Silicon Valley, and Wang Laboratories in Boston. They were more likely to be shy, antisocial engineering nerds in "coding caves" than the freewheeling "bros" who would characterize Silicon Valley startups in the Uber era.

The slowly accelerating numbers of women entering the industry peaked in the mid-eighties and then fell, never to recover. One factor for the declining female interest during the eighties may have been the emergence of personal computers and video games. Studies show that boys embraced these games more enthusiastically than girls, and effectively hogged the equipment from high school into college and beyond. The other reason is that as the economic recession and the slump in tech jobs in the eighties ended, and tech became hot, white men flooded the field, driving out everyone else. Men with bachelor's degrees in computer and informational sciences rose to approximately 7.5 percent of undergraduate degrees by 2004, while women never again cracked 2 percent. By 2021, men earned more than five times as many computer science degrees as women—a much bigger disparity than forty years earlier.

Part of what drove male interest during these times was soaring salaries. Salaries in the computer and engineering fields began to produce some of the highest entry-level wages available at college graduation. Indeed, salaries for "techies," particularly computer science majors,

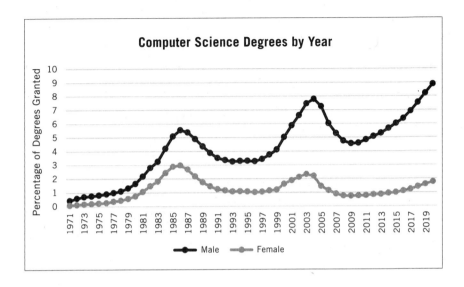

engineers, and math grads, have continued to increase faster than in other scientific fields, and these have been the STEM (science, technology, engineering, mathematics) fields where women's underrepresentation is greatest. Such trends may have, in turn, affected the nature of the men drawn to these fields. A fascinating study by the American Association of University Women found a link between the level of implicit bias and male overrepresentation in these fields. The study first measured the degree to which undergraduate students associate math and science with men, consciously and unconsciously. The researchers then linked the degree of implicit bias with particular majors. The study found that men who major in engineering, physics, and computer science have higher levels of implicit bias associating these fields with men than other male undergraduates, while the women who major in these fields have lower levels of such bias than other women.

In other fields, such as the humanities, the opposite results hold: the women who major in the humanities have higher levels of implicit bias, associating science and computing with men, while the men have lower levels of bias than the men in the more technical fields. What this means is that the male image of the fields becomes a self-fulfilling prophecy: the men attracted to the fields are more likely to be biased against women, suggesting they will be more likely to drive women out of the field, further increasing the perception that these are stereotypically "male" activities. Of course, we don't know which way the causal arrows run. Perhaps gamers are exactly the kind of boys likely to grow up to become sexual harassers at the likes of Uber, but it's perhaps more likely that the predominantly male atmosphere of college computer labs has its own reinforcing effects on male biases. Or, it could just be that as salaries in the field increased, the departments became harder to get into, keeping out art majors like Ingrid Avendaño and welcoming men like Travis Kalanick. Whatever the reason, the bias is there—and once you see it, it's impossible to ignore.

By the time Uber Technologies founder Travis Kalanick arrived on the Silicon Valley scene, the nerds had faded into the background and the bros were beginning to reign supreme. And Kalanick was the consummate tech bro. Born in 1976, he grew up in Los Angeles loving computers and he learned to code by the time he was in middle school. He majored in computer engineering at UCLA but dropped out in 1998 to devote his energies to a company he founded with some classmates at the height of the dot.com boom, a company that sold a Napster-like peer-to-peer file-sharing software. The initial "angel" funding came from a classmate's friends and family. The startup went bankrupt during the dot.com bust, in large part because the company faced $250 billion in copyright-infringement suits. Adding to the pain, some of Kalanick's own investors joined the suit; it became impossible to get new funding. Kalanick founded a "revenge business," designed to get the companies that had sued him to buy his new file-sharing product. That company, Red Swoosh, almost failed, too. At one point, there was no one left keeping the company afloat but Kalanick. He described the experience as a long six years that "meant not getting any girls, that's for sure." But, "through little else but the sheer force of his personality," he found a new investor, and he rebuilt the company and ultimately made it work, at least long enough to sell to a bigger company for $20 million.

When he came up with the idea for Uber, Kalanick was at a low point, burned out from his previous startups. He had just celebrated his thirtieth birthday and was living at home with his parents in his childhood bedroom, considering himself "practically middle-aged by Silicon Valley standards." The Uber origin story is that Kalanick and his co-founder, Garrett Camp, were in Paris on a snowy night in 2008. They couldn't get a cab. They thought: Why not solve the problem with an app? Push a button and get a car. They decided to start a company that would enable passengers to use their phones to summon a cab.

In the summer of 2010, Uber opened in San Francisco with a handful of cars. By then, Kalanick and Camp had attracted an angel investor to provide initial funding. They had created an innovative app that used the GPS system to find riders' locations and then transmitted the request to nearby drivers who had signed up to provide services. The drivers could signal their willingness to take the ride for a fixed price, and riders could pay by a credit card already on file. Camp crowed, "[E]veryone could ride like a millionaire." The app was handy. By itself, however, all it got them was a new technology that could be sold to the existing cab companies. That wouldn't be enough to make Kalanick and Camp billionaires. Instead, they opened their own company, called UberCab, designed to compete with (and ultimately replace) existing cab companies. But they weren't licensed to run a cab company. The San Francisco Municipal Transportation Agency and the California Public Utilities Commission sued, getting a court order against the company to cease operations. Kalanick, who loved a fight, ignored the order, but he changed the company name to "Uber."

To succeed, Uber aimed to circumvent the laws governing traditional taxi companies. "I think of them [Kalanick and his associates] as robber barons," says Barry Korengold, president of the San Francisco Cab Drivers Association. "They started off by operating illegally, without following any of the regulations and unfairly competing. And that's how they became big—they had enough money to ignore all the rules." Kalanick's startup model involved huge venture capital (VC) investments, Blitzkrieg growth tactics, "and an ethically questionable aggressive streak."

The hundreds of millions in VC funding, in turn, allowed Uber to very quickly ramp up its operations from a handful of cars in San Francisco to a global presence. It went from launching its first live rides via the app in 2010, to expanding to major cities in the United States and to Paris the very next year, to becoming "the most valuable startup in the world" (valued at $51 billion) by 2015. Yet managing that kind of growth is challenging. The lines between professional life and social life often blur. The entrance of stuffy human resources departments might put an end to the party atmosphere, constraining the entrepreneurs who believe that breaking rules is synonymous with innovation.

Meanwhile, like many Silicon Valley entrepreneurs, Kalanick wielded power more like a spiritual leader than a business leader, demanding nothing short of total devotion from his staff. The *New York Times*, in a 2019 article on Uber, described how Silicon Valley is built on this kind of "founder worship" as its "bedrock faith." According to reporter Mike Isaac, "Kalanick required an almost hypnotic level of obedience from his staff in order to build the company." The informality, the star system built around the winners of entrepreneurial competitions, and the lack of institutional rules (much less HR departments with the clout to enforce them) created all kinds of problems for women like Avendaño. When she experienced harassment, there was no effective way to complain about a company founder who sent emails encouraging his staff to get drunk and sleep around. And when she experienced discrimination from her fellow engineers and complained about it, she faced retaliation. "If your biggest priority is keeping your rock-star engineer happy, and you get a harassment complaint about him, you may ignore the written guidelines about what you're supposed to do," said Joelle Emerson, CEO of Paradigm, a diversity consultancy firm.

"Swashbuckling freedom" may be key to company growth, but it presents an impediment to accountability; if those in power think they can do no wrong, women trying to keep a toehold in a company like

Uber have no platform from which to argue otherwise. Above all, Kalanick seemed to want employees and managers to possess qualities not unlike his own. As is often the standard for startups, he was looking for the young, the brash, and the inexperienced. He offered them immediate responsibility and an open beer keg. He kept on the pressure to take risks, both at the Las Vegas gaming tables and in the office. He told employees they were brilliant, and that they must grow the business and increase revenues. And he was prepared to look the other way when his engineering crew adopted the kind of boorish behavior that goes with being twentysomething, entitled, and not entirely sober. Investor Mark Cuban explained, "Travis's biggest strength is that he will run through a wall to accomplish his goals. Travis's biggest weakness is that he will run through a wall to accomplish his goals." While toe-stepping was supposed to encourage workers to share ideas regardless of their rank, "too often it was used as an excuse for being an asshole," Kalanick's replacement later explained.

As we've seen in other sectors of the economy—everywhere from retail to GE—too many of the problems women face in the WTA workplace can be traced back to a culture defined by CEOs like Travis Kalanick. The startup world, much like GE's policy of rank-and-yank or the Wall Street bonus system, creates tournaments. These tournaments handsomely reward the winners. As they do, the competition to gain access to the multimillion-dollar rewards becomes even more intense, and the pathways to the top ranks become even more male dominated. Tech startups set the tone for Silicon Valley culture—and the toxic model for the treatment of women.

What's more, tournament winners in tech do not worry overly much about what law professor Larry Ribstein euphemistically refers to as "self-doubt and moral distractions." In Silicon Valley, the innovation mindset dovetails with a more general anti-establishment attitude. When you're reinventing the universe, you're unlikely to subscribe to what you may consider to be outdated rules of decorum. As *Vice News* explains, "That Uber regularly broke laws to cement its frontrunner status is not a controversial statement, it's a fact." And that mindset is easy to maintain when the company is on the line, when the ability to retain employees that have been recruited is in peril, and when it enters the founder's mind that he might not achieve what Kalanick outlined as his end goal: "utter domination."

All this creates the kind of self-reinforcing WTA culture that overwhelmingly selects for leaders with what are known as the "dark triad" personality traits—narcissism, psychopathy, and Machiavellianism—and whose leaders then select managers in their image, who go on to create highly toxic workplaces. The psychology studies on discrimination and harassment show that every element in the construction of these environments increases the likelihood of abuse. Workplaces that prize demonstrations of so-called masculine traits—who can work the longest hours, who is competitive, aggressive, and physically strong—define success not by a focus "on meeting performance goals, but on proving you are more of [a] man than the next guy." Studies that measure and rank highly competitive environments find that they correlate with increased sexual harassment and bullying. While acquiring more power generally increases arrogance and insensitivity, the effect is even more pronounced on those scoring high in dark-triad traits like narcissism—that is, the hard-charging "brilliant jerks" Uber prized. And it turns out that men with these characteristics, whether or not they are in managerial positions, prefer a larger number of sex partners. On top of that, narcissistic bosses display less awareness of the negative impact of sexual advances on their subordinates. Finally, the WTA economy creates more opportunities for this behavior. Tech startups, for example, take longer to create human resource departments than do larger, more established companies. It is hardly surprising therefore that these toxic environments disproportionately drive women out, undermining diversity in recruitment, retention, and expression. As Sheelah Kolhatkar of the *New Yorker* describes gender in the tech world, "many of these companies and their CEOs have created an internal culture that, at least when it comes to sexual harassment and gender inequality, resembles the Mad Men era, without the skinny ties and Martini lunches."

Avendaño's complaint against Uber provides us with a graphic description of a company that exists as a shrine to the founder, and that flouts the law and the civilized order that governs how people should treat each other. Even more than that, it drives out women drawn to tech, who love coding, who thrive on solving problems, and who want to join men in reshaping the world. In short, it promotes men like Travis Kalanick who see themselves as the rightful winners in the game of life, with little sympathy for those who are belittled by their unprofessional practices—and who go on to deeply traumatize women like Ingrid Avendaño.

Unlike Ellen Pao, the women of Uber won. Fowler's blog focused a powerful spotlight on Uber's dysfunctional operations. More women came forward. The company had no choice but to act. Kalanick was forced to resign. And startups, which depend on seizing the day, are also quite vulnerable to the wrong attention in critical moments of their development. The new management waived restrictive clauses in the women's employment agreements and quickly settled with Avendaño, Medina, and the other women who sued, agreeing not only to pay damages but also to reform its employee compensation, evaluation, and bonus system. Acting together, the women made a difference.

The challenge for women in tech remains the roller-coaster nature of the industry. The period after Avendaño's Uber departure were boom years for the industry. Tech workers were in demand, the industry faced a worker shortage, and women filled the pipeline. Surveys show that 74 percent of girls express some interest in STEM fields. In 2020, girls constituted 47.8 percent of AP Calculus test-takers and 30 percent of those taking the AP Computer Science exam, up from 20 percent in 2015.

In 2022, however, Silicon Valley's latest boom cooled off, triggering massive layoffs—and women were disproportionately among the casualties. According to eightfold.ai, a talent intelligence firm, women were 65 percent more likely than men to be laid off in the tech industry—and employees with ten to fifteen years of experience were hardest hit, constituting a fourth of the layoffs. Women in tech were once again being driven out, albeit for a very different set of reasons. But the result is the same: the talented female leaders who enter the industry will not be there to mentor and guide the next generation. At the same time, Silicon Valley appeared to be "slid[ing] back into 'Bro' culture."

The solution that some women have found, however, is to start their own tech companies and to band together to fight for progress in tech. Ellen Pao founded the nonprofit consulting company Project Include to promote diversity in Silicon Valley. And women continue to fight to lead their own companies. Startups founded by women in the health-tech space focus on using digital technology to help people monitor and manage their healthcare needs. Women have created incubators to develop online free educational resources to equip LGBTQ workers and allies with tech career skills, tech recruiting companies to manage talent globally and remotely, and angel fund and investor communities for women to receive global investor capital. A number of people in the next generation are creating startups to move more women and nonbinary people into Web3. Deana Burke, co-founder of Boys Club, a collective for women and nonbinary people, explains that Web3 is "the version of the internet that comes after the Facebooks and the Googles, the one where you, the user, can theoretically own your data—your art, your tweets, your selfies—and earn money from them." And, as we observed in Chapter 4, startups that included female founders fared better than male-only startups during in the downturn.

It is efforts like that one that are one reason we are optimistic. Startups actually make things. They create novel products, and the productivity and rigor that come from collaborative teams and diverse companies can improve those products and the workplaces in which they are created.

CHAPTER 7

Home Alone: Martinez v. Aspen Dental

I n May 2020, Lauren Martinez found herself faced with an impossible situation. She had been working as an assistant office manager in a dental practice in Lee County, Florida, for over a year. Although she was on maternity leave at the time the COVID-19 pandemic hit, having recently given birth to her son, she knew she was going to have to return to work when her office reopened at the end of April. Like the majority of middle-class families, the Martinezes needed every cent of their two incomes to make ends meet—her husband also worked at the dental office—and so both parents needed to be out of the house during the day at work. With schools and daycare centers shuttered because of the pandemic, Martinez and her husband made the difficult decision to leave their baby son, Luca, in the care of her 14-year-old daughter, Emily, who was at home doing school remotely, so that they wouldn't suffer any loss of income. The situation was far from ideal—what parents want to leave their baby in the care of another child?—but the Martinezes felt they had no other choice. "It was either go to work or get evicted," Lauren later pointed out.

In the weeks to come, their daughter, Emily, did her best to care for the baby while juggling schoolwork and online classes. Then, on May 26, 2020, Martinez returned home from work to find Emily running a temperature and throwing up. Martinez let the dental office know that

Emily was sick, possibly with COVID-19, and that she wouldn't be able to come into work. She asked if she could work remotely so she could stay home to take care of her children. She assumed this wouldn't be a problem since her job was essentially a sales position at a dentist's office, talking to customers on the phone about the services offered and encouraging them to sign up for different packages. It was work that could easily be done remotely—or so she thought. Her supervisor told her that he would check with the higher-ups to see what was possible. A few days later, she received a text telling her to either come back to work or risk being fired. "We cannot continue to have you just not come in to work and retain the spot," her supervisor texted. "The feedback from the higher-ups is if you cannot come in due to childcare . . . the position is vacated. Meaning you no longer have a job." After Martinez objected, the supervisor texted her again, warning her "not to question my professionalism or my intention," and "remember I am your boss."

Blindsided by the exchange, Martinez decided to send a written complaint to Aspen Dental, the dental services organization that manages the HR aspects of dental practices for individual dental providers, including the practice where she worked. Surely it must be against the rules to threaten someone with dismissal for not having adequate childcare during a pandemic. Martinez asked if it was still an option to work remotely for a few days so she could take care of her children while they were sick. She was told that she wouldn't get paid for doing that. Soon after that, Martinez was told to return to work, which she did on June 2, 2020, only to find she had been written up for poor attendance. When she protested again, she learned that she was being fired. After being escorted out of the building, Martinez was "so upset and humiliated," she went home and called a local attorney's office. The paralegal there connected her with a lawyer, Benjamin Yormak, who had previously sued Aspen Dental in a different matter.

That July, Lauren Martinez and her lawyer filed a suit against Aspen Dental and R. Dustin Dixon DMD Holdings, PLLC, claiming that the dental office had broken federal law by first refusing to grant her leave and then by firing her. She argued that Aspen Dental had interfered with her rights under the Family and Medical Leave Act (FMLA), which permitted employees working for employers with fifty or more employees to take up to twelve weeks of unpaid leave each year to care for sick children, and the Emergency Family Medical Leave Act (EFMLA), which allowed families to take paid leave (at two-thirds of the employee's salary) for up to ten weeks because of childcare issues during the pandemic. She also alleged that her employer retaliated against her when she tried to invoke her right to reinstatement, another violation of the FMLA.

Dental practices have become a growth field for women. Between 2010 and 2020, the percentage of dentists who are women increased from roughly one-fourth to over one-third, with the percentage of female dental school graduates exceeding 50 percent in 2019. Dental office support personnel are even more likely to be women, including dental office managers (90 percent female) and dental hygienists (93 percent female). Moreover, female dentists are more diverse than male dentists, including many people of color and recent immigrants.

At the same time the field has become more welcoming to women, however, private equity has been increasingly taking over dental practice management, with potentially negative consequences for employees and customers. Since the mid-2010s, private equity firms have been busily investing in medical practices, not only in the United States but also around the world. The private equity playbook has transformed the healthcare sector, bringing with it a WTA worldview that is entirely out of step with the needs of healthcare providers and patients. Private equity's playbook is simple: buy a company, dramatically reduce costs, boost reported earnings, and then sell for a profit. The overriding goal—theoretically—is to improve the companies' financial health, but pragmatically, their goal is to make a large return in a short period of time. Employee or patient satisfaction is beside the point. While this is less than ideal in an average company, it can have a downright lethal effect for the patients served by companies in healthcare. Studies are emerging that when private equity takes over sectors of healthcare, there are reasons for concern. After being acquired by private equity, "hospitals charged more and . . . compared with similarly sized and located hospitals, private equity–owned hospitals tended to have lower patient satisfaction," as well as lower numbers of full-time employees per hospital bed. And mortality rates increase. For example, researchers from the University of Pennsylvania, Chicago Booth, and NYU examined private equity–acquired nursing homes over a fifteen-year period. They found that the profit goals led to reduced staff providing basic hygiene, infection management, and monitoring, as well as a 50 percent increase in antipsychotic medications administered in those homes. The researchers found that these differences led to a 10 percent increase in mortality rates, which "translate[d] to more than 20,000 additional deaths relative to other homes during this time frame." And this is occurring in an industry where the value of private equity has increased more than fifty-fold since 2002, with private equity putting $206 billion into over 1,400 deals in healthcare acquisitions, just in 2021.

Aspen Dental is just such a private equity company. For its part, Aspen Dental denied any wrongdoing in the *Martinez* case, telling the press that dental practices operating under the Aspen brand had offered employees a number of generous benefits and programs during the pandemic, including enhanced sick pay and extended COVID-related leave. Professional service organizations like Aspen are supposed to be efficient and "run" dental practices for the dentists, ensuring compliance with a variety of legal mandates, such as the electronic records and privacy provisions that have transformed healthcare providers. But Aspen Dental is a company with a questionable track record, at best. In 2013, a PBS series produced by *Frontline* revealed that Aspen patients were routinely overcharged or given unnecessary treatments. A class action lawsuit accused Aspen of violating laws in twenty-two states (it was later dismissed). And in 2021, the Massachusetts attorney general sued Aspen for "bait and switch" advertising that promised free dental care for which the practice later billed the patients. The company settled with the attorney general's office in 2023 for $3.5 million and restrictions on its future advertisements.

In a privately managed dental office, without a private equity–funded dental services organization in the background, Martinez might have had a personal relationship with her boss—the dentist. An individual dentist might not have been able to afford to lose an office manager for an extended period, and that boss might have been willing to arrange things so she could work from home. Martinez had established her value as an employee, and so the dentist might also have been reluctant to let her go. But Aspen Dental did not have a personal relationship with Martinez. The private equity firm operated from a corporate office in New York, with little face-to-face contact or interaction with employees. When Martinez's childcare issues arose, a human resources office in New York, which was supposed to ensure compliance with laws such as those enacted to address the pandemic, apparently decided that Martinez was dispensable.

In the prior chapter, we focused on younger women in Silicon Valley who were forced to leave their jobs because they could no longer endure a toxic WTA workplace. In this chapter, we see what happens to women in the middle of the WTA economy who are being pushed out of the workplace for a very different reason: this country's failure to support working parents with adequate and affordable childcare. For as long as mothers have worked outside the home, it's been the case that our ability to hold down a job has been contingent on childcare affordability and availability. The reality is that women primarily bear the burden of arranging for childcare and staying home when childcare is unavailable. Even before the pandemic hit—virtually eliminating the option of daycare and other childcare supports—working mothers were dependent on a fractured system. A 2018 survey found that "mothers were 40 percent more likely than fathers to report that they had personally felt the negative impact of child care issues on their careers."

What does the WTA economy have to do with lack of childcare? The answer is—everything. The very definition of the WTA economy is that it fails to invest in the collective good, and instead a small group extracts immediate gains, leaving everyone else to fend for themselves in a negative-sum contest. Although family-friendly provisions are incredibly popular across the political spectrum, working mothers in the United States, especially those in the middle of the economy like Martinez, routinely find themselves living one childcare crisis away from being pushed out of the labor market. The 2020 COVID-19 crisis only exposed the many ways this country has been failing its women workers. During the first year of the pandemic, women lost 5.4 million jobs overall, compared with 4.4 million jobs lost by men, many of them because they had no choice but to stay home with their children after childcare became unavailable. With the recovery, college-graduate women were among the first to resume full-time employment, but women without college degrees, who have long been dependent on a jerry-rigged childcare support system, had a much slower return trajectory. They disproportionately worked in some of the sectors, such as the care economy, that were hardest hit by the pandemic. Working-class women are much more likely to quit or be fired when they get pregnant.

The pandemic exacerbated existing tensions and vulnerabilities for working parents, with many employers proving unsympathetic to family responsibilities. Mothers of young children, for example, reported they were concerned about their children interrupting them during Zoom calls at twice the rates of fathers. Employment for mothers with children under the age of 13 plummeted compared to fathers with similar-aged children during the first year and a half of the pandemic. Even mothers who remained in their jobs cut back on hours because of both childcare and housework. Although the pandemic has been responsible for revealing the fault lines in our broken childcare system, the reality is that the United States has never managed to sufficiently address the childcare needs of working families. While other countries around the world have systems of state-subsidized nurseries and daycares, in America childcare has, historically, been considered a private matter. In fact, we have to go all the way back to World War II to find a time when this country implemented anything like a comprehensive, federally funded childcare program. In the build-up to World War II, Congress passed the Defense Housing and Community Facilities and Services Act of 1940—popularly known as the Lanham Act—which authorized war-related government grants, including funding for daycares. The idea was to provide enough childcare resources that women could be released into the labor force to help with the war effort. Despite reluctance from many people (including New York's mayor, Fiorello La Guardia) to aid the entry of women with young children into the job market, the funding went ahead, and public and private entities came together to create new daycare centers and support existing ones. In the three years that followed, these centers took care of approximately 550,000 children—only an estimated 10 percent of those who needed such care—but still a marked improvement from what had been available before. Although many working mothers hoped the program would continue and expand, it wasn't to be. In 1946, with the war over and men coming home to retrieve their jobs, the money for childcare centers dried up. Women marched and protested to keep the program, but it was deemed no longer necessary.

In 1971, a little more than thirty years after the Lanham Act, America had its second brush with creating a universal childcare provision. In the late 1960s, women were entering the workforce in larger numbers than ever before, and child psychologists began to stress the vital importance of the early childhood years. During his 1970 presidential campaign, Richard Nixon had promised to "make a national commitment to providing all American children an opportunity for a healthful and stimulating development during the first five years of life." When the Comprehensive Child Development Act (CCDA) of 1971 came before Congress, it was met with broad support across both sides of the aisle. The bill was designed to create a national network of childcare centers, where the poorest children could attend for free and other children could join on a sliding scale. The Senate successfully passed the bill with a vote of 63 to 17. But when the CCDA reached President Nixon's desk, he decided to veto it. In explaining why, the president pointed to the "fiscal irresponsibility, administrative unworkability, and family-weakening implications of the system it envisions." In short, he tarred the proposal as too expensive, too bureaucratic, and too collectivist, invoking fears of communism and Soviet-style indoctrination of children. The message from the president was clear: a woman's place is in the home, and it wasn't up to the government to make it any easier for her to leave it.

Nixon's veto memo gave voice to free-market ideals that would become the rallying cry of the American right for the next fifty years. The Nixon presidency not only signed away government-mandated childcare provisions, but it also marked a new era in American politics—one in which conservative business interests began their concerted effort to undo New Deal regulation and restrictions on businesses. The same year of the Nixon childcare veto, in August 1971, the U.S. Chamber of Commerce—a pro-business American lobbying group—decided to commission Lewis Powell to write a confidential memo entitled: "Attack on the American Free Enterprise System." In his memo, Powell, who was about to accept Nixon's nomination to the Supreme Court, called for a far-reaching effort to disseminate conservative ideas via media and academia. The memo became a blueprint for conservative business interests and a rallying cry for right-wing corporations to "rescue" America from communists and New Deal democrats. Powell's words galvanized businessmen to oppose what Powell saw as a radical agenda undermining corporate interests and the free market.

With Powell's memo circulating, billionaire brothers David and Charles Koch sat up and took notice. As philanthropists of conservative causes, the brothers took the Powell memo as a "call-to-arms." David and Charles had inherited the family oil-refining business from their father, Fred Koch, after his death in 1967, and they had taken the company from regional bit player to what is currently ranked as the second largest private company in the United States. Like their father, who was a staunch member of the anti-communist John Birch Society, both brothers believed that "big government" was the enemy. When Nixon's tax cuts benefited big businessmen like them, they took those spoils and began pumping money into libertarian-conservative political advocacy groups, such as the U.S. Chamber of Commerce and Americans for Prosperity. In turn, these groups began working to block measures that increased the role of government or that imposed mandates on businesses.

With the election of Ronald Reagan in 1980, anti-government groups such as those funded by the Kochs began to gain even greater influence, and the ideological push for less regulation and less intervention steadily increased. Even Democratic president Bill Clinton declared in his 1996 State of the Union message that "[t]he era of big government is over." Meanwhile, the need for childcare and other family support grew exponentially. When Nixon had vetoed the comprehensive childcare bill back in 1971, only around 30 percent of married mothers of young children were in the labor market (although the percentage of Black mothers working outside the home has always been higher than the figure for white mothers). In the subsequent decades, the percentage of mothers in the labor market more than doubled, reaching a peak in the late 1990s. But the government failed to provide options for meeting the country's need for accessible and affordable childcare. Instead, conservatives reflexively opposed earmarking any government funds to provide for paid family leave or childcare (deeming it too irresponsible), and they blocked measures to compel employers to provide greater assistance (considering it government overreach). While Clinton's welfare reform law, the Personal Responsibility and Work Opportunity Act of 1996, had encouraged low-income women to enter the workforce by providing subsidized daycare for their children, the Newt Gingrich revolution continued its assault on government services, with the former Speaker of the House famously proposing a ban on welfare benefits altogether in order to use the money to create orphanages for the children of unwed mothers.

Subsequent presidents have varying records on this crucial child-care issue. Although First Lady Laura Bush was a former schoolteacher, President George Bush's proposed budgets did not expand assistance to childcare or Head Start; in fact, his 2009 budget would have ceased childcare assistance for 200,000 children. By the time President Barack Obama took office in 2009, his American Recovery and Reinvestment Act included an injection of funding for early childhood programs, providing $2 billion over two years for the childcare and development fund to help states facing fiscal challenges during the economic downturn. It also provided $2 billion over two years in additional Head Start funding, some of which was used to expand the program to include more babies and toddlers. But much like the program of the war years, it was a temporary measure that vanished after two years of stimulus.

In 2016, candidate Donald Trump promised to make childcare more affordable, with a proposal to spend $500 billion on childcare over ten years. What Trump proposed during the campaign, and what his daughter Ivanka Trump spearheaded, was a system of tax credits. Trump called for a "childcare tax deduction," allowing an individual earning less than $250,000 a year (or couples earning less than $500,000) to deduct a certain amount of their childcare costs from their taxes. When Ivanka's proposal was finally unveiled during her father's term, it turned out that, in classic WTA fashion, the $500 billion plan gave the largest benefits to wealthier families, proving that even Republicans believe in childcare—as long as it leads to tax cuts for people with nannies and au pairs. Trump's approach to childcare during the pandemic crisis echoed Nixon's veto message: childcare was a matter of individual responsibility. Families might need a small amount of temporary assistance, but the government had no overall responsibility to ensure that a childcare infrastructure existed—much less whether it would survive a disruptive, global event like the pandemic.

Not only did Trump fail to deliver on his campaign promise to make childcare affordable for families, but also his administration's failure to curb the pandemic or to provide funds so that childcare centers could safely reopen instead helped to bring the entire childcare industry to the brink of collapse. At a time when there was a desperate need for childcare centers, they began closing in unprecedented numbers, with researchers warning that nearly half of the U.S. childcare centers could be lost to the pandemic.

Even before COVID-19 struck, finding quality, affordable childcare had been extremely difficult, with 60 percent of the public reporting challenges. Middle-income women in particular have had to deal with a patchwork of private and public service, with many living in "child-care deserts" where it's almost impossible to find conveniently located care. These trends also disproportionally hit those with limited resources and those with lower levels of education—groups that had "the slowest return to work. These mothers have always had less access to paid leave, telework options, or affordable childcare."

Employers have long accorded highly skilled employees who are hard to replace more family benefits—even if they also create pressures not to fully utilize them. Low-wage employers like Walmart have long depended on women with limited options, often in part because of childcare responsibilities that limit their ability to work full time or to get the experience needed to obtain better jobs. If you're an employer like Aspen Dental, with employees you might consider easily replaceable, it's unlikely you'll provide accommodations unless forced to do so. Which is how Lauren Martinez got left out in the cold. Her employer seems to have found a worker with childcare issues an inconvenience to its monthly bottom line, so it fired her.

As Martinez's story and the stories of so many other women show us, parents with family responsibilities can participate in the workforce only if they have access to comprehensive childcare. Yet, high-quality childcare is expensive. One of the authors of this book spent her entire salary as a law professor on childcare during the years when her third child was a toddler. This lack of an affordable childcare infrastructure creates problems at every level of the economy—and it's holding us back. The United States emerged as the best-educated country in the world in the nineteenth century because it was one of the first countries in the world to embrace free secondary education. Today it lags behind comparable countries, in large part because of the failure to invest in early childhood care—the arena where public investment provides the biggest return on the dollars spent.

The failure to provide childcare increases economic inequality in the United States every bit as much as do those big bonuses for top executives. While it plays out in different ways for different groups in society, the common denominator is the way it limits women's options everywhere. Within a system that treats childcare solely as a matter of private responsibility, women have always borne the primary burden for providing the care. With the wholesale movement of mothers into the labor market, however, that inevitably means that women cannot participate on the same terms as men. There are many factors that drive the gender pay gap, but one of the most pervasive is the "motherhood penalty," through which having children negatively affects women's earnings in ways that are not true for men. These pressures—with salaries tied to "face time" in the office, diminished flexibility, and the sentiment that women who have children are less serious or committed workers—have increased with bonus pay that's contingent on working the longest hours.

The motherhood penalty, coupled with the absence of affordable childcare, affects women at every level of the economy. At the top, elite jobs place an increasing emphasis on long hours and "job above all." As a result, women employees in these workplaces are forced to either give up on having children, find a stay-at-home spouse, or constantly juggle competing responsibilities. It is hardly surprising that more mothers than fathers leave the labor force in the face of such pressure. Why not quit if you have to work at least twice hard as the men and don't get the same benefits—and if you happen to have a husband who makes more money than you do? According to Nextup (formerly the Network of

Executive Women), women who are at first- and mid-level manage-ment "exit at nearly double the rate of men (24.4 percent vs. 13.3 per-cent), while higher-level managers and executive and C-suite women leave their jobs nearly four times as often as men (26.9 vs. 7.3 percent)." Or, as Harvard economist and Nobel Prize winner Claudia Goldin tartly explains: "Something has to give. And with one really high income, the second income is less crucial."

At the bottom of the economy, the pressure is equal, but there are far fewer options. Quality childcare is unaffordable. The jobs that exist often lack flexibility. The absence of affordable housing, together with stagnant wages and a broken social safety net, means that if a parent has to stay home because the daycare is closed, that loss of pay might prove catastrophic. Given the lack of flexibility and benefits, many parents at the bottom economically cycle in and out of low-wage jobs. The women in this group frequently quit after childbirth (or are forced out), and then return to work full time when the children are older. And they may not have a second parent to provide any help.

Meanwhile, in the middle of the economy, most families are de-pendent on two incomes like the Martinezes, but often have trouble finding the kind of affordable, reliable, and flexible childcare that en-ables both parents to work. Ironically, middle-income areas (by which we mean areas where households make a combined annual income of around $75,000) are most likely to be located in childcare deserts. To make matters worse, the challenges of managing two incomes, a family, and financial tensions—and perceptions of an unfair division of fam-ily responsibilities—have contributed to much higher divorce rates for this group, which adds another level of financial pressure to already strapped families. Sociologists suggest that balancing work and fam-ily life is harder for less-educated women because these couples are less able "to afford services, such as high-quality child care, take-out meals, and home cleaning, that help to ease the family burdens asso-ciated with dual employment." Wives who work primarily for money rather than for career satisfaction have reported greater tension in their marriages—unsurprisingly, marital satisfaction increases when neither spouse has to clean the toilet.

The U.S. Supreme Court's 2022 decision, *Dobbs v. Jackson Women's Health Organization*, which overturned *Roe v. Wade* and returned the regulation of abortion to the states, is certain to make things worse. Following *Dobbs*, twenty-four states have moved to sharply restrict or ban abortions. The Guttmacher Institute estimated in February 2023 that 58 percent of women of child-bearing years live in states that are "hostile or extremely hostile" to abortion rights.

Restricting or banning abortion will dramatically impact women's ability to work. An amicus brief in the *Dobbs* case filed by 154 economists cited a robust body of studies conducted in the fifty years since *Roe*, showing that access to abortion "has had a significant impact on women's wages and educational attainment, with impacts most strongly felt by Black women." Without the ability to control their own reproductive lives, women will not only experience lower educational attainments but they will also have much lower labor force participation (and these effects will last for years), and be "less likely to move into higher-paid occupations." It is too early yet to ascertain the full effects of state control over women's reproductive healthcare and decision-making, but the cascade of restrictions after *Dobbs* will interact with the systematic lack of access to childcare support to compound the effects of the Triple Bind that we have identified.

When it comes to family and medical leave, of the kind that Lauren Martinez desperately needed so she could stay home to take care of her children, again, families are left to carry the burden and the cost. Across the board, only 50 percent of workers are even covered by the FMLA, and about three-fourths of those who are covered can't afford to take that leave because it's unpaid. The FMLA is further inaccessible to many because workers usually have to be employed for over a year before they become eligible for it; as any parent can tell you, most kids can't avoid getting sick for a month, let alone an entire year. Employers who do offer paid maternity leave tend to be those whose employees have skills. Two-thirds of new mothers with a college degree receive some kind of paid maternity leave—something that few states require. On the other hand, women with less than a college education were four times more likely to be let go because of pregnancy or childbirth, even though federal law protects against being fired because of pregnancy, childbirth, or related medical conditions. It was only because of a precise set of circumstances—thanks to the emergency COVID expansion of the FMLA, and because she had worked for the company for more than a year—that Lauren Martinez could even file her complaint.

By the time Martinez filed her lawsuit in July 2020, the family was in an even more precarious position. Not long after her dismissal, the dental office asked Martinez's husband to delete from her cellphone any texts the supervisor had exchanged with Martinez. The husband not only refused to do so, but he also quit his job in protest of such an invasion of privacy and in solidarity with his wife. Stripped of both their incomes, the family feared losing their home. Martinez's husband eventually found work at a food truck, but it was almost impossible for Lauren to find another job with a new baby in the middle of a pandemic. She received unemployment for a short period of time—and the family was eligible for food stamps and Medicaid—yet they struggled to pay the bills, getting their water shut off more than once.

Although a private person, Martinez decided to go public with her story, landing on the cover of *Time* magazine, and sharing her experiences of being laid off alongside other mothers with similar lawsuits. At the time of writing, she was still looking for work, aware that even if she found a job, it wasn't going to be easy to secure childcare. Many daycares had closed permanently during the COVID-19 outbreak, and those that stayed open had long waiting lists and high tuition fees. A federal district court ruled against her because she did not prove that either of her children had a "serious medical condition," as required by FMLA, nor did she specifically request FMLA leave or tell her employer she believed her child had COVID, for purposes of the EFMLA. Yet her determination to right the wrong of her unlawful termination is laudable, and she initially appealed this decision. When asked by a local news station about what she would teach her children about her experience, she said, "I want them to stand up for what's right. I want them to use their voice. . . .You just continue to move forward and do what's right."

The pandemic exposed the existing chasms in the makeshift childcare infrastructure, but it also showed us that, even in the middle of a national crisis, it can be difficult to muster the political will to address collective needs. Broader efforts to address childcare needs faced staunch opposition from the same forces that have opposed the expansion of government benefits since the Nixon administration—forces that remained sufficiently powerful to block congressional action

Despite this, we still have hope for a collective response. Postpandemic, a new view of childcare has begun to emerge, one that sees the development of a comprehensive childcare infrastructure as a "job creator" every bit as critical to the workforce infrastructure as public transportation, fair labor standards legislation, or high-speed broadband. Without childcare, parents with family responsibilities can't participate in the workplace as reliable employees. With childcare, they have the support they need to do their jobs, put food on the table, and keep the water from being shut off. If there is anything that scholars agree on, it is that the biggest payoff from public expenditures on children comes from early childhood investment, whether in the form of universal pre-K education or high-quality childcare. Investment in children, especially during times of crisis, pays off for society for a simple reason: it makes for happier, healthier, more productive adults down the line.

Future legislation may well recognize that investing in pregnancy support and early childhood care is necessary for improving the lives of working families. Congress passed the Providing Urgent Maternal Protections (PUMP) for Nursing Mothers Act in December of 2022; it requires employers to provide nursing mothers with a place other than a bathroom to pump at work and reasonable break time to do so. In addition, Congress passed the Pregnant Worker Fairness Act, which took effect in 2023, requiring employers to accommodate pregnant workers by permitting such things as small breaks unless the accommodation would impose undue hardship on the employer. States have begun to provide support for both pregnancy and early childcare. Moreover, with the tighter labor market that has emerged with the economic recovery from the pandemic, employers now have a stake in more available childcare; accessible childcare is essential for keeping all workers, but especially women, in the labor market. A comprehensive solution, however, can come only with recognition that childcare, like roads and schools, is a collective responsibility on which the well-being of families and the economy depend. Such recognition can't come soon enough for families like the Martinezes.

CHAPTER 8

Platform World:
Gig Workers v. Handy

O ver the course of this book, we have shown that modern workplaces have been increasingly untenable for women. Many of the highest-paying jobs require unforgiving hours and workplace competitions that pay off less well for women than for men. Lower-paying jobs, like those at Walmart, may involve exploitative practices, inflexible working conditions, and little hope for advancement. And women, who still bear the disproportionate burden of childcare, often find themselves pushed out or wanting out because of their childcare responsibilities. What do these women do? A growing number of workers have turned to flexible, temporary, or freelance jobs that offer few protections and uncertain pay. And while both men and women participate in the gig economy, their experiences differ considerably.

For many women, gig work may seem like a great alternative. As an independent contractor, you can set your own hours and operate on your own terms. This can feel liberating, especially for women who are still primarily responsible for childcare. To find some gig jobs, you need only access to the internet—which means you can work when your children are in school, fill in odd gaps between more permanent jobs, or continue to supplement your income by gigging even after you find another 9-to-5. And for many women, gig work might be the only work available in their communities, especially for those who have just been let go from a prior job.

The term "gig work" can be used to mean many things—everything from more traditional temporary or contract work, to the more novel online platform work, in which buyers and sellers are connected through an intermediary such as Uber, Airbnb, or TaskRabbit. In this chapter, we define a "gig" as any job that is not permanent and does not accrue benefits. The American workforce continues to lean toward gig work in greater numbers, with more people than ever earning a living, or supplementing their full-time job, without a conventional employer. Depending on how you count them (and counting them is difficult, because there are so many different types of alternative work), more than 30 percent of the population does some gig work and almost half of all millennials do so. This number comprises around 60 million Americans.

But while many have hailed gig work as the future of American employment—offering workers the freedom to work on their own terms and employers greater flexibility in hiring—such "advantages" do not come without costs. The reality is that gig workers are, of course, much more vulnerable to economic instability than their counterparts in conventional jobs. They're unlikely to have health insurance coverage or to contribute to retirement security. They don't get job-protected leave, much less paid leave, and employment discrimination laws don't apply because they are not considered employees. There's no workers' compensation or liability protection, and the pathways to advancement are difficult to navigate, if they exist at all. They are much more concerned than "permanent" workers about the stability of their work situation. Those at the bottom of the alternative-work world, without skills in high demand, generally cannot be sure whether they will have work hours at all, even at low pay. And although a majority of gig workers prefer the work they are doing to another type of work, when compared to traditional workers, gig workers are less likely to consider the job they are doing as a long-term career. All these facts are true of gig workers whether they are men or women, but women gig workers are also almost twice as likely as men to have hourly rates below minimum wage. And when women don't have the protections of the conventional workplace, they suffer in other ways, too.

For 34-year-old Patti Cris, signing up with the online marketplace Handy brought with it the promise of regular, flexible work funneled through an established industry leader. The Handy company, which was founded in 2012, sells household services to clients via an online site and app. If clients need a housecleaning or an odd job around the home, such as furniture assembly, they can go online and click to make an appointment for a cleaner or handy worker. On the other end, the Handy "Pro"—as Handy contractors are known—can "claim" the job using the app. Handy sets the costs of the service, billing its customers directly. The company tracks Pros and then pays them an amount that Handy determines. The platform has proved enormously popular with people who need domestic help; since Handy's founding in 2012, it has grown into a multimillion-dollar company acquired by the publicly traded Angi Homeservices that operates in hundreds of cities in the United States, as well as in Canada and Europe. In fact, in 2022, Handy's parent company reported annual revenues of over $1.8 billion.

Cris had been working for Handy for eight months in early 2018, when it became clear to her that although Handy could offer her flexible work, it wasn't going to offer her on-the-job protection. As she later described, she had accepted a Handy job cleaning an apartment in San Jose. That day, she drove to the client's home with her supplies (Handy required she fund both the gas and the cleaning products). According to the information she had received via the Handy app, she would be cleaning the client's home while he was out of the house, but even so, she knocked twice on the door before letting herself in. When she did, she found her client waiting for her, stark naked.

Stunned, Cris told the man that she was a Handy worker. He replied that he hadn't requested a cleaning. She fled. "I felt really violated," she remembered. That day, she emailed Handy to report the incident, and left voicemails and further emails when the company didn't respond.

Then she learned that, despite her complaint, Handy deducted $15 from her pay for leaving the harasser's residence early, classifying her behavior as canceling on short notice. Equally, cleaners who receive poor reviews from customers can earn less per hour and can be removed from Handy's service altogether.

In the coming weeks, Handy failed to start an investigation or take any corrective action about the incident. Cris says the company never provided any response to her report of harassment and refused to reverse the fee they had charged her for leaving early. Unlike some other gig companies, it had no rapid-response system in place to handle reports of safety issues, such as sexual harassment and assault. Eventually, Cris received a response from Handy: she was told they couldn't find a record of the booking. After this lackluster response, Cris quit the platform. She'd had enough. As a gig worker, Cris didn't have the traditional recourse of an employer—a manager, an HR department, or internal affairs—to turn to when things went wrong. Despite providing exceptional support to its customers—managing its workers closely and fining them if they step out of line—Handy failed to intervene on behalf of Cris when she was the one who needed support. The company washed its hands of Cris's reported harassment, and she was left on her own.

Although the term "gig work" is new, the phenomenon is anything but new. At one time, most wage labor was contingent and few jobs provided benefits; the history of the labor movement has involved a hard-fought battle to secure better jobs, with the federal government ultimately regulating hours and working conditions, and subsidizing benefits such as health insurance. Nonetheless, the early regulations deliberately excluded the types of jobs women traditionally held; as women finally won access to the workplace, businesses shifted to greater use of part-time and temporary employees to evade the federal requirements.

Some of us who came of age in the 1970s, like author Naomi Cahn, remember well the era of the Kelly Girl. Naomi was a temporary worker with what is now Kelly Services, a "temp" agency that provides short-term workers to companies. Naomi, who applied to be a Kelly Girl so she could earn money after school and during college vacations, was paid minimum wage, but she still earned more as a Kelly Girl than as a babysitter.

Kelly Services originated in 1946, although the first temporary agency had been around for twenty years at that point. By 1960, more than half of American businesses had used temp workers. The temp industry was deliberately feminized, with companies changing their names and advertising their "Girls." They did so, in part, to get around unions, and all the expensive protections that unions had bargained for that were typically available to full-time workers.

To avoid union wrath, the agencies developed a shrewd strategy, portraying temp work, such as retail sales or clerical work, as "women's work." Their ads featured young, white, and typically middle-class women handling short-term office work. They emphasized that temps were less expensive and, in the words of a Kelly Services 1971 ad, a temp:

> Never takes a vacation or holiday. Never asks for a raise. Never costs you a dime for slack time. (When the workload drops, you drop her.) Never has a cold, slipped disc or loose tooth. (Not on your time anyway!) Never costs you for unemployment taxes and Social Security payments. (None of the paperwork, either!) Never costs you for fringe benefits. (They add up to 30 percent of every payroll dollar.) Never fails to please. (If your Kelly Girl employee doesn't work out, you don't pay.)

Women, who have gained access to these jobs only in the last half-century, have long been relegated to contingent work, especially as in-home domestic workers (defined as those who work in private homes and who are paid directly by the care or cleaning recipient). In 1870, the census showed that "52 percent of employed women worked in 'domestic and personal service,'" and in 1880, almost all Black women engaging in paid labor were in domestic work. This country has a long history of leaving contingent workers out of workplace protections. When Congress passed the Fair Labor Standards Act (FLSA) in 1938, it introduced the forty-four-hour, seven-day work week, minimum wage, and guaranteed compensation for overtime work, as well as banning child labor—but domestic workers, farmworkers (another form of minority dominated contingent labor), and as we noted in Chapter 1, retail workers like those at Walmart were excluded. At the time it was passed, the FLSA covered only 20 percent of all workers, excluding 86 percent of women and almost all Blacks, male or female. Retail workers were finally included in 1963. And in 1964, Title VII of the Civil Rights Act barred employment discrimination on the basis of race, color, religion, sex, or national origin—which led to many women winning access to secure jobs—but domestic workers were again excluded, as the act applied only to employers with fifteen or more employees. It was not until 1974, when the Fair Labor Standards Act was amended, that domestic workers gained protections, including minimum wage and overtime pay, but they still had no legal protection from discrimination based on race, national origin, or sex. Today, the approximately 2 million domestic workers are mostly women, and often immigrants and people of color. They remain some of the most vulnerable workers in our economy, who have long been without developed paths to career advancement, labor protection, or the social safety net.

The precarity that household cleaners have experienced for over a hundred years has also increasingly become true of workers across sectors and classes. Since the 1970s, there has been a wholesale movement away from traditional employers who supply stable, full-time jobs with benefits and opportunities for advancement. This shift from a nation of conventional employment to gig work started with the changing management strategies and an emphasis on "lean" corporations. During the 1980s and 1990s, large manufacturers like General Electric, which we discussed in Chapter 2, felt pressure from increasing global competition, cut employment dramatically and outsourced anything that they could, whether abroad or to independent contractors at home. Within this new system, employees came to be viewed as dispensable. The result is a "new psychological contract." Employers no longer guarantee long-term employment; employees no longer feel loyal.

The most dramatic changes occurred in manufacturing, the focus of what had been the most successful unionization efforts. Manufacturing jobs peaked at 32 percent of nonfarm employment in 1953 and fell to 9 percent in 2019, with the absolute number of manufacturing jobs plummeting between 2001 and 2010. The largest job growth, in contrast, has occurred in jobs providing services, with the greatest gains occurring between 2000 and 2015. By 2015, retail jobs like the ones Betty Dukes held, constituted 11 percent of nonfarm employment and leisure and hospitality jobs an additional 10.7 percent, with food services and drinking places accounting for three-fourths of the growth in this sector. The demand for home-health and personal-care aides, another service category, was expected to increase by 22 percent between 2022 and 2032—much faster than other occupations. These service-sector jobs, even in good times, are more precarious than manufacturing jobs, even as they account for an increasing proportion of all employment. And the provision of services, from dog walking, to accounting, to digital marketing, is increasingly done by temporary or freelance workers.

Starting in the 1990s, the number of temporary workers employed each day almost tripled, from under 1 million to just under 3 million by 2000. And the post-recession recovery did not re-create the good middle-class jobs with benefits that had been cut. Instead, machines and temps increasingly performed the work that had been done by a stable workforce, with temporary employment of all kinds close to doubling between the depths of the recession in 2009 and the recovery in 2016. The Bureau of Labor Statistics indicates that temp jobs are typically more cyclical than other jobs; employers across all industries "shed temporary, contracted workers before their permanent employees" during downturns and hire such workers back before expanding their permanent workforce during recoveries, contributing to the expansion and importance of temp workers in the economy. Still, in 2019, with the economy in full recovery, Google had greater numbers of temporary and on-contract workers than full-time workers, and this pattern is repeated in many other tech firms; the companies may realize savings of $100,000 a year—per job—from this practice. LinkedIn reported the number of open contractor positions in tech tripled from January 2021 to October 2022.

In America, we have changed from "career to job to task."

If this story were just about the change from an industrial economy to one based on services, however, one could imagine a happy account of labor protections to fit the new work environments. Instead, as we saw with Walmart's success in stymieing unionization and the entrenched opposition to publicly funded childcare, the rise in service-based employment occurred as business power increased and a new anti-regulation, anti-labor coalition took hold: there is no happy account, as we know from the story of the Lewis Powell memo and subsequent developments in Chapter 7.

The triumph of this conservative coalition has eroded the legal and political protections that once made workers beneficiaries of corporate success. The labor market has been remade, ensuring most jobs are less secure and dramatically reducing benefits. And as good jobs—the ones offering security and benefits—have dried up, gig work has risen to fill in the gaps.

In other words, while flexible work may seem empowering to the average worker, in fact, the gig worker phenomenon is just another symptom of the WTA's reorganization of the economy; it matches employers who do not want to commit to full-time employees with workers who either want out of full-time-plus employment or who would prefer a full-time job and can't find one. The numbers are equally divided: 52 percent report taking a gig job because of economic necessity; 48 percent indicate it's a choice they prefer to other employment. When gig employees are asked why they prefer gig work, 39 percent indicate they want more free time and 34 percent indicate they want more control over their schedules. In contrast with traditional jobs, only 3 percent of gig employees work forty hours a week or more. The more flexible hours are a large part of the attraction, as is the ability to earn additional income.

Ana Medina, whom we discussed as being driven out of Uber in Chapter 6, provides an example; her LinkedIn page describes her as a "freelance software engineer" during the entire period in which she worked full time at Uber and in other positions.

What's going on here is a phenomenon that the political scientist Jacob Hacker has called "the Great Risk Shift." He describes it as playing out in "nearly every domain of economic life: job security, work–family balance, retirement, health care" and explains that the result has "forced working Americans to take on responsibilities that corporations and government once bore jointly." Hacker couples the growth of contingent employment with the increased family need to juggle work and caregiving, the decline of employment-based health benefits, and the near-extinction of defined-benefit pension plans to "mak[e] workers and their families bear more risk and responsibility on their own." Gig work exemplifies the change, as it shifts the cost of training and the search for opportunities for promotion onto workers—at the same time that states have underfunded public education and as college leads to a greater debt burden on those who seek higher education. In addition, workers are often confronted with hidden costs (e.g., the cost of purchasing car insurance, which all Uber drivers must have) that often result in net wages below the minimum wage. The results become mutually reinforcing. As secure jobs are harder to come by and fewer jobs provide full and secure benefits or promotion opportunities, workers in most parts of the economy switch jobs more often, further exacerbating the lack of investment from employers. Gig work, in filling in the gaps, then undercuts the price of labor, just as Uber undercut the wages of traditional taxi drivers. Indeed, Uber paid $20 million in 2017 to settle charges that it had exaggerated pay, and it agreed to cease making misleading or inflated claims about what drivers would earn.

Today, gig work is the new model of work, whether for cleaners, web designers, dog walkers, or cabbies. Even in more traditional companies, the use of temps, independent contractors, and other workers without security or benefits has increased. In these fissured workplaces, the ones who thrive are those with either "sharp elbows" who game the system or with the ability to work long and varying hours. The WTA economy has created insecurity, and the gig economy is symptomatic of that, but this insecurity also makes it easy to find workers who will take these jobs at low wages. Men and women who find themselves out at the end of the company's musical-chairs game are funneled to gigs. Many workers believe it's just temporary, and that it can tide them over until they find something more permanent. While all gig workers experience precarity, the uncertainty of episodic income, and overall job insecurity, female gig workers may be disadvantaged in ways that male gig workers are not.

Gig workers typically do their jobs away from any routine physical premises, which means they can be exposed to numerous hazards—physical, biological, and psycho-social—with women being particularly vulnerable. Workers like Cris have gig roles that require them to be alone with clients. Between 20 and 30 percent of gig workers say they have experienced harassment or unwanted sexual advances at work, but this number may be much higher, as gig workers don't always have conventional channels for reporting. Moreover, although platform workers are screened, gig customers typically are not. As was true with Patti Cris and Handy, when things go wrong for these workers, there is often little or no reporting structure. And an HR department, if one exists, may be online, remote, and inaccessible. These women experience greater physical and sexual vulnerability than men, and greater difficulty securing protection in less conventional work environments.

What's more, studies indicate that women gig workers do not charge as much for their services as do men. Gig jobs vary, but on most platforms, women make less money than men. The largest differences tend to come in the job categories that pay more. A 2022 study looking at freelance jobs on Upwork, a platform focusing on cognitive skills such as tech work, management advising, and graphic design, found that, overall, men charged 48 percent more than women in the same job categories. The largest disparities were for software engineers, with men charging $100.90 per hour on average, in comparison with $30 per hour for women. The smallest disparities were in writing. Women copywriters, for example, charged $6 per hour more than the men, but male business writers, the highest paid of the writing categories, charged $20 per hour more than the women in the same field. This study is not alone in finding that women are not paid as much for their gig work, although the studies vary in the extent of the disparities they find and whether the disparities are larger or smaller than exist in brick-and-mortar workplaces.

A major reason for the discrepancy is that women are more likely than men to take jobs that pay less. And they are less likely than men to do things like drive faster, as many Uber drivers do, to make more money. Customer preferences sometimes come into play, too; controlled studies in the lab show that men's work is valued more highly than women's work. But the single biggest reason for the differences may simply be that men have more alternatives than women. Men are more likely to be full-time workers who earn money on gig platforms on the side. These men won't take gig jobs that pay less than they can earn elsewhere. Women, on the other hand, may be more likely to take gig jobs because they have care responsibilities, or lost their job and don't have other options. These differences in motivation affect the prices women will accept on platforms; that is, women as a whole have different "reservation prices" than men.

Perhaps most insidiously, apps like Handy serve to atomize workers, pitting them against each other in competition for jobs. The COVID pandemic, which introduced whipsaw changes in the demand for online work, illustrates the challenges. The pandemic, because of the combination of layoffs and greater childcare demands, magnified worker demand for online work. The increased competition for the available jobs further pitted workers against each other, lowering wages, creating greater income insecurity as jobs became harder to get, and making the ability to cater the work to meet employer needs more important in securing job opportunities. The mothers of young children were disproportionately affected, and they reported less ability to find the jobs that best suited their family needs. Increased competition made the much-vaunted flexibility of gig work harder to realize during the COVID recession—it transferred the risks from a pandemic and the related economic downturn from employers to workers.

The key to worker strength comes from the ability to organize, and gig work makes that much harder. When you're working alone, without a place to meet other workers who share your experiences, it can be harder to learn that you're not the only one, and that problems you face are systemic rather than individualized. Moreover, when workers like those at Uber try to organize, their status as independent contractors has been held against them. Federal law allows employees to organize, to push for higher pay and better working conditions from their employers. When independent contractors do the same thing, it can be viewed as an illegal attempt to fix prices. Indeed, when the city of Seattle enacted legislation specifically allowing Uber drivers to bargain for higher wages, the U.S. Chamber of Commerce sued Seattle, alleging the local measure violated federal antitrust law. Uber workers fired back and insisted that, if they are independent contractors, then Uber's practice of setting platform prices violates antitrust law. The case against Seattle was settled in 2020, but the legal issues underlying the characterization of gig employees remain unresolved. Workers argue that they are in a no-win position—denied the protections of employees while also without the ability of true independent contractors to bargain for contract terms. Their claims show how the touted benefits of gig work—the flexibility, the ability to work on your own terms—can soon pale in comparison to the disadvantages of an unprotected workplace without benefits, stability, or the support of co-workers. In one sense, the gig economy is WTA at its finest—it truly is every man for himself.

But against all odds, gig workers are beginning to fight back. In 2019, Patti Cris gave evidence to lawyers working with a group called the Public Rights Project about her experiences working for Handy. The Public Rights Project works to ensure enforcement of civil rights, and it sought to hold Handy accountable for ignoring sexual harassment claims, filing a suit against them that accused the company of misclassifying their workers as gig workers rather than as employees. Although Handy did not technically employ its contractors, it certainly behaved like an employer in many respects. Every Handy worker is required to meet certain eligibility requirements before obtaining work through the app. For instance, they have to show they have prior cleaning experience, and they must pass a credential verification and a background check. They also have to complete a Handy orientation. Once the orientation is completed, they sign a standard contract, containing terms and conditions that designate them as an independent contractor. Handy workers must follow a long list of Handy rules, dictating what they wear, what cleaning supplies to bring to jobs, and how to interact with clients. The complaint argues that by forcing cleaners to perform their jobs to a certain standard, by making them attend training sessions, giving them checklists to follow, telling them which supplies to use and what to wear, what to say to customers and constantly micromanaging their work, Handy is treating them as employees while exploiting their labor as independent contractors.

The distinction between Handy's Pros being classified as employees and that of independent contractors is critical. California law (and indeed all states) affords employees a multitude of rights that independent contractors do not have. When employees are misclassified, they are unlawfully denied their guaranteed rights to minimum labor standards, including minimum wage and overtime pay, meal and rest breaks, workers' compensation coverage, paid sick leave, family leave, reimbursement for business expenses, and access to wage-replacement programs like disability insurance and unemployment insurance. Additionally, misclassified workers are not protected by most anti-discrimination laws, do not have as much protection from sexual harassment/assault, and do not have nearly as robust legal rights to unionize and to bargain collectively.

In addition to Cris's claim, other lawsuits have challenged Handy's practices. In October 2014, two former Handy cleaners filed a class action lawsuit in California, accusing the company of labor violations. Sisters Vilma and Greta Zenelaj, who brought the suit, claimed that Handy failed to pay minimum wage, plus overtime, and even failed to pay them their tips; above all, the suit stated that Handy was in violation of California law by misclassifying cleaners as independent contractors while treating them as employees. In 2015, another class action lawsuit was filed against Handy in U.S. District Court in Massachusetts, making similar claims. And then, in 2021, the district attorneys in both San Francisco and Los Angeles sued Handy, reiterating the Zenelaj sisters' claims that Handy should treat its workers as employees, with all of the protections that workers enjoy, rather than as independent contractors. Those protections include not just the right to a minimum wage but also, the lawsuit claimed, access to paid sick leave and unemployment insurance. In a wide-ranging 2023 settlement, Handy agreed to pay $4.8 million to workers who were part of the lawsuit and to allow Pros to negotiate directly with customers and not to face a penalty for rejecting a gig.

Handy is not alone in facing suits like these; a 2019 review of suits filed against Uber, Lyft, Handy, Doordash, Instacart, Postmates, Grubhub, and Amazon found "these companies have been sued at least 70 times by workers" who wanted protection under both federal and state labor laws.

What these lawsuits seek to do is give workers access to secure working conditions, with health benefits and safe workplaces. They are part of a larger movement of workers confronting companies that exploit their workers, from the Shirtwaist factory workers protesting unsafe sweatshop conditions at the turn of the twentieth century to Amazon warehouse workers uniting to strike during the pandemic. These efforts have not always been successful. Not only did the Amazon strikes fail to win workers the right to unionize as they had hoped, but in the year before, Californians voted in favor of Proposition 22, a ballot initiative that ensured gig drivers would not be classified as employees. Nonetheless, efforts like these are drawing attention to the needs of gig workers.

And there's a broader shift taking place. Instead of organizing labor within companies, the way traditional unions do, some labor advocacy groups are creating independent organizations that support workers with many different employers. For example, the NewsGuild of New York supports journalists across many different outlets, and the National Domestic Workers Alliance started its own platform so that payers could add $5 to normal fees to allow workers to buy benefits. Additionally, Bluecrew, a revolutionary temp agency, hires gig workers as employees, bridging the gap between the stability that employees need and the flexibility that employers want. The single development, however, that may change the gig economy is the tight labor market that began in 2021 and persisted into 2023. Workers saw better options, and accepted them. Gig employers are facing more competition and still need to attract workers, so now they have no choice but to create better working conditions.

In addition, public benefits can be designed to depend less on employee status. Indeed, the rise of the gig economy was a major impetus for the Affordable Care Act. As the number of workers with permanent jobs declined, employer-provided healthcare covered fewer and fewer workers, making it more expensive (and competitively disadvantageous) for low-wage employers to provide health insurance at all. As even traditional employers drop health insurance and other benefits, therefore, the need for comprehensive federal provisions addressing these needs has only grown. Yet, the very idea of expanding government benefits triggers an intense partisan divide. President Donald

Trump, for example, sought to undercut the Affordable Care Act, while the Biden administration tried to strengthen it.

In many ways, the fight over the gig economy symbolizes the larger—and longer—fight over the WTA economy. Since the 1970s, employers across sectors have systematically contrived to isolate workers in the marketplace. They've done this by decimating long-term employment, eroding union protections, embracing automation, and making employees expendable. As workers have more tenuous ties to their employers—and to each other—it has become more challenging, and often impossible, for workers to organize. If you have no contact with other people doing the same job as you, it is difficult to trust one another and then come together to demand better conditions. This precarity, which makes most workers feel more insecure, is not a side effect of the WTA economy; it is a key design feature that prevents collective action. And so the fight against the WTA economy *has* to be a fight against worker marginalization and for more robust federal guarantees of access to healthcare, adequate income, and decent working conditions. Otherwise, the winners in this new economy will continue to be large companies like Handy—ones that can shift the risks of the enterprise onto their employees while insulating themselves from responsibility for the consequences. Without changes to the current structure, the gig and platform economies will continue to amplify the already-growing financial insecurities of contemporary Americans. And women like Patti Cris will continue to be vulnerable.

PART 4

Taming the WTA Economy

In the first three parts of this book, we focused on the legal actions of women who have challenged the WTA workplace. We have analyzed their complaints for insight into what has happened to women in the twenty-first century, why progress has stalled after the striking gains in income and employment parity that followed the late twentieth-century women's movement. Through the stories of these women—and the studies that show their claims are not unique—we have seen the new barriers women face at every level of the WTA economy.

We have realized that these barriers exist because the WTA economy has fundamentally changed corporate America. It's not just that the upper reaches of the economy have become more competitive; it's also that the nature of the competition has changed. Women seeking to climb the corporate ladder are perceived to be poor candidates for the managerial positions that handsomely reward those who are willing to bend, or break, the rules and are then able get away with it. The women who try to compete on the new terms may find themselves convenient scapegoats for executives who need someone to blame, in environments in which misconduct is rife and regulators want to see signs of "progress" in cleaning up the fraud. Women who come to understand the rules of the game often decide they want nothing to do with toxic workplace environments. Even in less toxic environments, mothers faced with a choice between meeting their children's needs and inflexible workplaces are more likely than fathers to quit—or be forced out. Women in low-wage or gig jobs may have little choice but to cycle in and out of marginalized positions, with few benefits or prospects for advancement. All these factors add up to an unequal economy that bars women's access to the most lucrative new positions.

In this final part of the book, we look more closely at remedies for the WTA economy and mindset. In this section, we highlight women who are fighting back—by mobilizing a larger movement that puts women and women's values at the forefront of social change. These women have attempted to show the dark side of the WTA ethos, and their fight involves not just the litigation of individual wrongs but also the orchestration of media, community organizing, and voter mobilization to push back against those in power. Through their stories and actions, we show these powerful women-led countermovements that are rising up across the country and that provide hope for fighting the dominant WTA ethos.

When we started this book, we focused on the marketplace, on what was happening to businesses. Early in the process of writing the book, we realized that we are telling not just an economic story but also a political story: the WTA economy could only have thrived through the corruption and complicity of the political sphere. As we finish the book, however, we are also seeing the political sphere adopt the same winner-take-all tactics as the economic sphere, with even more pernicious results. Winner-take-all in the corporate sphere involves the ability of corporate leaders to appropriate a disproportionate share of institutional resources for themselves. In the political sphere, it refers to the ability of political winners to entrench their own power and that of their allies at the expense of everyone else. The tactics are remarkably similar. Personalized power replaces institutional authority, and systems that enshrine personalized power, in turn, select for dominance. In these systems, breaking the rules and getting away with it becomes a marker of status, while outright lies, whether about climate change or vaccine efficacy, replace "plausible deniability" as the rule-breaking becomes more brazen. Finally, winner-take-all regimes, in politics just as much as in business, enshrine traditional notions of masculinity—and encourage the hubris that equates success and wealth with a right of sexual access.

This toxic brand of politics threatens many of the arenas most important to women. While private business competition, after all, is often zero sum, the public sphere is supposed to be about the greater societal good. Women have historically been more attracted to public-sector than private-sector employment, in part because of their identification with professional cultures, like those of public school teachers and social workers, that prize dedication to community ahead of personal advancement and modest salaries in exchange for job security, respected status, and reliable benefits. WTA politics has launched a wholesale assault on these values. It has brought the same zero-sum mindset from the private sphere to the public sphere, treating benefits for some as an infringement on the rights of others. It treats those willing to accept less pay for job satisfaction and security as chumps, the modern equivalent of the fifties-era men William Whyte lambasted for their lack of competitive zeal. And rather than respect the professionalism of those who seek to advance the needs of others, it chastises them for their "greed" when they claim the taxpayer-funded employment benefits they have been promised. This clash of worldviews, which has been associated with stereotypically feminine versus masculine values, better predicts political loyalties today than simply being male or female. Those who identify with feminine values—with concern for the community over the individual, with care for the least fortunate, with equality over hierarchy, and with positive-sum (we are collectively better off) rather than negative-sum (when one person wins another loses) mindsets—are fifty points more likely to identify as Democrats than those with stereotypically masculine values.

In the face of these assaults on collective values, women have been fighting back, and what encourages us most about their fight is the anger. It's that same anger that we saw in the women's movement of our youth. Central to those efforts was consciousness raising. Women who joined together and talked to other women discovered—to their surprise—that their stories were remarkably parallel. The women in these consciousness-raising sessions learned that many in the group had been sexually abused, or experienced discrimination, or suffered a host of other indignities. Sharing their stories with each other led to the recognition that they were confronting a system of male dominance, and it focused and steeled their efforts to fight back.

Similarly, the stories of the women in this book are surprisingly alike. They are stories of much more than individual acts of discrimination; rather, they show systemic patterns of behavior associated with a winner-take-all ethos (that often embodies corruption) across different sectors of the economy, such as tech, finance, and education. Their fights are about more than individual grievances. They are about a system that has remade their lives—and the lives of those around them—for the worse.

In this section, we profile women fighting back against this system.

When we first interviewed Melissa Tomlinson, the teacher we profile in Chapter 9, we thought her description of the forces arrayed against her, the "corporate education agenda," was a bit over the top. By the time we finished the book, we realized that she was right—that understanding what was happening to public schools in New Jersey could be appreciated only in the context of the national drive to ensure tax cuts for the wealthy through the villainization of "government schools" and what is taught in them. Tomlinson found strength through working with a union, the New Jersey Education Association, and the more militant "Badass Teachers Association."

One of the most powerful forces in the fight for fair wages and representation on matters of policy has been unions—unions like the ones who stick up for teachers. When we came of age, unions were in retreat, charged by the left with maintaining racial privilege and by the right with protecting lazy and incompetent employees. Yet, unions are a necessary antidote to the unrestrained individualism and corruption of the WTA economy. They give workers a collective voice capable of confronting the powerful and buffering the excesses of the WTA economy. Unions, however, have been under continued assault, from Sam Walton, to the U.S. Supreme Court, to Silicon Valley, precisely because they are effective not just in advancing workers' rights but also in organizing coalitions that raise funds and mobilize the opposition to the WTA more generally. Chapter 9 describes why ambitious politicians like Chris Christie (and Glenn Youngkin in Virginia and Ron DeSantis in Florida) villainize public school teachers and seek to delegitimize the role of public schools in promoting racial equality. We also show how success in fighting back not only elects teacher-union-friendly politicians like Governor Phil Murphy of New Jersey but also strengthens support for increases in the minimum wage, paid family leave, affordable childcare, maternal health, and other issues that increase economic equality and women's full participation in society.

Chapter 10 examines a different kind of concerted action, symbolized by the #MeToo movement. We were inspired as we saw a grassroots movement that turned individual accounts of sexual assault into an avalanche capable of toppling the powerful and the entrenched. We nonetheless watched with concern as Brett Kavanaugh was confirmed as a Supreme Court Justice, without an investigation of Christine Blasey Ford's accusations of Kavanaugh's sexual misconduct, a raw assertion of political power on behalf of a coalition that has remade the Court in ways that undermine women's position in society. Even as the power of #MeToo as a mass movement seems to have waned, a further-reaching change is emerging: the role of sexual-harassment investigations in stemming abuses of power. Today, victims are fighting back by linking the abuse of power with sexual predation: the most effective lawsuits no longer rely on the compelling statistics of Walmart-style class actions. Instead, they reveal the ugliness that underlies abuses of power. Allegations of sexual harassment capture more headlines than statistics showing gender disparities. And as investors and stock exchanges like Nasdaq promote gender diversity, companies find it harder to cloak pervasive harassment. Women, fighting back against sexual exploitation, are leading a movement to bring back the rule of law to the C-suites that govern corporate America.

The #MeToo movement rests on power coming from the bottom up, and it can make change happen—changes that resonate across society. As these two chapters show, challenging the WTA economy will require a broader coalition of those who value equality, collaboration, and concern for everyone to fight back against the tiny percentage at the top. That coalition combines the fight to better the lot of teachers and to demand accountability for sexual predators with the need for economic and racial justice. While women and the issues important to women are at the forefront of the movements we describe in this section, success will require a broader coalition that unites the majority of the country behind the efforts to limit the abuses of power that come from the top.

CHAPTER 9

Fighting Back

Melissa Tomlinson, a teacher at Buena Regional Middle School in New Jersey, felt she had to fight back. In November 2013, Chris Christie was running for reelection as governor of New Jersey. He had made criticizing teachers a cornerstone of his campaign. Christie labeled the state's public schools "failure factories." While Christie knew that New Jersey public schools were some of the best in the nation, his real target was the heavily minority schools in Trenton and Newark that received a disproportionate share of state funding—funding Christie wished to cut. Tomlinson went to a campaign rally for the governor with her colleagues from a group called the Badass Teachers Association to defend themselves and make their voices heard. After Christie made his stump speech, Tomlinson managed to intercept the governor as he was walking toward his campaign bus, asking, "Why do you portray our schools as 'failure factories'?" Christie poked a finger in her face, raised his voice, and said he was "sick of you people." For the next ten minutes, the two argued about funding for public schools, with the crowd shouting at Tomlinson and cheering for Christie. Eventually Christie shut down the discussion, telling Tomlinson, "Do your job," before walking away. Throughout the altercation, Tomlinson found herself shaking, but she had stood her ground. She saw confronting Christie as part of a larger fight, not just for teachers but also for their values. It is also a battle for children, who have become pawns in a conflict that seeks to undermine public education. And it is also a fight for women—the women whose dedication and commitment have long defined public education at its best.

Tomlinson got to this point—to teaching, activism, and a confrontation with Chris Christie—because she had children. Before she became a mother, she had run bars and worked in restaurants. The hours didn't fit with family responsibilities, though, and once she gave birth, she quit. When her boys started preschool, she volunteered to work at their school and the preschool owner told her that she was a "natural," and that she should go back to school and get a teaching certificate. She did, working part time with children with special needs while she took classes. That led to an interest in special education, and eventually to a master's degree in that field. She discovered that she loved teaching, devoting herself to finding a way to reach every child in her class, to engage them, and to provide the support that would let them succeed.

She found, though, that it took a lot of hard work and sacrifice to get into the classroom—and to stay there. While she was earning her degrees, she worked three jobs, including teaching and waiting tables. By the time she finished, she had racked up student loans. There were times when she wondered if it was worth it. Tomlinson started teaching in the early years of No Child Left Behind, the effort pioneered by President George W. Bush to hold schools accountable for children's success. The result introduced a nationwide emphasis on high-stakes testing, using children's performance in those tests as the measure of a school's success. School funding and leadership, and often teachers' evaluations, came to depend on the test scores. Tomlinson soon realized that "the classroom was nothing like I thought education should be. It set off alarm bells." She started questioning the efficacy of such high-stakes testing, and began to feel that she was "spending all [her] time collecting data." Her ability to attend to her students' needs suffered.

When Christie became governor in 2010, things worsened. The state budget was in freefall because of the financial crisis. New Jersey lost out on the first two rounds of Obama administration educational funding, called Race to the Top, which encouraged states to adopt merit pay schemes tying teacher pay to test scores, and the state lost the potential for hundreds of millions in federal funding as a result. That loss was, according to the president of the New Jersey Education Association, because of Christie's failure to cooperate with school districts. Christie also cut school funding almost immediately upon becoming governor. "Class sizes went up," Tomlinson told us, "Extra programs—anything not tested—[were] cut. Anything creative or fun was cut. Art, music, building repair, assistance to schools with lead in the water." These budget cuts also meant teachers were losing money. If they got raises at all, they were a few hundred dollars per year. At the same time, New Jersey was making teachers pay more for healthcare and pensions. Tomlinson struggled to pay her student loans, maintain her mortgage, and provide for her kids on her salary. She saw teachers around her leaving the profession, replaced by newcomers who could be paid less and who would cycle out sooner rather than later. What particularly stung for Tomlinson, though, was Christie's attacks on teachers. She explained that he set a tone: "[H]is lack of respect for teachers, that's starting to transfer to the parents in society, which in turn is starting to transfer to the students." The crowd at Christie's rally had echoed that disrespect.

She decided she had to fight back to protect her students—and fellow teachers. She found that she was not alone in wanting change. She learned about the Badass Teachers Association, which seeks to promote professional practices within teaching and "reject racially and socially oppressive profit-driven education reform." Here was a group of people who had the same concerns she did. Tomlinson knew that New Jersey is a wealthy state, with some of the best public schools—and yes, highest test scores—in the country. She also knew that it had areas of entrenched poverty, and that Christie had undercut the schools' efforts to reach students in cities like Newark, Trenton, and Camden. For his part, Christie insisted he was not attacking teachers, but their unions. He said that teachers' unions deserved a "punch in the face." He explained that they are "not for education for our children. They're for greater membership, greater benefits, greater pay for their members. And they are the single most destructive force in public education in America."

When Tomlinson attended the Christie rally, she carried a cardboard sign that read, "I am a public school teacher! We are not failing our students! NJ is ranked 3rd in the US. Christie's refusal to finance public education is failing our students." She felt strongly about the need to counter Christie's negative portrayal of public school teachers. During her time working at bars and restaurants, she had learned how to stand up to bullies. "The advocacy part of this is my heart," she told us when we interviewed her for this book, "whether advocating for my students in the classroom or the profession." And her presence made a difference. The image of Chris Christie wagging his finger in her face went viral. Although he won reelection, when he left office in 2018 it was as the most unpopular governor in New Jersey history, with his image as a bully enshrined in the public imagination. Tomlinson's bravery in standing up for her profession and the quality of care she knows her students deserve had an effect.

———

Tomlinson's fight raises the questions "How did teachers become a punching bag?" and "What can we learn from their fights?" The answers involve understanding three factors: the clash of values that define the WTA economy, a fight over the status of women within the economy as a whole, and a toxic political mix produced by the intersection of race, taxes, and public school funding. At the core of the conflict between Christie and Tomlinson is a lie—the claim that public schools can be improved without raising taxes—and a political tactic that substitutes the villainization of an opponent for a discussion of the underlying issues. Tomlinson's awakening as an activist—and why her fight so inspires us—rests on her realization that key to fighting back requires confronting the lies and the clash of values that underlies them. More effectively than any union representative, Tomlinson, as an ordinary public school teacher, represented the teachers' values that Christie refused to address. The clash between Tomlinson and Christie also illustrates why a women-identified profession has become a political flashpoint in the WTA era.

First, the fight over teacher pay represents, in a microcosm, the battle between organizational values and the ethos of the winner-take-all economy. Public school teachers like Tomlinson symbolize communal values; Tomlinson saw her conflict with Christie as an effort to stand up for her students—the ones shortchanged by educational budget cuts and a mindless emphasis on testing. Chris Christie's brawling tactics in opposing teachers, in contrast, played to his white suburban base and the tax-opposing wealthy backers he needed to fund his presidential run, rather than the overall needs of the state.

The second factor involves the relationship between public school teachers and the changing status of women, a relationship that means those who choose to stay in teaching—a profession long associated with women and women's values—pay an increasingly high price in terms of pay, benefits, and working conditions for doing so. When we started looking at how this happened, we were surprised to find that in the era of sex-segregated jobs, women got a premium for going into teaching; they were paid 14.7 percent more than women in other jobs that required similar levels of education and experience. Women everywhere were paid badly, but it turned out that teachers were paid less badly than others. Since the 1960s, all kinds of professions have opened to women, and many women who might once have become teachers now go to medical school, or law school, or take tech jobs instead. School administrators no longer have access to a dedicated group of captive women with few other options; they have had to compete for teachers in a far more open market. Over the course of the seventies, twenty-eight state legislatures revised their school finance systems to be able to do so. Instead of depending on local property taxes to fund schools, "the state share of education spending increased from 38% in 1972 to 45% by 1979, and the state aid to elementary and secondary education doubled." State spending, funded by higher taxes, increased another 21 percent in the eighties, with the majority of states tying more funding to greater state oversight and more emphasis on testing. As the WTA economy was getting underway in the early nineties, teachers as a group made only slightly less (1.8 percent in 1994) than comparably qualified workers in other fields, and the percentage of male teachers had increased—to over a third of elementary and secondary teachers. Then, the WTA economy really took hold—and the teaching profession has yet to recover.

From 1996 to 2001, during a period of tighter labor markets and wage growth across many sectors of the economy, college grads who went into any field *other* than teaching enjoyed a remarkable 13.4 percent jump in pay. Instead, during this relatively prosperous period, teacher weekly wages fell by 0.4 percent. Some states cut salaries. Others simply failed to keep up with the private sector. Public school teachers today earn 23.5 percent less than do people with the same level of education in other fields, the highest teaching wage penalty economists have recorded in U.S. history. And as teachers lost ground in the economy, the profession again became more female, reaching 77 percent by 2019—levels comparable to the eras in which teaching was thought of as a woman's occupation. The fact that teachers dramatically lost ground *by standing still*, however, is largely invisible and expensive to address, making it easy for politicians like Christie to dismiss as "greedy" the unions seeking fair pay for teachers.

While women's increased status touched off challenges for state educational budgets, the failure of teacher salaries (and those in healthcare and other women-dominated occupations) to keep pace with male-dominated occupations has a lot to do with women's status in today's economy. Many of the gender pay gaps we have described in this book are differences in pay between men and women within various occupations. However, economists tell us that the greatest source of disparities between men and women does not really come from the differences in pay between male and female workers within a given field, though such differences exist. Instead, economists estimate that "differences in the type of work men and women do account for 51% of the pay gap." In the top ten most segregated jobs for women, for example, including preschool and kindergarten teachers and medical secretaries, compared to the top ten most segregated jobs for men, which include electrical power line installers and roofers, the average annual wage is higher for men than for women in all but one. Skincare specialists, in which 99 percent of the workforce is women, had annual wages of $24,706; for men, brick masons and related positions were the most segregated, also at 99 percent, with an annual wage of $39,391.

These differences have gotten worse since 1980 and now account for a larger portion of the overall gender pay gap than they once did. In other words, although overt discrimination has declined, women continue to work in professions with significantly lower paychecks than the professions their male counterparts choose. When salaries in finance, and tech, and corporate management ranks soar, those without access to such pay increases fall further behind. Gender integration in occupations, which had begun to improve in the 1980s, stalled with the rise of the WTA economy, and the renewed occupational segregation is an important factor in the pay gap between similarly educated men and women.

The third factor setting up the clash between Tomlinson and Christie involves race, taxes, and politics—a toxic brew in any era. As the push toward school integration waned in the seventies, states faced increasing pressure to equalize school spending across districts. The reliance on local property taxes made the inequalities worse. Parents who can afford to do so move to districts with better public schools. As they do, housing prices in the favored districts go up, property taxes increase with the higher valuations, and the school districts have more money to hire better teachers. The differences between wealthy districts and poor ones increase. The solution appeared to be simple: have the states pick up a larger share of the school finance budget so they can distribute it more equally. For the states to do so, they need to raise state taxes, and raise taxes paid by wealthier people to fund poorer—and much more heavily minority—districts.

The U.S. Supreme Court, when it examined the issue in the seventies, found that the most affluent school district in San Antonio, Texas, spent $594 per pupil compared to $356 per student in the least affluent. Still, the Court concluded, "no problem here"—that is, no constitutional violation that compelled action. Starting with the California decision in *Serrano v. Priest* in 1971, however, a number of state supreme courts compelled reforms on the basis of their state constitutions, and as we have noted, many states increased state educational funding voluntarily. The greater state responsibility, while it created greater equality between school districts, had two major drawbacks. State budgets, which rely on income taxes and sales taxes, are much more cyclical than property taxes; in a recession, state revenue plummets while property tax revenue tends to be more stable. In addition, voters are most likely to support the taxes that fund public schools when they see their tax dollars going to their own children and grandchildren. The more they see school expenditures going to other districts or groups different from their own, the less likely they are to support the taxes necessary to fund schools. In many states, increasing taxes to pay for education, particularly in response to courts' ordering school district equalization, became "political suicide."

The WTA economy made all this much worse. As private-sector salaries soared in the nineties, a rigidly uncompromising anti-tax movement took hold nationally that made it much harder to address the disparities in teacher salaries. In earlier decades, even conservative states like Texas had managed compromise efforts that increased the state role (and the necessary tax increases) promoting public education. Tax-reduction advocate Grover Norquist helped to change all that in the late eighties, with a "no new taxes" pledge that became de rigueur for Republican candidates. In the following years, billionaire-funded

PACs have used political contributions to enforce the new orthodoxy, threatening to mount primary challenges against Republican candidates who support tax increases.

These factors can produce education disasters during economic downturns. Public education remains primarily a state responsibility; the average state provides 47 percent of U.S. public school funding, with local governments providing most of the rest. State and local governments, however, must balance their budgets; unlike the federal government, they can't just print money. That means in good times when wages go up, they must come up with ways to raise teacher salaries if teaching positions are to be competitive with private-sector jobs. In bad times, the states must raise taxes to replace declining revenue and keep public schools afloat.

Ideally, during national downturns, the federal government, which does not have to balance its budget, offsets the state revenue losses. With the rise of the WTA economy, however, the same wealthy conservatives who oppose state tax increases have also opposed any federal fiscal stimulus designed to cushion state budgets during hard times. The recent Great Recession provides a dramatic illustration. The 2009 federal stimulus package that followed the financial crisis had included money that cushioned the impact of the recession on the states, and economists agree that the policy worked. The spending bolstered state budgets, helping to prevent massive layoffs, and prompted the start of a recovery. But with the Republican congressional sweep in 2010, Congress put an abrupt end to stimulus measures, producing a "fiscal cliff" that upended state education budgets.

Collectively, the states spent billions less for K-12 education in 2012 than they had in 2011. The budget cuts eliminated nearly 351,000 teaching jobs across the country and almost certainly contributed to prolonging the recession. Public school teachers paid a disproportionate price, contributing to the record teaching penalty we described earlier. By 2015, more than half the states were "still providing less total school funding per student than they were in 2008," and that included

New Jersey. As of the 2017–18 school year, well into the economic recovery, twelve states had cut state support for elementary and secondary schools by dramatic amounts over the preceding decade, with seven
of the twelve—Arizona, Idaho, Kansas, Michigan, Mississippi, North
Carolina, and Oklahoma—doing so because of income-tax rate slashes.
Other states, like New Jersey, cut funding indirectly by requiring teachers to pay more for health insurance or to contribute a higher percentage of their salaries to pension funds. These actions meant reducing
the number of teachers, scrimping on school maintenance and supplies,
and leaving many public school teachers scraping to get by. In 2018,
Arne Duncan, the U.S. Secretary for Education during the Obama administration, recalled meeting a teacher from North Carolina. From a
state that was once a leader in education, this teacher was now "selling plasma to make ends meet." Duncan commented, "Unfortunately,
many teachers have to work second jobs. Many teachers work over the
summer. But when you're selling blood to stay in the classroom? That's
unconscionable."

These factors frame the clash between Christie and Tomlinson and explain why collective organizations are essential to any effort to improve
the status of teachers—and women's lot in the center of the economy.
Christie took office in 2010, at the height of the Great Recession. As
a Republican governor eyeing higher office, he could not raise taxes.
Attacking teachers' unions proved a way out of a box that was decades
in the making.

At the time Christie took office, New Jersey was hampered because
of how it funded its public schools. New Jersey still relied on local
property taxes to a greater degree than most other states to fund public
education. Property taxes, however, as we explained in greater detail
earlier, vary with the wealth of the locality: richer districts have more
expensive property, by definition, and that means that property taxes in

such districts generate more revenue than poorer districts, even if the assessments on individual properties are calculated in accordance with the same formula.

In the early 1990s, New Jersey became one of a number of states to rule that such disparities between wealthy suburban school districts and other areas of the state violated the state constitution. Jim Florio, the governor at the time, tried to address the issue the way other states had—by raising state income taxes and sales taxes to increase the state's share of educational funding. He was roundly defeated for reelection in 1993, and no subsequent New Jersey governor has been willing to raise taxes to increase education funding. As a result, the state has left the local property-tax system in place as the principal source of educational funding, while using remedial state funds to bolster resources in the neediest districts. At the time Christie took office, New Jersey had the highest *local property taxes* in the country, with the bulk of *state funding* going to equalize disparities in the local tax base.

An important result of the inability to raise taxes has been the impact on the state's pension fund, which has been underfunded ever since. Fiscally prudent states, like Tennessee and South Dakota, put aside funds to pay for teacher pensions at the time they enter into their employment contracts. New Jersey, in contrast, promised teachers future pension benefits without putting the money into the teachers' pension fund—in spite of state law requiring that the state do so, and during a prosperous period in the late nineties when the state could have afforded to earmark the funds. By shortchanging the pension fund, New Jersey governors engaged in a form of winner-take-all behavior: they broke the rules that pensions be funded and found that they could get away with it. Voters rewarded politicians like Christie, who promised—in defiance of state law—to cheat teachers of the benefits they had been promised. In the meantime, teachers, with underfunded pension benefits, received an effective pay cut whether they realized it or not.

When Chris Christie became governor in the beginning of 2010, he therefore inherited a genuine budget crisis. New Jersey faced a deficit equal to a fourth of its entire budget, with education spending making up a substantial part of state expenditures. Local governments had already raised property taxes to make up some of the shortfall, and Christie had been elected at least in part because he had run against raising taxes in the state. His goal, like that of governors throughout the country, was to figure out how to cut spending.

By 2013, at the time of his confrontation with Tomlinson, Christie viewed the state budget crisis as an opportunity to implement a privatization agenda that might make him a hero among those opposed to government spending and provide him with a platform to run for president. To implement that agenda he needed a foil, and he found one in the state's public school teachers and their unions. Upon taking office, Christie declared, "I love the public schools, but the fact of the matter is there is excess and greed there." In an era before Donald Trump became a political figure, he created a Trumpian image: that of a fighter sticking up for the oppressed (and relatively well-off) taxpayers who saw their hard-earned tax dollars going to the undeserving. When people like Tomlinson stood up to him, he cultivated his image as the straight-talking, *Fox News* pundit, ex-prosecutor, by shouting them down. Wagging a finger in Tomlinson's face, as though he were administering a scolding, was pure political theater. Christie even had an aide follow him around with a camcorder, ready to record moments when the governor let loose on unsuspecting citizens like Tomlinson who dared to question him. He would then post the videos on YouTube, to be circulated among conservatives across the country, "the way tween girls circulate Justin Bieber videos," as the journalist Ezra Klein noted in the *Washington Post*. One of his drubbings of another aggrieved public school teacher at a town hall racked up over 750,000 views.

For her part, Melissa Tomlinson saw Christie's attacks on teachers as attacks on women, fueling her determination to fight back. In a blogpost in 2015, she wrote that "the rhetoric we hear [is] being driven by the corporate education agenda (which is the house of mostly white wealthy males) [and] is a direct attack on a profession that is over 75% women." When we interviewed her, she explained to us that although many teachers leave because of low pay, the teachers who remain are stuck in the middle, and are forced to absorb the pressures of schools being squeezed out of funding and support. "When a mandate comes down from the top, that puts stress on the district," she explained. "The district administrators put stress on the principals, who then put stress on the teachers. The teachers try not to put stress on the students, the students whom they are forced to put through repeated rounds of high stakes testing." Most teachers, Tomlinson said, internalize the stress, and some "suffer from something like PTSD. If they push back against the administrators, they will be let go or moved into a teaching position they won't like."

In many ways, her decision to question Christie was as calculated as his decision to have an aide follow him and video his interactions. The teachers' association to which Tomlinson belonged had encouraged its members to confront Christie. It provided fliers to hand out and gave advice about what to say. Their goal was to educate the public about what was really happening—and to show Christie's bully image in its most unflattering light.

The teachers' campaign ultimately had an effect: the more Christie attacked teachers, the more his poll numbers fell. New Jersey voters initially saw Christie as a truth teller standing up on behalf of New Jersey's beleaguered taxpayers. He succeeded in using his barrage of insults to push through cuts. Teachers' unions and other associations tried to counter Christie's claims that unions are greedy and that teachers were overcompensated. Nonetheless, the result of Christie's "reforms," as Tomlinson has emphasized, was to further squeeze teachers, many of whom were already driving for Uber or Lyft in their spare time just to stay in the classroom. At the time Christie left office, New Jersey's pension fund remained the most underfunded in the country.

Tomlinson also tried to expose the racist nature of Christie's attacks. His references to "failure factories" set the stage for his "solutions": get rid of the state funding, especially that going to low-income schools, while letting wealthy districts keep their higher property tax revenues; get rid of teachers by abolishing tenure; and ultimately, get rid of the low-income schools, replacing them with vouchers or charter schools. This last "solution" disproportionately affected Black women teachers, who have long been the mainstay of schools in their communities. After her confrontation with Christie, Tomlinson sent him a follow-up letter in which she squarely asked him: "Why do you portray schools as failure factories? What benefit do you reap from this? Have you acquired financial promises for your future campaigns as you eye the presidential nomination?" She suggested that in order to score political points, "you are setting up the teachers to take the blame."

Tomlinson links Christie's assault on public schools to attacks on public-sector unions generally. With a profession made up overwhelmingly of women, she comments, "we don't think it's a coincidence that misogynistic politicians like Scott Walker and Chris Christie target our public-sector unions first. Why go after the police or firemen, when teachers are perceived to be such an easy target?" Teachers account for a large percentage of state budgets, about 30 percent calculated nationally, with 21 percent going to primary and secondary schools. Police departments, in contrast, account for less than 4 percent of state expenditures. Governors who are serious about cutting taxes find the most expedient way to reduce state budgets is by slashing education funding. Teachers' unions thus become a convenient target.

Today, Tomlinson is the Executive Director of the Badass Teachers Association, the organization that had given her hope when Christie first took office. She is also more optimistic than she was a decade ago. She explained that she saw the answer in a long-term campaign to get parents and voters to see what is really going on with public education—and to stand up for the women in the trenches who care deeply about their students and their profession. She feels that effort is succeeding. In 2017, the voters of New Jersey elected a new governor,

Phil Murphy—and he made opposing Christie's attacks on public education, and the unions supporting them, a central issue in his campaign. When Murphy won reelection in 2021, in a hotly contested race, the state's largest teachers' union claimed credit: they believed that their support made the difference. New Jersey's 2022–23 budget has been hailed as a "positive surprise," as it substantially increased state aid for underfunded districts, promoting educational equity in the state.

While the controversies over public education have been the most dramatic, they are part of a wholesale attack on public-sector unions, which disproportionately represent women. At the state and local level, women constitute 60.3 percent of public-sector employees (such as clerks, administrators, and human resource managers), even though they are just under half the overall workforce. The starving of public-sector budgets, therefore, has only served to worsen the gender pay gap—and teachers in particular have lost ground in the states that place restrictions on unions' ability to organize and engage in collective bargaining. Traditionally, unions have been a significant bulwark against the wholesale dismantling of public education and worker protections. They provide solidarity and protection to individuals who would be vulnerable—to pay disparities, to overwork, to unscrupulous employers—on their own. Accordingly, unions have long had a target on their backs, placed there by corporations and the politicians they fund.

Since we started this book, the attacks on public school teachers have intensified. While to some extent, frustration with pandemic school shutdowns served as an initial impetus, the subsequent attacks resulted from an ideologically based assault on public spending, and they channel the politics of grievance. Rather than seriously address state funding crises or the effectiveness of public schools, ambitious governors and legislators look for targets they can hit to stoke voter anger. By reinforcing the message that public spending is wasteful, and that public school teachers push liberal agendas about race or sexuality onto their students, politicians divide the electorate. The result undermines concern for teachers and communities by suggesting that collective approaches coddle the incompetent.

The attack on teachers has also been part of the fight against unionization, as we have seen from the beginning of this book. The Supreme Court, stacked with pro-business appointees, has been complicit in supporting this dismantling of union protections. In Illinois, for example, Bruce Rauner, a hedge-fund multimillionaire, won the governorship in 2014, blaming public-sector unions for the state's fiscal crisis, which was at its height during that time. Illinois, like New Jersey, had underfunded its pension obligations for years. The Great Recession, together with the end of federal stimulus, turned the chronic underfunding into a crisis.

Rauner decided to attack the foundation of union funding—the requirement that all workers in a bargaining unit pay union dues once the union, through an election, acquires the exclusive right to represent the workers. He argued that civil servants—those employed by the state—shouldn't be required to pay dues to a union, as it compels them to subsidize union positions with which they disagree and thereby violates their freedom of speech. His argument completely overlooked the "free rider" problem: that if employees can opt out of union membership, they would reap the benefits from collective bargaining for free. The case Rauner inspired—*Janus v. American Federation of State, County and Municipal Employees*—made it all the way to the Supreme Court.

In 2018, the Court's 5 to 4 conservative majority sided with Rauner and overturned a longstanding precedent validating Illinois's law governing union dues. Justice Elena Kagan's dissent outlined the stakes of this decision, and explained that the precedent had been designed to deal with a "collective action problem of nightmarish proportions." Unions, she explained, once they acquire exclusive bargaining-agent status, become legally compelled to fairly represent all the workers in a bargaining unit, whether they join the union or not. If individuals could gain all the benefits of union representation without paying dues, every worker would have a financial incentive to opt out—even if they supported the union's activities.

Justice Samuel Alito's majority opinion dismissed the "free rider" problem as simply not that important, certainly not important enough to violate workers' First Amendment rights to refuse to contribute dues to a union whose positions they oppose. Precisely because public unions address a broad range of policy issues, such as taxes, "education, child welfare, healthcare, and minority rights," the majority concluded that every employee has a First Amendment right to opt out of paying dues, despite a longstanding line of cases that have maintained that such dues are critical to union vitality. The opinion challenged core principles of workplace governance that had allowed unions, on the basis of worker elections, to act on behalf of employees as a whole, giving the workers an effective collective voice to counter management power.

The Illinois unions lost key protections after the Supreme Court's decision. But in another respect, they carried the day. Bruce Rauner, who sought to eliminate public-sector union collective bargaining altogether, lost his bid for reelection in 2018, in a landslide. And at least to date, the *Janus* ruling has not had as large an effect on union funding as Justice Kagan feared, though state restrictions on unions' collective bargaining rights have been linked to falling teacher income.

Modern unions have built broad coalitions addressing important policy issues—and have shown their influence in modern politics. Workers in the public sector are five times as likely to be union members as those in the private sector. And while the percentage of workers in unions has declined since 1983, it has declined far less precipitously in public-sector unions. Teachers' unions are a case in point. Beginning in 2018, teacher union activism spread across the country, supported by many parents who were tired of policies that focused on high-stakes testing to the detriment of more meaningful educational funding and support. This was the year of many teachers' strikes, with teachers walking out in West Virginia, Kentucky, Oklahoma, and elsewhere, in some cases despite state laws that gave them no protection if the state decided to retaliate.

In Arizona, Rebecca Garelli, a teacher inspired by Melissa Tomlinson's Badass Teachers Facebook page, trained colleagues to organize protests in about 1,200 Arizona schools. The teachers wore red T-shirts to show their solidarity and eventually called a weeklong strike. They won a promise for a 20 percent pay hike over three years. The head of the state teachers' union credited the victory to the activist newcomers like Garelli, inspired by Tomlinson's example.

In recent history, unions have also been influential in promoting gender equity, and have been vital to women's ability to win a seat at the table in matters of public policy. Women constitute 58 percent of state and local public-sector union members, including many nurses, first responders, and healthcare and social workers, as well as teachers. These professions depend on state funding, and in many states, they are underfunded in good times and cut to the bone in hard times. As we've observed, the underfunding of professions dominated by women has contributed to the persistence of the gender wage gap. Yet unions help reduce these gaps. Women represented by public-sector unions are paid 23 percent more than their public-sector counterparts who are not represented by unions. And part of the reason that pensions have been a flashpoint is that public-sector unions and politicians agreed to a trade: below-market salaries today in exchange for more generous pension rights later, with a bill that would come due during someone else's governorship. Pensions have been vital to recruiting and retaining the best public-sector employees. Just as critically, the gender wage gap among union-represented public-sector workers is about half that among their public-sector counterparts who are not represented by unions.

Public-sector unions have thus played an essential role in fighting back, by linking the well-being of the women who staff the nations'

schools and social welfare organizations to essential public needs. They
have argued that emphasis on reductionist metrics such as testing undermine teachers' professional autonomy in addressing students' needs,
and become an excuse for cutting teacher pay in order to reduce taxes.
Bonus pay tied to test scores, which is supposed to reward the most
effective teachers, in fact makes things worse. It reduces teaching from
a calling that values professional judgment, to a video game designed to
garner the highest number of points before the next merit evaluation. It
contributes to teacher turnover, attracting those most willing to game
the system and driving out those driven by more altruistic motives. It
undercuts the role of public school personnel in creating a stable, secure, middle class. And just as rank-and-yank pay systems did in the
corporate ranks, it increases gender disparities. Teachers' unions have
effectively made the point that with the combination of budget cuts
and high-stakes testing, teachers will vote with their feet. According
to the Bureau of Labor Statistics, teacher resignation and retirement
rates reached an all-time high in August 2020, six months after acknowledgment of the pandemic; and while many teachers returned to
the classroom, amid the persistence of the pandemic, school violence,
and stagnated wages, the leaving rates are again at twenty-year highs.
"In Washington state, more teachers left the classroom after last school
year than at any point in the last three decades." And in Florida, a 2023
report indicated that vacant teaching positions rose by 21 percent compared to the previous year "and more than 200 percent since 2018." The
attacks on teachers that followed the pandemic have contributed to a
nationwide teacher shortage—one that disproportionately affects rural,
urban, and high-poverty areas.

Since COVID, the cultural fight over education has shifted into
a higher gear. Politicians celebrating "parental rights" are fighting to
restrict what teachers can present in the classroom, particularly on
controversial issues such as race or gender, and the Christie types who
once tried to replace traditional public schools with charter schools
now want simply to give parents vouchers. Parents can then pick the

schools of their choice, including private schools that do not have to comply with state educational mandates. Many see the new movement as another attack "on the foundational idea of public education itself, in effect transferring a public good to a private benefit," and one that celebrates parental choice without addressing the educational needs of students.

Unions, often led by enterprising women such as Melissa Tomlinson, offer the promise of offsetting the entrenched power of those who would undermine public education. And since education is often the single biggest responsibility of state governments, the strength of unions becomes a tool to counter anti-democratic measures. Governor Ron DeSantis of Florida, for example, borrowed from the Chris Christie playbook in preparing his 2024 run for the presidency. DeSantis has made public schools and their teachers a target of his efforts to remake Florida. In this fight, public-sector unions, which include not only primary and secondary teachers but also university instructors, are "the only organized statewide force that stands between DeSantis and his agenda." Paul Ortiz, a Florida history professor active in a teachers' and faculty union, explained that DeSantis's backers have long made the elimination of public education a prime objective, and he emphasized that "DeSantis is trying to abolish unions, critical race theory and gender studies because these are institutions and theories that help people challenge state power." In Florida and elsewhere, unions have been a powerful force in combating the injustices of the WTA economy. Today, they also play a critical role in preserving our democracy.

CHAPTER 10

#MeToo

Marlyn Perez was an undocumented immigrant from Guatemala who harvested vegetables in Florida. A profile of her in the *Atlantic* reported that her crew chief put together crews that consisted almost entirely of recent, undocumented immigrants. The article explained that the crew chief forced the workers to put in ten- to twelve-hour days picking produce, work nights at a packinghouse, and work overtime compensated at less than minimum wage. He limited their access to water and food, and they were sold drinks and meals at increased prices. He paid them less than they were promised, and less than the law required.

Perez was earning about $35 per day, but as she later recounted, the crew boss took out money for rent, transportation to and from work, food, and water, reducing the pay to about $20 per day. When Perez protested that she had not received full pay, her boss told her that "she had no rights and no papers, so she shouldn't complain." After her additional requests for full pay, the crew boss suggested he might pay her more if she had sex with him. She refused. When he caught her alone in an isolated area, he grabbed her and fondled her. She again refused to have sex with him, so he showed her the pistol he carried. When she said she would quit, the boss threatened to burn her in her trailer. She feared him, and she feared the police. She had nowhere to go.

Actor Salma Hayek, despite working in a different industry thousands of miles away, also felt trapped. She had entered into a deal with studio head Harvey Weinstein to produce the movie *Frida,* about the life of Mexican artist and feminist icon Frida Kahlo. Hayek had developed the project and cared about it passionately. She was excited about working with Weinstein's studio, which had a reputation for producing high-quality artistic films. But once the deal was struck, Weinstein would show up unannounced at her door. He would ask her to take a shower with him. When Hayek refused, he blocked the efforts to produce her movie. He said he would replace her with another actress. He threatened to kill her. She fought Weinstein at every turn to get *Frida* produced. She gave in to his demands for certain movie scenes designed to titillate him, and she experienced a breakdown in producing them. In spite of all the obstacles he put in front of her, she succeeded. The movie was nominated for multiple Academy Awards, including one for Hayek as Best Actress. The American Film Institute included *Frida* in its 2002 list of Movies of the Year. Yet, she remained silent about Weinstein's behavior for years. She reports, "In his eyes, I was not an artist. I wasn't even a person. I was a thing: not a nobody, but a body." She wasn't a marginalized, undocumented farmworker, but she still felt she had nowhere to go.

But then something happened. The *New York Times* published a front-page story highlighting, with sordid detail, the many allegations against Weinstein. More women began to speak out. Many prominent men supported them. Reporters reached out to Hayek. Initially, she refused to talk to them. As she saw the other women come forward, she decided to go public with her own experiences.

Hayek wrote a full account in the *New York Times* two months after the *Times*'s initial story. Her voice joined others. Unlike the untold number of women before them who were harassed without ever telling anyone, or complained and were fired, or pursued a legal course of action only to see their allegations swept under the rug, or were placated or paid to go quietly, these women were heard. The call for consequences grew to a crescendo. In 2017, *Time* magazine named the "Silence Breakers" its "Person of the Year." Included were celebrities Taylor Swift and Ashley Judd, an anonymous young hospital worker, former Uber engineer Susan Fowler, lobbyist Adama Iwu, and a farmworker not so different from Perez, identified with an assumed name to protect her confidentiality. Iwu organized a group of women to expose the culture of sexual harassment in California politics. Latina farmworkers wrote a "letter of solidarity" referencing some of their own experiences of sexual harassment, and how keenly they appreciated the risk of coming forward.

Once they publicized their stories, these women were no longer alone, no longer powerless. Women came together, showing how the power of collective action could shine a spotlight on systemic abuses. Making public these stories resulted in an accounting for the abuses. Perez became connected with the Coalition of Immokalee Workers, a farmworkers' rights organization, that helped her and other workers in her camp find a lawyer. Perez won a liquidated damage award of $959,644.24 from the crew boss; Harvey Weinstein, accused by scores of women in addition to Hayek, received a twenty-three-year prison sentence in New York in 2020. He received another sixteen-year sentence in February 2023 for sexual assault charges against different women in Los Angeles. With the #MeToo movement, accountability became possible.

When faced with harassment claims in the past, Weinstein had settled. To cover his tracks, he had used nondisclosure agreements "with employees, business partners, and women who made allegations—women who were often much younger and far less powerful than Weinstein, and who signed under pressure from attorneys on both sides." Weinstein was so successful in keeping the allegations secret that Hayek said she had heard nothing about them when she entered into a contract with Weinstein's movie studio to produce *Frida*. And, indeed, even after a young model, Ambra Battilana Gutierrez, went to the police in 2015 and with their help produced a recording in which Weinstein admitting that he had groped her, the New York City District Attorney Cyrus Vance declined to prosecute. Vance, who later brought the prosecution that obtained the twenty-three-year prison sentence against Weinstein, explained that #MeToo had made the difference. Not only had numerous women come forward, but their accounts had educated the public to better understand the nature of sexual assault. Individual women with considerably more resources than farmworkers like Perez had found it daunting to pursue their claims for justice—so long as they were isolated and alone. But #MeToo put not only the abusers but also the prosecutors on the defensive.

The #MeToo movement touched off cascading allegations of harassment. Using the hashtag #MeToo, millions of women—and some men—came forward to call out their harassers, famous or not. Many allegations (like Hayek's) reached back decades. They carried weight because they described a common pattern, repeated with each new person who came forward. Once the dam burst, harassers and abusers across industries were finally named: Amazon Studios head Roy Price, actor Kevin Spacey, NPR News head Michael Oreskes, Alabama judge Roy Moore, comedian Louis C.K., financier Jeffrey Epstein, TV hosts Charlie Rose and Matt Lauer, and even the "wholesome" radio personality Garrison Keillor. The allegations included: propositions for sex during discussions about job prospects, lewd phone calls, men exposing themselves and masturbating in front of subordinates, pictures of male genitalia sent to co-workers, groping, blackmail, and rape.

The #MeToo movement seemed spontaneous, gaining traction after actor Alyssa Milano urged victims of sexual assault or harassment to tweet #MeToo to show how widespread the problem is. But it draws on centuries of frustration and anger, and even the term "Me Too" had been around for more than a decade (unbeknownst to Milano). In 2006, social activist Tarana Burke originated the phrase "Me Too." She used it to signify that sexual harassment and assault victims were not alone. She sought to forge connections among women of color, lesbians, and people in economically disadvantaged communities, emphasizing that the indignities they often suffered in silence were commonplace and should be seen not as a source of shame but as a call to action. But it took more than a decade for that movement to result in 2017's public accounting.

The immediate reaction to Milano's tweet drew on women's experiences with "bosses and co-workers who not only cross boundaries but don't even seem to know that boundaries exist." There was a firestorm of collective anger from women who were weary of "going along to get along," tired of living in fear that they would be fired from a job they could not afford to lose, and exhausted from keeping quiet about the sexual violence they suffered. Within one year, 19 million tweets had been posted using the hashtag, some simply saying that they too had experienced sexual assault or harassment, others telling their stories in graphic detail.

Perhaps it was the magnitude of the claims of the #MeToo movement (including allegations of rape and pedophilia), perhaps it was multiple victims coming forward (safety in numbers), perhaps the prominence of some of the abusers and the access to resources on the part of some of the victims, perhaps it was time for a public acknowledgment of the anger, but the year emerged as a pivotal time of reckoning. CBS fired Charlie Rose, Roger Ailes was pressured to resign as CEO of Fox News, media companies cut ties with Louis C.K., Kevin Spacey was suspended from *House of Cards*, Michael Oreskes resigned from NPR, and Republican judge Roy Moore lost his race for a seat representing Alabama in the U.S. Senate to Doug Jones (the first time a Democrat had won a Senate race in the state in twenty years). And in 2021, Andrew Cuomo resigned as governor of New York, following allegations that he sexually harassed eleven women, groping them, subjecting them to unwanted kisses, and making inappropriate remarks about their sex lives.

#MeToo signaled something more than women simply getting fed up with this type of treatment; it involved turning the tables on those who have used the accumulation of power to ensure their own invulnerability. Thus, #MeToo served as a form of jujitsu, turning the power of celebrated men to act with impunity into a weapon against them, using their very celebrity to topple them.

So, #MeToo had a stunning impact. In 2018, the *New York Times* documented over two hundred men who had been brought down by reports of misconduct, many of whom were then replaced by women. While some cynics may see the advancement of women during a time of crisis as only window dressing, the promotion of women to positions of power tends not only to reduce the incidence of sexual harassment but also to encourage the adoption of other pro-social policies, leading to better employee relationships, greater attention to employee health and safety, and improved management of diversity challenges. Just the presence of women in leadership has a profound impact on how much harassment occurs, and how it's dealt with when it does happen. The tactic of fighting back on social media, naming alleged perpetrators and describing abuses, has gone mainstream and worldwide, and it can empower women not only to expose abuses but also to assume more prominent roles in righting the abuses.

As lawyers and law professors, we've read or litigated hundreds of cases involving sex discrimination and sexual harassment. When #MeToo gained steam, we felt its power. We realized that the very success of the WTA economy in evading the rule of law fueled the energy behind the #MeToo movement in opposing it. To appreciate why requires understanding how the meaning of sexual harassment, legally and symbolically, has changed with time and how the #MeToo movement empowers women to fight back not just against the more egregious sexual predators like Harvey Weinstein but also against the everyday harassment that marginalizes women's place in the workforce.

Sexual harassment in the workplace is not new, and even after the 1964 Civil Rights Act banned sex discrimination in the workplace, it was another two decades before the Supreme Court decided that the statute reached sexual harassment. Indeed, early cases dismissed claims of sexual harassment, arguing that boys will be boys and boys chase girls. That's what happened to Adrienne Tomkins, an office worker at the Public Service Electric and Gas Company in Newark, New Jersey. In 1976, Tomkins, in accordance with the complaint she later filed in federal court, reported that she had lunch with her supervisor and rejected his demand that, if she wanted to keep her job, she needed to have sex with him. When she refused, he restrained her from leaving the restaurant and later fired her. A federal judge stated that a "physical attack motivated by sexual desire on the part of a supervisor and which happened to occur in a corporate corridor" was not sex discrimination. He continued: "The abuse of authority by supervisors of either sex for personal purposes is an unhappy and recurrent feature of our social experience."

It took a determined fight to get sexual harassment recognized by the law as a form of sex discrimination that marginalized women in the workplace. One of the first appearances of the term "sexual harassment" was in the mid-1970s, during a course that journalist Lin Farley taught at Cornell University on women and work—just around the time of the Tomkins case. During a "'consciousness-raising' session," female students recounted the disturbingly sexualized experiences they had at work, ranging from verbal references to rape. Farley noted that "[e]very single one of these kids had already had an experience of having either been forced to quit a job or been fired because they had rejected the sexual overtures of a boss." The term "sexual harassment" resonated with women's experiences. Law professor Catharine MacKinnon published her groundbreaking book, *Sexual Harassment of Working Women*, in 1979, and it made the case that sexual harassment was endemic and existed as a form of sex discrimination that blocked women's workforce progress. The fight in that era was for recognition that sexual attention intrinsically prevents women's full acceptance in the workplace. By 1986, the Supreme Court agreed that Title VII's anti-discrimination provisions addressed workplace sexual harassment and workers could sue for redress. The Supreme Court's opinion was an early example of how putting a name to the wrongdoing is often the first step toward accountability. Indeed, once the Court recognized sexual harassment as sex discrimination, the Court also quickly held that an employee's reluctant consent to sexual advances from a more powerful employer did not undermine a sexual harassment claim. The Court recognized that sexual harassment was an abuse of power and one that served to marginalize or exclude women from the workplace.

Celebrated cases define sexual harassment in the popular imagination. Earlier generations cite Justice Clarence Thomas and Anita Hill, or Bill Clinton and Monica Lewinsky. More recently, Supreme Court Justice Brett Kavanaugh and Christine Blasey Ford, Weinstein and Bill Cosby and multiple women have been the landmark cases for a younger generation. Yet, just as the first consciousness-raising sessions indicated in the seventies, workplace harassment remains shockingly routine across almost every industry. Harassment flourishes in organizations that are male dominated, hierarchical, and tolerant of bad behavior, whether that is Weinstein studios, General Motors factories, or an Uber engineering team.

The Equal Employment Opportunity Commission (EEOC) points out that the vast majority of incidents still go unreported. Rather than turn in their harasser, most victims resort to self-help—they try to avoid the harasser, downplay the seriousness of the situation, or simply attempt to ignore the behavior. An overwhelming number (79.5 percent) of women who were targets of harassment change jobs within two years of the harassment; this is more than six times the usual rate of job churning. Some of them were trying to avoid the harasser; others were unhappy with the employer's response. People who have experienced harassment continue to report psychological consequences, such as depression, a decade later.

Women are not the only victims, although the Supreme Court did not recognize that same-sex sexual harassment was legally actionable until 1998. Each year in the past decade, men have filed between 16 and 17 percent of the EEOC charges for sexual harassment. Yet claims are more likely to be successful where the defendants are male and the victims are female; the public has yet to recognize that male-on-male sexual harassment is just as much an abuse of power—and not just an exercise of coercive sexuality—as men sexually harassing women

Sexual harassment—for both men and women—is especially prevalent in low-wage industries, such as accommodations and food services, with decentralized operations (restaurant owners are typically answerable to no one) and power imbalances between male managers and their predominantly female workforces. Two-thirds of female workers and more than half of the men have experienced sexual harassment from restaurant managers, and 80 percent of the women and 70 percent of the men report sexual harassment from co-workers.

While large corporations have more internal controls, today's corporate "tournament" increases the risk of sexual harassment, as such work environments select for the ambitious, the aggressive, and the confident. The most competitive environments breed sexual harassment in all its forms. They attract and promote "toxic leaders" who rank low in empathy and high in the willingness to harass or bully others to protect their own egos. This tendency to select for bullying and harassment is built into the fabric of the WTA economy every bit as much as traditional sexism was built into the gender-segregated workplaces of the industrial era. Men may harass women (and sometimes men) to establish their superiority over their subordinates—or they may harass women to establish their superiority over other men. Ingrid Avendaño's experiences illustrate how intense workplaces like Uber breed constant efforts at one-upmanship and how much more abusive the behavior can become when women try to challenge it in ways that threaten to undermine the men around them.

Sexual harassment is thus both a symptom and a consequence of a WTA economy. Narcissists (mostly men) accumulate power, often by taking risks, breaking the rules of a civilized order, and exploiting those around them. Their success convinces them they are entitled to take the spoils that come with their status and to dismiss the pain of those they hurt in the process. The victims of harassment are silenced as they defer to the overwhelming forces they see arrayed against them. The sexual harassment may, indeed, be about sex, as Marlyn Perez found out, but it is also about power, as Salma Hayek observed.

Sexual harassment law, by itself, failed to empower plaintiffs in part because sexual harassment was initially conceived as part of the effort to fight sex discrimination—that is, to undo the wholesale exclusion of women from the workplace. In contrast, courts were reluctant to police what they saw as sexual attraction; the courts simply did "not want to police office flirtations motivated by personal affection." To distinguish between the two, the courts required that plaintiffs show the harassment they experienced was a form of sex discrimination that affected their employment. This means that a plaintiff could receive relief if they made one of two showings. The first is called quid pro quo harassment and it occurs, for example, when a boss says to an employee "you don't get a promotion unless you sleep with me." The second involves creation of a "hostile work environment," such as the environment that occurs when co-workers so mercilessly harass employees of another sex that they drive them out of the workplace altogether. As the EEOC explains, sexual harassment is only illegal "when it is so frequent or severe that it creates a hostile or offensive work environment or when it results in an adverse employment decision (such as the victim being fired or demoted)." The courts, in contrast, have never been willing to police more prosaic workplace conduct that threatens or marginalizes women. Persistent and belittling sexual comments or expressions of sexual interest without coercion may not be actionable sexual harassment at all.

Of course, even if plaintiffs make it to court and win under Title VII, the total amount of compensatory and punitive damages a plaintiff can recover from smaller employers (with between fifteen and one hundred employees) is $50,000; for the largest employers (those with more than five hundred employees), that damage cap is $300,000. These caps have remained unchanged since 1991, and have not accounted for growth in the economy and inflation over the past thirty years. Even if this amount of money would be worthwhile to a victim, these kinds of suits are often not worthwhile for lawyers to take. While $300,000 might seem like a lot, lawyers may have to spend years in litigation, interviewing witnesses, conducting discovery, preparing pleadings, and fighting in court, often against a much better-financed defendant represented by multiple lawyers. And the proof requirements for hostile environment cases require the plaintiff to prove the offensive conduct was unwelcome. Thus, many victims are stuck; prosecutors like Cyrus Vance initially did not think they could win even egregious cases of sexual assault against powerful men like Harvey Weinstein, and women in the workforce like Perez had little ability to sue their bosses. This is one of the reasons why the vast majority of sexual harassment incidents go unreported—and it is a reason that the #MeToo movement has proved so powerful: it is much harder to dismiss as isolated incidents a cacophony of claims in a given workplace or against a particular boss.

Overall, the studies show that sexual harassment remains pervasive, that many victims find it difficult to access the available remedies, and that workplaces with higher risks of harassment include those that lack diversity, prize "high-value employees," and create significant power disparities between employees—in short, the classic attributes of the WTA workplaces we have presented here. A 2019 *Investment News* survey of financial advisors found that half of them had either experienced harassment or witnessed it more than once. And the Egan study we discussed in Chapter 5 found that the finance firms with the greatest gender disparities in terminations for misconduct also had the highest rates of sexual harassment complaints. As Catharine MacKinnon, the foremother of sexual harassment law, explained, "[T]he more power a man has, the more sexual access he can get away with compelling." That power can be exercised in any industry—on the casting couch, in an Olympic doctor's "examination" room, or in the tomato-picking fields.

Indeed, some men see greater sexual access as a major purpose of gaining power.

Accordingly, #MeToo was a response to the power structure that gave harassers immunity. The movement arose as a reaction to the ineffectiveness of law and the invisibility of the unaccountable power of today's WTA economy. It has created opportunities for women to speak up and to engage in broader actions. Sexual harassment persists when its victims are isolated and powerless. Harassment diminishes when it is illuminated and identified. So, #MeToo inspired publicity that made the harassment—and the patterns that silenced the victims—visible to the public. Once the public recognizes the patterns, lawsuits can often address the wrong in tangible ways: the accusations against Harvey Weinstein led to the bankruptcy of his studio and damages being awarded to at least some of those wronged.

This has been one of the biggest changes wrought by the #MeToo movement: the public—and prosecutors and juries—now recognizes the patterns and is willing to return jury verdicts that once were inconceivable. Consider the case of magazine writer E. Jean Carroll. In 2019, Carroll wrote an article in *New York* magazine describing how then president Donald Trump had sexually assaulted her in the nineties, in a New York department store. The case is the type that victims of sexual assault have long believed they could not win. The assault occurred while the two were alone; there were no witnesses. And while Carroll told close friends about the incident just after it happened, she did not report it to the authorities. By the time she was willing to go public with her story in 2019—after she recognized that what she had experienced had happened to a number of other victims of Donald Trump—the statute of limitations had passed for any type of civil redress. Yet, remarkably, in May 2023, a Manhattan jury (that reportedly included a juror who had voted for Trump) unanimously found that the former president had sexually abused her, then defamed her by calling her a liar when she wrote about the attack in her memoir, and awarded her millions of dollars in damages.

Carroll's success could have happened only because of her courage in facing the threats, expense, and trauma of bringing such a case and the #MeToo movement's role in the changes that made the jury verdict possible. First, the New York legislature, recognizing that women have historically been discouraged from coming forward with such charges, suspended the statute of limitations for bringing the sexual assault suit decades after the event happened. Second, the court allowed multiple witnesses who were not parties in the case to testify that Trump had assaulted them in similar ways. Instead, of a "he said, she said" case with no witnesses, Carroll was able to put on the testimony of confidants who described how she had told them of the assault at the time it had happened and other women who were able to establish that Trump had a pattern of engaging in such conduct. Third, Trump's belief in his own impunity contributed to the verdict. The jury was allowed to hear his boasts on tape that: "I just start kissing them. It's like a magnet. Just kiss. I don't even wait. And when you're a star they let you do it. You can do anything. . . . Grab 'em by the pussy." At a deposition in the Carroll case, Trump doubled down on the comments, saying, "Well, historically, that's true with stars . . . if you look over the last million years, I guess that's been largely true. Not always, but largely true. Unfortunately or fortunately." And when Carroll's lawyer then asked, "And you consider yourself to be a star?" Trump responded, "I think you can say that, yeah." Trump's own words reinforced the pattern that emerged from the witnesses' testimony.

Finally, and most notably, the jury, which delivered its verdict after a relatively short deliberation, had no trouble believing Carroll, despite the fact that she could not remember the exact year in which the assault took place and that she had waited more than twenty years before coming forward with her accusations. On the witness stand, Carroll described herself as a member of the "silent generation," who were taught to blame themselves for such events and to keep their chins up and not complain. What Carroll described was credible partly because of the legal changes that allowed her to bring the suit in the way she did and partly because the behavior she described is now recognizable to the public as characteristic of sexual harassment—and, indeed, in this instance, sexual assault—cases.

That's why the #MeToo movement has seemed so promising; it—at least for a while—has made sexual harassment more visible and provided opportunities to point out other barriers in the workplace. All the factors we have identified in this book indicate that sexual harassment is most likely to occur in environments that breed narcissism, masculinity displays, and abuse of power. And as we have shown, conservative courts have limited the use of once powerful tools such as class actions to fight wholesale gender disparities like those that existed at Walmart. Fighting those wholesale gender disparities helps expose the abuses of power, and the #MeToo movement has resulted in a new set of tactics that go beyond traditional sex discrimination suits to show the different ways that abuses of power come together in the workplace.

Consider the case of Lauren Bonner. Bonner was the head of talent analytics at Point72 Asset Management, a prominent New York hedge fund, that is part of one of the most male-dominated and opaque sectors of the economy. Hedge funds are a creation of financial deregulation. In 2003, the 3,000 hedge funds in the United States managed roughly $500 billion in assets. Two decades later, there were approximately 12,000 lightly regulated hedge funds, with roughly $4.3 trillion under management. And white men manage 97 percent of industry assets, in spite of the fact that women do as well or better than the men. What we find fascinating about her case is that the sexual harassment allegations she included proved to be a powerful tool in the litigation arsenal—even in a case that we would have predicted might lose in court.

As a recruiter for Point72, Bonner's job gave her access to the company's data, which provided a detailed account of discrimination against women. She reported that of the firm's 125 portfolio managers, only one was a woman. And thirty-one of the hedge fund's thirty-two managing directors were men. "I see things like female candidates coming out of college have to have GPAs and SATs that are 20 percent to 25 percent higher than their male peers to get the exact same job," Bonner stated in an interview with *CNBC*. Well-qualified women like Bonner were shunted into human resources or marketing, while less qualified men were promoted ahead of them.

After four years with the hedge fund, she had become increasingly frustrated with the lack of opportunities for advancement. She decided to sue. The problem for her lawyers was that the statistics that compellingly showed the firm engaged in sex discrimination did not prove that Bonner would have received a promotion but for her sex. That is, even if the firm was more likely to promote men than women, she had to prove that she herself had experienced discrimination. And her claim that Point72 promoted unqualified men who had no more relevant finance experience is a hard claim to win. Bonner and her lawyers designed a complaint that highlighted sexual harassment claims and allowed her to capture the abuse of power in the company in a way that a simple allegation of unequal treatment would not have done.

The *New Yorker* described Bonner's lawsuit as "#MeToo Comes to Wall Street." She alleged that Point72 president, Douglas Haynes, wrote the word "PUSSY" on the whiteboard hanging in his office and left it there for weeks. For female employees who participated in meetings in his office, "the PUSSY Board drifted above them, taunting them with repulsive references to their own bodies." She described attending a fundraiser with a colleague and being introduced to a Point72 consultant whom she understood was to be treated with the utmost respect. He had walked over with a woman neither Bonner nor her colleague knew. Later, after the woman left, Bonner's colleague innocently asked who the woman was. According to Bonner's complaint, the consultant replied, "Why? Do you want to fuck her? You can, she works for me." Overall, she alleged a "boys' club" atmosphere was present at Point72 that was hostile to women—and, she added, to anyone other than white men who had succeeded in being admitted to the club.

To counter the legal obstacles to winning the sex discrimination case, Lauren Bonner used #MeToo movement tactics to tie her experiences at the firm to abuses of power. Bonner's hedge fund was best known because of its founder's past. Stephen Cohen had headed S.A.C. Capital Advisers. A *New Yorker* article noted that S.A.C. "had been known as one of the most aggressive and successful hedge funds in the industry, producing impossible-sounding returns year after year." That prompted the Securities and Exchange Commission (SEC) to launch an insider-trading investigation, resulting in criminal convictions against numerous S.A.C. employees, with a number receiving significant jail terms, though the Second Circuit reversed the convictions on appeal. Cohen, despite the fact that he oversaw the system that encouraged the insider trading, escaped prosecution. The SEC merely banned him from investing other people's money for two years. Cohen founded Point72 to invest his own money, the $10 billion the SEC let him keep. Bonner filed her lawsuit just before the two-year ban was set to expire, at a point of maximum leverage.

"This case is important," Bonner's complaint explained, "precisely because it shows that, in 2018, wealthy, financially sophisticated, global companies such as Point72 continue to believe that they operate above the law." Continuing the not-so-veiled references to what happened at S.A.C, the complaint concluded, "Rather than learning from past failures to supervise potential wrongdoing, P72's conduct shows that earning profits trumps any need to follow statutory rules, including the applicable discrimination laws."

In another era, class action lawsuits offered the hope of real reform for women. Bonner understood that by the time of her 2018 suit, decisions like *Wal-Mart v. Dukes* and others upholding mandatory arbitration provisions limited the chances that a court would order wide-reaching reform of the entire company and its culture. She knew her best hope for change was to focus media attention on Point72's practices. Once the complaint was filed, she worked to generate publicity. "I certainly tried to make change internally," Bonner explained in her first television interview. "I just couldn't let it go. I couldn't walk away from the problem. It's too important. It was too blatant, and it's been going on for way too long. I just couldn't help but fight it."

Bonner's courage had tangible results. She settled her case for an undisclosed sum, and the hedge fund, at least initially, hired more women. Douglas Haynes, the Point72 president with the PUSSY white-board, resigned just weeks after Bonner filed her lawsuit. And when Steve Cohen proposed to buy the New York Mets, the discrimination allegations once again became fodder for the press. While they did not derail Cohen's $2.4 billion acquisition of the baseball team, they did prompt an investigation into allegations that the Mets organization had engaged in sexual harassment. Two prominent members of the Mets, including the general counsel, were soon gone as well.

The #MeToo tactics—focusing on unsavory practices, generating publicity, and tying together different kinds of misconduct—offer new weapons in the fight against discriminatory workplaces. Bonner might have had a hard time winning either a simple sex discrimination case or a sexual harassment case. She experienced no quid pro quo harassment propositioning her and the incidents she described might not have been pervasive enough to be a hostile work environment. By combining the allegations of discrimination and harassment, though, she increased the ability to win a more favorable settlement—and to encourage Point72 to take sexual harassment considerations more seriously. Once a company feels it has to address the negative publicity, it settles and strengthens the hand of HR. The legal weaknesses that allow a company to block individual cases that seek individual remedies become much less important.

Bonner's case illustrates why individual sexual harassment claims on their own may not be enough to make structural change. The hedge fund dealt with Bonner's allegation by firing Haynes, but it's not clear that the hedge-fund culture changed. Employers also became more concerned—rightly, in our opinion—with fair process for those accused of harassment. But the case does show why #MeToo provides a critical opening to reforms to the culture in which sexual harassment thrives.

The first step toward reform has been this visibility and the accompanying idea of accountability that have sifted into public consciousness. In a Pew Research survey, seven out of ten people responding said that those who commit sexual harassment at work are more likely now to be held responsible than prior to the #MeToo movement. Prominent people who assault and harass women are being held responsible. For example, a targeted grassroots internet campaign, #MuteRKelly, was effective in pressuring the music industry to end sponsorship for the R & B singer in 2019. Kelly was later convicted of the serial abuse of young girls, and in February 2023, he received an additional twenty-year sentence on top of the earlier convictions.

Unions joined these efforts. Organizers found that #MeToo can be an effective organizing tool, particularly with female workers all too aware of the harassment in their workplaces. And women organizers have used the movement to push for "the idea of a female-led labor movement focused on obtaining free childcare, schedule control, and family leave," particularly in areas "such as education and healthcare where women employees comprise the majority." Union organizer Jane McAlevey argued that, "Naming and shaming is not sufficient. Women need to translate the *passion* of this moment into winning the solution that will help end workplace harassment." She concludes that a "good union radically changes workplace culture for the better" and one of the ways is by standing up for employees who claim harassment.

Just as unions can help with collective support, EEOC enforcement is useful in taking the pressure off individual victims. The EEOC investigates complaints and bears the costs involved in bringing actions. In the immediate aftermath of #MeToo, sexual harassment charges filed with the EEOC increased by 13.6 percent in 2018. The EEOC itself filed 50 percent more lawsuits than in the prior year. And the total amount recovered by the EEOC in 2018 for sexual harassment victims jumped to nearly $70 million, up from $47.5 million the prior year. While these cases still represent only a small percentage of the total number of potential charges, they show the impact of the #MeToo movement on victims' willingness to come forward. The fact that the number of charges has decreased since then may show that focusing attention on the abuses supports those who want to report and need allies.

The second reform has been changing the laws that allow mandatory arbitration and nondisclosure agreements to cloak serial abuses. Successful lawsuits can bring pressure on a company to discipline or dismiss repeat offenders, but that is much harder to do if the facts remain secret. For decades, a key tool for keeping abuse quiet was to have employees sign mandatory arbitration agreements during their on-boarding. Sixty million workers in this country—more than half of all private-sector, nonunion employees—are subject to forced arbitration clauses. Under these arbitration agreements, employees cannot go to court; they can only resort to less formal proceedings that can be kept secret. And these proceedings often end with nondisclosure agreements (NDAs) that give women limited relief in exchange for their silence.

Consider what happened at Sterling Jewelry, which sells most recognizably under the name brands of Kay Jewelers and Zales. For more than fifteen years, an alleged 70,000 women who worked there had been systematically denied fair pay and promotions, and hundreds more had been groped, propositioned, pressured to have sex, and raped. When these women were hired, one piece of the flurry of paperwork that each signed was a mandatory arbitration agreement. These agreements forced any employee with a complaint to use Sterling's in-house investigation process. If the results were unsatisfactory, the employee could request a hearing panel—but Sterling picked the employee's peers and lawyers who would serve on it. The hearings were conducted in private and "if there was a settlement, the employee often had to sign a nondisclosure agreement that prohibited the employee from speaking about the case again." Other employees were unaware of the allegations because the one-sided arbitrations played out in secret.

Also, #MeToo has had an impact on the continued secrecy surrounding sexual harassment cases. California enacted legislation in 2018 that banned nondisclosure agreements for sexual harassment, and expanded that in 2021 to cover NDAs in other proceedings; in 2022, Congress followed suit and partially banned NDAs in sexual harassment cases through what is known as the federal "Speak Out Act." To be sure, it only bans the enforcement of confidentiality provisions regarding sexual assault and sexual harassment that were signed before the dispute arose—in other words, employers are free to bargain for silence in the arbitration process.

But even the impact of arbitration agreements on sexual harassment claims was finally blunted in 2022, in large part—as was true with NDAs—because of the publicity from the #MeToo movement: Congress enacted and President Biden signed into law the Ending Forced Arbitration of Sexual Assault and Sexual Harassment Act, which banned employers from forcing workers who alleged sexual misconduct to arbitrate their claims. Employers are still free to force arbitration and NDAs in numerous other types of workplace discrimination claims. Even tax law changed to accommodate this new era; settlements of sex discrimination suits that include nondisclosure agreements can no longer be deducted as a business expense.

One intended consequence of #MeToo—employees acting more carefully with respect to the potential for sexual harassment in the workplace—seems to be occurring, but so are some unintended consequences. One year after #MeToo spread across Twitter, LeanIn.Org reported survey results from male managers demonstrating a 32 percent jump in a Pence-ian unwillingness to "participat[e] in a common work activity with a woman, such as mentoring, working alone, or socializing together." Not only did that mean excluding women from the one-on-one mentoring that might be available to men, but it also seemed to blame women for inevitably serving as temptresses.

Over time, though, the movement has the potential to change social practices and norms, even though there are questions about whether the immediate effectiveness is limited to high-profile abusers, with multiple victims, most of whom are straight white women. Whether any new laws will be effectively enforced depends on whether they become part of broader efforts to impose accountability on those who have been able to act with impunity. The kickstart of #MeToo through social media avoided the delays and barriers to access that lawsuits would have required. The future of safeguards against harassment and abuse will depend, though, on embodying these protections in law. The public could lose interest, and laws are needed to shore up protections and guard against the whims of public outrage.

The third and most fundamental step is changing the WTA culture in which sexual harassment thrives by challenging companies that breed harassment on multiple fronts. That means not just going after individuals but also using sexual harassment to change the WTA culture. McDonald's provides a case in point. In the aftermath of the #MeToo movement, allegations of sexual harassment forced a shake-up of corporate management, individual liability for top executives, and widespread protests targeting the abuse of teen workers at McDonald's restaurants. McDonald's CEO Stephen J. Easterbrook had been forced to resign in 2019, "after he acknowledged exchanging videos and text messages in a non-physical, consensual relationship with an employee." When the McDonald's board subsequently discovered that Easterbrook had also engaged in several physical relationships with other employees that he had failed to disclose, the board obtained a clawback of over $100 million in compensation Easterbrook had been paid. Shareholders followed up with a suit against McDonald's human resources director at the time, David Fairhurst, alleging that he had ignored red flags about the party atmosphere, and personally engaged in several instances of sexual harassment, "allowing a corporate culture to develop [at McDonald's] that condoned sexual harassment and misconduct." The shareholder action (brought by shareholders on behalf of the corporation, arguing that officers and directors breached their fiduciary duties and harmed the corporation) detailed how a "party atmosphere" existed at McDonald's corporate headquarters, with "alcohol fueled corporate events" in which "[m]ale employees (including senior corporate executives) engaged in inappropriate behavior . . . routinely making female employees feel uncomfortable." In a precedent-setting 2023 opinion, the Delaware Chancery court ruled that allegations of sexual harassment can constitute a "breach of the duty of loyalty" and that corporate officers like Fairhurst, as well as directors, can be held individually liable for their actions. As the headline in a law firm blog explained, "For the First Time, a Delaware Court Holds that Corporate Officers Have a Duty of Oversight."

Cases such as these against corporate officers are significant because they indicate a duty to investigate and police such claims. Fairhurst was sued not just for his participation in the sexual harassment but also for allowing the climate in which it occurred to flourish. Shareholders' actions are not classic Title VII employment discrimination cases, and so are not subject to those damages caps. Whether or not these cases result in individual damages awards, however, they constitute clear notice that high-profile executives who engage in or conceal sexual harassment— including consensual sexual activities—may lose their jobs.

In the meantime, employees were also filing their own actions against McDonald's, with less far-reaching consequences. They "filed more than 100 complaints and lawsuits alleging workplace sexual harassment, such as groping, propositions for sex (sometimes in exchange for hours), and rape," and won a number of important victories. The EEOC brought additional claims, and in 2023 the EEOC obtained a $2 million settlement from one McDonald's franchise that encompassed harassment allegations at eighteen separate restaurants. The combination of the individual lawsuits, EEOC involvement, bad publicity, a 2018 strike, and the ability to enlist the assistance of lawyers from public-interest organizations like the ACLU have increased the capacity of otherwise isolated McDonald's workers to fight back.

While individual cases can bring relief to particular employees, they have not served as the catalyst to fundamental reforms. Instead, treating sexual harassment as a corporate responsibility rather than as a matter of individual cases might be the force that leads companies to reform their corporate cultures. At McDonald's and many other corporations, however, this requires a change in attitudes not just toward women but also toward labor relationships more generally. McDonald's, like Walmart and Amazon, has vigorously fought unionization and any claim that the corporation is responsible for what the individual franchises that operate the restaurants do. McDonald's franchise structure, like many other aspects of the WTA economy, allows the few to reap the profits from the enterprise with limited responsibility for what happens to the workers or the customers at individual stores. The rampant sexual harassment at some of the restaurants has served as a rallying point for unionization and other labor-protection effects. And while we are optimistic about the impact #MeToo has had on workplaces, we see the larger political struggle in starker terms. The ability to engage in sexual harassment—and get away with it—remains a potent symbol of power.

The #MeToo Movement can only have a long-term impact on the workplace and the culture that tolerates sexual harassment if the ability to confront attackers unites women and connects them to a larger constituency for reform. Precisely because sexual harassment is raw and inexcusable, it can be a counterpoint for the organization of a new set of forces to contest what has been the lawlessness of the WTA economy. While sexual harassment allegations can now force the ouster of top-ranking CEOs, such allegations can change nationwide practices only if sexual harassment is seen as part of a broader set of injustices that result from the power imbalance of the WTA economy.

A Future Without WTA Excesses: Escaping the Triple Bind

In the introduction to this book, we met A. J. Vandermeyden, the Tesla engineer who charged her employer with sex discrimination, sexual harassment, and retaliation for pointing out quality control issues—and possible fixes—in the cars her plant was making. We asked the question why, at a time when women had won entry to male bastions such as automotive engineering, are women still not gaining ground in the American workplace?

The answer—discovered over the course of the book—is that women are the canaries in the coal mine that signal the entrenched existence of the winner-take-all (WTA) economy, and its many abuses. Vandermeyden, after all, thought she understood the first leg of the Triple Bind: she succeeded when she played on the same terms as Tesla's male engineers and won a promotion by putting in the kind of twenty-six-hour shifts that impress bosses. Vandermeyden's downfall came when she discovered that thriving required playing by a hidden set of rules, ones that placed the boss's demands for faster production over concerns for customers and workers.

In the second leg of the Triple Bind, when women attempt to play the game, as Ellen Pao did at Kleiner Perkins, they run up against the double standard: women are treated more harshly for engaging in the same conduct as men. In the third leg of the Triple Bind, when women see that the game is rigged against them, they take themselves out—if they haven't been shoved out already. But Pao took her fight public and moved on to start a new organization that advocates for diversity and inclusion. It is those challenges from people like Pao that give us hope.

The story of Vandermeyden's experiences at Tesla connects the dots between women and a WTA economy that prioritizes individual advancement at the expense of employees and consumers. We've shown how this same economy fosters negative-sum competitions in the workplace that actively shortchange workers, while disproportionately costing female employees pay, promotions, leadership opportunities, and sometimes their very jobs. We have identified the specific force that has become more powerful: the ability of those at the top to rig institutions to advance their own interests at the expense of everyone else. We have shown that women's lost ground is a product of those developments and that the treatment of women is an early indicator of a system that benefits the few at the expense of the many, not just women. That economy has given Elon Musk the ability to introduce a more environmentally friendly car to the automotive market and start a privately run space program. But what makes Musk's ventures possible in this era is not the brilliance of his ideas nor the importance of his projects. Instead, it's his ability to turn celebrity and audacity into funding, to turn funding into personal riches, and to use his riches to cow a Securities and Exchange Commission that had asserted grounds to remove him from Tesla's helm for repeated securities violations into a favorable settlement. He sees correctly that the ability to realize his bold dreams requires, as Mark Zuckerberg pointed out, moving fast and breaking things.

Musk's riches allowed him to buy Twitter (now known as X) for $44 billion in late 2022. Once he acquired the company, he quickly imposed his will there the way he had at Tesla. He fired top executives; he told managers to "stack-rank" their employees to cut the low performers;

he ordered several rounds of layoffs, and there were numerous resignations; then Musk emailed the remaining 2,900 employees and gave them one day to decide if they wanted to sign a pledge to commit to Twitter 2.0 with an "extremely hardcore" work ethic that would involve "logging 'long hours at high intensity.'" A 2022 lawsuit unsurprisingly alleged that women were among the prominent casualties; even before the work-ethic pledge, 57 percent of Twitter's women were pushed out, compared to less than half the men. Twitter became the company that could win the Model WTA Award for 2022–23.

Elon Musk also changed Twitter's mission to reflect his own priorities. When he feared that President Biden's tweets supporting the Eagles in the Super Bowl were getting more traction than his, "Musk asked eighty engineers on Sunday night to begin working on a project that would ensure his tweets would . . . get significant engagement—and if they didn't they would lose their jobs." In May 2023, Musk decided to promote an anti-trans film, which led to the resignations of several top Twitter women responsible for content moderation. Musk has given new meaning to the concept of "winner take all," using his winnings at Tesla to impose his idiosyncratic views on the media universe. As Paul Krugman observed, "[H]uge disparities in income and wealth translate into comparable disparities in political influence." And, as we realized by the time we reached the final section of this book, the women who are fighting back are not fighting to enjoy the spoils of the new, stratified economy. They are fighting, alongside like-minded men, to change the very terms on which society is conducted.

———

Today, we have a system of winner-take-all politics that complements the winner-take-all economy. We see the same patterns in politics as we've seen throughout the book: political winners rig the system through gerrymandering, placing restrictions on the vote, and aggressively using the filibuster to keep power, even when they lose the majority of the vote. The political "winners" take all, explaining how public opinion—such as that the majority of the public supports higher taxes on the wealthy, background checks for gun purchases, and higher minimum wage laws—has little to no bearing on the policies that are implemented. A powerful minority uses the levers of power to block popular measures such as universal childhood education, in ways that are often invisible to the general public. Moreover, as dental-office worker Lauren Martinez discovered, even when Congress passes protective legislation, as it did during the COVID-19 period, business-friendly administrations may choose not to enforce the laws and business friendly judges may undercut them

Meanwhile, economic winners like the Koch brothers, the Walton family, Elon Musk, Wall Street firms, and a large swath of American corporations use their winnings to influence the political system. These forces have played a long game, promoting a free-market economic ideology, funding grassroots groups from the National Rifle Association to local school-board candidates, using control of state legislatures to create low-tax, anti-union jurisdictions that lure businesses from other states, and stacking the courts with conservative justices. Indeed, over a thirty-year period, the judiciary has steadily and quietly made it harder to bring bribery cases against public officers, insider-trading cases against hedge-fund owners like Stephen Cohen, and securities-fraud actions against anyone. Employment discrimination suits like the one Betty Dukes brought against Walmart are no longer levers for system-wide reforms. Instead, WTA politics award power to those willing to seize it, which enables them to perpetuate their economic agendas.

Today, these efforts—to game the political system, to stack the courts with ideological extremists, and to allow billionaires to act with impunity—are increasingly coming out of the shadows and moving into the open, and they are increasingly successful. No case is more symbolic of the move out of the shadows—and no case is more important for women's futures—than the Supreme Court's 2022 opinion in *Dobbs v. Jackson Women's Health Organization*, which reverses the 1973 *Roe v. Wade* case that recognized abortion as a fundamental right.

Before the *Dobbs* decision, the Supreme Court, most recently led by Chief Justice John Roberts, had quietly chipped away at abortion access, routinely upholding ever more restrictions on abortion providers without overruling *Roe* itself. Once conservative jurists acquired a 6 to 3 majority through the gaming of the appointments process, the Court took the final step of overturning entirely the constitutional right to abortion and returning the issue to the states. It is hard to overstate the affront to women that is embedded in the decision and its aftermath.

Many states immediately made it difficult to obtain an abortion even when necessary to save the life of the mother. And a number of states make no exceptions for rape, incest, or fetal birth defects. Yet the reaction to *Dobbs* showed that women's outrage has the power to change the political landscape. The decision mobilized voters, and candidates ran—and won—on abortion-access platforms. A study of ten states showed that the total number of women registering to vote shot up by 35 percent after the *Dobbs* decision, while men registering to vote over the same time frame increased by only 9 percent. The *Dobbs* decision prompted elections and referendums in individual states, and voters largely rebuked the ruling. In August 2022, right after the decision, Kansas voters rejected a proposed state constitutional amendment that would have said there is no right to abortion. In November 2022, voters in Michigan and Kentucky also adopted abortion-supportive measures, and these helped drive overall voter turnout; indeed, a reproductive-rights advocacy group in Kentucky emphasized that "[a]bortion transcends party lines." In 2023, Wisconsin voters flipped the political direction of their state's highest court by electing to the Wisconsin Supreme Court a liberal judge who ran on abortion rights. This was a voters' backlash against taking away rights and telling women what to do with their bodies, and it indicates the strength of a group that is primed to fight for their rights.

Women, of course, don't speak with one voice; married women's political leanings have historically been far more aligned with their husbands' leanings than with their sex, and Black and Latina women tend to vote differently from white women. Still, the gap between men and women voters has been growing—women were 7 percent more likely than men to vote for Joe Biden than Donald Trump in 2020. But it's not just a gender gap in partisan identification; there is also a gender gap in policy preferences. Women are more likely to be aligned with what has historically been labeled "feminine values"—the values of cooperation, community, and equality. To be sure, they are part of a broader coalition on these values, a coalition that also supports more egalitarian gender roles. Today, voters' views on gender (i.e., their views "that men should be masculine, act masculine and hold masculine roles; women should be feminine, act feminine, hold feminine roles") have become a major predictor of political loyalties and are a better predictor than whether a voter is male or female of policy views on issues that range from climate change to government support for healthcare.

Abortion is symbolic of this divide. Beliefs about gender roles influence support for abortion rights, and the restriction of abortion rights in turn is likely to have a profound effect on traditional gender roles and women's labor-force participation. Those who favor more traditional gender roles are also less likely to support government childcare spending and parental leave, and to oppose gender pay equity laws—protections that become that much more important when the state limits reproductive rights. Both gender (whether someone is male or female) and gendered views (whether someone supports traditional gender roles) are also likely to correlate with support for government aid to the poor. At the same time, evidence is mounting that one of the most likely consequences of *Dobbs* is sharp class and regional divisions in access to contraception and abortions, with only the well-off able to obtain the healthcare they need. This is likely to further lock poor women into poverty, as poor women are more likely than wealthier women to elect abortion, because they cannot afford to support the children they already have. Women generally are more likely to support the government's role in providing services in areas such as health and education; they are more likely than men, regardless of racial group, to support providing more services, even though that may mean a spending increase. Accordingly, the question of whether we will become a more or less equal society depends on the strength of those who champion the values traditionally associated with women.

Yet, a determined—and powerful—minority blocks the implementation of these values, even where they command the support of a broad majority of the public, as is true on issues such as abortion. The question then becomes: How can we harness the values of a women's coalition—which combines women's leadership and their ballot power, together with the support of their allies—in the broader fight against the excesses of the WTA economy?

Through stories and data, this book has shown the relationship between the political and the economic forces that allow the select few like Musk to win big and that result in the treatment of women in modern American society. Women's fates are tied to the abuse of power that the WTA economy fosters. But the book also points to solutions, placing women at the vanguard of a countermovement fighting back, as we saw in the stories of teachers and #MeToo survivors. Indeed, this countermovement may already have started. Elite investors are recognizing the connection between diversity, particularly gender diversity, and adherence to the rule of law in ways that reduce potential liability. We are heartened to see that a higher percentage of women became tech founders and general partners at venture capital firms during the boom in tech funding between 2017 and 2022. We found encouraging the greater recruitment of women into entry-level jobs in finance, and we cheered that women are reaching parity with men as law firm associates.

And we were stunned to see that in 2022, the CEOs of major companies like McDonald's could be fired for sexual misconduct that fell well short of the sexual assaults that had inspired the #MeToo movement. These changes seemed to be signs that institutionalized corporate America—the large companies, banks, venture capitalists, investment funds such as BlackRock, and traditional law firms—has gotten the message that greater diversity is a positive good and that human resources departments need to address sexual misconduct. In 2021, Nasdaq adopted a Diversity Rule, approved by the Securities and Exchange Commission, that requires disclosure of diversity metrics in order to "encourage board diversity; it also allows stakeholders to track the composition of boards." The Nasdaq Diversity Rule concluded that: "There is substantial evidence that board diversity enhances the quality of a company's financial reporting, internal controls, public disclosures and management oversight."

We believe that the continued success of this fight rests on three steps.

The first step is making visible the injustices of the WTA economy. We have found, whether in court or out of court, that the key to success in the new era is enlisting a sense of outrage at the abuses of the WTA economy. As we finished our work on this book, we wanted to talk to someone with insight into how this fight can be waged. Debra Katz is a lawyer who has spent three decades bringing sex discrimination cases and is known as the "feared attorney of the #MeToo movement." She recognizes the power in focusing public attention on abuses of power, wherever they occur.

The founder of her own law firm, Debra Katz has represented numerous high-profile people. Her clients have included Christine Blasey Ford, the Stanford research psychologist who testified that U.S. Supreme Court nominee Brett Kavanaugh sexually assaulted her when they were in high school. She has also represented one of the accusers of former New York governor Andrew Cuomo, and another accuser of his brother, former CNN anchor Chris Cuomo. And she has represented one of the witnesses against Harvey Weinstein.

Katz learned early on in her career that part of being effective means being willing "to shed light on the issues to ensure accountability." Young lawyers are often told to restrict their advocacy to the courtroom, but Katz disagrees. For people who are working to promote social change, she says, "silence has never helped us." She and her firm take a "multi-tiered approach" to discrimination cases; she views these cases as about changing practices and minds, while also seeking redress for her clients. Associating with groups that use organizing as a tool is another key tactic for Katz, who points out, "There are lots of ways to use the legal system without litigating." When there is a judiciary that's hostile to civil rights, and you're up against companies who see even substantial settlements as the cost of doing business, you need more firepower than just legal skills. Thus, publicity can be a powerful tool. In some cases, shining a light on abuses of power has a more immediate impact in effecting reforms than jury verdicts. The law usually lags behind social progress, and lawsuits can take a long time to wind their way through the courts. Bad publicity is much more painful and immediate. Mobilizing public outrage can lead to both short-term gains—think of the end of NDAs in sexual harassment cases—and long-term changes.

The second step is showing the links between sex discrimination and WTA practices that are counterproductive to society. As we looked at complaint after complaint, we found that unethical practices in companies and discrimination against women go hand in hand. Katz echoed the same patterns we have pointed to in this book: corporations involved in corporate wrongdoing are also workplaces that are hostile to women. "Of course, harassment and bullying are ultimately about power dynamics," she notes. "Having power can make an individual feel 'uninhibited' and more likely to engage in inappropriate behaviors." She also emphasizes that women are held to a different standard than the men who have become the winners in the WTA economy. That double standard persists when women try to fight back. In her experience, plaintiffs have to be without blemish to prevail. This helps explain why it is particularly hard to win cases like Ellen Pao's (Chapter 4) or Misha Patel Terrazas's (Chapter 5) that involve discriminatory terminations. Juries are often unforgiving of women who are alleged to have done something wrong, like having an affair, even if the men who work next to them are excused for engaging in similar—or worse—behavior.

Workplaces ought to have a single set of standards that identify the most egregious abuses and hold everyone to the same degree of accountability.

The third step is empowering women's voices. Katz observed that "#MeToo has had a profound impact: Women are feeling emboldened to come forward because they have a sense that people will actually now believe them. [And women] who do come forward tend to find more people who are willing to support them." She described her delight at seeing some of the accusers in the Harvey Weinstein case taken seriously, even though they were not the "perfect victims." And at the same time, companies have grown less willing to protect harassers. Today wrongdoers are losing their jobs. "That's a sea change," Katz says. It reflects the power of the #MeToo movement in showing how the abuses occur. The women accusing Weinstein are no longer isolated individuals that defense lawyers could portray as vengeful liars. The stories they told fit into a pattern that the #MeToo movement made visible. Because of the movement, E. Jean Carroll "took on a former president with virtually unlimited resources—and won," netting a multimillion-dollar jury verdict for Trump's sexual abuse of Carroll in a Bergdorf Goodman department-store dressing room and then for defaming her when she reported it. The public—including judges and juries—can respond to the patterns once they can see them.

Such visibility comes with its own risks, however. In representing Christine Blasey Ford at the time she testified against Kavanaugh, Katz faced anti-Semitic death threats for the first time in her thirty-five years of being a lawyer, forcing her to have armed security at both her home and her office. Despite the real physical dangers, Katz is hopeful about being on the right side of history in a world that is changing, pointing out that "you can't do civil rights work and not be an optimist." In all her cases, Katz believes that educating the public, the courts, and potential jurors makes a difference. She wants them to be aware of how what they are seeing in individual cases is part of a larger pattern.

Katz sees a generational shift occurring, in part because of the changing nature of work. Unlike prior generations, today's young workers are less worried about not having a job or about the stigma of changing jobs. Recently, in remote work, people may feel greater safety. Katz views the next generation as empowered and full of energy. Growing up with technology, this next generation focuses on innovation and knows how to communicate concerns across multiple platforms.

Women like Debra Katz point the way forward, giving us tools to bring down the WTA economy by using publicity and legal action to reveal the system's abuses.

Still, we know that we live in a world where the Supreme Court has made it harder to bring sex discrimination cases like the one against Walmart or to protect whistle-blowers in the nation's banks. That means bringing individual cases will not be sufficient. It is not enough to chip away at a fundamentally corrupt system through solitary cases that win relief, even if they do provide support for the wronged individuals themselves. Nor can the secret be to "lean in," joining the wrongdoers in the process, and trying to win at their corrupt game. Those who try will find themselves, like Terrazas at Wells Fargo, complicit in a system that will not respect their efforts to thread an ethical needle whose eye is continually shrinking. Nor can the secret be to lean out and quit jobs—or the economy—entirely.

Collective action provides the best model for how resistance to the powerful can succeed. The #MeToo movement showed how it was possible to create the political will necessary to make change. It is women and their allies coming together to make abuse visible. It is using outrage to put in place collective solutions. The strength and safety found in numbers fueled headlines on the abuses that women long thought were a matter of their individual misfortune.

Changing the political conversation has ripple effects that go well beyond politics; it can lead to the changes we advocate for the WTA economy. Using publicity, lawsuits, and the ballot box can achieve the following:

Cap the accumulation of power at the top. A critical step in the fight to curb these WTA forces will be limiting the power of those at the top of corporations. General Electric ultimately faced security-fraud charges for the accounting manipulation that Jack Welch implemented, but the slap on the wrist that GE received did not prevent Welch from remaining a very wealthy man. And Megan Messina may have successfully settled her case with Bank of America (described in Chapter 2), but it seems clear that the type of unethical activities she described in her complaint were not meaningfully addressed. Indeed, public reports indicate that the Trump administration scaled back the banking investigations that were underway when it came into office. Redressing these abuses, just like fighting sex discrimination, will thus be futile if it requires rooting them out one case a time. Instead, it will require changing the ability to profit from the break-the-rules mindset that has taken hold at the core of the WTA economy. Capping the power of those at the top gives them less incentive to set up these illegitimate business practices.

In looking back at the remarkable period of relative economic equality in mid-century America, it is important to consider its origins in the New Deal. Franklin D. Roosevelt took office as the Great Depression discredited the financiers who had produced the stock market crash of 1929. Revelation of their outsized pay—a million dollars a year in 1929—generated headlines that sent shockwaves across America. In the minds of the American public, outsized Wall Street salaries became associated with the will to fleece widows and orphans. The discrediting of the wealthy bankers laid the groundwork for the New Deal's creation of the administrative state and the adoption of comprehensive financial regulation—including the Glass-Steagall Act, which separated commercial and investment banking, the Federal Deposit Insurance Corporation and the Securities and Exchange Commission—and an improved social safety net. It also contributed to the creation of a governing coalition that lasted from 1932 to 1980 that countered the power of big business.

While accounts of these developments highlight different reforms, they rarely emphasize the cap on executive pay. A lasting effect of the Great Depression was to delegitimize the large salaries of the financiers as a corrupting influence in themselves. World War II did the rest, as an era of shared sacrifice produced high marginal tax rates. During the decades from the New Deal to the rise of the WTA economy, marginal taxes were as high as 90 percent on income over $2 million and limited the concentration of power. It's those tax rates that made possible the era of the "organization man," in which institutions became more prominent than individuals. While fifties corporations did not open their executive ranks to women or to people of color, they embraced the collective values that have long been identified with women. Even the head of General Motors thought in the 1950s that what was good for General Motors and what was good for America were the same. The win-win mindset that replaced the zero-sum thinking of earlier eras helped fuel the fight for racial and gender equality that would gather steam in the sixties.

While some economists today may worry that such high tax rates discourage work, it turns out that in earlier eras, they were associated with greater investment in institutions. The organization man of the 1950s and '60s, after all, gained more in status from the prestige of his company than the size of his bonus. The average CEO of the 1950s earned 20 times more than the average worker; today, a CEO earns 399 times that of a company's workers. We need to return to the high marginal tax rates that produced investment in institutions or, alternatively, to impose caps on pay. This would specifically target the executives who get to set their own pay and use it to produce a "heads I win, tails I win big" system. It would also target one of the biggest sources of the gender gap in pay—the rigged bonus system. Limiting the wealth at the top has the potential to set in motion a series of cascading effects that would positively influence everything from climate change, to funding for public schools, to improved access to healthcare.

Reset labor markets and reform management practices. Supporting the middle class means developing more equitable economic policies to reset labor markets. The federal government, through monetary and fiscal policies, charts a course for the economy as a whole. With the rise of the WTA era, it has tended to prioritize keeping a lid on inflation, which helps creditors, rather than promoting full-employment policies. Yet, the single biggest jump in the fortunes of low-income women in decades came from the tight labor markets that followed the recovery from the COVID recession. Employers like Walmart now pay more than the minimum wage in entry-level positions. Workers with needed skills in tight labor markets find it easier to switch jobs, making it easier to say no to employers who abuse or shortchange them. And if companies have to pay more to hire workers, they invest more in worker training and retention. In this sense, greater support for families, in the form of greater public support for children, healthcare, and childcare, increase women's ability to say no to bad jobs, reducing women as the reserve army of the unemployed in the modern era, and shrinking the supply of marginal workers who will take jobs with few benefits and little security. If companies were then forced to address productivity and profits rather than short-term gains in stock prices, they would also have an incentive to adopt better management practices.

We can learn much from management theory when it comes to restructuring competition. Management theorists reject a dichotomy between women's stereotypical strengths and effective management techniques. For the last half-century, well before the entry of women into executive ranks, standard management advice counseled attention to the creation of cooperative teams, focused on accomplishing business objectives. Today, diverse groups do better for similar reasons: consensus-based decision-making with a broader base of people produces better decisions. In contrast, workplaces that pit workers against each other lower morale, produce higher turnover, and increase in-group favoritism, disproportionately driving women and minorities out of such workplaces. Yet, given a more diverse American population and the greater importance of global markets, maintaining a diverse workforce is essential to recruiting workers and reaching a more diverse customer base. It can also lead to greater product innovation and the promotion of new services, as more diverse companies identify a broader range of problems and solutions. Recognizing the benefits of diversity, major investment funds have already made diversity a factor in picking their investments. A business world focused on performance rather than on the short-term enrichment of top executives will be an increasingly diverse one.

Raise the floor. The WTA economy intentionally breeds insecurity, keeping wages and benefits artificially low. Increasing the minimum wage would help ensure that a significant number of workers do not need public benefits, such as the Supplemental Nutrition Assistance Program, to boost their salaries. Increasing wages has ripple effects in local communities and businesses and can help reduce pay inequities, particularly for women of color. A new social compact would guarantee everyone a minimum income, whether through universal employment or simply universal basic income. Greater income security would in turn increase the ability to say no to WTA-negative competitions and provide stability for families at all socioeconomic levels.

While some economists argue that greater worker support, whether through a higher minimum wage or through income guarantees, would reduce overall employment, studies generally show that modest increases in the minimum wage have little effect; even were they to reduce employment, greater worker supports have offsetting benefits. As the famed Stockton, California, experiment illustrates, in which a random group of residents were given $500 per month for two years, a no-strings-attached stipend can improve financial security, increase job possibilities, and promote general well-being. Participants spent their money on necessities such as food and gas, with under 1 percent being spent on items like cigarettes and alcohol. The percentage who had a full-time job increased while they received the cash supplement— much more quickly than the control group's employment. Providing economic security resulted in better health as well, and giving money to poor mothers may even, as another study found, help with children's brain development. More than thirty such pilot projects across the country confirm that income guarantees have reinforcing effects that improve people's lives.

Invest in individuals, children, and communities. The WTA economy has cut investment in individuals, children, and communities. At the same time, women fulfill a disproportionate share of domestic obligations at the expense of their personal interests and advancement. So long as women remain the chief operating officers of their households, they will not become chief operating officers outside their homes. Critical to creating a winning economy is the rebirth of a social community that provides stable employment for every able adult, enmeshes new parents in community networks that strengthen their ability to care for their children, and treats every child as a valued member of society. Women—and their children, and the larger society—will win only if there is greater public investment in childcare, universal pre-K, paid family leave, and family-friendly workplaces. Investment in children, as the workers of tomorrow, pays off for society as a whole.

The expansion of the child tax credit during the COVID pandemic demonstrated how quickly government policy can slash child poverty and provide stability to families so they can weather job crises or economic downturns. Even before taxpayers filed their returns, the government sent checks to many people of $600 per month for each child under the age of 6. The child tax credit was a significant factor in reducing the child poverty rate by 46 percent in a single year, to its lowest rate ever, 5.2 percent. After the child tax credits and other COVID relief programs ended, the child poverty rate more than doubled, to 12.4 percent. If *just* the child tax credit had continued, the poverty rate would have been 8.4 percent. Numerous other countries, including Canada, Australia, and many in Europe, have child allowances that are similar to the expanded child tax credit, and these have succeeded in significantly reducing child poverty.

Parents spend the money on the children or to improve the family conditions, and expenditures on risky behavior or frivolous items do not increase. Economists calculate that the net aggregate benefit of cash-assistance policies would bring a more than tenfold gain in social capital, such as increased tax revenue and decreased child health costs; in particular, a permanent expansion of the 2021 Child Tax Credit would "cost $97 billion per year and generate social benefits with net present value of $982 billion per year."

Investing in prekindergarten will help prepare children for school, leading to better educational outcomes for them; it will also provide care for children so their parents can enter the workforce. Offering high-quality preschool helps parents participate in the workforce, as Washington, D.C., found when it implemented a universal preschool program: the labor force participation rate of mothers with children under 5 increased by 12 percentage points. Greater support may also reduce the churn that occurs as mothers cycle in and out of dead-end jobs, in response to pregnancy-hostile employers and the lack of adequate childcare.

Strengthen the rule of law. The WTA economy benefits those who can break the rules and get away with it. While the practices of the Wall Street traders, the Walmart managers, the top executives at GE, the venture capitalists in Silicon Valley, and the HR managers at Aspen Dental look different, they are all part of the same system that celebrates deceit and rule-breaking for short-term gains. No one should be able to violate the rules of a civilized society with impunity, whether the violations involve securities fraud, wage theft, groping, or paying women less than men for the same work.

Central to reinstituting the rule of law will be eliminating certain practices, such as deferred prosecution, mandatory arbitration, and confidentiality agreements, that allow companies to minimize wrongdoing; an end to confidentiality agreements can empower others to come forward with claims of discrimination and fraud. What can't be seen and can't be understood can't be prosecuted—and is almost impossible to fight.

Reforms of this magnitude take congressional hearings, Supreme Court opinions, and public outrage manifested in conversations, on social media, in grassroots political actions, and in voting. And they may not ultimately occur until a calamity strikes that makes the WTA abuses impossible to ignore. The individual women in this story, and the innumerable women who are behind them, the #MeToo movement, and the post-*Dobbs* activism nonetheless give us inspiration. They are not just waging individual battles to right wrongs committed against them; they are also committed to a long-term struggle for fundamental reform.

Taken together, the reforms outlined here would change the game for this generation of working women, as well as for generations to come. They would tame the excesses of the WTA economy, creating a level playing field—and promoting competence over connivance, cronyism, and machismo culture. They would also remove historic obstacles to gender equality so that women would be empowered, uplifted, and better able to thrive in the new American workplace. Men would be freer to invest more in their children, and children would enjoy a more open future. These reforms would lead to an economy in which every person gets a fair shake. And we would all be better off.

Acknowledgments

This book has been a collaborative project, with each chapter vetted and revetted by each of us numerous—sometimes seemingly endless—times. As a result, each chapter reflects our collective thoughts, energy, and research, as well as our joint values of care, communication, co-operation, and empathy.

We thank the women who spoke to us, whose voices are reflected in every chapter.

In writing this book we received support and collegiality from many sources.

We thank Bill Black, who contributed to the intellectual genesis of the book, and Tony Gambino, who helped us work through the ideas in this book. Thanks to David Cay Johnston for his leads—and his support. For helpful comments and conversations, we thank Afra Afsharipour, Katharine Baker, Brian Bix, Eleanor Brown, the Castelbaums, Danielle Citron, Jessica Clarke, Philip Cohen, Doriane Lambelet Coleman, Marie-Therese Connolly, Gerald Davis, Scott Dewey, Lisa Fairfax, Martha Fineman, Emily Glazer, Barbara Glesner Fines, Anne Goldstein, Sarah Haan, Cindy Handler, Jill Elaine Hasday, Joan Heminway, Claire Hill, Cathy Hwang, George Jerkovich, Aliza Knox, Howard Lavine, Martha McCluskey, Joan Meier, Alan Morrison, Fionnuala Ní Aoláin, Wendy Paris, Jonathan Rauch, Rachel Rebouché, Darren Rosenblum, Joseph N. Sellers, Kim Shafer, Barb Snell, Faith Stevelman, Lynn Stout, Jenny Montoya Tansey, Deborah Tuerkheimer, Joan

Williams, and Andrew Yarrow. We thank participants in faculty workshops and symposia held at the Association of American Law Schools, Emory University School of Law, George Washington University Law School, Northwestern University's Law & Gender Colloquium, and the University of Minnesota's *Journal of Law and Inequality*. These conversations enriched our ideas, and the participants inspired and supported us.

We are grateful for research assistance from David Edholm, Audrey Hutchinson, Elizabeth Mansfield, and Emma Kruger. We received stellar technical and administrative support from the University of Virginia School of Law Library. Billi Jo Morningstar provided exceptionally helpful manuscript services.

Eve Claxton of Unfurl Productions provided excellent editorial guidance as we wrote the manuscript. We thank Dawn Davis and Emily Simonson of Simon & Schuster for their belief in this project. Thanks also to those involved in the copy-editing process: Carole Berglie and Amy Medeiros. We are grateful to Elisa Rivlin for her careful review of the manuscript.

We also thank Bridget Matzie, agent extraordinaire, for seeing this project as possible and shepherding us through the proposal, writing, and editing processes.

We are deeply appreciative of editors Abigail Cahn-Gambino and Aaron Geary, business consultant Dylan Geary, psychologists Vincent Carbone and Louisa Flynn, professor Sheryl Asen, and Jewel Madsen, senior academic advisor.

Finally, we thank those who have supported and inspired us throughout our work on this book, most especially our families.

Notes

INTRODUCTION

1 *She was so inspired:* Sheelah Kolhatkar, "The Tech Industry's Gender-Discrimination Problem," *New Yorker*, November 13, 2017, https://www.newyorker.com/magazine/2017/11/20/the-tech-industrys-gender-discrimination-problem.

1 *"Tesla is one of the most":* Jose Moran, "Time for Tesla to Listen," *Medium* (blog), February 9, 2017, https://medium.com/@moran2017j/time-for-tesla-to-listen-ab5c6259fc88 [https://perma.cc/LNR9-TECM].

2 *"pervasive harassment":* Sam Levin, "Female Engineer Sues Tesla, Describing a Culture of 'Pervasive Harassment,'" *Guardian*, February 28, 2017, https://perma.cc/JC4U-5668.

2 *When Vandermeyden became:* Levin, "Female Engineer."

2 *In the complaint: Vandermeyden v. Tesla Motors, Inc.,* No. RG16831835, Second Amended Complaint (Alameda Cnty., Cal. Dec. 2, 2016); Levin, "Female Engineer."

2 *The not-so-secret key:* Technology writer Will Oremus explained that what drives Musk's "insane-seeming ambitions" is not just the desire to motivate his employees and suppliers: "Musk is the kind of person who runs on adrenaline, works best—or perhaps only—under insane pressure, and is gripped by existential dread the moment he finds himself working on a problem that feels the slightest bit quotidian or mundane. And he expects the same of the people who work for him." Will Oremus, "Why Elon Musk Keeps Promising the Impossible," *Slate*, May 5, 2016, 2:43 p.m., https://slate.com/technology/2016/05/teslas-elon-musk-keeps-promising-the-impossible-i-think-i-know-why.html; Matt Pressman, "How Tesla CEO Elon Musk Makes Impossible Goals Possible," *Evannex* (blog), May 2016, https://evannex.com/blogs/news/117140997-how-tesla-ceo-elon-musk-makes-impossible-goals-possible-infographic.

2 *Under Musk:* Mike Murphy, "Tesla Stock Soars as Deliveries Surge 87% in 2021, Smash Quarterly Record," *MarketWatch*, January 3, 2022, 10:47 a.m. ET, https://www.marketwatch.com/story/tesla-smashes-quarterly-delivery

-record-sees-sales-surge-87-in-2021-11641150700#:~:text=The%20price
%20gain%20added%20about,exercising%20even%20more%20stock%20
options.

2   *ultimately producing more cars:* Jessica Bursztynsky, "Tesla Stock Closes
Up 13% After Reporting Record Vehicle Deliveries for 2021," *CNBC*, January 3, 2022, 4:00 p.m., ET, https://www.cnbc.com/2022/01/03/tesla-stock
-jumps-after-reporting-record-vehicle-deliveries-for-2021.html (describing
how Tesla's market valuation [and stock price] soared after Tesla announced
that the auto company had increased deliveries of its electric cars by 87%
over the preceding year, beating expectations).

2   *Musk admitted:* On December 30, 2021, Tesla announced that it was recalling 475,000 cars because of safety issues. Hyunjoo Jin, "Tesla Recalls
Almost Half a Million Electric Cars over Safety Issues," *Reuters*, December 31, 2021, https://www.reuters.com/business/autos-transportation/tesla
-recalls-over-475000-electric-vehicles-2021-12-30/. *See also* Chris Isidore,
"Elon Musk Admits Tesla Has Quality Problems," CNN, February 3, 2021,
https://www.cnn.com/2021/02/03/business/elon-musk-tesla-quality-prob
lems/index.html. The business press speculated that it would have little effect on Tesla's share price. "Tesla Recall Won't Materially Affect the Stock,
Says Mizuho's Vijay Rakesh," *CNBC*, December 30, 2021, 9:32 a.m. ET,
https://www.cnbc.com/video/2021/12/30/tesla-recall-wont-materially-af
fect-the-stock-says-mizuhos-vijay-rakesh.html. And it didn't. Tesla's announcement a few days later that it had exceeded production expectations
sent the share price soaring, notwithstanding the product safety defects.
Bursztynsky, "Tesla Stock Closes Up."

2   *A profile of Musk:* Oremus, "Why Elon Musk Keeps Promising."

3   *A spokesperson said:* Kolhatkar, "The Tech Industry's Gender-Discrimination
Problem."

3   *Ultimately, after Tesla insisted:* "Biggest California Wrongful Termination
Lawsuits and Settlements," *1000Attorneys*, December 31, 2022, https://
perma.cc/PUX2-YU8N.

3   *except that:* From 1948 to 1973, hourly compensation for a typical worker
rose 91.3%; from 1973 to 2013, it rose 9.2%. Lawrence Mishel et al., "Wage
Stagnation in Nine Charts," Economic Policy Institute, report, January 6,
2015, https://www.epi.org/publication/charting-wage-stagnation/. A 2019
U.S. Census report is headlined "College Degree Widens Gender Earnings
Gap," U.S. Census Bureau, May 2019, https://www.census.gov/library/sto
ries/2019/05/college-degree-widens-gender-earnings-gap.html.

4   *Then when we looked at the numbers:* Elise Gould, "State of Working America Wages 2019," Economic Policy Institute, report, February 20, 2020,
https://www.epi.org/publication/swa-wages-2019/. Older data is at Elise
Gould, "State of Working America Wages," Economic Policy Institute, report, February 20, 2019, https://www.epi.org/publication/state-of-american
-wages-2018/.

4   *In 2019, a Goldman Sachs study:* "Closing the Gender Gaps 2.0: Fresh Data Show

More Work to Do," Goldman Sachs, report, October 23, 2019, https://www.goldmansachs.com/insights/pages/gender-pay-gap-2.0-f/report.pdf. *See also* "2022 State of the Gender Pay Gap Report," *Payscale*, [no date], https://www.payscale.com/research-and-insights/gender-pay-gap/ (last visited May 13, 2022).

4   *By the time:* Elise Gould and Katherine deCourcy, "Gender Wage Gap Widens Even as Low-Wage Workers See Strong Gains," Economic Policy Institute (blog), March 23, 2023, https://www.epi.org/blog/gender-wage-gap-widens-even-as-low-wage-workers-see-strong-gains-women-are-paid-roughly-22-less-than-men-on-average/.

5   *The gender pay gap:* Rakesh Kochhar, "The Enduring Grip of the Gender Pay Gap," Pew Research Center, report, March 1, 2023, https://www.pewresearch.org/social-trends/2023/03/01/the-enduring-grip-of-the-gender-pay-gap/.

5   *Women make up 87 percent:* "Nurse Salary Research Report 2022," *Nurse.com* (blog), May 2022, https://www.nurse.com/blog/wp-content/uploads/2022/05/2022-Nurse-Salary-Research-Report-from-Nurse.com.pdf.

5   *they don't explain why:* Kochhar, "The Enduring Grip of the Gender Pay Gap."

5   *The United States has lagged:* Macy Alcideo et al., "The Reality of Child Care in America Without Paid Family Leave," *TheSkimm*, December 22, 2021, https://www.theskimm.com/news/the-reality-of-child-care-in-america-without-paid-family-leave; Gretchen Livingston and Deja Thomas, "Among 41 Countries, Only U.S. Lacks Paid Parental," Pew Research Center, report, December 16, 2019, https://www.pewresearch.org/fact-tank/2019/12/16/u-s-lacks-mandated-paid-parental-leave/; Olivia B. Waxman, "The U.S. Almost Had Universal Childcare 50 Years Ago. The Same Attacks Might Kill It Today," *Time*, December 9, 2021, 11:18 a.m. EST, https://time.com/6125667/universal-childcare-history-nixon-veto/.

5   *Indeed, the gender wage gap:* Gould and deCourcy, "Gender Wage Gap Widens."

6   *Yes, childcare explains:* Richard W. Johnson et al., "Unpaid Family Care Continues to Suppress Women's Earnings," *Urban Institute*, June 9, 2023, https://www.urban.org/urban-wire/unpaid-family-care-continues-suppress-womens-earnings.

6   *For most people, men and women: See above* for p. 3, *except that.*

6   *during the 1990s:* Mishel et al., "Wage Stagnation in Nine Charts," at Figure 3 (showing the annual pay increases for the top 1% were almost 100% during the 1990s, compared to a mere 15% for the bottom 90%).

6   *we were surprised:* Tim Walker, "Who Is the Average U.S. Teacher?," National Education Association, report, June 8, 2018, https://www.nea.org/advocating-for-change/new-from-nea/who-average-us-teacher; *See also* Shelby LeQuire, "The History of Women as Teachers," *Western Carolina Journalist*, May 4, 2016, https://thewesterncarolinajournalist.com/2016/05/04/the-history-of-women-as-teachers/; Alia Wong, "The U.S. Teaching Population Is Getting Bigger, and More Female," *Atlantic*, February 20, 2019, https://

www.theatlantic.com/education/archive/2019/02/the-explosion-of-wom
en-teachers/582622/.

6   *teachers' salaries:* Walker, "Who Is the Average U.S. Teacher?"

6   *the percentage of women in computer science:* Steve Henn, "When Women
Stopped Coding," NPR, October 21, 2014, https://www.npr.org/sections
/money/2014/10/21/357629765/when-women-stopped-coding. *See also* "The
Current State of Women in Computer Science," Computer Science.org, report,
[no date], https://www.computerscience.org/resources/women-in-computer
-science/ (last visited September 26, 2019) (in 1984, women were 37% of
computer science graduates; now they constitute 18% of such graduates);
Sapna Cheryan et al., "There Are Too Few Women in Computer Science
and Engineering," *Scientific American*, July 27, 2022, https://www.scientific
american.com/article/there-are-too-few-women-in-computer-science-and
-engineering/.

7   *And for those women who stuck it out:* Mary Biekert, "Female MBA Graduates Earn \$11,000 Less Than Male Peers, Finds Global Study," *Business
Standard*, September 23, 2021, https://www.business-standard.com/article
/current-affairs/female-mba-graduates-earn-11-000-less-than-male-peers
-finds-global-study-121092300302_1.html.

7   *six of the top seven categories: See* Alexander Eichler, "Gender Wage Gap
Is Higher on Wall Street Than Anywhere Else," *Huffington Post*, March
19, 2012, http://www.huffingtonpost.com/2012/03/19/gender-wage-gap
-wall-street_n_1362878.html; Kathy Haan, "Gender Pay Gap Statistics in
2023," *Forbes*, February 27, 2023, https://www.forbes.com/advisor/business/
gender-pay-gap-statistics/. *See also* Connie Loizos, "In Tech, the Wage Gender Gap Worsens for Women over Time, and It's Worst for Black Women,"
TechCrunch, April 4, 2017, https://techcrunch.com/2017/04/04/in-tech-the
-wage-gender-gap-worsens-for-women-over-time-and-its-worst-for-black
-women/.

7   *It turns out that the parts:* Rani Molla, "The Gender Gap Is Smaller in Tech,
but It Will Hurt the Economy More," *Vox*, April 2, 2019, 7:00 a.m., https://
www.vox.com/2019/4/2/18290482/gender-wage-tech-economy-hired
("And the difference in absolute dollar amount between what men and
women make in tech on a weekly basis is larger than in other major employment sectors, according to data from the Bureau of Labor Statistics.").

7   *After all, women's representation:* McKinsey & Co., "Women in the Workplace 8," report, 2021, https://wiw-report.s3.amazonaws.com/Women_in
_the_Work place_2021.pdf; Emma Hinchliffe, "Women CEOs run more
than 10% of Fortune 500 Companies for the First Time in History," *Fortune*, January 12, 2023, https://fortune.com/2023/01/12/fortune-500-com
panies-ceos-women-10-percent/.

7   *In our field:* "Profile of the Legal Profession," American Bar Association, report, 2023, 75, https://www.americanbar.org/content/dam/aba/administra
tive/news/2023/potlp-2023.pdf.

7   *While the percentage of women:* Laina Hammond, "The Pay Gap Between

Male and Female Law Partners Is Real—Litigation Finance Can Help Women Close It," *Law.com/Texas Lawyer*, October 22, 2021, 10:32 a.m., https://www.law.com/texaslawyer/2021/10/22/the-pay-gap-between-male -and-female-law-partners-is-real-litigation-finance-can-help-women -close-it/?slreturn=20210927214429; "Women in the Legal Profession," ABA Profile of the Legal Profession, 2022, https://www.abalegalprofile.com /women.php.

7   *And many are being forced out:* Jossie Haines, "Why Women Leave Tech— and How We Can Fix It," *EMHub*, July 13, 2022, https://emhub.io/arti cles/why-women-leave-tech-and-how-we-can-fix-it (noting that "56% of women leave the tech industry 10-20 years into their careers [double the rate of men]").

8   *Yet, they are also substantially:* Mark Egan et al., "When Harry Fired Sally: The Double Standard in Punishing Misconduct," National Bureau of Economic Research, report, March 2017, https://www.nber.org/papers/w23242.

8   *Today, the biggest beneficiaries: See, e.g.,* AFL-CIO, "Union Jobs Offer Women, Minorities Better Life," Boilermakers.org, report, August 31, 2017, https://boilermakers.org/news/headlines/labor-day-facts-union-jobs-offer -women-minorities-better-life ("Black women in unions earn an average of $21.90 an hour while non-union women earn $17.04"); Elise Gould and Celina McNicholas, "Unions Help Narrow the Gender Wage Gap," Economic Policy Institute, report, April 3, 2017, https://www.epi.org/blog /unions-help-narrow-the-gender-wage-gap/.

8   *winning benefits such as health insurance:* AFL-CIO, "Union Jobs Offer Women."

8   *Yet, the war against unions:* Union membership has dropped from 20% of the workforce to 10.8%. Ben Finley and Tom Krisher, "Labor Shortage Leaves Union Workers Feeling More Emboldened," *PBS*, September 6, 2021, 12:06 p.m. EDT, https://www.pbs.org/newshour/economy/labor-shortage -leaves-union-workers-feeling-more-emboldened.

8   *The story of unions is a prime example:* Gordon Lafer and Lola Loustaunau, "Fear at Work," Economic Policy Institute, report, July 23, 2020, https:// www.epi.org/publication/fear-at-work-how-employers-scare-workers-out -of-unionizing/.

9   *Outright misogyny has increased:* Kathryn Joyce, "Misogyny and 'Male Supremacism': Central Driving Force in the Rise of the Far Right," *Salon*, May 10, 2022, 6:30 a.m., ET, https://www.salon.com/2022/05/10/misogyny-and -male-supremacism-central-driving-force-in-the-rise-of-the-far-right/ (reviewing Emily Carian et al., eds., *Male Supremacism in the United States: From Patriarchal Traditionalism to Misogynist Incels and the Alt-Right*).

9   *Indeed, women are no longer: See, e.g.,* Michael Heise and David Sherwyn, "Sexual Harassment: A Doctrinal Examination of Employer Liability, and a Question About NDAs—Because Complex Problems Do Not Have Simple Solutions," *Indiana Law Journal* 96 (2021): 969.

10   *Even the Black–white wage gap:* David Leonhardt, "The Black-White Wage Gap Is as Big as It Was in 1950," *New York Times*, June 25, 2020, https://www.nytimes.com/2020/06/25/opinion/sunday/race-wage-gap.html.

10   *In contrast, the winner-take-all era:* Joseph Bachelder, "Growth in CEO Pay Since 1990," Harvard Law School Forum on Corporate Government, September 19, 2018, https://corpgov.law.harvard.edu/2018/09/19/growth-in-ceo-pay-since-1990/ (projection from 2018 to 2020).

11   *Musk has been termed:* Charles Duhigg, "Dr. Elon & Mr. Musk: Life Inside Tesla's Production Hell," *Wired*, December 13, 2018, 6:00 a.m., https://www.wired.com/story/elon-musk-tesla-life-inside-gigafactory/?utm_source=twitter&utm_social-type=owned&mbid=social_twitter&utm_medium=social&utm_campaign=wired&utm_brand=wired.

11   Wired *magazine's article:* Duhigg, "Dr. Elon & Mr. Musk."

11   *This is a "zero-sum game":* Jennifer L. Berdahl et al., "Work as a Masculinity Contest," *Journal of Social Issues* 74 (2018): 422, 430.

11   *Amping up production schedules:* David Lumb, "The Case for Setting Impossible Deadlines," *Fast Company*, May 14, 2015, https://www.fastcompany.com/3046316/the-case-for-setting-impossible-deadlines.

11   *Masculinity contest cultures:* Jennifer L. Berdahl et al., "How Masculinity Contests Undermine Organizations and What to Do About It," *Harvard Business Review*, November 2018, https://hbr.org/2018/11/how-masculinity-contests-undermine-organizations-and-what-to-do-about-it (emphasis omitted).

11   *Such environments:* Berdahl et al., "How Masculinity Contests."

11   *Inside such organizations:* Berdahl et al., "How Masculinity Contests."

12   *Musk and Tesla, for example:* Dorothy Atkins, "Tesla Hit with $3.2M Bias Verdict After $137M Award Nixed," *Law360.com*, April 3, 2023, 4:53 p.m. EDT, https://www.law360.com/articles/1593085/tesla-hit-with-3-2m-bias-verdict-after-137m-award-nixed.

12   *of repeated labor violations:* Tyler Sonnemaker, "Elon Musk Illegally 'Threatened' to Retaliate Against Workers and Tesla Repeatedly Violated Labor Laws, NLRB Says," *Business Insider*, March 25, 2021, 6:51 p.m., https://www.businessinsider.com/elon-musk-tesla-nlrb-labor-law-violations-tweet-retalition-rehire-2021-3.

12   *efforts to cover up the violations:* "Is Elon Musk a Fraud?," *The Intercept*, May 14, 2020, https://theintercept.com/2020/05/14/is-elon-musk-a-fraud/.

12   *In 2018, the Securities and Exchange Commission:* "Elon Musk Settles SEC Fraud Charges: Tesla Charged with and Resolves Securities Law Charge," U.S. Securities and Exchange Commission, press release, September 29, 2018, https://www.sec.gov/news/press-release/2018-226.

12   *Musk took over Twitter:* Kate Conger et al., "Two Weeks of Chaos: Inside Elon Musk's Takeover of Twitter," *New York Times*, November 11, 2022, https://www.nytimes.com/2022/11/11/technology/elon-musk-twitter-takeover.html.

12   *But Musk is still winning:* Kia Kokalitcheva, "Elon Musk Wins Securities

Fraud Case over 2018 Tweet," *Axios*, February 4, 2023, https://www.axios
.com/2023/02/03/elon-musk-not-liable-securities-fraud-tweet.

16   *Management gurus stress:* Jim Collins, "Level 5 Leadership," Jim Collins website, [no date], https://www.jimcollins.com/concepts/level-five-leadership
.html (last visited February 7, 2023); Ryan Scott, "Employee Engagement
vs. Employee Experience," *Forbes*, May 4, 2017, 8:00 a.m., ET, https://
www.forbes.com/sites/causeintegration/2017/05/04/employee-engage
ment-vs-employee-experience/?sh=730f7cd78834 ("Companies with highly
engaged workforces outperform their peers by 147% in earnings per
share"); Ruth Umoh, "PepsiCo CEO Indra Nooyi: 5 Powerful Career Hab-
its that Drove Her Success," *CNBC*, October 2, 2018, https://www.cnbc
.com/2018/10/02/pepsico-ceo-indra-nooyis-last-day-5-habits-that-drove
-her-success.html.

PART 1: When Women Don't Compete on the Same Terms as Men, They Lose

19   *The new era of deregulation:* Greg Smith, "Why I Am Leaving Goldman
Sachs," *New York Times*, March 14, 2012, https://www.nytimes.com/2012
/03/14/opinion/why-i-am-leaving-goldman-sachs.html.

1. The Hidden Rules: Wal-Mart Stores, Inc. v. Dukes

21   *She was born:* Michael Corkery, "Betty Dukes, Greeter Whose Walmart Lawsuit Went to Supreme Court, Dies," *New York Times*, July 18, 2017, https://
www.nytimes.com/2017/07/18/business/betty-dukes-dead-walmart-work
er-led-landmark-class-action-sex-bias-case.html.

21   *She had minor brushes:* Liza Featherstone, *Selling Women Short: The Landmark Battle for Workers' Rights at Wal-Mart* (New York: Basic Books, 2004),
36 (noting that Betty Dukes "has what she frankly refers to as a 'dark past': numerous misdemeanor convictions, mostly for firearms possession, and DUI").

21   *She told a local newspaper:* Rowena Coetsee, "All Are Welcome to Her Party,"
Ledger Dispatch, December 19, 1998.

21   *So, she accepted a job*: U.S. Department of Labor, Changes in Basic Minimum
Wages in Non-Farm Employment Under State Law: Selected Years 1968 to
2016, [no date], https://www.dol.gov/whd/state/stateMinWageHis.htm (last
visited December 8, 2023). *See also* Corkery, "Betty Dukes, Greeter Whose
Walmart Lawsuit."

21   *She was certain:* Monee Fields White, "Meet Betty Dukes, the Black Woman
Who's Taking on Walmart," *IMDiversity*, 2012, https://imdiversity.com
/villages/women/meet-betty-dukes-the-black-woman-whos-taking-on
-walmart/.

22   *When she complained to her supervisors:* Nicholas Copeland and Christine
Labuski, *The World of Wal-Mart: Discounting the American Dream* (New
York: Routledge, 2013), 58.

22 *After that, she was informed:* Wal-Mart Stores, Inc. v. Dukes, 564 U.S. 338, 344 (2011).

22 *As she later explained:* Ellen Hawkes, "Betty Dukes," *Ms.*, Winter 2004, http://www.msmagazine.com/winter2004/womenoftheyear.asp.

22 *She saw herself and her family:* Featherstone, *Selling Women Short*, 37.

23 *Dukes's initial legal claim:* Dukes v. Wal-Mart Stores, Inc., No. C 01-2252 MJJ, 2002 WL 32769185 (N.D. Cal. Sept. 9, 2002), at *1.

23 *Indeed, she initially assumed:* Featherstone, *Selling Women Short*, 3.

24 *From the outset:* "Walmart and Low Wage America: High Expectations," *Economist*, January 28, 2016, http://www.economist.com/news/united-states/21689607-what-big-pay-rise-walmart-means-minimum-wage-debate-high-expectations. *See also* "Sam Walton: Bargain Basement Entrepreneur," *Entrepreneur*, October 9, 2008, https://www.entrepreneur.com/article/197560.

24 *In the forties and fifties:* Featherstone, *Selling Women Short*, 59 (observing that wage work by farm women tripled in the thirty years following the end of World War II).

24 *Walton saw his women employees:* Sam Walton and John Huey, *Sam Walton: Made in America, My Story* (New York: Doubleday, 1992), 99, 281, 37 ("And if the associates treat the customers well, the customers will return again and again, and that is where the real profit in this business lies, not in trying to drag strangers into your stores for one-time purchases based on splashy sales or expensive advertising. Satisfied, loyal, repeat customers are at the heart of Wal-Mart's spectacular profit margins, and those customers are loyal to us because our associates treat them better than salespeople in other stores do"; "we go out of our way to instill a sense of community involvement.")

24 *Walton thought of management:* Nelson Lichtenstein, *The Retail Revolution: How Wal-Mart Created a Brave New World of Business* (New York: Metropolitan, 2009), 74.

24 *he explained that:* Walton and Huey, *Sam Walton*, 218.

24 *And it could mean:* Walton and Huey, *Sam Walton*, 218.

25 *He liked to brag:* Nelson Lichtenstein, "Is Walmart Good for America?," *PBS*, June 9, 2004, https://www.pbs.org/wgbh/pages/frontline/shows/walmart/interviews/lichtenstein.html.

25 *The Labor Department:* Lichtenstein, *Retail Revolution*, 89–90; Rick Wartzman, *The End of Loyalty: The Rise and Fall of Good Jobs in America* (Washington, D.C.: Public Affairs, 2017), 331.

25 *Its store managers and assistant managers:* Lichtenstein, *Retail Revolution*, 103.

26 *Walmart had engineered low-price products:* Lichtenstein, *Retail Revolution*, 106.

26 *It had pioneered:* Beth Lewallan, "Walmart and the Bar Code," *Frontline*, November 16, 2004, https://www.pbs.org/wgbh/pages/frontline/shows/walmart/secrets/barcode.html.

26   *Around the time of the* Dukes *litigation:* Lichtenstein, *Retail Revolution*, 92; Complaint, *Dukes et al. v. Wal-Mart Stores, Inc.*, No. 3:01CV02252 (N.D. Cal. filed Oct. 27, 2011), https://perma.cc/DD2N-2D7F.

26   *The managers "are relentlessly and mercilessly graded":* Lichtenstein, *Retail Revolution*, 60.

26   *Should their labor costs rise:* Lichtenstein, *Retail Revolution*, 88.

26   *As Walmart expanded nationally:* Walton and Huey, *Sam Walton*, 218.

27   *Still, the Supreme Court's opinion: Wal-Mart Stores, Inc. v. Dukes*, 564 U.S. 338, 343 (2011) (stating that "[a]dmission to Wal-Mart's management training program, however, does require . . . a willingness to relocate").

27   *some managers continued:* Naomi Schoenbaum, "The Family and the Market at Wal-Mart," *DePaul Law Review* 62 (2013): 759, 760 n. 5. *See also* Walton and Huey, *Sam Walton*, 218. ("In the old days, retailers felt the same way about women that they did about college boys, only more so. In addition to thinking women weren't free to move, they didn't think women could handle anything but the clerk jobs because the managers usually did so much of the physical labor—unloading trucks and hauling merchandise out of the stockroom on a two-wheeler, mopping the floors and cleaning the windows if necessary.")

27   *This meant there were:* Lichtenstein, *Retail Revolution*, 103–106.

27   *Assistant managers reportedly worked:* Lichtenstein, *Retail Revolution*, 103–106.

27   *Within this system:* Laura Clawson, "This Week in the War on Workers: Walmart Loses $54 Million Wage Theft Lawsuit," *Daily Kos*, November 26, 2016, https://www.dailykos.com/story/2016/11/26/1603451 /-This-week-in-the-war-on-workers-Walmart-loses-54-million-wage -theft-lawsuit. As this book goes to press, Walmart raised pay well above the federal minimum wage of $7.25 per hour in a tight labor market to reduce employee turnover. *See* Sharon Edelson, "Walmart Raises Average Hourly Pay to over $17.50, Improvements to Working Conditions," *Forbes*, January 24, 2023, 1:41 p.m., ET, https://www.forbes.com /sites/sharonedelson/2023/01/24/walmart-announces-average-us-hourly -wage-hike-to-over-1750-and-other-new-investments-in-associates/?sh =34612f011a1e.

27   *Some managers, trying to reconcile:* Steven Halebsky, review of *The Retail Revolution, Sociological Forum* 27, no. 1 (March 2012): 255.

27   *As the* New York Times *reported:* Steven Greenhouse, "Suits Say Wal-Mart Forces Workers to Toil Off the Clock," *New York Times*, June 25, 2002, https://www.nytimes.com/2002/06/25/us/suits-say-wal-mart-forces-work ers-to-toil-off-the-clock.html.

27   *simply "adjusted" the time cards:* Lichtenstein, *Retail Revolution*, 107. Lichtenstein was writing in 2009. There are still numerous wage and hour cases being filed against Walmart alleging misclassification and time-shaving. *See, e.g., Quiles v. Wal-Mart Store, Inc.*, No. 16-9479, 2020 WL 1969940 (D. N.J. Apr. 24, 2020); "Wal-Mart Hit with Time-Shaving and Misclassification Lawsuits," Pechman Law Group (blog), November 29, 2018,

https://pechmanlaw.com/blog/walmart-hit-with-time-shaving-and-mis classification-lawsuits; *Braun v. Wal-Mart Stores, Inc.*, 106 A.3d 656, 658 (Pa. 2014).

28 *Walmart, in turn, accepted*: Wayne F. Cascio, "The High Cost of Low Wages," *Harvard Business Review*, December 2006, https://hbr.org/2006/12/the -high-cost-of-low-wages.

28 *Workers who stepped*: See, e.g., *McPadden v. Wal-Mart Stores E., L.P.*, No. 14 -CV-475-SM, 2017 WL 61933 (D.N.H. Jan. 5, 2017); Chris Morran, "Walmart Ordered to Pay $31 Million for Retaliating Against Pharmacist Whistleblower," *Consumerist*, January 29, 2016, https://consumerist .com/2016/01/29/walmart-ordered-to-pay-31-million-for-retaliating-against -pharmacist-whistleblower/; "EEOC Sues Walmart for Sexual Harassment and Retaliation," U.S. Equal Employment Opportunity Commission, press release, September, 19, 2023, https://www.eeoc.gov/newsroom/eeoc-sues -walmart-sexual-harassment-and-retaliation.

28 *While these abuses were not targeted at women*: Brad Seligman, "Patriarchy at the Checkout Counter: The *Dukes v. Wal-Mart Stores, Inc.* Class Action Suit," in *Wal-Mart: The Face of Twenty-First-Century Capitalism*, ed. Nelson Lichtenstein (New York: New Press, 2006), 238.

28 *Meanwhile, Walmart's loyal*: The nonpartisan Government Accountability Office issued a report in late 2020 on full-time workers who rely on federal benefit programs; in a number of states, including Arkansas, Walmart was the employer of the largest number of food stamp recipients. Government Accountability Office, Federal Social Safety Net Programs: Millions of Full-Time Workers Rely on Federal Health Care and Food Assistance Programs, table 25 (2020), https://www.gao.gov/assets/gao-21-45.pdf. This was also true in Georgia and Indiana, for example, according to tables 27 and 29.

28 *Out of the goodness of their hearts*: Hayley Peterson, "Wal-Mart Asks Workers to Donate Food to Its Needy Employees," *Business Insider*, November 20, 2014, 11:56 a.m., https://www.businessinsider.com/walmart-employee-food -drive-2014-11.

28 *In 2018, a report*: See Philip Mattera, "Grand Theft Paycheck: The Large Corporations Shortchanging Their Workers' Wages," Corporate Research Project, report, Good Jobs First website, June 2018, 8, https://www.good jobsfirst.org/sites/default/files/docs/pdfs/wagetheft_report.pdf.

29 *When Dukes started at Walmart*: Walmart Digital Museum, [no date], https://www.walmartmuseum.com/content/walmartmuseum/en_us/time line/decades/1980.html (last visited November 30, 2023).

29 *They were stunned*: *Dukes v. Wal-Mart Stores, Inc.*, 222 F.R.D. 137, 146 (N.D. Cal. 2004), *aff'd*, 474 F.3d 1214 (9th Cir. 2007), *opinion withdrawn and superseded on denial of reh'g*, 509 F.3d 1168 (9th Cir. 2007), *on reh'g en banc*, 603 F.3d 571 (9th Cir. 2010), *rev'd*, 564 U.S. 338 (2011). ("In general, roughly 65 percent of hourly employees are women, while roughly 33 percent of management employees are women . . . [of] store manager[s]—14 percent [are women].")

29   *By contrast, in the retail industry:* The plaintiff's expert in the Walmart lit-
     igation concluded that among Walmart's top twenty competitors in the re-
     tail industry, women were 56.5% of store managers, but he noted Walmart's
     claims that if it "had counted its highest-level hourly-wage supervisors as
     'managers' . . . the way it believes several of [the] comparator firms do, the
     entire purported disparity [vis-à-vis those firms] vanishes." Richard A.
     Nagareda, "Class Certification in the Age of Aggregate Proof," *New York
     University Law Review* 84 (2009): 97, 173, 223.

30   *With 1.6 million plaintiffs:* Declaration of Richard Drogin, PhD, in Support
     of Plaintiffs' Motion for Class Certification 14, April 23, 2003, https://www
     .cohenmilstein.com/sites/default/files/Drogin.pdf, table 7. *See also* Richard
     Drogin, "Statistical Analysis of Gender Patterns in Wal-Mart Workforce,"
     Portland Mercury, February 2003, 15, https://www.portlandmercury.com
     /images/blogimages/2011/09/15/1316128387-r2.pdf.

30   *At a press conference:* "Wal-Mart Hit with Lawsuit," CNN, June 19, 2001,
     http://www.cnn.com/2001/BUSINESS/06/19/walmart.reut/.

30   *Walmart's Employment of Women in Various Positions:* Chart is based on
     data from *Dukes*, 222 F.R.D. at 146–147 (light gray positions are salaried;
     dark gray positions are hourly).

31   *Yet only one-third of the managers: Dukes*, 564 U.S. at 370 (Ginsburg, J., dis-
     senting). ("Women fill 70 percent of the hourly jobs in the retailer's stores
     but make up only '33 percent of management employees.'")

31   *Another manager told a female employee:* Deborah Thompson Eisenberg,
     "*Wal-Mart Stores v. Dukes*: Lessons for the Legal Quest for Equal Pay," *New
     England Law Review* 46 (2012): 229, 245 n. 90, 258.

31   *"Men need to be":* Eisenberg, "*Wal-Mart Stores v. Dukes*," 258.

31   *"Retail is for housewives":* Eisenberg, "*Wal-Mart Stores v. Dukes*," 244 n. 87.

31   *According to a Utah:* Eisenberg, "*Wal-Mart Stores v. Dukes*," 244 n. 87.

31   *A store manager in Texas:* "Wal-Mart's Violation of US Workers' Rights to
     Freedom of Association," Human Rights Watch, report, April 30, 2007,
     https://www.hrw.org/report/2007/04/30/discounting-rights/wal-marts-vio
     lation-us-workers-right-freedom-association.

32   *The lawyers found evidence that Walmart:* Melissa Hart, "Learning from
     Walmart," University of Colorado Law Legal Studies Research Paper No. 06-
     36, 2006, https://papers.ssrn.com/sol3/papers.cfm?abstract_id=936771.

32   *Lichtenstein, who has written extensively:* Lichtenstein, ed., *Wal-Mart*, 15.

32   *That effort required political lobbying:* Drew Desilver, "5 Facts About the
     Minimum Wage," Pew Research Center, report, January 4, 2017, https://
     www.pewresearch.org/fact-tank/2017/01/04/5-facts-about-the-minimum
     -wage/.

32   *By 2018, 303 of the Fortune 500 companies:* When companies are at risk of
     not meeting their financial forecasts . . . they turn to wage theft. Clark Mer-
     refield, "When Companies Barely Meet or Beat Earnings Forecasts, Watch
     Out for Wage Theft," Journalist's Resource website, August 5, 2021, https://

journalistsresource.org/economics/wage-theft-earnings-pressure/. *See also* Aneesh Raghunandan, "Financial Misconduct and Employee Mistreatment: Evidence from Wage Theft," *Review of Accounting Studies* 26 (2021): 867 (finding "firms whose CEOs have greater risk-related incentives [i.e., higher vega] are more likely to engage in wage theft").

32   *And while wage theft*: Ihna Mangundayao et al., "More Than $3 Billion in Stolen Wages Recovered for Workers Between 2017 and 2020," Economic Policy Institute, report, December 22, 2021, https://www.epi.org/publica tion/wage-theft-2021/.

33   *And, although women made up less*: Jasmine Tucker and Kayla Patrick, "Low-Wage Jobs Are Women's Jobs: The Overrepresentation in Low Wage Work," National Women's Law Center, report, [no date], https://nwlc.org/res ources/low-wage-jobs-are-womens-jobs-the-overrepresentation-of-women -in-low-wage-work/ (last visited July 29, 2018). *See also* "Percent Distribu- tion of Workers Paid Hourly Rates with Earnings at or Below Minimum Wage in the U.S. 2020, by Full and Part Time Status and Gender," *Statista*, 2021, https://www.statista.com/statistics/299318/percent-distribution-of-us -minimum-wage-workers-by-gender-and-working-hours/.

33   *Meanwhile, most women*: Desilver, "5 Facts About Minimum Wage."

33   *Mr. Sam hated unions*: Lichtenstein, *Retail Revolution*, 156. *See also* Walton and Huey, *Sam Walton*, 164.

33   *"Labor unions are nothing"*: Matthew Schoenfeld, "Hillary Clinton's Wal-Mart Duplicity," *USA Today*, February 22, 2016, 6:00 a.m., ET, https://www.usa today.com/story/opinion/2016/02/22/hillary-clinton-wal-mart-minimum -wage-layoffs-store-closures-column/80225734/.

33   *Studies show*: Elise Gould and Celine McNicholas, "Unions Help Narrow the Gender Wage Gap," Economic Policy Institute, report, April 3, 2017, https:// www.epi.org/blog/unions-help-narrow-the-gender-wage-gap/.

33   *Union membership increases the wages*: Gould and McNicholas, "Unions Help Narrow."

33   *Unionized women*: Wendy Chun-Hoon and Liz Shuler, "Want Equal Pay? Get a Union," U.S. Department of Labor (blog), February 15, 2022, https:// blog.dol.gov/2022/02/15/want-equal-pay-get-a-union#:~:text=Being%20 represented%20by%20a%20union,the%20course%20of%20their%20careers.

34   *In addition, unions*: Chun-Hoon and Shuler, "Want Equal Pay?"

34   *Declines in union membership*: "Unions Help Reduce Disparities and Strengthen Our Democracy," Economic Policy Institute, report, April 23, 2021, https://www.epi.org/publication/unions-help-reduce-disparities-and -strengthen-our-democracy/.

34   *During the Reagan era*: During the eighties, Walton created two foundations, one controlled by his family and a second controlled by Walmart, that would ultimately channel millions in tax-free money to charitable and political causes, including opposition to raises in the minimum wage and anti-union ef- forts. *See* "Walmart Foundation: History," Influence Watch website, [no date], https://www.influencewatch.org/non-profit/walmart-foundation/#history

(last visited May 17, 2022); "Walton Family Foundation," Influence Watch website, [no date], https://www.influencewatch.org/non-profit/walton-fam ily-foundation-inc-walmart/ (last visited May 17, 2022).

34 *Bush administration even placed:* Lichtenstein, *Retail Revolution*, 242. Indeed, when the NLRB threatened Walmart with an "extraordinary nationwide remedy" that could have resulted in personal fines of over $10,000 each for store managers engaged in illegal union suppression, the Bush administration simply replaced the NLRB General Counsel preparing to bring the action. His successor dropped the case. Lichtenstein, *Retail Revolution*, 181.

34 *Making an all-out effort:* "Discounting Rights: Wal-Mart's Violation of US Workers' Right to Freedom of Association," Human Rights Watch, report, April 30, 2007, https://www.hrw.org/report/2007/04/30/discounting-rights /wal-marts-violation-us-workers-right-freedom-association#. *See also* Lichtenstein, *Retail Revolution*, 136, 188–189.

34 *Empirical studies show:* Lee Epstein and Mitu Gulati, "A Century of Business in the Supreme Court, 1920–2020," *Minnesota Law Review Headnotes* 107 (2022): 49, 57. *See also* William M. Landes and Richard A. Posner, "How Business Fares in the Supreme Court," *Minnesota Law Review* 97 (2013): 1431, 1449, 1471.

35 *and that the Court's pro-business:* Epstein and Gulati, "A Century of Business," 59.

35 *Moreover, law professor:* Elizabeth Pollman, "The Supreme Court and the Pro-Business Paradox," *Harvard Law Review* 135 (2021): 220, 225.

35 *The Court has produced:* Janus v. AFSCME, 585 U.S. 2448 (2018); Joan Biskupic, "John Roberts Is All Business in His Conservatism," CNN, June 23, 2021, https://www.cnn.com/2021/06/23/politics/john-roberts-conser vative-california-unions/index.html. *See also* Scott A. Budow, "How the Roberts Court Has Changed Labor and Employment Law," *Illinois Law Review Online* (2021): 281, 282. ("Over the last sixteen years, the Roberts Court has reshaped the balance of power between employers and employees through these closely divided decisions, often in measurable ways.")

35 *make it harder to bring:* Epic Sys. Corp. v. Lewis, 138 S. Ct. 1612 (2018).

35 *The Supreme Court's:* Andrea Flynn, "The Supreme Court's War on Women Is Also a War on Workers," *Washington Post*, July 23, 2018, https://www .washingtonpost.com/news/posteverything/wp/2018/07/23/the-su preme-courts-war-on-women-is-also-a-war-on-workers/?utm_term= .d75788c4e092.

35 *The changes not only:* Katherine Anne Long, "New Amazon Data Shows Black, Latino, and Female Employees Are Underrepresented in Best-paid Jobs," *Seattle Times*, April 14, 2021, 1:42 p.m., https://www.seattletimes.com /business/amazon/new-amazon-data-shows-black-latino-and-female-em ployees-are-underrepresented-in-best-paid-jobs/; Alex N. Press, "Amazon Waged a Brutal Anti-Union Campaign. Unsurprisingly, They Won," *Jacobin*, April 9, 2021, https://www.jacobinmag.com/2021/04/amazon-bessemer -union-drive-vote-nlrb; David Streitfeld, "How Amazon Crushes Unions,"

New York Times, March 16, 2021, https://www.nytimes.com/2021/03/16/technology/amazon-unions-virginia.html.

35 *The effort to keep out unions:* Celine McNicholas et al., "Employers Are Charged with Violating Federal Law in 41.5% of All Union Election Campaigns," Economic Policy Institute, report, December 11, 2019. https://www.epi.org/publication/unlawful-employer-opposition-to-union-election-campaigns/.

35 *In 2022:* Justin McCarthy, "U.S. Approval of Labor Unions at Highest Point Since 1965," Gallup, report, August 30, 2022, https://news.gallup.com/poll/398303/approval-labor-unions-highest-point-1965.aspx.

35 *And the unionization victory:* Coco McPherson, "Amazon Employees: Victory Is Inspiring Workers at Other Retailers. Could a Walmart Union Be Next?," *Capital & Main*, April 26, 2022, https://capitalandmain.com/amazon-employees-victory-is-inspiring-workers-at-other-retailers-could-a-walmart-union-be-next.

35 *Given entrenched industry:* Greg Rosalsky, "You May Have Heard of the 'Union Boom.' The Numbers Tell a Different Story," NPR, February 28, 2023, https://www.npr.org/sections/money/2023/02/28/1159663461/you-may-have-heard-of-the-union-boom-the-numbers-tell-a-different-story.

36 *On June 20, 2011: Wal-Mart Stores, Inc. v. Dukes,* 564 U.S. 342 (2011).

37 *For example, in a 2004 case:* Steven Greenhouse, "Abercrombie & Fitch Bias Case Is Settled," *New York Times*, November 17, 2004, https://www.nytimes.com/2004/11/17/us/abercrombie-fitch-bias-case-is-settled.html.

37 *Justice Antonin Scalia's opinion:* See, e.g., Elizabeth J. Cabraser, "The Class Abides: Class Actions and the 'Roberts Court,'" *Akron Law Review* 48 (2015): 757, 759; A. Benjamin Spencer, "Class Actions, Heightened Commonality, and Declining Access to Justice," *Boston University Law Review* 93 (2013): 441, 443.

37 *In her dissent: Dukes,* 564 U.S. at 372 (Ginsburg, J., concurring in part and dissenting in part).

37 *She added that: Dukes,* 564 U.S. at 371 (citations omitted).

37 *He insisted that: Dukes,* 564 U.S. at 355 (emphasis in original).

38 *It also meant:* Rick Wartzman, *Still Broke: Walmart's Remarkable Transformation and the Limits of Socially Conscious Capitalism* (Washington, D.C.: Public Affairs, 2022), 117.

38 *"But, there is no doubt":* Statement of Betty Dukes, Lead Plaintiff in *Wal-Mart v. Dukes*, Before the Committee on the Judiciary United States Senate, *Barriers to Justice: How the Supreme Court's Recent Rulings Will Affect Corporate Behavior*, June 29, 2011, 5, https://www.judiciary.senate.gov/imo/media/doc/11-6-29%20Dukes%20Testimony.pdf.

38 *Although some of the women:* See, e.g., Edward Segal, "Walmart Is Sued for Gender and Race Discrimination by EEOC," *Forbes.com*, February 11, 2022, 4:08 p.m., https://www.forbes.com/sites/edwardsegal/2022/02/11/wal

mart-is-sued-for-gender-and-race-discrimination-by-eeoc/?sh=b7cb1d4
56143.

39   *In its obituary:* Corkery, "Betty Dukes, Greeter Whose Walmart Lawsuit."

39   *number of female managers:* Walmart website, Culture, Diversity Equity, and Inclusion Report, 2023, 4, https://corporate.walmart.com/purpose/be longing-diversity-equity-inclusion/belonging-diversity-equity-and-inclu sion-report (showing that 44.07% of "Management" and 36.75% of "Officer" positions are held by women, with 18.07% and 9.87% respectively held by women of color).

39   *It now issues:* Walmart website, Culture, Diversity, Equity and Inclusion Report, [no date], https://corporate.walmart.com/purpose/culture-diversity -equity-and-inclusion-report#cdei-report (last visited April 24, 2023).

39   *Walmart's CEO:* Lauren Thomas, "Walmart CEO Says Congress Should Fix the 'Lagging' Minimum Wage," *CNBC,* June 5, 2019, 3:51 p.m., ET, https:// www.cnbc.com/2019/06/05/walmart-ceo-federal-minimum-wage-is-lag ging-congress-should-act.html.

39   *Particularly in the aftermath:* U.S. Government Accountability Office, "Which Workers Are the Most Affected by Automation and What Could Help Them Get New Jobs?," GAO.gov (blog), August 23, 2022, https://www.gao.gov/blog /which-workers-are-most-affected-automation-and-what-could-help-them -get-new-jobs ("Researchers estimate that anywhere from 9% to 47% of jobs could be automated in the future").

39   *Walmart has accelerated:* Hope King, "Walmart Defines Timeline for Automation Push," *Axios,* April 6, 2023, https://www.axios.com/2023/04/06 /walmart-automation-logistics.

40   *used his riches to entrench:* Catherine Ruetschlin, "How Walmart and Home Depot Are Buying Huge Political Influence," *American Prospect,* December 3, 2014, https://prospect.org/justice/walmart-home-depot-buying-huge-politi cal-influence/.

41   *As Union Membership Declines, Income Inequality Decreases:* Data on union membership follow the composite series found in Historical Statistics of the United States through 1982, updated through 2021 using Bureau of Labor statistics, series ID: LUU0204899600. Income inequality (share of income to top 10%) data are from the World Income Database. From Josh Bivens et al., "What to Know About This Summer's Strike Activity," Economic Policy Institute, report, August 30, 2023, https://www.epi.org/publication/summer -strike-activity/#fig-a. Reprinted with permission of Economic Policy Institute.

2. How to Rig the Game: Schaefer v. General Electric

44   *Welch, disgruntled about:* David Gelles, *The Man Who Broke Capitalism: How Jack Welch Gutted the Heartland and Crushed the Soul of Corporate America—and How to Undo His Legacy* (New York: Simon & Schuster, 2022), 28.

45 *To understand what happened*: Tony Dobrowolski, "The Rise and Fall of GE's Empire," *Berkshire Eagle*, July 1, 2011, https://www.berkshireeagle.com /archives/the-rise-and-fall-of-ges-empire/article_3003a24a-6974-594a -9303-537cd1c4ee69.html#:~:text=From%20its%20beginnings%20in%20 the,part%20of%20life%20in%20Pittsfield.

45 *A young man was taught*: Gelles, *The Man Who Broke Capitalism*, 124.

45 *GE considered the "acid test"*: Rick Wartzman, *The End of Loyalty: The Rise and Fall of Good Jobs in America* (Washington, D.C.: Public Affairs, 2017), 135.

45 *These executives "belonged" to companies*: William H. Whyte, *The Organization Man* (New York: Simon & Schuster, 1956), 6–8.

45 *"an IBM man"*: John Kenneth Galbraith, *The New Industrial State* (Boston: Houghton Mifflin, 1967), 188.

46 *Pay levels did not vary*: Galbraith, *New Industrial State*, 147–148, 138–139.

46 *Today it's a mind-blowing*: Josh Bivens and Jori Kandra, "CEO Pay Has Sky-rocketed 1,460% Since 1978," Economic Policy Institute, report, October 4, 2022, https://www.epi.org/publication/ceo-pay-in-2021/.

46 *Instead, the executives of the era*: June Carbone and Nancy Levit, "The Death of the Firm," *Minnesota Law Review* 101 (2017): 963, 990.

46 *Modern management theorists argue*: See, e.g., Lynn Stout, *Cultivating Conscience: How Good Laws Make Good People* (Princeton, NJ: Princeton University Press, 2010), 169 (describing how firms influence team unity and bonding by encouraging loyalty to the firm).

46 *Critics, on the other hand*: Gary Sernovitz, "What 'The Organization Man' Can Tell Us About Inequality Today," *New Yorker*, December 29, 2016, https://www.newyorker.com/business/currency/what-the-organization -man-can-tell-us-about-inequality-today. ("To Whyte, the central problem was that the organization men actually liked being organization men.")

47 *He disliked that the average 1950s executive*: Whyte, *Organization Man*, 77, 131, 137.

48 *Winning the competition*: Richard Bernstein, "Winning the Business Game with a Few Basic Principles," review of *Jack: Straight from the Gut* by Jack Welch, with John Byrne, *New York Times*, September 14, 2001, http://www .nytimes.com/2001/09/14/books/books-of-the-times-winning-the-business -game-with-a-few-basic-principles.html [https://perma.cc/SS4G-PQAW].

48 *Indeed, during his*: John Holusha, "A Softer 'Neutron Jack' at G.E.," *New York Times*, March 4, 1992, https://www.nytimes.com/1992/03/04/business/a -softer-neutron-jack-at-ge.html.

48 *"I've never seen a business ruined"*: Richard Bernstein, "'Jack: Straight From the Gut' by Jack Welch, with John A. Byrne," *Chron.com*, September 23, 2001, https://www.chron.com/life/article/Jack-Straight-From-the-Gut-by-Jack -Welch-with-2073763.php.

48 *By 1999, Welch's*: Brian J. Hall, "What You Need to Know About Stock Options," *Harvard Business Review*, March 2000, https://hbr.org/2000/03/what -you-need-to-know-about-stock-options.

48 *During the eighteen-year*: Barry Ritzholtz, "Judging GE's Jeff Immelt Versus

Jack Welch," *Bloomberg.com*, June 12, 2017, https://www.bloomberg.com /view/articles/2017-06-12/judging-ge-s-jeff-immelt-versus-jack-welch.

48   *Welch had figured out:* Roger F. Martin, *Fixing the Game: Bubbles, Crashes, and What Capitalism Can Learn from the NFL* (Cambridge, MA: Harvard Business Review Press, 2011), 29, 97 (detailing during the Jack Welch era, General Electric was able to meet or beat earnings forecasts an unbelievable 96% of the time, with earnings from 89% of those quarters hitting analysts' forecasts to the exact penny).

49   *"What a kick":* Wartzman, *End of Loyalty*, 134, 135.

49   *Every year, Welch:* Dave Davies, "Short-Term Profits and Long-Term Consequences—Did Jack Welch Break Capitalism?," NPR, June 1, 2022, 1:22 p.m., EDT, https://www.npr.org/2022/06/01/1101505691/short-term -profits-and-long-term-consequences-did-jack-welch-break-capitalism.

49   *With large bonuses:* Jack Welch, "Jack Welch: 'Rank-and-Yank'? That's Not How It's Done," *Wall Street Journal*, November 14, 2013, https://www .wsj.com/articles/8216rankandyank8217-that8217s-not-how-it8217s-done -1384473281.

50   *Economists and business school professors:* Milton Friedman, "The Social Responsibility of Business Is to Increase Its Profits," *New York Times*, September 13, 1970, https://www.nytimes.com/1970/09/13/archives/a-friedman -doctrine-the-social-responsibility-of-business-is-to.html. *See also* Milton Friedman, *Capitalism and Freedom*, 40th edition (Chicago: University of Chicago Press, 2002), 133 (originally published in 1962).

50   *It wasn't just about:* "'Neutron Jack' Exits," *New York Times*, September 9, 2001, https://www.nytimes.com/2001/09/09/opinion/neutron-jack-exits.html. *See also* John Holusha, "A Softer 'Neutron Jack' at G.E.," *New York Times*, March 4, 1992, https://www.nytimes.com/1992/03/04/business/a-softer-neu tron-jack-at-ge.html. ("In the 1980's, Mr. Welch exemplified the relentless executive willing to mow down any employees standing between him and a brighter bottom line. Through layoffs, plant closings and the sale of busi- nesses, he eliminated 100,000 jobs, leaving 284,000. As profits increased, his style was widely respected and imitated.")

50   *Jeff Skilling at Enron:* Alan Murray, "Should I Rank My Employees?," in *Wall Street Journal Guide to Management* (New York: Harper Business, 2009). Adapted as an online excerpt at http://guides.wsj.com/management/re cruiting-hiring-and-firing/should-i-rank-my-employees/ [https://perma.cc /7Q99-AULE] (last visited May 12, 2022).

50   *We think it can better: See, e.g.,* Jennifer L. Berdahl et al., "Work as a Mascu- linity Contest," *Journal of Social Issues* 74 (2018): 422, 430; Kenneth Matos et al., "Toxic Leadership and the Masculinity Contest Culture: How 'Win or Die' Cultures Breed Abusive Leadership," *Journal of Social Issues* 74 (2018): 500, 502.

50   *But the closer:* Susan Chira, "Why Women Aren't C.E.O.s, According to Women Who Almost Were," *New York Times*, July 21, 2017, https://www.ny times.com/2017/07/21/sunday-review/women-ceos-glass-ceiling.html?

login=email&auth=login-email (a female executive described how although she hadn't felt "handicapped" before she made it "to the C-suite . . . the next rungs of the ladder depend not only on results but also on prevailing in an environment where everyone is competing for a chance at the top job.")

51   *Despite her consistent:* Complaint at 20, ¶ 62. *Schaefer v. Gen. Elec. Co.*, Case No. 307-cv-00858-PCD (D. Conn. May 31, 2007), http://s3.amazonaws .com/fcmd/documents/documents/000/000/745/original/general-electric -schaefer_complaint.pdf?1423019518 [hereafter, Schaefer Complaint].

51   *The only reason:* Schaefer Complaint at 5, ¶ 10.

51   *Capito acknowledged that "this":* Claudia H. Deutsch, "Lawyer Files Bias Suit Against G.E.," *New York Times*, June 1, 2007, http://www.nytimes.com /2007/06/01/business/01bias.html.

51   *Even worse:* Schaefer Complaint at 9, ¶ 24.

51   *Schaefer hired her own lawyers: Schaefer v. Gen. Elec. Co.*, No. 3:07–CV–0858 (PCD), 2008 WL 649189 (D. Conn. Jan. 22, 2008) at *1.

52   *In an interview with:* Deutsch, "Lawyer Files Bias Suit."

52   *Schaefer's complaint stated that:* Schaefer Complaint, at 3, ¶ 9.

52   *Schaefer expressed pride at the time:* "Former GC Settles Gender Discrimination Suit Against General Electric," *Law.com*, January 28, 2009, https://www .law.com/almID/1202427825855/Former-GC-Settles-Gender-Discrimina tion-Suit-Against-General-Electric/?slreturn=20220214174502.

52   *In a joint statement:* John Christofferson, "Former GC Settles Gender Discrimination Suit Against General Electric," *Law.com*, January 28, 2009, https://www.law.com/almID/1202427825855/; *General Electric Gender Discrimination Class Action* (2017), http://umkclaw.link/gegenderclassac tion.

52   *Like most such settlements:* Debra Cassens Weiss, "Ex-General Counsel of GE Unit Settles Gender Bias Case," *ABA Journal*, January 27, 2009, https:// www.abajournal.com/news/article/ex-general_counsel_of_ge_unit_settles _gender_bias_case#google_vignette.

52   *The clue in the complaint:* Deutsch, "Lawyer Files Bias Suit."

52   *An important Welch move:* Dexter Van Dango, "The House that Jack Built," *Monitor Daily*, [no date], https://www.monitordaily.com/article-posts/ge -capital-the-house-that-jack-built/ (last visited April 3, 2023).

53   *if Welch had trouble:* James B. Stewart, "Did the Jack Welch Model Sow Seeds of G.E.'s Decline?," *New York Times*, June 15, 2017, https://www.nytimes.com /2017/06/15/business/ge-jack-welch-immelt.html?_r=0.

53   *As one CNN reporter:* Terence P. Pare, "GE Monkeys with Its Money Machine," *CNN Money*, February 21, 1994, https://money.cnn.com/magazines /fortune/fortune_archive/1994/02/21/78990/index.htm.

53   *GE Capital had:* Schaefer Complaint at ¶¶ 34–37, 58, *Securities & Exchange Comm'n v. General Elec. Co.*, Civil Action No. 3:09-CV-01235 (D. Conn. Aug. 4, 2009), https://www.sec.gov/litigation/complaints/2009/comp21166.pdf.

53 *According to* New York Times *business reporter*: Gelles, *The Man Who Broke Capitalism*, 147.

53 *with GE spending $200 million:* Floyd Norris, "Inside G.E., a Little Bit of Enron," *New York Times*, August 7, 2009, https://www.nytimes.com/2009/08 /07/business/07norris1.html.

53 *ultimately paying a:* U.S. Securities and Exchange Commission, "SEC Charges General Electric with Accounting Fraud: GE Agrees to Pay $50 Million to Settle SEC's Charges," SEC, press release, August 4, 2009, https://www .sec.gov/news/press/2009/2009-178.htm.

54 *GE's regulatory filings:* Tim Reason and Marie Leone, "GE Settles Accounting Fraud Charges," *CFO.com*, August 4, 2009, https://www.cfo.com/accounting -tax/2009/08/ge-settles-accounting-fraud-charges/.

54 *Dineen had taken charge:* U.S. Securities and Exchange Commission, "SEC Charges General Electric."

54 *Dineen needed a subordinate:* "Through the Looking Glass," KPMG, report, (2016): 17, https://assets.kpmg/content/dam/kpmg/xx/pdf/2016/0 8/through-the-looking-glass.pdf ("[CEOs] acknowledg[e] the importance of a confident and trusted GC in a crisis").

54 *his highly touted proteges:* Gelles, *Man Who Broke Capitalism*, 80, 84, 106–107.

54 *And those lies:* Michael C. Jensen, "Paying People to Lie: The Truth About the Budgeting Process," *European Financial Management* 9 (2003): 379, https://papers.ssrn.com/sol3/papers.cfm?abstract_id=267651.

55 *And although most companies:* "Stack Ranking—All You Need to Know," *Corvisio.com*, April 3, 2020, https://medium.com/@corvisio/stack-ranking -all-you-need-to-know-a5339c27ad83 (by one estimate, about 30% of Fortune 500 companies currently use stack ranking as a method of performance evaluation). *See also* A. J. Hess, "Ranking Workers Can Hurt Morale, Productivity. Companies Are Doing It Anyway," *Fast Company*, February 16, 2023, https://www.fastcompany.com/90850190/stack-ranking -workers-hurt-morale-productivity-tech-companies (noting that stack ranking is a method that is again taking hold in the tech industry).

55 *the reciprocal loyalty:* Wartzman, *End of Loyalty*, 312.

55 *In 1990, more than a third:* Jordan Pfuntner, "Percent of Private Industry Workers Participating in Retirement Plans, Selected Periods, 1990–2003," U.S. Bureau of Labor Statistics, report, 2004, https://www.bls.gov/opub/mlr /cwc/percent-of-private-industry-workers-participating-in-retirement -plans-selected-periods-1990-2003.pdf.

55 *Today, that is true:* U.S. Department of Labor, "Retirement Plans for Workers in Private Industry and State and Local Government in 2022," U.S. Bureau of Labor Statistics, report, February 1, 2023, https://www.bls.gov/opub /ted/2023/retirement-plans-for-workers-in-private-industry-and-state -and-local-government-in-2022.htm.

55 *First, changing to a system:* Marta M. Elvira and Mary E. Graham, "Not Just a Formality: Pay System Formalization and Sex-Related Earnings Effects,"

Organization Science 13 (2002): 601, 614 (finding a 25% difference in bonus pay among men and women holding the same jobs).

55 *indeed, differences in incentive awards:* Stefania Albanesi, Claudia Olivetti, and María José Prados, "Gender and Dynamic Agency: Theory and Evidence on the Compensation of Top Executives," Federal Reserve Bank of New York Staff, report no. 718, March 2015, https://www.newyorkfed.org /medialhttps://www.sec.gov/litigation/complaints/2009/comp21166.pdf .ibrary/media/research/staff_reports/sr718.pdf.

55 *A 2018 study tracking: See, e.g.,* Mita Goldar et al., "Rethinking Gender Pay Equity in a More Transparent World," ADP Research Institute, report 110, 3 (2019), https://www.adp.com/-/media/ri/pdf/rethinking%20 gender%20pay%20inequity%20in%20a%20more%20transparent%20 world.ashx (reporting in 2018 that a study tracking 11,000 employees found that women's bonuses were 69% of men's).

55 *While the stakes are lower: See, e.g.,* Paul A. Gompers et al., "Gender Effects in Venture Capital," unpublished manuscript, May 12, 2014, https://papers .ssrn.com/sol3/papers.cfm?abstract_id=2445497 (observing "that women tend to perform better in firms that have more formal processes and greater bureaucracy"). See Chapter 1, this book, for differences in bonus pay awards to Walmart managers.

56 *Sociologists find:* Claire Cain Miller, "Women Did Everything Right. Then Work 'Got Greedy,'" *New York Times,* April 26, 2019, https://www.nytimes .com/2019/04/26/upshot/women-long-hours-greedy-professions.html.

56 *Before the WTA economy:* Miller, "Women Did Everything Right" (emphasis added).

56 *Those who work:* Miller, "Women Did Everything Right."

56 *"After 55 hours":* Kabir Sehgal and Deepak Chopra, "Stanford Professor: Working This Many Hours a Week Is Basically Pointless," *CNBC,* March 21, 2019, 6:29 p.m. EDT, https://www.cnbc.com/2019/03/20/stanford-study -longer-hours-doesnt-make-you-more-productive-heres-how-to-get -more-done-by-doing-less.html (citing John Pencavel, "The Productivity of Working Hours," Discussion Paper No. 8129, April 2014, https://docs. iza.org/dp8129.pdf).

56 *Instead, overwork and busyness:* Silvia Bellezza et al., "Conspicuous Consumption of Time: When Busyness and Lack of Leisure Time Become a Status Symbol," *Journal of Consumer Research* 44 (2017): 118.

56 *and performing overwork:* Alex Christian, "How Working Unpaid Hours Became Part of the Job," *BBC,* October 19, 2021, https://www.bbc.com/work life/article/20211013-how-working-unpaid-hours-became-part-of-the-job.

56 *"The reward to become":* Miller, "Women Did Everything Right."

56 *Instead, male nurses:* Paige Minemyer, "Survey: Pay Gap Between Male and Female Nurses Persists," *Fierce Health Care,* October 4, 2017, 12:55 p.m., https://www.fiercehealthcare.com/finance/nurse-salary-pay-gender-wage -gap.

56 *Male nurses today earn more*: Kathleen Gaines, "Male Nurses Earn $5,000 More Per Year Than Female Nurses, Study Finds," *Nurse.com* (blog), 2023, https://perma.cc/37GQ-RKG8/; https://www.nurse.com/blog/report-shows -increase-in-nurse-gender-pay-gap/.

57 *Second, competitive pay:* Andrea S. Gunik and Zsófia Vörös, "Why Narcissists May Be Successful Entrepreneurs: The Role of Entrepreneurial Social Identity and Overwork," *Journal of Business Venturing Insights* 19 (2023): e00364*3, *7 (finding that narcissists "are more likely to overwork than their peers" and that "this drive will eventually be reflected in higher venture performance").

57 *University of Chicago economists*: Ann Bares, "Competitive Incentives: A Turn off for Women, A Turn on for Men?," *Compensation Café*, January 28, 2011, https://www.compensationcafe.com/2011/01/competitive-incentives -a-turn-off-for-women-a-turn-on-for-men.html (quoting Jeffrey A. Flory et al., "Do Competitive Workplaces Deter Female Workers? A Large-Scale Natural Field Experiment on Job Entry Decisions," *Review of Economic Studies* 82 (2015): 122, https://doi.org/10.1093/restud/rdu030).

57 *Indeed, women may have*: Emily Grijalva et al., "Gender Differences in Narcissism: A Meta-analytic Review," *Psychology Bulletin* 141 (2015): 261, 283. *See also* Lynn A. Stout, "Killing Conscience: The Unintended Behavioral Consequences of 'Pay for Performance,'" *Journal of Corporate Law* 39 (March 2014): 2, 11, 35.

57 *As law professor Donald Langevoort*: Donald C. Langevoort, "Resetting the Corporate Thermostat: Lessons from the Recent Financial Scandals About Self-Deception, Deceiving Others and the Design of Internal Controls," *Georgetown Law Journal* 93 (2004): 285, 288.

57 *When Jack Welch*: Tomas Chamorro-Premuzic, *Why Do So Many Incompetent Men Become Leaders (and How to Fix It)* (Cambridge, MA: Harvard Business Review Press, 2019), 53.

57 *Finally, negative-sum competitions*: Berdahl et al., "Work as Masculinity Contest," 432; Naomi Cahn, June Carbone, and Nancy Levit, "Gender and the Tournament: Reinventing Antidiscrimination Law in an Age of Inequality," *Texas Law Review* 96 (2018): 425, 458–463.

57 *Research has shown*: Meera Jagannathan, "Do You Want to Be a CEO? Women Face These Extra Obstacles on Their Way to the C-Suite," *MarketWatch*, July 21, 2019, https://www.marketwatch.com/story/do-you-want-to -be-ceo-your-chances-are-much-better-if-youre-a-man-2019-06-27.

57 *Managers in intensely:* Berdahl et al., "Work as a Masculinity Contest," 435.

58 *such environments:* Stout, "Killing Conscience," 525, 534 ("incentive pay has been statistically linked with opportunistic, unethical, and even illegal executive behavior, including earning manipulations, accounting frauds, and excessive risk-taking").

58 *Multiple studies:* Alice H. Eagly, "Women as Leaders: Leadership Style vs. Leaders' Values and Attitudes," Harvard Business School Research

Symposium, *Gender & Work: Challenging Conventional Wisdom*, 2013, http://www.hbs.edu/faculty/conferences/2013-w50-research-symposium /Documents/eagly.pdf [https://perma.cc/UCJ9-G53Z]; Shankar Vedantam, "Women Held to Higher Ethical Standard Than Men, Study Shows," NPR, June 2, 2016, https://www.npr.org/2016/06/02/480487259/women-held-to -higher-ethical-standard-than-men-study-shows (study showing that when men and women were punished for ethical violations, "females had a 106 percent higher likelihood of being disbarred than males"). *See also* Laura Kray et al., "Are Women More Ethical then Men?," *Greater Good,* March 8, 2017, https://greatergood.berkeley.edu/article/item/are_women_more_eth ical_than_men; Katie Shonk, "Moral Leadership: Do Women Negotiate More Ethically Than Men?," Harvard Law School (blog), August 24, 2020, https://www.pon.harvard.edu/daily/leadership-skills-daily/moral-leader ship-do-women-negotiate-more-ethically-than-men/; Damodar Suar and Jyotiranjan Gochhayat, "Influence of Biological Sex and Gender Roles on Ethicality," *Journal of Business Ethics* 134 (March 2016): 199 (citations omit-ted) ("In a meta-analysis of 14 studies, women were found to be more ethical than men in seven of the studies, and no difference was observed in seven other studies. In another meta-analytic study of 66 pre-career student sam-ples, women were found to have higher ethical standards than men, but the difference between women and men declined as work experience increased. In still another meta-analysis of 47 studies, 49% of the studies yielded a difference between women and men in ethical behavior, 34% yielded no difference, and 17% provided mixed results. Furthermore, in a qualita-tive review of the literature, while some studies showed little or no differ-ence between men and women, none found higher standards of ethicality among men than among women. Combining the empirical, meta-analytic, and qualitative studies, the weight of the evidence suggests that women are more ethical than men."). *See also* Robert A. Peterson et al., "Effects of Nationality, Gender, and Religiosity on Business-Related Ethicality," *Jour-nal of Business Ethics* 96 (2010): 573, 574, 582 (citing cross-cultural studies showing that "females exhibit higher ethical standards and behaviors than do males" in numerous contexts). *But see* Maryam Kouchaki, "Women Act More Ethically than Men when Representing Themselves—but Not when Representing Others," *Harvard Business Review,* November 1, 2018, https:// hbr.org/2018/11/men-are-more-likely-to-act-unethically-on-their-own-be half-women-on-someone-elses.

58   *Studies also show:* Meredith Somers, "Women Are Less Likely to Be Pro-moted. Here's One Reason Why," MIT Sloan School of Management website, April 12, 2022, https://mitsloan.mit.edu/ideas-made-to-matter/women-are -less-likely-men-to-be-promoted-heres-one-reason-why.

58   *a trait often:* Chamorro-Premuzic, *Why Do So Many Incompetent Men,* 53 ("when it comes to leadership, the only advantage that men have over women [e.g., from Argentina to Norway and the United States to Japan] is the fact that manifestations of hubris—often masked as charisma or charm—are

commonly mistaken for leadership potential, and that these occur much more frequently in men than in women").

58 *men can more easily schmooze:* Dina Gerdeman, "How Schmoozing with the Boss Helps Men Get Promoted," *Harvard Business School Working Knowledge,* March 4, 2020, https://hbswk.hbs.edu/item/how-schmoozing-with-the-boss-helps-men-get-promoted.

58 *"in fact, social bonding":* Gerdeman, "How Schmoozing with the Boss."

58 *Highly competitive workplaces:* Berdahl et al., "Work as a Masculinity Contest," 431; Yasin Koc, Duygu Gulseren, and Zhanna Lyubykh, "Masculinity Contest Culture Reduces Organizational Citizenship Behaviors Through Decreased Organizational identification," *Journal of Experimental Psychology: Applied* 27 (2021): 408 (finding that masculinity contest cultures reduce organization identification in both men and women and are associated with promoting individual gains over collective or pro-social actions).

58 *In such environments:* Elaine Howard Ecklund and Di Di, "A Gendered Approach to Science Ethics for US and UK Physicists," *Science and Engineering Ethics* 23 (2017): 183, 185, https://doi.org/10.1007/s11948-016-9751-8 (if women are viewed as less willing to engage in "ethically gray conduct," they may be viewed as unwilling to do what it takes to "get ahead of the competition").

58 *Johanna Harris:* Johanna Harris, "Why Some Men Don't Trust Women in the Workplace," LinkedIn, April 16, 2014, https://www.linkedin.com/pulse/20140416103709-275490660-why-some-men-don-t-trust-women-in-the-workplace/.

59 *They often get promotions:* Quentin Fottrell, "The Controversial Theory Why More Women Have Replaced Male CEOs Since the Great Recession," *MarketWatch,* July 29, 2019, https://www.marketwatch.com/story/the-number-of-new-female-ceos-has-almost-doubled-since-2010-heres-whats-behind-that-dramatic-growth-2019-07-18?mod=mw_latestnews.

59 *The record high, set in 2023:* Emma Hinchliffe, "Women CEOs Run More than 10% of Fortune 500 Companies for the First Time in History," *Fortune,* January 12, 2023, https://fortune.com/2023/01/12/fortune-500-companies-ceos-women-10-percent/. In 2022, white women represented 21% of the C-suite generally, while women of color represented 5%. "Women in the Workplace, 2022," McKinsey & Co., report, October 18, 2022, https://www.mckinsey.com/featured-insights/diversity-and-inclusion/women-in-the-workplace.

59 *And the pipeline is leaky:* Claire Cain Miller, "The Number of Female Chief Executives Is Falling," *New York Times,* May 23, 2018, https://www.nytimes.com/2018/05/23/upshot/why-the-number-of-female-chief-executives-is-falling.html.

59 *Women are 30 percent:* Miller, "Women Did Everything Right"; Nikki Waller, "How Men and Women See the Workplace Differently," *Wall Street Journal,* September 27, 2016, http://graphics.wsj.com/how-men-and-women-see-the-workplace-differently/ (discussing 30% figure).

59   *And of the women:* Miller, "The Number of Female Chief Executives Is Falling."

59   *Over the ten-year:* Jeremy Schneider, "Are Female CEOs Better than Male CEOs?," Personal Finance Club (blog), March 7, 2023, https://www.personal financeclub.com/are-female-ceos-better-than-male-ceos/.

60   *Chart—Are Women Better?:* Schneider, "Are Female CEOs Better than Male CEOs?"

60   *A larger study of almost:* Marcus Noland et al., "Is Gender Diversity Profitable? Evidence from a Global Survey," Peterson Institute for International Economics website, February 2016, https://piie.com/publications/wp/wp 16-3.pdf. *See also* Aimee Picchi, "In Business, More Women at the Top Means More Profits," *CBS News*, February 9, 2016, https://www.cbsnews .com/news/more-women-more-profits/.

60   *Critics have condemned the myopic focus:* David Gelles and David Yaffe-Bellany, "Shareholder Value Is No Longer Everything, Top C.E.O.s Say," *New York Times*, August 19, 2019, https://www.nytimes.com/2019/08/19/business /business-roundtable-ceos-corporations.html.

60   *The Business Roundtable, an association:* Gelles and Yaffe-Bellany, "Shareholder Value."

60   *Even conservative Republican:* "Rubio Sounds Alarm on U.S. Business Investing," *Tampa Bay Times*, June 20, 2019, https://www.tampabay.com /florida-politics/buzz/2019/06/20/rubio-sounds-alarm-on-us-business-in vesting-the-stock-market-is-not-the-economy/.

61   *Influenced by the studies:* Saijel Kishan, "BlackRock Plans to Push Companies on Racial Diversity in 2021," *Bloomberg.com*, December 10, 2020, 9:06 a.m., CT, https://www.bloomberg.com/news/articles/2020-12-10/black rock-plans-to-push-companies-on-racial-diversity-in-2021.

61   *Diversity within this movement:* Naomi Cahn, June Carbone, and Nancy Levit, "The Instrumental Case for Corporate Diversity," *Minnesota Journal of Law & Inequality* 40 (2022): 117.

61   *So have several:* Michael Hatcher and Weldon Latham, "States Are Leading the Charge to Corporate Boards: Diversify!," Harvard Law School Forum on Corporate Governance, May 12, 2020, https://corpgov.law.harvard .edu/2020/05/12/states-are-leading-the-charge-to-corporate-boards-di versify/.

61   *And the Nasdaq exchange has endorsed:* Nasdaq Stock Market LLC, Self-Regulatory Organization Filing of Proposed Rule Changes (Form 19b-4) 27-28 (Dec. 1, 2020), https://listingcenter.nasdaq.com/assets/Rule Book/Nasdaq/filings/SR-NASDAQ-2020-081.pdf [https://perma.cc/6ML8 -98PG]. *See also* U.S. Securities and Exchange Commission, No. 34-90574, Self-Regulatory Organizations; Nasdaq Stock Market LLC, Notice of Filing of Proposed Rule Change to Adopt Listing Rules Related to Board Diversity 22 (2020), https://perma.cc/9MHQWJ9J.

61   *We doubt that:* Cahn, Carbone, and Levit, "Instrumental Case for Corporate Diversity."

61   *At the time of his death:* "Jack Welch Net Worth, Richest," The Richest website,

[no date], https://www.therichest.com/celebnetworth/celebrity-business/ceo/jack-welch-net-worth/ (last visited September 12, 2019).

61 *By 2022, even that:* Allan Sloan, "Jack Welch's GE Legacy Ended Last Week: R.I.P.," *Yahoo! News,* March 15, 2023, https://finance.yahoo.com/jack-welchs-ge-legacy-ended-last-week-rip-134345986.html.

62 *She founded her own:* "About Lorene Schaefer, Esq.," *Win-Win HR,* [no date], https://winwinhr.com/about-lorene-schaefer/ (last visited May 14, 2023).

3. Counting on Wall Street: Messina v. Bank of America Corp.

63 *Messina, a top female banker:* Renae Merle, "Bank of America Accused of Running a 'Bros Club' that Underpaid Female Executives," *Washington Post,* May 17, 2016, https://www.washingtonpost.com/news/business/wp/2016/05/17/bank-of-america-accused-of-running-a-bros-club-that-underpaid-female-executives/?utm_term=.4a4a15a2236c; *Messina v. Bank of Am. Corp.,* No. 1:16-cv-03653 (S.D.N.Y. 2016), Complaint, at ¶ 1, https://perma.cc/T6YU-LASB [hereafter, Messina Complaint].

63 *Further, she claimed:* Jonathan Stempel, "Former Top BofA Female Banker Settles 'Bro's Club' Bias Lawsuit," *Reuters,* September 21, 2016, 3:18 p.m., https://www.reuters.com/article/us-bank-of-america-lawsuit-genderbias/former-top-bofa-female-banker-settles-bros-club-bias-lawsuit-idUSKCN11R2P6.

63 *She was a 42-year-old single mother:* Messina Complaint, at ¶¶ 27–29.

63 *She had graduated from Marymount College:* Messina Complaint, at ¶¶ 32–33.

63 *She moved to Salomon Smith Barney:* Messina Complaint, at ¶ 35.

63 *She established her financial career:* Amy J. Binder, "Why Are Harvard Grads Still Flocking to Wall Street?," *Washington Monthly,* August 21, 2014, https://washingtonmonthly.com/2014/08/21/why-are-harvard-grads-still-flocking-to-wall-street/ (stating that in 2007, 58% of Harvard men, and 43% of Harvard women took jobs on Wall Street at graduation); Ezra Klein, "Wall Street Steps in When Ivy League Fails," *Washington Post,* February 16, 2012, https://www.washingtonpost.com/business/economy/wall-street-steps-in-when-ivy-league-fails/2012/02/16/gIQAX2weIR_story.html.

64 *women like Messina were shunted:* Matt Wirz, "Female CLO Managers Tend to Outperform Men," *Wall Street Journal,* February 8, 2019, 8:00 a.m., https://www.wsj.com/articles/female-clo-managers-tend-to-outperform-men-11549630802.

64 *In 2011, she was promoted:* Messina Complaint, at ¶¶ 37–41.

64 *GlobalCapital, which styles:* "About Us," *GlobalCapital,* [no date], https://www.globalcapital.com/about-us (last visited April 26, 2023).

64 *announced the two new:* Will Caiger-Smith, "BAML Reshuffles NY Structured Credit," *GlobalCapital,* February 26, 2015, 9:30 p.m., https://www.globalcapital.com/article/28mxnybllcep3amq75pmo/people-news/baml-reshuffles-ny-structured-credit-with-new-co-heads.

64   *She "consistently received stellar performance reviews"*: Messina Complaint, at ¶ 38.

64   *During that meeting:* Messina Complaint, at ¶ 45.

65   *As she spoke:* Messina Complaint, at ¶ 47.

65   *Twice, he stopped Messina:* Messina Complaint, at ¶ 52.

65   *Messina was the only:* Messina Complaint, at ¶ 44.

65   *He even left Messina:* Messina Complaint, at ¶ 48.

65   *According to the lawsuit:* Messina Complaint, at ¶ 58.

65   *Messina's lawsuit:* Michael J. de la Merced, "Goldman Sachs to Pay $215 Million to Settle Gender Bias Suit," *New York Times*, May 9, 2023, https://www.nytimes.com/2023/05/09/business/dealbook/goldman-sachs-discrimination-lawsuit.html.

65   *In fact, only four days:* Janet Adamy and Paul Overberg, "Women in Elite Jobs Face Stubborn Pay Gap," *Wall Street Journal*, May 17, 2016, 12:59 p.m., ET, https://www.wsj.com/articles/women-in-elite-jobs-face-stubborn-pay-gap-1463502938.

66   *In response:* Messina Complaint, at ¶ 66.

66   *As he glanced:* Messina Complaint, at ¶ 92.

66   *He also reluctantly:* Messina Complaint, at ¶ 93.

66   *In the suit, Messina's lawyers:* Messina Complaint, at ¶ 107.

66   *In 2015, Kotsen:* Messina Complaint, at ¶ 94.

66   *Trepanier was awarded this compensation:* Messina Complaint, at ¶¶ 62, 84.

66   *The complaint also specifically:* Messina Complaint, at ¶ 188.

66   *Not only was Messina's 2015 bonus:* Messina Complaint, at ¶ 96.

66   *Messina's complaint suggests:* Messina Complaint, at ¶ 84.

67   *When she and Trepanier:* See Messina Complaint, at ¶ 133.

67   *His reported response:* Messina Complaint, at ¶ 134.

67   *Given the nature:* Messina Complaint, at ¶ 135.

67   *Her complaint indicates:* Messina Complaint, at ¶¶ 132–142, 153–235.

67   *Elsewhere in the complaint:* Messina Complaint, at ¶¶ 143–157.

67   *When Messina accused him*: Messina Complaint, at ¶ 154.

67   *But Messina cared:* Messina Complaint, at ¶¶ 72, 73, 77, 93.

67   *Trepanier was also alleged to have conducted an auction:* Messina Complaint, at ¶¶ 164, 165. *See also* Messina Complaint, at ¶¶ 143–157, 166–181.

67   *The complaint describes*: Messina Complaint, at ¶¶ 248–250.

67   *In the coming weeks:* Messina Complaint, at ¶¶ 80, 82, 84, 236, 238.

68   *when Messina recounted:* Messina Complaint, at ¶ 193.

68   *Not only did the complaint allege:* Messina Complaint, at ¶¶ 11, 16, 87. When companies face lawsuits alleging any form of employment discrimination or harassment, best practices involve rearranging work locations for the accused or putting the accused on leave, not the complainant. Christine M. Meadows, "Best Practices for Managing Staff in the #MeToo Era," 35

GPSolo 35 (May/June 2018): 36, 38. ("Unless the complainant requests reassignment, the accused should always be the party who is moved out of the situation.")

68 *Messina's complaint says:* Messina Complaint, at ¶ 240.

68 *It had restricted those activities:* Annie Tsang, "Morning Agenda: A Tale of Two Silicon Valleys," *New York Times*, May 18, 2016, https://news.blogs.nytimes.com/2016/05/18/morning-agenda-a-tale-of-two-silicon-valleys//.

68 *Those allegations and her reference:* Merle, "Bank of America Accused."

68 *she had reached a settlement:* "Goldman Sachs in Talks to Settle Gender Discrimination Lawsuit," *Reuters*, May 3, 2023, 8:10 p.m. EDT, https://www.reuters.com/legal/goldman-sachs-talks-settle-gender-discrimination-lawsuit-source-2023-05-03/ (discussing the settlement of a twelve-year-old class action lawsuit).

68 *As with many such settlements:* Stempel, "Former Top BofA Female Banker Settles 'Bro's Club' Bias Lawsuit."

69 *We can assume only:* Messina Complaint, at ¶ 271 (severance package offer of $500,000); at ¶ 269 (lost back pay in the amount of $8.25 million); at ¶ 273 (lost bonus pay in the amount of $6 million).

69 *Perhaps the most notorious:* Susan Antilla, "25 Years After the 'Boom Boom Room' Lawsuit, Wall Street Still Has a Long Way to Go," CNN, May 27, 2021, 9:59 a.m., https://www.cnn.com/2021/05/27/perspectives/boomboom-room-lawsuit-wall-street/index.html.

69 *Suits against Merrill Lynch:* Cremin v. Merrill Lynch, Inc., 957 F. Supp. 1460 (N.D. Ill. 1997); Complaint of Plaintiff-Intervenor Allison Schieffelin at 4–5, EEOC v. Morgan Stanley & Co., No. 01 CV 8421, 324 F. Supp. 2d 451 (S.D.N.Y. 2004). *See also* Christine Sgarlata Chung, "From Lily Bart to the Boom-Boom Room: How Wall Street's Social and Cultural Response to Women Has Shaped Securities Regulation," *Harvard Journal of Law and Gender* 33 (2010): 175, 230.

69 *including pornographic pictures:* Contardo v. Merrill Lynch, Pierce, Fenner & Smith, Inc., 753 F. Supp. 406, 408 (D. Mass. 1990); Bethany McLean, "'We All Wear All Black Every Day': Inside Wall Street's Complex, Shameful, and Often Confidential Battle with #MeToo," *Vanity Fair*, February 27, 2018, https://www.vanityfair.com/news/2018/02/inside-wall-street-complex-shameful-and-often-confidential-battle-with-metoo.

69 *But what she found worse:* Contardo, 753 F. Supp. at 409.

69 *In a bench trial, the judge:* Contardo, 753 F. Supp. at 411–412.

70 *However, though women:* Antilla, "25 Years After the 'Boom Boom Room' Lawsuit."

70 *Researchers have found:* Olle Folke et al., "Women in Leadership Positions Face More Sexual Harassment," Swedish Institute for Social Research, report, January 16, 2020, https://www.sofi.su.se/english/2.17851/research/research-news/women-in-leadership-positions-face-more-sexual-harassment-1.479264; Aimee Picchi, "Women in Leadership Roles Sexually

Harassed More Than Other Women," *MoneyWatch*, January 16, 2020, 1:29 p.m., https://www.cbsnews.com/news/women-in-leadership-are-harassed-more -than-other-female-employees/.

70 *powerful men on Wall Street:* Hugh Son, "Goldman Sachs Paid $12 Million to Female Partner to Settle Sexism Complaint, Bloomberg Reports," *CNBC*, November 15, 2022, 4:30 p.m., https://www.cnbc.com/2022/11/15/goldman -paid-12-million-to-settle-sexism-complaint-bloomberg-reports.html.

70 *By the late 1980s:* Margo Epprecht, "The Real Reason Women Are Leav- ing Wall Street," *Quartz*, September 5, 2013, https://qz.com/121085/the-real -reason-women-are-opting-out-of-wall-street/.

70 *That number took a nosedive:* Epprecht, "The Real Reason"; Kyle Stock, "Ranks of Women on Wall Street Thin," *Wall Street Journal*, September 20, 2010, https://www.wsj.com/articles/SB10001424052748704858304575498071732136704.

71 *"Catalyst . . . blogged in 2010":* Epprecht, "The Real Reason."

71 *"Women in financial services":* Epprecht, "The Real Reason." *See also* Claire Zillman, "Wall Street Has Never Had a Female CEO. Why Not?," *Fortune*, September 19, 2019, https://fortune.com/longform/banking-finance-wom en-ceos-wallstreet/.

71 *Although women are in the game:* Kweilin Ellingrud et al., "Closing the Gen- der and Race Gaps in North American Financial Services," McKinsey & Co., report, October 21, 2021, https://www.mckinsey.com/industries/fin ancial-services/our-insights/closing-the-gender-and-race-gaps-in-north -american-financial-services. ("Women, particularly women of color, con- tinue to be underrepresented in financial-services roles above entry level.")

71 *An analysis of personal financial advisors:* Derek Thompson, "Why the Gender-Pay Gap Is Largest for the Highest-Paying Jobs," *Atlantic*, December 2014, http://www.theatlantic.com/business/archive/2014/12/the-sticky-floor -why-the-gender-wage-gap-is-lowest-for-the-worst-paying-jobs/383863/. *See also* Katherine Haan, "Gender Pay Gap Statistics in 2023," *Forbes*, February 27, 2023, https://www.forbes.com/advisor/business/gender-pay-gap-statistics/.

71 *other surveys found similar gaps:* Indeed, one study found that the six oc- cupations with the largest gender gaps were all in the financial sector. Alexander Eichler, "Gender Wage Gap Is Higher on Wall Street than Any- where Else," *Huffington Post*, March 19, 2012, http://www.huffingtonpost .com/2012/03/19/gender-wage-gap-wall-street_n_1362878.html. *See also* relevant data at *Payscale*, https://www.payscale.com/research-and-insights /gender-pay-gap/ (showing, in a 2021 study, finance and insurance to be the industry with the largest gender gaps in pay).

71 *Despite increasing numbers of female MBAs:* William Alden, "Wall Street's Young Bankers Are Still Mostly White and Male, Report Says," *New York Times*, September 30, 2014, https://dealbook.nytimes.com/2014/09/30/wall -streets-young-bankers-are-still-mostly-white-and-male/; Epprecht, "The Real Reason"; T. Clifton Green et al., "Gender and Job Performance: Evidence from Wall Street," National Bureau of Economic Research, Working Paper

No. 12897, 2007, https://www.nber.org/papers/w12897. On enrollment, see "Forté Foundation Reports Women's MBA Enrollment Hits Historic 42% in 2023," Forté Foundation, press release, November 2, 2023, https://www .fortefoundation.org/site/DocServer/ForteWomensEnrollment_2023-FI NAL-PR-20231030.pdf.

72 *They jumped even more:* See June Carbone, "Once and Future Financial Crises: How the Hellhound of Wall Street Sniffed Out Five Forgotten Factors Guaranteed to Produce Fiascos," *University of Missouri-Kansas City Law Review* 80 (2012): 1021, 1058.

72 *And while wages plummeted:* Donald Tomaskovic-Devey and Ken-Hou Lin, "Financialization: Causes, Inequality Consequences, and Policy Implications," *North Carolina Banking Institute* 18 (2013): 167, 175–176.

72 *Looking at* Forbes's *annual list:* Howard R. Gold, "Never Mind the 1 Percent," *Chicago Booth Review,* November 29, 2017, https://review.chicagobooth .edu/economics/2017/article/never-mind-1-percent-lets-talk-about-001 -percent.

72 *Women are said to:* Thekla Morganroth et al., "The Gendered Consequences of Risk-Taking at Work: Are Women Averse to Risk or to Poor Consequences?," *Psychology of Women Quarterly* 46 (September 2022): 257 (finding that, contrary to the findings of other studies, women are not in fact more risk averse than men, but rather become more risk averse as their experiences differ from men's).

72 *Indeed, in 2021:* Ellingrud et al., "Closing the Gender and Race Gaps."

72 *Instead, McKinsey consultants:* Ellingrud et al., "Closing the Gender and Race Gaps."

73 *taking risks meant:* Claire Hill and Richard W. Painter, "Berle's Vision Beyond Shareholder Interests: Why Investment Bankers Should Have (Some) Personal Liability," *Seattle University Law Review* 33 (2010): 1173, 1177–1178.

73 *Merrill Lynch, Pierce, Fenner & Smith, engaged in brokering:* James B. Stewart, *Den of Thieves* (New York: Touchstone, 1992), 26.

73 *The ethnically identified companies:* Landon Thomas Jr., "Whatever Happened to Mother Merrill?," *New York Times,* August 3, 2003, http://www .nytimes.com/2003/08/03/business/whatever-happened-to-mother-merrill .html.

74 *As one banker explained:* Chris Arnade, "What I Saw as a Wall Street Trader: A Culture of Bad Behavior," *Guardian,* October 1, 2013, https://www.the guardian.com/global/2013/oct/01/wall-street-banks-shared-responsibility -risks-investing.

74 *Known for their cocksure arrogance:* Frank Partnoy, *Infectious Greed: How Deceit and Risk Corrupted the Financial Markets* (Washington, D.C.: Public Affairs, 2009), 13.

74 *This was the year that:* Hill and Painter, "Berle's Vision," 1177–1178.

74 *In increasing numbers in the 1980s:* Hill and Painter, "Berle's Vision," 1177– 1178.

75 *By the 1990s, as law professor:* Frank Partnoy, *Infectious Greed: How Deceit*

and Greed Corrupted the Financial Markets (New York: Times Books, 2003), 3.

75   *This increase in: See, e.g.,* Donald C. Langevoort, "Chasing the Greased Pig Down Wall Street: A Gatekeeper's Guide to the Psychology, Culture, and Ethics of Financial Risk Taking," *Cornell Law Review* 95 (2011): 1209.

75   *Michael Lewis's 1989 book:* Michael Lewis, *Liar's Poker: Rising Through the Wreckage on Wall Street* (New York: Norton, 1989), 56.

75   *The well-paid class:* Claire A. Hill and Richard Painter, *Better Bankers, Better Banks: Promoting Good Business Through Contractual Commitment* (Chicago: University of Chicago Press, 2015), 98.

75   *Firms like Salomon:* Hill and Painter, *Better Bankers*, 90–92.

76   *And, as the commercial banks:* Aimee Picchi, "Years After the Housing Crash, the Specter of 'Too Big To Fail' Still Haunts the Banking Industry, *CBS News*, March 21, 2023, 6:21 p.m., https://www.cbsnews.com/news/too-big-to-fail-banks-2008-financial-crisis-credit-suisse-silicon-valley-bank/.

76   *"That's where your bonus":* Arnade, "What I Saw."

76   *An employee's incentive was not:* Arnade, "What I Saw."

76   *As the financial crisis loomed:* Sam Gustin, "Not So 'Fabulous' Fab: Ex–Goldman Sachs Trader Fabrice Tourre Found Liable for Fraud," *Time*, August 1, 2013, http://business.time.com/2013/08/01/not-so-fabulous-fab-ex-goldman-sachs-trader-found-liable-for-fraud// (stating in fact the customer was a German bank).

77   *Wall Street's traders, addicted:* Gustin, "Not So 'Fabulous'"; Matt Taibbi, "Looting the Pension Funds," *Rolling Stone*, September 26, 2013, https://www.rollingstone.com/politics/politics-news/looting-the-pension-funds-172774/; *Securities and Exchange Commission v. Goldman Sachs & Co. and Fabrice Tourre* (S.D.N.Y. April 16, 2010) at ¶¶ 52–60, https://www.sec.gov/files/litigation/complaints/2010/comp-pr2010-59.pdf.

77   *Rather than facing:* The banks faced millions in civil penalties but none of the major players in the financial crisis were prosecuted. Stephen Neukam, "5 Things to Know About the Silicon Valley Bank Investigation," *The Hill*, March 15, 2023, 2:38 p.m., ET, https://thehill.com/business/3901751-5-things-to-know-about-the-silicon-valley-bank-investigation/#:~:text=Even%20though%20the%20Financial%20Crisis,the%20collapse%20were%20ever%20prosecuted.

77   *In fact, post-2008, Wall Street:* Pedro Nicolaci da Costa, "Big Banks and the White House Are Teaming Up to Fleece Poor People," *Foreign Policy*, February 23, 2016, https://foreignpolicy.com/2016/02/23/big-banks-and-the-white-house-are-teaming-up-to-fleece-poor-people/ (discussing fleecing the "unbanked" in the post-2008 era).

77   *Yet, financial-sector bonus systems: See, e.g.,* Sanjai Bhagat and Brian J. Bolton, "Misaligned Bank Executive Incentive Compensation," Social Science Research Network paper, June 11, 2013, http://dx.doi.org/10.2139/ssrn.2277917.

78   *Research shows that workplaces: See* Kenneth Matos et al., "Toxic Leadership and the Masculinity Contest Culture: How 'Win or Die' Cultures Breed Abusive Leadership," *Journal of Social Issues* 74 (2018): 422, 502–503 (listing four dimensions, including "Show No Weakness").

78   *Such managers play favorites:* Shannon L. Rawski and Angela Workman-Stark, "Masculinity Contest Cultures in Policing Organizations and Recommendations for Training Interventions," *Journal of Social Issues* 74 (2018): 607; *see also* Berdahl et al., "Work as a Masculinity Contest," 435.

78   *The companies overlook the negative side:* Peter Glick, Jennifer L. Berdahl, and Natalya Alonso, "Development and Validation of the Masculinity Contest Culture Scale," *Journal of Social Issues* 74 (2018): 449.

78   *And Wall Street has not been kind:* Geraldine Fabrikant, "When Citi Lost Sallie," *New York Times*, November 16, 2008, https://www.nytimes.com/2008/11/16/business/16sallie.html. *See also* John Carney, "How Moynihan Forced Sallie Krawcheck Out," *CNBC*, September 22, 2011, 9:40 a.m., https://www.cnbc.com/id/44417689; Halah Touryalai, "Sallie Krawcheck Out at Bank of America Merrill Lynch," *Forbes*, September 6, 2011, https://www.forbes.com/sites/halahtouryalai/2011/09/06/sallie-krawcheck-out-at-bank-of-america-merrill-lynch/#7ec0cda17d80.

79   *A variety of studies have debunked the idea:* Cordelia Fine, *Testosterone Rex: Myths of Sex, Science, and Society* (New York: Norton, 2017), 151–170.

79   *women, if anything, do a little better:* Cindy Chen Delano, "Hedge Funds Have a Missed Opportunity that Could Be Hurting Results," *Barron's*, November 23, 2018, https://www.barrons.com/articles/hedge-funds-gender-gap-could-be-hurting-performance-1543017569.

79   *Meredith Jones, director at Rothstein Kass:* Eric McWhinnie, "Women Are Mostly Better Investors than Men," *USA Today*, March 9, 2014, https://www.usatoday.com/story/money/personalfinance/2014/03/09/women-better-investors-than-men/6176601/. *See also* Steve Garmhausen, "Women: Better Advisors?," *Barron's*, June 2, 2012, https://www.barrons.com/articles/SB50001424053111904081004577438301140635494.

79   *Those findings are:* Jacob Wolinsky, "Here Is Why Female Hedge Fund Managers Outperform Men," *Forbes*, July 13, 2021, https://www.forbes.com/sites/jacobwolinsky/2021/07/31/female-hedge-fund-managers-get-boost-from-are-less-confident-which-may-boost-returns/?sh=770182981796.

79   *Such traits certainly pay off:* Matt Wirz, "Female CLO Managers Tend to Outperform Men," *Wall Street Journal*, February 8, 2019, 8:00 a.m., https://www.wsj.com/articles/female-clo-managers-tend-to-outperform-men-11549630802.

79   *In a 2014* Bloomberg *article:* Michael Lewis, "Eight Things I Wish for Wall Street," *Bloomberg*, December 15, 2014, https://www.bloomberg.com/opinion/articles/2014-12-15/michael-lewis-eight-things-i-wish-for-wall-street.

80   *Sallie Krawcheck, after being:* Jeff J. Roberts, "I Was Fired for Being a Woman, Sallie Krawcheck Tells Crowd," *Fortune*, October 8, 2016, http://fortune.com/2016/10/08/sallie-krewcheck-fired/.

80   *She speculated that the differences:* Roberts, "I Was Fired."

81   *And numerous studies have found:* Tomaskovic-Devey and Lin, "Financialization": 167, 169 ("Financialization goes beyond the financial system and distorts income distributions, job creation, and investment throughout the economy").

See also Stephen G. Cecchetti and Enisse Kharroubi, "Why Does Credit Growth Crowd Out Real Economic Growth?," *The Manchester School* 87 (2019): 1.

81   *The bank, threatened:* Board of Governors, Federal Reserve System, Review of the Federal Reserve's Supervision and Regulation of Silicon Valley Bank, April 28, 2023, 3, https://www.federalreserve.gov/publications/files/svb -review-20230428.pdf.

81   *over the last three:* Ellingrud et al., "Closing the Gender and Race Gaps."

81   *increased volatility and uncertainty:* Neukam, "5 Things to Know."

4. Sharp Elbows: Pao v. Kleiner Perkins

85   *She arrived in Silicon Valley:* Ellen Pao, *Reset: My Fight for Inclusion and Lasting Change* (New York: Random House, 2017), 43.

85   *Raised to think that she could overcome:* Jessica Bennett, "Ellen Pao Is Not Done Fighting," *New York Times*, September 8, 2017, https://www.nytimes .com/2017/09/08/style/ellen-pao-gender-discrimination-silicon-valley-reset .html.

85   *As she later described:* Ellen Pao, "This Is How Sexism Works in Silicon Valley," *Magzter*, September 3, 2017, https://www.magzter.com/stories/Life style/New-York-magazine/This-Is-How-Sexism-Works-In-Silicon-Valley.

86   *The recruiter who interviewed her:* Pao, *Reset*, 62.

86   *She had loved working:* Pao, *Reset*, 63.

86   *Raising money from university endowments:* Charles Duhigg, "How Venture Capitalists Are Deforming Capitalism," *New Yorker*, November 23, 2020, https://www.newyorker.com/magazine/2020/11/30/how-venture-capital ists-are-deforming-capitalism [https://perma.cc/L55L-TBXV]. Lee Hower, "Where Do Venture Capital Dollars Actually Come From? This Visual Ex- plains," *Nextview*, Agile VC (blog), October 29, 2019, https://agilevc.com /blog/2014/10/29/where-do-venture-capital-dollars-actually-come-from/.

86   *In return, they take an equity stake:* Bob Zider, "How Venture Capital Works," *Harvard Business Review*, December 1998, https://hbr.org/1998/11 /how-venture-capital-works.

86   *She was also worried that:* Pao, *Reset*, 63.

86   *But Doerr, a consummate salesman:* Pao, *Reset*, 63.

87   *When Pao pitched Twitter to her bosses:* Colleen Taylor and Kim-Mai Cutler, "Ellen Pao 'Owns the Room,'" *TechCrunch*, March 9, 2015, 9:14 p.m., https:// perma.cc/K2RS-NBAP.

87   *Three and a half years later:* Pao, *Reset*, 84.

87   *Nonetheless, the male partner:* Ruth Reader, "Ellen Pao's Lawyer Concludes: Kleiner Perkins Is a Boys' Club," *Venture Beat*, March 24, 2015, http://ven turebeat.com/2015/03/24/ellen-paos-lawyer-concludes-kleiner-perkins-is -a-boys-club/; https://perma.cc/MP62-5T9S. Pao, *Reset*, 84.

87   *Pao received no:* First Amended Complaint at ¶¶ 28, 40, *Pao v. Kleiner Per- kins Caufield & Byers LLC*, No. CGC-12-520719 (San Francisco Cnty. Cal.

Oct. 16, 2013), https://s3.amazonaws.com/s3.documentcloud.org/docu ments/1672582/pao-complaint.pdf [hereafter, Pao Complaint]; Pao, *Reset*, 84.

87   *Pao explained that:* Pao, "This Is How Sexism Works"; *see also* Pao, *Reset*, 72.

88   *And Pao noted:* Pao, *Reset*, 75; Pao, "This Is How Sexism Works."

88   *While the firm claimed:* Trial Brief of Defendant Kleiner Perkins Caufield & Byers, LLC at 3, *Pao v. Kleiner Perkins Caufield & Byers*, No. CGC-12-520719 (Cal. App. Dep't Super. Ct. Feb. 17, 2015) [hereafter, Kleiner Perkins Trial Brief]; Patrick Kulp, "5 Things We Learned About Silicon Valley Culture from the Ellen Pao Trial," *Mashable*, March 29, 2015, http://mashable .com/2015/03/29/ellen-pao-trial-recap/#obaH6S8iSkq5 [https://perma.cc/5W 5F-N9VJ].

88   *being too territorial and untrustworthy:* Kulp, "5 Things We Learned," 6.

88   *Her male peers, who started when she did:* Nitasha Tiku, "The Ellen Pao Trial Is Spilling Silicon Valley Secrets," *The Verge*, March 3, 2015, 2:26 p.m., https://www.theverge.com/2015/3/3/8141053/ellen-pao-kleiner-perkins -venture-capital.

88   *Pao received conflicting messages:* Bennett, "Ellen Pao Is Not Done."

88   *Ultimately, after trying:* Mary Louise Kelly, "Silicon Valley's Ellen Pao Tackles Sex Discrimination, Workplace Diversity in Memoir," NPR, September 19, 2017, https://www.npr.org/sections/alltechconsidered/2017/09 /19/551810814/silicon-valley-s-ellen-pao-tackles-sex-discrimination -workplace-diversity-in-mem#:~:text=In%202012%2C%20tech%20investor %20Ellen,against%20her%20when%20she%20complained.

88   *As Margaret O'Mara, who wrote:* Stephen Mihm, "How the Department of Defense Bankrolled Silicon Valley," *New York Times*, July 9, 2019, https:// www.nytimes.com/2019/07/09/books/review/the-code-margaret-omara .html.

89   *The venture capital model:* Margaret O'Mara, *The Code: Silicon Valley and the Remaking of America* (New York: Penguin, 2019), 7. ("Innovation blossomed within a small, tightly networked community where friendship and trust increased people's willingness to take professional risks and tolerate professional failure.")

89   *The venture capitalists, the seasoned repeat players:* O'Mara, *The Code*, 75.

90   *accepted Kleiner's funding offer:* John Cassidy, *Dot.Con: The Greatest Story Ever Told* (New York: HarperCollins, 2002), 141.

90   *They backed people they got to know:* O'Mara, *The Code*, 75.

90   *He reported in wonder:* Cassidy, *Dot.Con*, 61.

90   *Driven and competitive, he was:* Tom Nicholas, *VC: An American History* (Cambridge, MA: Harvard University Press, 2019), 262.

90   *He became known as a kingmaker:* O'Mara, *The Code*, 307.

90   *Tens of billions of dollars:* O'Mara, *The Code*, 314–315.

90   *reaching a height in 2000:* "Done Deals: Venture Capitalists Tell Their Story: Featured HBS John Doerr," excerpt from the book *Done Deals*, Udayan Gupta, ed., *Working Knowledge*, Harvard Business School, December 4, 2000,

https://hbswk.hbs.edu/archive/done-deals-venture-capitalists-tell-their
-story-featured-hbs-john-doerr.

90 *It was a decade in which:* "Done Deals."

90 *Clark, a driven man:* Cassidy, *Dot.Con,* 61.

91 *The* New York Times *hailed:* Cassidy, *Dot.Con,* 85.

91 *Netscape's success on Clark's terms:* Cassidy, *Dot.Con,* 62.

91 *The founders came to display:* Emily Chang, *Brotopia: Breaking Up the Boys' Club of Silicon Valley* (New York: Portfolio, 2019), 37.

91 *In 1999, at the height:* Candida Brush et al., "Women Entrepreneurs 2014: Bridging the Gender Gap in Venture Capital," Media Services, Babson College, September 2014 [hereafter, Babson Report], https://www.babson.edu/media/babson/site-assets/content-assets/about/academics/centres-and-institutes/blank-institute/global-research/diana-project/diana-project-executive-summary-2014.pdf.

91 *The number of VC firms also fell:* In 2012, there were 462 active U.S. venture capital firms ("active" is defined as investing at least $5 million in companies in the year). By contrast, there were 1,022 such firms at the height of the technology bubble in 2000. Babson Report.

92 *At the time of Pao's trial:* Gené Teare, "Sole Female Founders Raised $1B Less in 2020 Despite Record Venture Funding Surge in the US," *Crunchbase,* March 24, 2021, https://news.crunchbase.com/news/sole-female-founders-raised-1b-less-in-2020-despite-record-venture-funding-surge-in-the-us/ (discussing if women founders had male partners, the women did better, garnering 10% of venture capital funding from 2012 through 2016).

92 *at Pao's trial:* Davey Alba, "How to Succeed in Venture Capitalism the John Doerr Way," *Wired,* March 4, 2015, 9:53 p.m., https://www.wired.com/2015/03/succeed-venture-capital-john-doerr-way/.

92 *"Male partners did not want":* Jodi Kantor, "Harvard Case Study: Gender Equity," *New York Times,* September 8, 2013, https://www.nytimes.com/2013/09/08/education/harvard-case-study-gender-equity.html.

92 *Facebook's IPO in 2012:* Kantor, "Harvard Case Study"; Sheela Kolhatkar, "The Tech Industry's Gender-Discrimination Problem," *New Yorker,* November 13, 2017, https://www.newyorker.com/magazine/2017/11/20/the-tech-industrys-gender-discrimination-problem.

92 *"Now you had the frat boys":* Kolhatkar, "The Tech Industry's Gender-Discrimination Problem."

92 *Pao points out that at Kleiner:* Kolhatkar, "The Tech Industry's Gender."

92 *The venture capitalists' new culture, in turn:* Kolhatkar, "The Tech Industry's Gender."

93 *In the early 2000s:* O'Mara, *The Code,* 397–402.

93 *In her first five years at Kleiner:* Kleiner Perkins Trial Brief, at 4, line 5.

93 *Doerr likely hoped that:* "There's no reason a venture group need be more than an episodic collection of talented individuals. But since its founding in 1972 by Eugene Kleiner and Tom Perkins, KP has been committed to the training, development, and transition of generations of partners." "Done Deals."

93   *As she writes in her memoir:* Pao, *Reset*, 8.

93   *"White men dominate the field":* Pao, *Reset*, 70.

94   *Women were told their:* Pao Complaint, at ¶ 29.

94   *In her complaint, Pao alleges:* Pao Complaint, at ¶¶ 24, 28.

94   *In her memoir, Pao describes:* Ellen Pao, "This Is How Sexism Works in Silicon Valley: My Lawsuit Failed. Others Won't.," *The Cut*, August 21, 2017, https://www.thecut.com/2017/08/ellen-pao-silicon-valley-sexism-reset-excerpt.html [excerpting the book *Reset* by Ellen Pao].

94   *"It felt good to have an ally":* Pao, *Reset*, 97.

95   *He became increasingly hostile to her:* Avery Hartmann, "Ellen Pao Explains How the Affair She Had at Work Led to Her High-Profile Gender Discrimination Lawsuit," *Business Insider*, August 21, 2017, 1:29 p.m., http://www.businessinsider.com/ellen-pao-reset-book-excerpt-gender-discrimination-lawsuit-2017-8; Colleen Taylor and Kim-Mai Cutler, "Ellen Pao 'Owns the Room,'" *TechCrunch*, March 9, 2015, https://techcrunch.com/2015/03/09/ellen-pao-owns-the-room/.

95   *Soon after, Nazre was promoted:* Pao, *Reset*, 116.

95   *When she pointed out:* Hartmann, "Ellen Pao Explains How"; Pao, *Reset*, 123.

95   *More pointedly, she was:* Pao, *Reset*, 124.

95   *When, in 2009, Pao asked:* Pao Complaint, at ¶ 26.

95   *This is how she learned:* Sara McBride and Dan Levine, "Silicon Valley Gender Trial Enters Final Stages," *Yahoo News*, March 24, 2015, https://www.yahoo.com/news/silicon-valley-gender-lawsuit-heads-closing-arguments-005628500--sector.html.

95   *Vassallo sent him packing:* David Streitfeld, "Ellen Pao Loses Silicon Valley Bias Case Against Kleiner Perkins," *New York Times*, March 28, 2015, https://www.nytimes.com/2015/03/28/technology/ellen-pao-kleiner-perkins-case-decision.html; https://perma.cc/LXQ3-Z9BJ; Pao, *Reset*, 129.

96   *Two months later, he left the firm:* Pao, *Reset*, 131, 153.

96   *"I want no less":* Pao, *Reset*, 132.

96   *But whereas Nazre got:* Pao, *Reset*, 116, 132.

96   *Office romances are dicey:* See, e.g., Deborah M. Weiss, "Sexual Harms Without Misogyny," *University of Chicago Legal Forum* 2019: 299, 341 (noting that "9% of women have left work because of failed romance compared to 3% of men," citing the "2018 Vault Office Romance Survey Results," *Vault Career Advice* [blog], February 12, 2018, http://www.vault.com/blog/workplace-issues/2018-vault-office-romance-survey-results/; https://perma.cc/E44D-Z42Q).

97   *Yahoo's former president:* Jessica Guynn, "Ellen Pao's Suit Was Wake Up Call for Silicon Valley," *USA Today*, March 27, 2015, https://www.usatoday.com/story/tech/2015/03/27/ellen-pao-kleiner-perkins-verdict-silicon-vallley/70557912/.

97   *Facebook COO:* Terry Collins, "Facebook's Sandberg Says She Identifies with Ellen Pao," *CNET*, April 24, 2015, 3:15 p.m., PT, https://www.cnet.com/culture/facebooks-sandberg-says-she-identifies-with-ellen-paos-experiences/.

97 *Law professor Joan Williams:* Jessica Bennett, "Ellen Pao Is Not Done Fighting," *New York Times*, September 8, 2017, https://www.nytimes.com/2017/09/08 /style/ellen-pao-gender-discrimination-silicon-valley-reset.html?.

97 *"When I see that pattern":* Pao, *Reset*, 116.

98 *They found that where:* Emilio J. Castilla and Stephen Benard, "The Paradox of Meritocracy in Organizations," *Administrative Science Quarterly* 55, no. 4 (December 1, 2020): 543, https://doi.org/10.2189/asqu.2010.55.4.543.

98 *The paradox is:* Melissa Sandgren, "The Paradox of Meritocracy," World Economic Forum, report, March 21, 2016, https://www.weforum.org/agenda /2016/03/the-paradox-of-meritocracy/.

98 *In the study:* Sandgren, "Paradox of Meritocracy" ("both men and women will prefer to hire a male applicant—even when the academic record is the same").

98 *"Homophily," in which venture capitalists:* Sophie Calder-Wang, Paul Gompers, and Patrick Sweeney, "Venture Capital's 'Me Too' Moment," National Bureau of Economic Research, Working Paper No. 28679, 2021, 5, https://www.nber .org/system/files/working_papers/w28679/w28679.pdf. Gompers apparently received $900/hour for his testimony. Noah Kulwin, "A Re/code Timeline: The Ellen Pao v. Kleiner Perkins Trial," *Vox*, March 13, 2015, 2:59 p.m., https:// www.vox.com/2015/3/13/11560180/a-recode-timeline-the-ellen-pao-vs -kleiner-perkins-trial.

98 *Paul Gompers, the expert:* Paul Gompers et al., "Gender Gaps in Venture Capital Performance," paper, July 7, 2020, https://papers.ssrn.com/sol3 /papers.cfm?abstract_id=2445497.

99 *He and his co-authors concluded:* Gompers et al., "Gender Gaps."

99 *However, the researchers:* Gompers et al., "Gender Gaps."

99 *The authors emphasize that research:* Gompers et al., "Gender Gaps."

99 *witnesses testified:* Claire Cain Miller, "What Silicon Valley Learned from the Kleiner Perkins Case," *New York Times*, March 28, 2015, https://www .nytimes.com/2015/03/28/upshot/what-silicon-valley-learned-from-the -kleiner-perkins-case.html.

100 *Large institutions have policies:* Arthur H. Kohn, Jennifer Kennedy Park, and Armine Sanamyan, "Companies Anti-Fraternization Policies: Key Considerations," *Harvard Law School Forum: Corporate Governance*, January 26, 2020, https://corpgov.law.harvard.edu/2020/01/26/companies-anti -fraternization-policies-key-considerations/ (indicating that about half of companies have such policies between employees and more have them forbidding relationships between supervisors and subordinates).

100 *Such policies tend to:* Vicki Schultz, "The Sanitized Workplace," *Yale Law Journal* 112 (2003): 2061, 2187. ("The effort to prohibit romance may lead to discriminatory outcomes because in many firms, for employees in heterosexual couples, women will be more likely than men to be fired or transferred.")

100 *Sarah Lacy, the founder and editor:* Bennett, "Ellen Pao Is Not Done."

100 *"There are no smoking guns":* Vauhini Vara, "The Ellen Pao Trial: What Do We Mean by 'Discrimination'?," *New Yorker*, March 14, 2015, https://www

.newyorker.com/business/currency/the-ellen-pao-trial-what-do-we-mean
-by-discrimination.

100 *One of the jurors who believed:* Streitfeld, "Ellen Pao Loses Silicon Valley."

101 *Journalists began referring:* Jessi Hempel, "The Pao Effect Is What Happens
     After Lean In," *Wired*, September 28, 2017, 6:15 a.m., https://www.wired
     .com/story/the-pao-effect-is-what-happens-after-lean-in/.

101 *They called their 2015 report:* Trae Vassallo et al., "Elephant in the Valley,"
     dedicated website, [no date], https://www.elephantinthevalley.com/ (last
     visited April 19, 2023).

101 *Eighty-four percent of the participants:* Vassallo et al., "Elephant."

101 *Most of the advances:* Vassallo et al., "Elephant."

101 *Almost 40 percent:* Vassallo et al., "Elephant."

101 *"The asymmetry of power":* Kolhatkar, "The Tech Industry's Discrimination
     Problem."

102 *The most recent development:* Pam Kostka, "More Women Became VC Part-
     ners Than Ever Before in 2019 but 65% of Venture Firms Still Have Zero
     Female Partners," *Medium* (blog), February 7, 2020, https://medium.com/all
     raise/more-women-became-vc-partners-than-ever-before-in-2019-39cc
     6cb86955.

102 *The* New York Times *reported:* Alisha Haridasani Gupta, "VC Funding for
     Start-Ups Founded by Women Is Surging," *New York Times*, November 2, 2021,
     https://www.nytimes.com/2021/11/02/business/dealbook/female-founded
     -startups-vc-funding.html.

102 *At under 20 percent, however:* Deloitte, "VC Human Capital Survey," 3rd ed.,
     March 2021, 5, https://www2.deloitte.com/content/dam/Deloitte/us/Doc
     uments/audit/vc-human-capital-survey-3rd-edition-2021.pdf.

102 *When female venture capitalists:* Ashley Bittner and Bridget Lau, "Women-
     Led Startups Received Just 2.3% of VC Funding in 2020," *Harvard Business
     Review*, February 25, 2021, https://hbr.org/2021/02/women-led-startups
     -received-just-2-3-of-vc-funding-in-2020.

102 *Project Include:* About Project Include, [no date], https://projectinclude.org
     (last visited November 6, 2023).

103 *Over the last decade:* Isabelle Solal and Kaisa Snellman, "For Female Found-
     ers, Fundraising Only from Female VCs Comes at a Cost, *Harvard Business
     Review*, February 1, 2023, https://hbr.org/2023/02/for-female-founders-only
     -fundraising-from-female-vcs-comes-at-a-cost ("Women are massively under-
     represented among both venture-backed entrepreneurs and VC inves-
     tors, with companies founded solely by women receiving less than 3% of
     all venture capital investments and women accounting for less than 15% of
     check-writers.")

103 *All-women teams:* "2022 Review of Funding for Female Founders," Female
     Founders Fund website, April 3, 2023, https://blog.femalefoundersfund
     .com/2022-review-of-funding-for-female-founders-e928f8072655.

103 *Industry analysts observe:* Dominic-Midori Davis, "Women-Founded Start-
     ups Raised 1.9% of All VC Funds in 2022, a Drop from 2021," *TechCrunch*,

January 18, 2023, 3:00 p.m CST, https://techcrunch.com/2023/01/18/women
-founded-startups-raised-1-9-of-all-vc-funds-in-2022-a-drop-from-2021/.

103   *They received 17.2 percent:* Davis, "Women-Founded Start-ups." *See also* "2022 Review of Funding."

103   *Overall, firms with:* Davis, "Women-Founded Start-ups."

103   *Startups that included:* "2022 Review of Funding."

103   *For one thing:* "2022 Review of Funding."

103   *From 2021 to 2022:* "2022 Review of Funding."

103   *Overall, female founders:* "2022 Review of Funding."

104   *"In Pao's case, the sunlight":* Anita Hill, "Anita Hill Speaks: How to Avoid the Next Ellen Pao Case," *Fortune,* April 6, 2015, https://fortune.com/2015/04/06 /anita-hill-ellen-pao/.

104   *U.S. VC Deal Activity in Companies with All-Female Founders:* PitchBook– NVCA Venture Monitor, December 31, 2022, 31, https://nvca.org/wp-con tent/uploads/2023/01/Q4_2022_PitchBook-NVCA_Venture_Monitor.pdf. Reprinted with permission of PitchBook Data, Inc.

5. Women Make the Best Scapegoats: Terrazas v. Wells Fargo

105   *Misha Patel Terrazas:* Complaint, at ¶¶ 13, 31, *Terrazas v. Wells Fargo Bank, N.A.,* No. 2:17-cv-04275-JAT, 2017 WL 5713394 (D. Ariz. Nov. 21, 2017) [hereafter, Terrazas Complaint].

105   *helping to turn around:* Russ Wiles, "Report Cites Arizona as an 'Epicen- ter' in Wells Fargo's Fake-Accounts Scandal," *AZCentral (Arizona Republic),* April 10, 2017, 5:15 p.m., https://www.azcentral.com/story/money/busi ness/consumers/2017/04/10/report-cites-arizona-epicenter-wells-fargos -fake-accounts-scandal/100303116/.

105   *She was also rated:* Terrazas Complaint, at ¶ 21.

105   *Terrazas loved:* Dale Quinn, "Wells Fargo Mulls Debit Card Fees," *Tucson .com (Arizona Daily Star),* October 17, 2011, https://tucson.com/business /local/wells-fargo-mulls-debit-card-fees/article_7177971b-dd96-5a73 -b604-747ed14804cb.html.

105   *and she assumed that she had:* Terrazas Complaint, at ¶ 21.

105   *The scandal broke in 2013:* E. Scott Reckard, "Wells Fargo Accuses Workers of Opening Fake Accounts to Meet Goals," *Los Angeles Times,* October 3, 2013, 12:00 a.m., https://www.latimes.com/business/la-xpm-2013-oct-03-la -fi-1004-wells-fargo-firings-20131004-story.html.

106   *In September 2016:* Office of the Comptroller of the Currency, OCC As- sesses Penalty Against Wells Fargo, Orders Restitution for Unsafe or Un- sound Sales Practices, press release, September 8, 2016, https://www.occ .gov/news-issuances/news-releases/2016/nr-occ-2016-106.html; U.S. De- partment of Justice, Wells Fargo Exhibit A Statement of Facts, press release, [no date], https://www.justice.gov/opa/press-release/file/1251346/down load (last visited July 27, 2022).

106   *A November 2016:* Emily Glazer, "How Wells Fargo's Problems Flourished

in Arizona," *Wall Street Journal*, November 6, 2016, 5:11 p.m., https://www.wsj.com/articles/how-wells-fargos-problems-flourished-in-arizona-1478470259.

106 *In response to the publicity:* Terrazas Complaint, at ¶ 31. Emily Glazer, "Wells Fargo Names Cravath Partner as New Top Lawyer," *Wall Street Journal*, March 6, 2017, 5:39 p.m., https://www.wsj.com/articles/wells-fargo-names-cravath-partner-as-new-top-lawyer-1488827101.

106 *In February 2017:* Matt Egan, "Wells Fargo Fallout: Execs Reshuffled, 3 Managers Out," CNN Money, March 9, 2017, https://money.cnn.com/2017/03/09/investing/wells-fargo-reshuffles-executives-scandal/index.html.

106 *Terrazas believed that she:* Terrazas Complaint, at ¶ 27. The sentence continues "who, in turned [sic], allocated and pushed those goals down to the front-line employees. In addition to the aggressive sales goals, corporate stressed that Associates had to achieve their sales goals using all available means to forestall negative consequences."

107 *Her suit was one:* Terrazas Complaint, at ¶ 44; *Krestovnikov v. Wells Fargo Bank, N.A.*, No. 20ST-CV30296 (Los Angeles Cnty. Cal. Aug. 10, 2020) https://perma.cc/X9ZR-KGB8 [hereafter, Krestovnikov Complaint].

107 *Yet they are more likely:* Mark Egan et al., "When Harry Fired Sally: Uncovering the Gender Punishment Gap," *Principles for Responsible Investing* (blog), June 19, 2020, https://www.unpri.org/pri-blog/when-harry-fired-sally-uncovering-the-gender-punishment-gap/5951.article.

107 *And Wells Fargo's record:* Matt Egan, "Women Financial Advisers at Wells Fargo 27% More Likely to Lose Their Jobs: Study," CNN Money, March 16, 2017, 3:24 p.m. EDT, https://money.cnn.com/2017/03/16/investing/wells-fargo-gender-gap-bank/index.html. ("Wells Fargo Advisors had the highest rate of female workers leaving among the 44 firms studied between 2005 and 2015.")

107 *For us, Pao's story:* Trae Vassallo et al., "Elephant in the Valley," dedicated website, [no date], https://www.elephantinthevalley.com/ (last visited February 9, 2022) (finding that 84% of Silicon Valley women had been told that they were too aggressive).

107 *Pao's biggest sin, after all:* Adam Lashinsky, "Why Ellen Pao's Case Against Kleiner Perkins Is No Slam Dunk," *Fortune*, March 3, 2015, https://fortune.com/2015/03/03/ellen-pao-kleiner-perkins-facts/.

108 *"the supervisor may communicate":* Donald C. Langevoort, "Organized Illusions: A Behavioral Theory of Why Corporations Mislead Stock Market Investors (and Cause Other Social Harms)," *University of Pennsylvania Law Review* 146 (1997): 101, 123.

108 *Critically, the supervisor:* Langevoort, "Organized Illusions," 123.

108 *When executives want:* Allison Taylor, "What Do Corrupt Firms Have in Common?," Center for the Advancement of Public Integrity (April 2016).

108 *Plausible deniability:* Charles W. Calomiris, "The Subprime Turmoil: What's Old, What's New, and What's Next," *Journal of Structured Finance* 15 (Spring 2009): 6, 12.

108 *those who complained about:* June Carbone and William K. Black, "The

Problem with Predators," *Seattle University Law Review* 43 (2020): 441, 490–491. Wells Fargo also routinely pushed out those who complained about the fake accounts. *See* "Wells Fargo Employees Claim They Were Fired for Reporting 'Gaming' of Sales Quotas," *Money.com*, Sept. 29, 2016, https://money.com/wells-fargo-employees-sales-quotas/.

108 *CEO John Stumpf testified:* Susan M. Ochs, "The Leadership Blind Spots at Wells Fargo," *Harvard Business Review*, October 6, 2016, https://hbr .org/2016/10/the-leadership-blind-spots-at-wells-fargo.

108 *Within such a system: See* In the Matter of Tolstedt et al., U.S. Department of Treasury, AA-EC-2019-82, Notice of Charges for Orders of Prohibition, No. N20-001 at ¶¶ 29–58, https://www.occ.gov/static/enforcement-actions /eaN20-001.pdf (describing how complaints were derailed or discounted). See, in particular, ¶ 48, observing that the head of community banking thought such complaints "reflected poorly on the Community Bank" and "[s]aving face prevailed over determining and fixing the root cause of the sales practices misconduct problem."

109 *Among large banks, Wells Fargo:* Brayan Tayan, "The Wells Fargo Cross-Selling Scandal," *Harvard Law School Forum on Corporate Governance*, February 6, 2019, https://corpgov.law.harvard.edu/2019/02/06/the-wells-fargo -cross-selling-scandal-2/.

109 *"It very much was":* Bethany McLean, "How Wells Fargo's Cutthroat Corporate Culture Allegedly Drove Bankers to Fraud," *Vanity Fair*, May 31, 2017, https://www.vanityfair.com/news/2017/05/wells-fargo-corporate-culture -fraud.

109 *"The reason for eight?":* McLean, "How Wells Fargo's Cutthroat."

110 *While other financial institutions:* Adam Lashinsky, "Riders on the Storm," *Fortune*, November 21, 2012, 3:25 p.m., https://fortune.com/2012/11/21 /riders-on-the-storm/.

110 *and* American Banker *magazine called:* Tayan, "Wells Fargo Cross-Selling Scandal."

110 *It came out of the crisis:* Tayan, "Wells Fargo Cross-Selling Scandal."

110 *Like other mortgage lenders:* Hefler v. Wells Fargo, No. 3:16-cv-05479-JST (Mar. 15, 2018), Second Class Action Complaint at 6, https://www.wells fargosecuritieslitigation.com/Content/Documents/Second%20Consol idated%20Class%20Action%20Complaint.pdf. *See also* Michael W. Hudson, "Silencing the Whistleblowers," *Type Investigations*, May 10, 2010, https:// www.typeinvestigations.org/investigation/2010/05/10/silencing-whis tle-blowers/.

110 *In 2016, the bank was forced:* Jose Pagliery, "Wells Fargo to Pay $1.2 Billion for Hiding Bad Loans Before Housing Crash," CNN Money, April 8, 2016, 7:34 p.m., https://money.cnn.com/2016/04/08/news/companies/wells-fargo -bad-loans-settlement/index.html.

110 *and in 2018, in a different suit:* Ben Lane, "Wells Fargo to Pay $2 Billion for Allegedly Lying About Subprime Mortgages," *HousingWire*, August 1,

2018, 1:59 p.m., https://www.housingwire.com/articles/46335-wells-fargo
-to-pay-2-billion-for-allegedly-lying-about-subprime-mortgages/.

110   *She wrote a letter:* Office of Senator Elizabeth Warren, Letter from Senator
Warren to Federal Reserve Chairman Jerome Powell, September 13, 2021,
https://www.warren.senate.gov/imo/media/doc/Letter%20from%20Sen
ator%20Warren%20to%20Fed%20on%20Wells%20Fargo%20FHC%20
Status%2009.13.2021.pdf.

111   *Everyone's success, from CEO Stumpf:* Emily Glazer, "How Wells Fargo's
High-Pressure Sales Culture Spiraled Out of Control," *Wall Street Journal,*
September 16, 2016, 3:10 p.m., https://www.wsj.com/articles/how-wells
-fargos-high-pressure-sales-culture-spiraled-out-of-control-1474053044.
("Bankers in branches who hit sales targets could earn bonuses of $500 to
$2,000 per quarter, while district managers could get $10,000 to $20,000 a
year, according to six Wells Fargo employees. Bonuses made a big difference
in the paychecks of branch employees, whose base salaries often were about
$30,000 a year.")

111   *It thus sets up conflicts:* Veronica Dagher, "How Bank Cross-Selling Can
Help, Hurt You," *Wall Street Journal,* September 16, 2016, 10:56 a.m., ET,
https://www.wsj.com/articles/how-cross-selling-can-help-hurt-consumers
-1474037775.

111   *Sallie Krawcheck:* Janet Aschkenasy, "What Really Prompted Sallie Krawcheck's Departure from BofA?," *efinancialcareers,* September 12, 2011, https://
www.efinancialcareers.com/news/2011/09/what-really-prompted-sallie
-krawchecks-departure-from-bofa.

111   *Branch offices are expensive to operate:* Arca, "Cutting Branches to Cut Costs—
Does It Work?," *Arca.com* (blog), [no date], https://arca.com/resources/blog
/cutting-branches-to-cut-costs-does-it-work (last visited May 23, 2022).

111   *Wells Fargo in contrast:* "Leading Banks in the United States in 2021, by
Number of Branches," *Statistica,* [no date], https://www.statista.com/statis
tics/935643/banks-with-the-most-branches-usa/ (noting that Wells Fargo was
the third largest bank by assets, although it trailed the top bank by a trillion
dollars, just under $2 trillion to JP Morgan at $3 trillion) (last visited May
23, 2022); Alicia Phaneuf, "Top Ten Biggest US Banks by Assets in 2022,"
Insider Intel, January 2, 2022, https://www.insiderintelligence.com/insights
/largest-banks-us-list/. Wells Fargo closed branches from 2009 to 2010, for
example, during the depths of the financial crisis. Douglas Blakey, "US Branch
Numbers Decline," *Retail Banker International,* July 23, 2010, https://www
.retailbankerinternational.com/news/us-branch-numbers-decline/.

111   *Described as the "Most Powerful":* Tayan, "Wells Fargo Cross-Selling Scandal."

112   *For instance, when:* In the Matter of Tolstedt et al., at ¶¶ 16–17.

112   *Former CEO Richard Kovacevich:* See Chris Arnold, "Former Wells Fargo
Employees Describe Toxic Sales Culture, Even at HQ," NPR, October 4, 2016,
5:04 a.m., https://www.npr.org/2016/10/04/496508361/former-wells-fargo
-employees-describe-toxic-sales-culture-even-at-hq ("During a sales push

called 'Jump into January' former employees say they were expected to sell 20 products a day."); McLean, "How Wells Fargo's Cutthroat."

112 *According to an* NPR *report:* Arnold, "Former Wells Fargo Employees."

112 *In the period between 2011 and 2015:* Michael Corkery, "Wells Fargo Fined $185 Million for Fraudulently Opening Accounts," *New York Times*, September 9, 2016, https://www.nytimes.com/2016/09/09/business/dealbook /wells-fargo-fined-for-years-of-harm-to-customers.html.

112 *Customers complained that they:* McLean, "How Wells Fargo's Cutthroat."

112 *Clearly this wasn't just:* Justin Peters, "How Wells Fargo Became Synonymous with Scandal," *Slate*, November 28, 2020, 6:00 a.m., https://slate.com /business/2020/11/wells-fargo-scandal-history-karen-attiah.html.

112 *In fact, in the period:* McLean, "How Wells Fargo's Cutthroat." ("The fraud was not only big, but blatant, with 193,000 non-employee accounts opened between 2011 and 2015 for which the only e-mail domain name listed was @wellsfargo.com.")

112 *By the time the various investigations:* Uri Berliner, "Wells Fargo Admits to Nearly Twice as Many Possible Fake Accounts—3.5 Million," NPR, August 31, 2017, https://www.npr.org/sections/thetwo-way/2017/08/31/547550804/wells -fargo-admits-to-nearly-twice-as-many-possible-fake-accounts-3-5-million.

112 *These aggressive sale goals:* Terrazas Complaint, at ¶ 27.

112 *A 2017 independent Wells Fargo investigation:* Independent Directors of the Board of Wells Fargo & Company, "Sales Practices Investigation Report," SEC Form DEF 14A (April 10, 2017), 19, https://www.sec.gov/Archives /edgar/data/72971/000119312517118654/d375947ddefa14a.htm. The Community Bank, which Tolstedt ran from 2007 to 2016, "implemented the following philosophy to drive sales results: 'A whole bunch of management gurus say you need BHAGs—bold, hairy, audacious goals. That's a technique of management— to give troops a goal that looks unattainable and flog them heavily. And according to that line of thought, you will do better chasing a BHAG than you will a reasonable objective.'" In the Matter of Tolstedt et al., at 20.

113 *Terrazas dealt with a high-pressure:* Peters, "How Wells Fargo Became Synonymous." ("Further investigations revealed that Wells Fargo branch employees were under incredible pressure to sell more products to more customers. Senior executives threatened branch managers, branch managers threatened their staff—they were pushed to go for great, as if their jobs were on the line every day.")

113 *While the scandal broke:* Reckard, "Wells Fargo Accuses Workers."

113 *Wells Fargo did not:* Susan M. Ochs, "The Leadership Blind Spots at Wells Fargo," *Harvard Business Review*, October 2016, https://hbr.org/2016/10 /the-leadership-blind-spots-at-wells-fargo.

113 *unlike some of them:* Terrazas Complaint, at ¶¶ 29, 37, 38.

114 *while retaining men:* Terrazas Complaint, at ¶¶ 29, 37, 38.

114 *Yet, others at Wells Fargo:* Terrazas Complaint, at ¶¶ 29, 37, 38.

114 *Some have witnessed colleagues:* Emily Flitter and Stacy Cowley, "Wells Fargo Says Its Culture Has Changed. Some Employees Disagree," *New York Times*, March 9, 2019, https://perma.cc/D9HM-SZF3.

114 *Even after:* Kevin Wack, "Wells Fargo Employees Feared for Their Jobs, Consumer Banking Head Says," *American Banker*, November 1, 2021, 9:00 p.m. ET, https://www.americanbanker.com/news/wells-fargo-employees -feared-for-their-jobs-consumer-banking-head-says.

114 *Wells Fargo fired more women:* Susan Antilla, "When Brokers Act Badly at Wells Fargo, Women Take the Fall," *The Intercept*, July 1, 2019, https://the intercept.com/2019/07/01/wells-fargo-brokers-gender-bias/.

115 *Egan and his co-authors:* Egan et al., "When Harry Fired Sally: Uncovering the Gender Punishment Gap"; Emily Glazer, "Wells Fargo Ends Investigation over Bias Against Women," *Wall Street Journal*, November 9, 2018, 5:30 a.m., https://www.wsj.com/articles/wells-fargo-ends-investigation-over-bias -against-women-1541759400.

115 *Strikingly, they found:* Mark Egan et al., "When Harry Fired Sally: The Double Standard in Punishing Misconduct," National Bureau of Economic Research, Working Paper No. 23242, March 2017, revised December 2021, 3–4, https:// www.nber.org/system/files/working_papers/w23242/w23242.pdf.

115 *Wells Fargo had all:* Egan et al., "When Harry Fired Sally: The Double Standard," 18 nn. 23–24.

115 *the average settlement:* Antilla, "When Brokers Act Badly."

115 *And in a subsequent investigation:* Antilla, "When Brokers Act Badly." Indeed, Egan points out that many firms tolerate and retain high numbers of financial advisors with established records of misconduct, and Wells Fargo's financial advisors had some of the highest levels of misconduct. Mark Egan et al., "The Market for Financial Adviser Misconduct," *Journal of Political Economy* 127 (2019): 233, 248–258, https://www.journals.uchicago.edu/doi /pdf/10.1086/700735.

115 *At Wells Fargo, 72 percent of women:* Antilla, "When Brokers Act Badly"; *see generally* Egan et al., "The Market."

115 *When the women did leave:* Antilla, "When Brokers Act Badly." ("Likewise, leaving Wells was a more significant career-stopper for women than it was for men: We found that 75 percent of women who had negative disclosures resulting in a termination or resignation did not find work in the industry again, compared to 59 percent of the men.")

The study by Mark Egan and colleagues similarly found that despite women committing types of misconduct that was 20% less costly than men's, when women were terminated for that misconduct, they were 30% less likely than male advisors to find new employment. Egan et al., "When Harry Fired Sally," 28.

115 The Intercept *found that:* Antilla, "When Brokers Act Badly."

116 *Indeed, Egan's research:* Egan et al., "When Harry Fired Sally: The Double Standard," 4, 49; Egan et al., "The Market."

116 *Women who commit misconduct:* Joseph Shapiro, "Federal Report Says Women in Prison Receive Harsher Punishment Than Men," NPR, February 26, 2020, 5:05 a.m., https://www.npr.org/2020/02/26/809269120/federal -report-says-women-in-prison-receive-harsher-punishments-than-men. ("Women in prison, when compared with incarcerated men, often receive

disproportionately harsh punishments for minor violations of prison rules, according to a report released" by the U.S. Commission on Civil Rights.) Women who commit misconduct defy stereotypes that women are empathetic and submissive, and because women are scrutinized more closely, their behavior is analyzed more sharply, and they are treated more harshly. Catherine H. Tinsley and Robin J. Ely, "What Most People Get Wrong About Men and Women," *Harvard Business Review*, May 2018, https://hbr.org/2018/05/what-most-people-get-wrong-about-men-and-women. ("Several studies have found that because women operate under a higher-resolution microscope than their male counterparts do, their mistakes and failures are scrutinized more carefully and punished more severely.")

116 *Instead, according to both:* Lynne L. Dallas, "A Preliminary Inquiry into the Responsibility of Corporations and Their Officers and Directors for Corporate Climate: The Psychology of Enron's Demise," *Rutgers Law Journal* 35 (2003): 1; *See, e.g.,* Lynn A. Stout, "Killing Conscience: The Unintended Behavioral Consequences of 'Pay for Performance,'" *Journal of Corporate Law* 39 (2014): 525, 555–556.

116 *These environments produce abusive managers:* Jennifer L. Berdahl et al., "Work as a Masculinity Contest," *Journal of Social Issues* 74 (2018): 422, 435.

117 *Her supervisor told her:* Krestovnikov Complaint, at ¶¶ 35, 28.

117 *Moreover, a worker fired for misconduct:* Egan et al., "When Harry Fired Sally," 1. *See also* Peter Siegleman, "Protecting the Compromised Worker: A Challenge for Employment Discrimination Law," *Buffalo Law Review* 64 (2016): 565.

117 *Finally, Egan's other work:* Egan et al., "The Market."

117 *A Wells Fargo affiliate:* Egan et al., "The Market," Table 6, 258.

117 *The study observes that:* Egan et al., "The Market," 288.

117 *the ones who commit more:* Egan et al., "The Market," 275. ("Overall, the results presented in both panels of Table 12 suggest that firms with a higher proportion of advisers with misconduct are more tolerant of misconduct in their hiring and firing decisions.")

118 *The attitude inside Wells Fargo:* McLean, "How Wells Fargo's Cutthroat."

118 *Cross-selling became central:* Center for Progressive Reform, Wells Fargo Fake Account Scandal, report, [no date], http://progressivereform.org/our-work/consumer-protection/civjustice_wellsfargo/ (last visited September 27, 2021). ("Beginning in the early 2000s, corporate managers at Wells Fargo bank began pressuring branch employees to engage in aggressive "cross-selling"—marketing multiple financial products such as bank accounts, credit cards, or overdraft protection services to customers.")

118 *The abusive practices:* Reckard, "Wells Fargo Accuses Workers."

118 *Even then, the scale:* Berliner, "Wells Fargo Admits."

119 *In 2020:* U.S. Department of Justice, "Wells Fargo Agrees to Pay $3 Billion to Resolve Criminal and Civil Investigations into Sales Practices Involving the Opening of Millions of Accounts Without Customer Authorization,"

press release, February 21, 2020, https://www.justice.gov/opa/pr/wells-fargo -agrees-pay-3-billion-resolve-criminal-and-civil-investigations-sales-prac tices.

119   *In 2021, Wells Fargo:* Richard Craver, "Wells Fargo Ends 2021 with 7.1% Re-duction in Overall Job Positions," *Winston-Salem Journal,* January 14, 2022, https://journalnow.com/business/local/wells-fargo-ends-2021-with-7-1-re duction-in-overall-job-positions/article_6c490a86-7547-11ec-96fb-ef6ee 0bcb791.html, and the layoffs continued during 2022. *See also* Dan Ennis, "Wells Fargo Starts Layoffs in Home Lending Unit,: *Banking Dive,* April 25, 2022, https://www.bankingdive.com/news/wells-fargo-starts-layoffs-in-home -lending-unit/622632/. ("Wells Fargo CEO Charlie Scharf has been leading an effort, since at least 2020, to review the bank's business model, cutting units that are seen as "non-core" and embarking on periodic but substantial rounds of job cuts.")

119   *and in September 2021:* Hugh Son, "Wells Fargo Hit with Another Fine, But Also Says CFBP Order from 2016 Sales Practices Has Ended," *CNBC,* September 9, 2021, 5:08 p.m., https://www.cnbc.com/2021/09/09/wells-far go-hit-with-another-fine-but-also-says-cfpb-order-from-2016-sales-prac tices-has-ended.html.

119   *In December of 2022:* Emily Flitter, "Wells Fargo to Pay $3.7 Billion over Con-sumer Banking Violations," *New York Times,* December 20, 2022, https:// www.nytimes.com/2022/12/20/business/wells-fargo-consumer-loans-fine .html.

119   *CFPB director:* Richard Craver, "Wells Fargo Acknowledges Asset Cap to Last into 2024; Share Repurchases May Resume in First Quarter," *Winston Salem Journal,* January 16, 2023, https://journalnow.com/business/local /wells-fargo-acknowledges-asset-cap-to-last-into-2024-share-repurchases -may-resume-in-first/article_c6b86004-951f-11ed-b6a4-0b705651a895.html.

119   *He was not only fired:* Gabrielle Olya, "Former Wells Fargo CEO John Stumpf Banned from Banking Industry and Ordered to Pay $17.5 Million," *GO Banking Rates,* January 24, 2020, https://www.gobankingrates.com/net -worth/business-people/wells-fargo-john-stumpf-money/.

119   *Carrie Tolstedt:* Kevin Wack, "Judge's Report Hammers Three Ex-Wells Fargo Executives," *American Banker,* December 8, 2022, 6:13 a.m., ET, https://www .americanbanker.com/news/judges-report-hammers-three-ex-wells-fargo -executives. ("The OCC has also sought to collect $25 million in penalties from Carrie Tolstedt, the onetime head of Wells Fargo's retail banking unit, known as the Community Bank.") *See also* Stacy Cowley, "Former Wells Fargo Executive to Plead Guilty in Sham Accounts Scandal," *New York Times,* March 15, 2023, https://www.nytimes.com/2023/03/15/business/wells-fargo -carrie-tolstedt-jail.html#:~:text=six%20years%20ago.-,Carrie%20L.,of%20 five%20years%20in%20prison.

119   *Over his last ten years:* Martha C. White, "$41 Million Is Chicken Scratch Compared to What Stumpf Earned at Wells Fargo," *NBC,* September 29,

2016, 1:31 p.m., https://www.nbcnews.com/business/business-news/41-mil
lion-chicken-scratch-compared-what-stumpf-earned-wells-fargo-n656901.

119 *In 2020, his net worth:* Olya, "Former Wells Fargo CEO John Stumpf Banned."

120 *The asset cap:* Authors' interview with UMKC economics professor William
K. Black, July 23, 2022; Federal Deposit Insurance Corporation, "Consumer
Protection Is not Part of the FDIC Charge: About the Federal Deposit Insurance Corporation," FDIC website, [no date], https://www.fdic.gov/about/
(last visited July 21, 2022).

120 *Elizabeth Warren responded:* Lauren Muskett, "House Report Says Wells
Fargo Continues to 'Abuse' Customers," CFO website, report, March 5, 2020,
https://www.cfo.com/news/house-report-says-wells-fargo-continues-to
-abuse-customers/656841/.

120 *While the agency:* The CFPB faces a new threat, with the Supreme Court
having granted certiorari in February 2023 to a challenge to the constitu-
tionality of its funding mechanism that could dismantle the agency. John
L. Culhane et al., "SCOTUS Agrees to Decide Whether CFPB's Funding
Is Unconstitutional but Will Not Hear Case until Next Term," *Consumer
Finance Monitor,* February 27, 2023, https://www.consumerfinancemon
itor.com/2023/02/27/scotus-agrees-to-decide-whether-cfpbs-funding-is
-unconstitutional-but-will-not-hear-case-until-next-term/.

120 *These workers were supported by others:* Committee for Better Banks, "About
Us," Better Banks website, [no date], https://www.betterbanks.org/better
-banks-0/about-us-0 (last visited June 15, 2022).

121 *an initial civil suit:* E. Scott Reckard, "L.A. Sues Wells Fargo, Alleging 'Unlawful and Fraudulent Conduct,'" *Los Angeles Times,* May 4, 2015, 8:39 p.m.,
https://www.latimes.com/business/la-fi-wells-fargo-suit-20150505-story
.html.

121 *Congressional hearings later helped:* "Senator Elizabeth Warren Grills Wells
Fargo CEO John Stumpf on WFC Cross-Selling," *CNBC,* September 20, 2016,
available on Youtube, https://www.youtube.com/watch?v=iCLIyXpV5K0.

6. Tech Pushes Women Out: Women v. Uber

125 *Avendaño talked to the computer science department:* Ingrid Avendaño,
"My Tech Journey: From Art to Engineering and Getting Started in Silicon
Valley," *Model View Culture,* February 3, 2014, https://archive.ph/a3MkE.
("When I met with the CS department I had a very upsetting experience
with the administration. Within 10 minutes of meeting with the CS faculty
it felt like they were already expecting me to fail in their program and were
very standoffish. It didn't help that they had given me a 'pep talk' that actively discouraged me from joining their department. I was treated as if the
only reason I was interested in the major was just to make money.")

126 *Computer coding culture:* Clive Thompson, "The Secret History of Women in
Coding," *New York Times Magazine,* February 13, 2019, https://www.nytimes
.com/2019/02/13/magazine/women-coding-computer-programming.html.

126   *As computer programming became:* Thompson, "Secret History."

126   *Those students most likely:* Thompson, "Secret History."

126   *And even when their abilities:* Shana Vu, "Cracking the Code: Why Aren't More Women Majoring in Science?," *UCLA Newsroom*, June 26, 2017, https://newsroom.ucla.edu/stories/cracking-the-code:-why-aren-t-more-women-majoring-in-computer-science.

126   *Avendaño, however, demonstrated:* Avendaño, "My Tech Journey."

126   *Fortuitously, a three-month programming bootcamp:* Avendaño, "My Tech Journey."

126   *Indeed, when Avendaño started:* *Avendaño v. Uber Technologies, Inc.,* No. CGC18566677 (Cal. Super. Ct. May 21, 2018) [hereafter, Avendaño Complaint], at ¶ 22.

127   *mentor other women:* Avendaño Complaint, at ¶ 1.

127   *She gushed on her Twitter page:* Screenshot preserved from https://twitter.com/ingridavendano?lang=en.

127   *Like all new employees:* Mike Isaac, "Inside Uber's Aggressive, Unrestrained Workplace Culture," *New York Times,* February 22, 2017, https://www.nytimes.com/2017/02/22/technology/uber-workplace-culture.html.

127   *After she complained:* Avendaño Complaint, at ¶¶ 23, 24, 26.

127   *Women in tech receive:* Connie Loizos, "In Tech, the Wage Gender Gap Worsens for Women over Time, and It's Worst for Black Women," *TechCrunch,* April 4, 2017, https://techcrunch.com/2017/04/04/in-tech-the-wage-gender-gap-worsens-for-women-over-time-and-its-worst-for-black-women/.

127   *But in a field like tech:* "The Gender Pay Gap in Tech," *Comparably* (blog), June 13, 2016, https://www.comparably.com/blog/the-gender-pay-gap-in-tech/ (last visited Sept. 13, 2019).

127   *Banning employees from discussing:* Michael Baker et al., "Can Transparency Laws Fix the Gender Wage Gap?," *Harvard Business Review,* February 26, 2020, https://hbr.org/2020/02/can-transparency-laws-fix-the-gender-wage-gap. *See also* Susan R. Fiorentino and Sandra M. Tomkowicz, "Can Millennials Deliver on Equal Pay? Why the Time Is Finally Right for Pay Transparency," *Hofstra Labor and Employment Law Journal* 38 (2021): 253, 267–268. ("[A]n employer policy that bans employees from discussing wages violates the [National Labor Relations] Act.") Yet, so many employers are not covered by the National Labor Relations Act: public sector employees (although they may have pay transparency), agricultural, domestic workers, independent contractors, religious organizations, and retailers with less than $500,000 in annual sales. National Labor Relations Board, "Jurisdictional Standards," National Labor Relations Board website, [no date], https://www.nlrb.gov/about-nlrb/rights-we-protect/the-law/jurisdictional-standards (last visited January 12, 2024).

128   *During Avendaño's first year:* Kara Swisher and Johana Bhuiyan, "Uber CEO Kalanick Advised Employees on Sex Rules for a Company Celebration in 2013 'Miami Letter,'" *Vox,* June 8, 2017, https://www.vox.com/2017/6/8/15765514/2013-miami-letter-uber-ceo-kalanick-employees-sex-rules-company-celebration.

128 *Initially prepared the previous year:* Swisher and Bhuiyan, "Uber CEO Kalanick."

128 *And the email also made light:* Avendaño Complaint, at ¶ 13.

128 *Finally, it urged the employees:* Swisher and Bhuiyan, "Uber CEO Kalanick."

128 *In front of the Berkeley students:* Avendaño Complaint, at ¶ 11.

128 *When Avendaño reported:* Avedaño Complaint, at ¶ 12.

128 *A few months later:* Avendaño Complaint, at ¶ 15.

128 *Avendaño began to experience:* Avendaño Complaint, at ¶¶ 18, 39, 51, 63.

128 *Meanwhile, the sexual harassment:* Emily Chang, *Brotopia: Breaking Up the Boys' Club of Silicon Valley* (New York: Portfolio, 2019), 112–118.

129 *Employees sometimes got drunk:* Chang, *Brotopia*, 116–117; Avendaño Complaint, at ¶ 20.

129 *all, she believed:* Avendaño Complaint, at ¶ 37.

129 *Yet, despite informing her manager:* Avendaño Complaint, at ¶ 39.

129 *She also found it hard:* Chang, *Brotopia*, 116–117, 126.

129 *Like Avendaño, she eventually:* Chang, *Brotopia*, 126.

129 *This was the month:* Susan Fowler, "Reflecting on One Very, Very Strange Year at Uber," Susan Fowler (blog), February 19, 2017, https://www.susanjfowler.com/blog/2017/2/19/reflecting-on-one-very-strange-year-at-uber.

130 *Fowler had caught them:* Fowler, "Reflecting"; Chang, *Brotopia*, 107.

130 *Eventually, an outside law firm:* Avendaño Complaint, at ¶ 64; Joseph Menn and Heather Somerville, "Uber Fires 20 Employees After Harassment Probe," *Reuters*, June 6, 2017, https://www.reuters.com/article/us-uber-sexual-harassment-idUSKBN18X2GZ.

130 *Twenty employees:* Menn and Somerville, "Uber Fires 20 Employees."

130 *After three years at the company:* Avendaño Complaint, at ¶¶ 9, 64–66.

130 *Kalanick was forced to resign:* "Travis Kalanick to Depart Uber Board of Directors," *Uber Investor*, December 24, 2019, https://investor.uber.com/news-events/news/press-release-details/2019/Travis-Kalanick-to-Depart-Uber-Board-of-Directors/default.aspx. *See also* Anita Balakrishnan, "Here's the Full 13-Page Report of Recommendations for Uber," *CNBC*, June 13, 2017, 2:20 p.m. EDT, https://www.cnbc.com/2017/06/13/eric-holder-uber-report-full-text.html. (Covington and Burling report on more than 3 million documents and 200 interviews.)

130 *Women began to stand up:* Kia Kokalitcheva, "Timeline: Susan Fowler's Memo and a Year of Tech Reckoning," *Axios*, February 19, 2018, https://www.axios.com/2018/02/18/one-year-since-susan-fowler-timeline.

131 *"This culture was perpetuated":* Avendaño Complaint, at ¶ 1.

131 *Avendaño sought compensation:* Avendaño Complaint, at ¶ 152.

131 *Her suit sought an order:* Avendaño Complaint, at ¶ 152(h). *See also* Heather Somerville, "Three Women Sue Uber in San Francisco, Claiming Unequal Pay, Benefits," *Reuters*, October 25, 2017, 3:17 p.m., https://www.reuters.com/article/us-uber-lawsuit/three-women-sue-uber-in-san-francisco-claiming-unequal-pay-benefits-idUSKBN1CU2Z1 (illustrating that Avendaño was a part of two suits against Uber).

131   *Avendaño and Medina:* A McKinsey report shows that one out of four women
       of color who start at McKinsey-surveyed firms make it to the C-suite (the
       percentage goes from 17% to 4%), while for white women, it narrows from
       30% to 20%. McKinsey & Co., "Women in the Workplace," 2021, 8, https://
       wiw-report.s3.amazonaws.com/Women_in_the_Workplace_2021.pdf.

131   *By the time:* Avedaño Complaint, at ¶ 22.

131   *She wrote in 2018:* Avendaño screenshot.

131   *After moving to Netflix:* "Ingrid Avendaño," *Crunchbase* website, [no date],
       https://www.crunchbase.com/person/ingrid-avenda%C3%B1o (last visited
       June 15, 2022).

131   *"Now that I had a job":* Avendaño screenshot.

131   *It "takes over a year":* Avendaño screenshot.

131   *When the* New York Times *interviewed:* Isaac, "Inside Uber's Aggressive,
       Unrestrained Workplace Culture."

132   *The 2015 "Elephant in the Valley" report:* "Women in Tech," "Elephant in the
       Valley" dedicated website, [no date], https://www.elephantinthevalley.com/
       (last visited September 19, 2019).

132   *citing lack of career growth:* "Women in Tech: How to Attract and Retain
       Top Talent," *Indeed* (blog), November 6, 2018, https://www.indeed.com/lead
       /women-in-tech-report?co=US.

132   *Instead, as a study by the Center for Talent Innovation found:* Liza Mundy,
       "Why Is Silicon Valley So Awful to Women?," *Atlantic,* April 2017, https://
       www.theatlantic.com/magazine/archive/2017/04/why-is-silicon-valley-so
       -awful-to-women/517788/.

132   *If they are startup founders:* Mundy, "Why Is Silicon Valley So Awful."

132   *These negative perceptions:* Kapor Center for Social Impact, "Tech Leavers
       Study," April 27, 2017, https://www.kaporcenter.org/wp-content/uploads
       /2017/08/TechLeavers2017.pdf.

133   *the number of women:* National Academies of Science, Engineering, and
       Medicine et al., *Assessing and Responding to the Growth of Computer Sci-
       ence Undergraduate Enrollments* (Washington, D.C.: National Academies
       Press, 2018), 29, https://www.nap.edu/read/24926/chapter/4#29; "Declining
       Number of Women Studying Computer Science," *The Evolving Ultrasaurus,*
       November 20, 2008, https://www.ultrasaurus.com/2008/11/declining-num
       ber-of-women-studying-computer-science/.

133   *They were more likely:* Chang, *Brotopia,* 23–25.

133   *Studies show that boys:* Randall Stross, "What Has Driven Women Out of
       Computer Science?," *New York Times,* November 15, 2008, http://www.ny
       times.com/2008/11/16/business/16digi.html.

133   *Men with bachelor's degrees:* Stuart Reges, "Why Women Don't Code," *Quil-
       lette,* June 19, 2018, https://quillette.com/2018/06/19/why-women-dont-code/
       (charting the percentage of women in the computer science field over time).

133   *By 2021, men earned more:* "Women in Computer Science: Getting Involved in
       STEM," ComputerScience.org, resources, November 8, 2023, https://www.com

puterscience.org/resources/women-in-computer-science/ (asserting women only earn 18% of computer science bachelor's degrees in the United States).

133 *Salaries in the computer and engineering fields:* Peter Jacobs, "Science and Math Majors Earn the Most Money After Graduation," *Business Insider*, July 9, 2014, 9:56 a.m., http://www.businessinsider.com/stem-majors-earn-a-lot-more -money-after-graduation-2014-7. ("In other words, some people don't want women who ask for more money on their team. That's the double bind.")

133 *Indeed, salaries for "techies":* Wage data show that employers are paying more— often far more—for techies (i.e., computer science majors), engineers, and math grads. Krystle Dodge, "What Is the Benefit of an Engineering Degree vs a Science Degree," *Degree Query*, [no date], https://www.degreequery.com /what-is-the-benefit-of-an-engineering-degree-vs-a-science-degree/ (last visited July 22, 2022).

134 *Computer Science Degrees by Year:* Data derived from Scott Jaschik, "Furor on Claim Women's Choices Create Gender Gap in Comp Sci," *Inside Higher Education*, June 24, 2018, https://www.insidehighered.com/news/2018/06/25 /lecturers-explanation-gender-gap-computer-science-it-reflect-womens -choices. Updated from data in *Digest of Education Statistics; see* "Table 251. Degrees Conferred by Degree-Granting Institutions, by Level of Degree and Sex of Student: Selected Years, 1869–70 through 2015–16," https://nces.ed.gov/programs/digest/d06/tables/dt06_251.asp; "Table 277. Earned Degrees in Computer and Information Sciences Conferred by Institutions of Higher Education, by Level of Degree and Sex of Student: 1970–71 to 1993–94," https://nces.ed.gov/programs/digest/d96/d96t277.asp; "Table 279. Degrees in Computer and Information Sciences Conferred by Degree-Granting Institutions, by Level of Degree and Sex of Student: 1970–71 through 2003–04," https://nces.ed.gov/programs/digest/d05/tables/dt05_279.asp; "Table 282. Earned Degrees in Computer and Information Sciences Conferred by Institutions of Higher Education, by Level of Degree and Sex of Student: 1970–71 to 1995–96," https://nces.ed.gov/programs/digest/d98/d9 8t282.asp; "Table 322.20. Bachelor's Degrees Conferred by Postsecondary Institutions, by Race/Ethnicity and Sex of Student: Selected Years, 1976–77 through 2019–20," https://nces.ed.gov/programs/digest/d21/tables/dt21_322 .20.asp?current=yes; and "Table 325.35. Degrees in Computer and Information Sciences Conferred by Postsecondary Institutions, by Level of Degree and Sex of Student: 1964–65 through 2019–20," https://nces.ed.gov/pro grams/digest/d21/tables/dt21_325.35.asp?current=yes.

134 *The study found that men:* American Association of University Women, *Solving the Equation: The Variables for Women's Success in Engineering and Computing* (Washington, D.C.: AAUW, 2015), 3, 56, https://www.aauw.org /app/uploads/2020/03/Solving-the-Equation-report-nsa.pdf.

134 *In other fields:* AAUW, *Solving the Equation*, 56.

135 *He majored in computer engineering:* Sherman Hollar, "Travis Kalanick: American Entrepreneur," *Encyclopædia Britannica*, https://www.britannica .com/biography/Travis-Kalanick (last updated August 11, 2023).

135   *The initial "angel" funding*: Avery Hartmans, "Inside the Crazy-Successful, Controversial Life of Billionaire Uber CEO Travis Kalanick," *Business Insider,* May 4, 2017, https://www.businessinsider.com/life-of-uber-ceo-travis-kalanick-2017-5.

135   *Adding to the pain*: Max Chafkin, "What Makes Uber Run," *Fast Company,* September 8, 2015, https://www.fastcompany.com/3050250/what-makes-uber-run.

135   *He described the experience*: Chafkin, "What Makes Uber Run."

135   *But, "through little else"*: Chafkin, "What Makes Uber Run."

136   *He had just celebrated*: Kara Swisher, "Man and Uber Man," *Vanity Fair,* November 5, 2014, https://www.vanityfair.com/news/2014/12/uber-travis-kalanick-controversy.

136   *Push a button*: Swisher, "Man and Uber Man."

136   *Camp crowed*: Swisher, "Man and Uber Man."

136   *Kalanick, who loved a fight*: Swisher, "Man and Uber Man."

136   *"They started off by operating illegally"*: Swisher, "Man and Uber Man."

136   *Kalanick's startup model*: Mike Isaac, "How Uber Got Lost," *New York Times,* August 23, 2019, https://www.nytimes.com/2019/08/23/business/how-uber-got-lost.html.

137   *The hundreds of millions*: Dan Blystone, "The History of Uber," *Investopedia,* April 28, 2023, https://www.investopedia.com/articles/personal-finance/111015/story-uber.asp.

137   *It went from launching*: Sara Ashley O'Brien, "Uber Is the Most Valuable Startup in the World," CNN Business, July 31, 2015, 3:47 p.m. ET, https://money.cnn.com/2015/07/31/technology/uber-50-billion-valuation/index.html.

137   *The* New York Times: Isaac, "How Uber Got Lost."

137   *According to reporter Mike Isaac*: Isaac, "How Uber Got Lost."

137   *"If your biggest priority"*: Carol Hymowitz, "Uber-Like Bad Behavior Thrives in Absence of Human Resources," *Economic Times,* February 28, 2017, https://economictimes.indiatimes.com/small-biz/startups/uber-like-bad-behavior-thrives-in-absence-of-human-resources/articleshow/57386265.cms.

137   *"Swashbuckling freedom"*: Erin Griffith, "The Other Tech Bubble," *Wired,* December 16, 2017, https://www.wired.com/story/the-other-tech-bubble/. *See also* Chang, *Brotopia,* 40 ("from its earliest days, the industry has self-selected for men: first, antisocial nerds, then, decades later, self-confident and risk-taking bros").

138   *Above all, Kalanick seemed*: Jena McGregor, "'Hustlin' Is Out. Doing 'the Right Thing' Is In. Uber Has Rewritten Its Notorious List of Core Values," *Washington Post,* November 8, 2017, https://www.washingtonpost.com/news/on-leadership/wp/2017/11/08/hustlin-is-out-doing-the-right-thing-is-in-uber-has-rewritten-its-notorious-list-of-core-values/.

138   *And he was prepared*: Isaac, "Inside Uber's Aggressive, Unrestrained Workplace Culture."

138   *Investor Mark Cuban explained*: Eric Siu, "10 Lessons Startups Can Learn from Uber's Growth," *Single Grain* (blog), [no date], https://www

.singlegrain.com/blog-posts/business/10-lessons-startups-can-learn-ubers -growth/ (last visited September 13, 2019).

138   *While toe-stepping was*: Dara Khosrowshahi, "Uber's New Cultural Norms," LinkedIn, November 7, 2017, https://www.linkedin.com/pulse /ubers-new-cultural-norms-dara-khosrowshahi/.

138   *What's more, tournament winners*: Larry E. Ribstein, "Market vs. Regulatory Responses to Corporate Fraud: A Critique of the Sarbanes-Oxley Act of 2002," *Journal of Corporation Law* 28 (2002): 1, 9.

138   *As Vice News explains*: Edward Ongweso Jr. and Jason Koebler, "Uber Became Big by Ignoring Laws (and it Plans to Keep Doing That)," *Vice News*, September 11, 2019, 4:33 p.m., https://www.vice.com/en/article/8xwxyv/uber -became-big-by-ignoring-laws-and-it-plans-to-keep-doing-that.

139   *And that mindset is easy*: Isaac, "How Uber Got Lost"

139   *Workplaces that prize demonstrations*: Jennifer L. Berdahl et al., "Work as a Masculinity Contest," *Journal of Social Issues* 74 (2018): 422, 428–430.

139   *Studies that measure and rank*: Berhdahl et al., "Work as a Masculinity Contest"; Shannon L. Rawski and Angela L. Workman-Stark, "Masculinity Contest Cultures in Policing Organizations and Recommendations for Training Interventions," *Journal of Social Issues* 74 (2018): 607.

139   *While acquiring more power*: Isaac, "Inside Uber's Aggressive, Unrestrained Workplace Culture." *See also* Barbara Wisse and Ed Sleebos, "When the Dark Ones Gain Power: Perceived Position Power Strengthens the Effect of Supervisor Machiavellianism on Abusive Supervision in Work Teams," *Personality and Individual Differences* 299 (September 2016): 122.

139   *And it turns out*: Daniel Nelson Jones and Aurelio Jose Figueredo, "The Core of Darkness: Uncovering the Heart of the Dark Triad," *European Journal of Personality* 27 (2013): 521.

139   *Tech startups, for example*: Hymowitz, "Uber-like Bad Behavior."

139   *As Sheelah Kolhatkar of the* New Yorker *describes*: Sheelah Kolhatkar, "The Tech Industry's Gender-Discrimination Problem," *New Yorker*, November 13, 2017, https://www.newyorker.com/magazine/2017/11/20/the-tech-indu strys-gender-discrimination-problem.

140   *Surveys show that 74 percent*: Swati Mylavarapu, "The Lack of Women in Tech Is More than a Pipeline Problem," *TechCrunch*, May 10, 2016, https:// techcrunch.com/2016/05/10/the-lack-of-women-in-tech-is-more-than-a -pipeline-problem/.

140   *up from 20 percent in 2015*: Berkeley School of Information, "Changing the Curve: Women in Computing," Berkeley School of Information website, July 14, 2021, https://ischoolonline.berkeley.edu/blog/women-computing -computer-science/.

141   *According to eightfold.ai*: "What Tech Layoffs Mean for the Labor Market at Large," *eightfold.ai* (blog), November 22, 2022, https://eightfold.ai/blog /tech-layoffs-labor-market-talent-management/.

141   *At the same time*: Erin Griffith, "Silicon Valley Slides Back into 'Bro' Culture,"

New York Times, September 24, 2022, https://www.nytimes.com/2022/09/24
/technology/silicon-valley-slides-back-into-bro-culture.html.

141 *Startups founded by women:* "Meet the Female-Founded Start-ups Taking
the Health Tech Space by Storm in 2023," *SheCanCode* (blog), February 7,
2023, https://www.shecancode.io/blog/meet-the-female-founded-start-ups
-taking-the-health-tech-space-by-storm-in-2023.

141 *Women have created:* Emily Stevens, "9 Women Founders & Tech Entrepreneurs to Watch in 2023," *Career Foundry* (blog), April 24, 2023, https://
careerfoundry.com/en/blog/career-change/women-to-watch-in-tech/.

141 *Deana Burke, co-founder:* Rebecca Jennings, "Crypto, for Cool Girls," *Vox*,
February 15, 2022, 9:00 a.m., ET, https://www.vox.com/the-goods/22933633
/crypto-nfts-women-boys-club-web3.

141 *And, as we observed in Chapter 4:* "2022 Review of Funding for Female
Founders," Female Founders Fund (blog), April 3, 2023, https://blog.fe
malefoundersfund.com/2022-review-of-funding-for-female-founders-e9
28f8072655.

7. Home Alone: Martinez v. Aspen Dental

143 *That July, Lauren Martinez: Martinez v. Aspen Dental Mgmt., Inc.*, No. 2:20-CV-
545-JES-MRM, 2022 WL 523559 (M.D. Fla. February 22, 2022), at *9.

144 *the percentage of dentists who are women:* Mary Beth Veraci, "HPI: Women
Make Up Growing Percentage of Dental Workforce," American Dental Association, *ADA News*, March 30, 2021, https://www.ada.org/publications
/ada-news/2021/march/women-make-up-growing-percentage-of-dental
-workforce.

144 *Dental office support personnel:* "Dental Office Manager Demographics
and Statistics in the US," Zippia website, [no date], https://www.zippia.com
/dental-office-manager-jobs/demographics/ (last visited January 5, 2024);
"Dental Hygienist Demographics and Statistics in the US," Zippia website, [no
date], https://www.zippia.com/dental-hygienist-jobs/demographics/ (last visited January 5, 2024).

144 *Private equity's playbook:* Emily Stewart, "What Is Private Equity, and Why
Is It Killing Everything You Love?," *Vox*, January 6, 2020, https://www.vox
.com/the-goods/2020/1/6/21024740/private-equity-taylor-swift-toys-r-us
-elizabeth-warren.

144 *Employee or patient satisfaction:* Eileen O'Grady, "Deceptive Marketing,
Medicaid Fraud, and Unnecessary Root Canals on Babies: Private Equity
Drills into the Dental Care Industry," Private Equity Stakeholder Project
website, July 2021, https://pestakeholder.org/wp-content/uploads/2021/08
/PESP_DSO_July2021.pdf. This report found that:

> The private equity investment model, which typically targets out-
> sized returns over relatively short time horizons, may incentiv-
> ize profit-seeking tactics that are harmful to patients. Payment

structures between DSOs and dentists have been found to create perverse incentives that lead to overtreatment of patients, misleading advertising schemes, Medicaid fraud, and other problematic practices in order to reach revenue targets set by DSOs and maximize profit.

See also Heather Perlberg, "How Private Equity Is Ruining American Health Care," *Bloomberg*, May 20, 2020, 4:00 a.m., https://www.bloomberg.com/news/features/2020-05-20/private-equity-is-ruining-health-care-covid-is-making-it-worse.

145 *After being acquired:* Joseph Bruch et al., "COVID-19 and Private Equity Investment in Health Care Delivery," *JAMA Health Forum* 2 (2021), https://jamanetwork.com/journals/jama-health-forum/fullarticle/2777170; Fred Schulte, "Sick Profit: Investigating Private Equity's Stealthy Takeover of Health Care Across Cities and Specialties," *KFF Health News*, November 14, 2022, https://kffhealthnews.org/news/article/private-equity-takeover-health-care-cities-specialties/.

145 *And mortality rates:* Aine Doris, "When Private Equity Takes over Nursing Homes, Mortality Rates Jump," *Chicago Booth Review*, May 18, 2021, https://www.chicagobooth.edu/review/when-private-equity-takes-over-nursing-homes-mortality-rates-jump.

145 *They found that the profit goals:* Doris, "When Private Equity Takes."

145 *The researchers found:* Doris, "When Private Equity Takes."

145 *And this is:* Schulte, "Sick Profit." *See also* Nirad Jain et al., "Healthcare Private Equity Market 2022: The Year in Review and Outlook," Bain & Company, report, January 9, 2023, https://www.bain.com/insights/year-in-review-global-healthcare-private-equity-and-ma-report-2023/.

145 *Aspen Dental:* Aspen Dental Management, *Crunchbase* website, [no date], https://www.crunchbase.com/organization/aspen-dental-management-inc (last visited June 14, 2022).

145 *For its part, Aspen Dental:* Jack Lowenstein, "Working Mom Says She Lost Her Job Due to Need to Care for Her Sick Children," *WINK-TV News*, March 10, 2021, 5:48 p.m., https://www.winknews.com/2021/03/10/working-mom-says-she-lost-her-job-due-to-need-to-care-for-her-sick-children/.

145 *In 2013, a PBS series:* David Heath, "Dental Chain Violated New York Law, Settlement Says," *Frontline*, June 22, 2015, https://www.pbs.org/wgbh/frontline/article/dental-chain-violated-new-york-law-settlement-says/.

145 *A class action lawsuit:* David Heath, "Aspen Dental Facing Class-Action Lawsuit," *Frontline*, October 19, 2012, https://www.pbs.org/wgbh/frontline/article/aspen-dental-facing-class-action-lawsuit/.

145 *And in 2021:* Joe DiFazio, "Mass. Attorney General Suing Aspen Dental, Alleging 'Bait and Switch' Ad Campaigns," *Patriot Ledger*, December 11, 2021, https://www.patriotledger.com/story/news/2021/12/11/state-ag-suing-aspen-dental-accusing-company-deceptive-marketing/6460176001/.

146   *settled with the attorney general's office:* Office of the Attorney General, "Attorney General's Office Reaches $3.5 Million Settlement with Aspen Dental over Claims of Deceptive Advertising," Mass.gov, January 5, 2023, https://www.mass.gov/news/attorney-generals-office-reaches-35-million-settlement-with-aspen-dental-over-claims-of-deceptive-advertising.

146   *The reality is that women:* Claire Cain Miller, "The Pandemic Created a Child-Care Crisis. Mothers Bore the Burden," *New York Times,* May 17, 2021, https://www.nytimes.com/interactive/2021/05/17/upshot/women-workforce-employment-covid.html. ("When schools and child care centers shut down last spring, 5.1 million American mothers stopped working for pay. Today, 1.3 million of them remain out of work.")

146   *"mothers were 40 percent more likely":* Leila Schochet, "The Childcare Crisis Is Keeping Women Out of the Workforce," Center for American Progress, report, March 28, 2019, https://www.americanprogress.org/issues/early-childhood/reports/2019/03/28/467488/child-care-crisis-keeping-women-workforce/.

147   *During the first year of the pandemic:* Diana Boesch and Shilpa Phadke, "When Women Lose All the Jobs: Essential Actions for a Gender-Equitable Recovery," Center for American Progress, report, February 21, 2021, https://www.americanprogress.org/issues/women/reports/2021/02/01/495209/women-lose-jobs-essential-actions-gender-equitable-recovery/. Do note that women with young children, whose job loss rate was 50% above men at the height of the pandemic, have now come back. Misty L. Heggeness et al., "Tracking for Job Losses for Mothers of School-Age Children During a Health Crisis," U.S. Census Bureau, report, March 3, 2021, https://www.census.gov/library/stories/2021/03/moms-work-and-the-pandemic.html.

147   *women without college degrees:* Lydia DePillis, "Who Are America's Missing Workers?," *New York Times,* September 12, 2022, https://www.nytimes.com/2022/09/12/business/economy/labor-participation-covid.html.

147   *They disproportionately worked:* Sarah Jane Glynn and Mark DeWolf, "Black Women's Economic Recovery Continues to Lag," U.S. Department of Labor (blog), 2022, https://blog.dol.gov/2022/02/09/black-womens-economic-recovery-continues-to-lag; Stephanie H. Murray, "The Pandemic Exposed the Inequality of American Motherhood," *Atlantic,* November 28, 2022, https://www.theatlantic.com/family/archive/2022/11/covid-impact-women/672251/.

147   *Working-class women:* U.S. Census Bureau, "Are Women Really Opting Out of Work After They Have Babies?," news story, August 19, 2019, https://www.census.gov/library/stories/2019/08/are-women-really-opting-out-of-work-after-they-have-babies.html.

147   *Mothers of young children:* Marianne Cooper, "Mother's Careers Are at Extraordinary Risk Right Now," *Atlantic,* October 1, 2020, https://www.theatlantic.com/family/archive/2020/10/pandemic-amplifying-bias-against-working-mothers/616565/.

147   *Employment for mothers with children:* Caitlyn Collins, Leah Ruppanner, and William J. Scarborough, "Why Haven't U.S. Mothers Returned to Work? The Child-Care Infrastructure They Need Is Still Missing," *Washington Post,*

November 8, 2021, https://www.washingtonpost.com/politics/2021/11/08/why-havent-us-mothers-returned-work-child-care-infrastructure-they-need-is-still-missing/.

147 *Even mothers who:* Collins et al., "Why Haven't U.S. Mothers Returned?"

148 *we have to go all the way back:* Lydia Kiesling, "Paid Child Care for Working Mothers? All It Took Was a World War," *New York Times,* October 2, 2019, https://www.nytimes.com/2019/10/02/us/paid-childcare-working-mothers-wwii.html.

148 *Despite reluctance:* Kiesling, "Paid Child Care."

148 *In the three years that followed:* Rhaina Cohen, "Who Took Care of Rosie the Riveter's Kids?," *Atlantic,* November 18, 2015, https://www.theatlantic.com/business/archive/2015/11/daycare-world-war-rosie-riveter/415650/.

148 *Richard Nixon had promised:* "The Nation: Child Care Veto," *Time* magazine, December 20, 1971, https://content.time.com/time/subscriber/article/0,33009,878957,00.html.

149 *"fiscal irresponsibility, administrative unworkability":* Emily Schroeder, "The Crucial Juncture of Early Education Reform," *Trinity Reporter,* May 2, 2018, https://commons.trincoll.edu/edreform/2018/05/the-crucial-juncture-of-early-education-reform/.

149 *"Attack on American Free Enterprise System":* Lewis F. Powell Jr., "Powell Memorandum: Attack on American Free Enterprise System," August 23, 1971, https://scholarlycommons.law.wlu.edu/powellmemo/1/.

149 *As philanthropists of conservative causes:* Eric Rubenstein, "The Business of Conservative Politics: Jane Mayer on the Koch Brothers' Buying of the Republican Party," *Northwestern Business Review,* February 15, 2018, https://northwesternbusinessreview.org/the-business-of-conservative-politics-jane-mayer-on-the-koch-brothers-buying-of-the-republican-c38f18ebc477.

149 *David and Charles had inherited:* "America's Largest Private Companies: 2023," *Forbes,* November 14, 2023, https://www.forbes.com/largest-private-companies/list/.

150 *When Nixon had vetoed:* Institute of Education Sciences, "Youth Indicators 1996/Indicator 19. Mothers' Employment," National Center for Education Statistics, report, https://nces.ed.gov/pubs98/yi/yi19.pdf (1970 statistics).

150 *Instead, conservatives reflexively opposed:* Marianne Levine, "Paul Ryan Prizes Family Time, Opposes Family Leave," *Politico,* October 21, 2015, 6:06 p.m., https://www.politico.com/story/2015/10/paul-ryan-family-leave-speaker-house-215034.

150 *While Clinton's welfare reform:* Liz Halloran, "Gingrich's Proposals on Child Labor Stir Attacks, but Raise Issues," NPR, December 7, 2011, 10:34 a.m., https://www.npr.org/sections/itsallpolitics/2011/12/07/143258836/gingrichs-proposals-on-child-labor-stir-attacks-but-raise-real-issues.

151 *Although First Lady Laura Bush:* "A Legacy of Failure: Millions of Children and Families Still Struggling," Children's Defense Fund, report, February 13, 2018, https://www.childrensdefense.org/wp-content/uploads/2018/08/2009-Presidents-fy-Budget-Analysis.pdf.

151 *By the time President Barack Obama:* Sara Mead, "Obama's Early Childhood Education Legacy," opinion, *U.S. News & World Report*, January 13,
2017, 7:00 a.m., https://www.usnews.com/opinion/knowledge-bank/articles
/2017-01-13/obamas-leaves-a-lasting-legacy-on-early-childhood-education.

151 *When Ivanka's proposal was finally unveiled:* Sara Mead, "Ivanka's Tax Credit Won't
Help Kids" opinion, *U.S. News & World Report*, October 19, 2017, 4:30 p.m.,
https://www.usnews.com/opinion/economic-intelligence/articles/2017-10-19
/ivanka-trumps-child-care-tax-credit-doesnt-help-working-families.

151 *Not only did Trump fail:* Katie Hamm et al., "The Truth About President Trump's
Track Record on Childcare," Center for American Progress, news report, September 14, 2020, https://www.americanprogress.org/issues/early-childhood
/news/2020/09/14/490332/truth-president-trumps-track-record-child-care/.

152 *At a time when there was:* Kavitha Cardoza, "Researchers Warn Nearly Half
of U.S. Child Care Centers Could Be Lost to Pandemic," NPR, September 7,
2020, 4:02 p.m., https://www.npr.org/2020/09/07/909634878/researchers
-warn-about-half-of-child-care-centers-in-u-s-could-be-lost-to-pandemic.

152 *Even before COVID-19 struck:* John Halpin et al., "What Do Voters Want on
Child Care Ahead of the 2020 Elections?: Results from a National Survey of
Registered Voters," Center for American Progress, report, September 25, 2020,
https://www.americanprogress.org/issues/early-childhood/reports/2020
/09/25/490772/voters-want-child-care-ahead-2020-elections/.

152 *Middle-income women:* Michelle Fox, "Billions of Covid Relief Dollars Are
Going to Child Care. Here's Why Advocates Say More Needs to Be Done to
Fix the Crisis," *CNBC*, March 18, 2021, 9:41 a.m., https://www.cnbc.com/2021
/03/18/despite-billions-in-relief-advocates-say-more-needs-to-be-done-to
-fix-the-child-care-crisis.html.

152 *These mothers have always had:* Caitlyn Collins, "Why Haven't US Mothers Returned to Work?," *Washington Post*, November 8, 2021, https://
www.washingtonpost.com/politics/2021/11/08/why-havent-us-mothers
-returned-work-child-care-infrastructure-they-need-is-still-missing/.

152 *If you're an employer:* Martina Hund-Mejean and Marcela Escobari, "Our
Employment System Has Failed Low-Wage Workers. How Can We Rebuild?," Brookings Institution (blog), April 28, 2020, https://www.brookings
.edu/blog/up-front/2020/04/28/our-employment-system-is-failing-low-wage
-workers-how-do-we-make-it-more-resilient/. ("[T]he poor quality of low-
wage employment leads to a cycle of attrition and replacement that drives
the labor market toward a less-than-optimal equilibrium with neither firms
nor workers incented to invest in the job. This takes a steep toll on workers'
skills and opportunities for training: Low wage earners have little incentive
to spend scarce time and hard-earned money building skills; meanwhile,
employers, though frequently lamenting skills gaps, have little incentive to
train workers who they expect to leave. The labor market arrives at a 'low
skill equilibrium.'") Higher-paid employees have more access to leave. Kathleen Romig and Kathleen Bryant, "A National Paid Leave Program Would
Help Workers, Families," Center on Budget & Policy Priorities, report,

April 27, 2021, https://www.cbpp.org/research/economy/a-national-paid -leave-program-would-help-workers-families.

153 *Today it lags behind:* Tim Walker, National Education Association, "U.S. Lags Far Behind Other Countries in Access to Early Childhood Education," *NEA Today*, September 21, 2016, https://www.nea.org/advocating-for-change/new -from-nea/us-lags-far-behind-other-countries-access-early-childhood.

153 *There are many factors:* Abigail Johnson Hess, "Women's Earnings Drop After Having a Child—But Men's Do Not," *CNBC*, October 16, 2019, 9:00 a.m., https://www.cnbc.com/2019/10/16/womens-earnings-drop-after -having-a-childbut-mens-do-not.html; Paul Krugman, "Good Luck to Republicans if Biden's Family Plan Becomes Law," opinion, *New York Times*, April 29, 2021, https://www.nytimes.com/2021/04/29/opinion/child-care -biden.html; Claire Cain Miller, "The Gender Pay Gap Is Largely Because of Motherhood," *New York Times*, May 13, 2017, https://www.nytimes.com /2017/05/13/upshot/the-gender-pay-gap-is-largely-because-of-mother hood.html.

153 *According to Nextup:* "The Female Leadership Crisis 5," *Nextup News*, March 2018, https://www.nextupisnow.org/research/the-female-leadership-crisis -report/.

154 *Or, as Harvard economist Claudia Goldin:* Claudia Goldin, *Career and Family: Women's Century-Long Journey Toward Equality* (Princeton, NJ: Princeton University Press, 2021), 167. ("Having a husband who is hopping across continents means he cannot be home every day and possibly not every week.")

154 *The women in this group:* Robin Shulman, "If You're Pregnant and Working, Know Your Rights," *New York Times*, April 18, 2020, https://www.nytimes .com/article/pregnancy-discrimination-work.html.

154 *Ironically, middle-income areas:* Amanda Becker, "Middle-Income and Rural Families Disproportionately Grapple with Child-Care Deserts, New Analysis Shows," *Washington Post*, June 22, 2020, 7:00 a.m., https://www.washington post.com/nation/2020/06/22/middle-income-rural-families-disproportion ately-grapple-with-child-care-deserts-new-analysis-shows/.

154 *To make matters worse:* June Carbone and Naomi Cahn, *Marriage Markets: How Inequality Is Remaking the American Family* (New York: Oxford University Press, 2014), 100–101.

154 *Sociologists suggest that balancing work:* Paul Amato et al., *Alone Together: How Marriage in America Is Changing* (Cambridge, MA: Harvard University Press, 2007), 123–124.

154 *Wives who work primarily:* Carbone and Cahn, *Marriage Markets*, 100.

155 *The U.S. Supreme Court's 2022:* 142 S. Ct. 2228 (2022).

155 *Following* Dobbs: Elizabeth Nash and Isabel Guarnieri, "Six Months Post-Roe, 24 US States Have Banned Abortion or Are Likely to Do So: A Roundup," Guttmacher Institute, report, January 10, 2023, https://www.gutt macher.org/2023/01/six-months-post-roe-24-us-states-have-banned-abortion -or-are-likely-do-so-roundup.

155 *The Guttmacher Institute estimated:* "State Policies on Abortion," Guttmacher

Institute, report, [no date], https://www.guttmacher.org/united-states/abor
tion/state-policies-abortion (last visited February 4, 2023).

155 *An amicus brief:* Brief of Amici Curiae Economists in Support of Respondents at 12, *Dobbs v. Jackson Women's Health Org.*, No. 19-1392 (Sept. 20,
2021), https://www.supremecourt.gov/DocketPDF/19/19-1392/193084/2021
0920175559884_19-1392bsacEconomists.pdf. "For instance, one such study
showed that young women who utilized legal abortion to delay an unplanned
start to motherhood by just one year realized an 11% increase in hourly wages
later in their careers. Another found that, for young women who experienced
an unintended pregnancy, access to abortion increased the probability they
finished college by nearly 20 percentage points, and the probability that they
entered a professional occupation by nearly 40 percentage points."

155 *they will also have much lower:* "The Harms of Denying a Woman a Wanted
Abortion: Findings from the Turnaway Study," Advancing New Standards in
Reproductive Health, University of California, San Francisco, report, 2020,
https://www.ansirh.org/sites/default/files/publications/files/the_harms_of
_denying_a_woman_a_wanted_abortion_4-16-2020.pdf.

155 *be "less likely to move":* Rani Molla, "5 Ways Abortion Bans Could Hurt
Women in the Workforce," *Vox*, June 24, 2022, 5:15 p.m., ET, https://www
.vox.com/recode/23074696/abortion-illegal-supereme-court-women-work
(citing research from the nonprofit Washington Center for Equitable
Growth).

155 *Across the board, only 50 percent:* Ann O'Leary, "How Family Leave Laws
Left Out Low-Income Workers," *Berkeley Journal of Employment and Labor
Law* 28 (2007): 1, 45.

156 *Two-thirds of new mothers:* The number of states with paid family leave is
inching upward, but as of this writing only thirteen states and D.C. require it
(and the percentage of income supplementation varies among jurisdictions).
Bipartisan Policy Center, "State Paid Family Leave Across the U.S.," January 12, 2024, https://bipartisanpolicy.org/explainer/state-paid-family-leave
-laws-across-the-u-s/.

156 *On the other hand:* Julia Isaacs, Olivia Healy, and H. Elizabeth Peters, "Paid
Family Leave in the United States," Urban Institute, report, May 10, 2017,
fig. 1, https://www.urban.org/sites/default/files/publication/90201/paid_family
_leave_0.pdf.

156 *A federal district court ruled against her: Martinez*, 2022 WL 523559, at *9.

157 *Yet her determination: Martinez v. Aspen Dental Mgmt., Inc.*, No. 22-10906
(11th Cir. Mar. 23, 2022). The Eleventh Circuit Court of Appeals subsequently
dismissed the case for failure to timely file an appeal brief. *Martinez v. Aspen
Dental Mgmt., Inc.*, No. 22-10906BB, 2022 WL 19229076 (11th Cir. Sept. 28,
2022).

157 *When asked by a local news station:* Lowenstein, "Working Mom Says."

157 *settled with the attorney general's office:* Ryan Cooper, "How Joe Manchin Killed
Biden's Child Tax Credit," *MSNBC*, April 12, 2021, 1:41 p.m., CDT, https://www
.msnbc.com/opinion/msnbc-opinion/how-joe-manchin-killed-biden-s

-child-tax-credit-n1294320; Oliver O'Connel, "J.D. Vance Blasted After He Equates Biden's Free Childcare to 'Class War,'" *Independent*, April 29, 2021, 10:21 p.m., https://www.independent.co.uk/news/world/americas/us-poli tics/jd-vance-universal-childcare-criticism-b1839903.html; Jonathan Weisman and Emily Cochrane, "Benefits for All or Just the Needy? Manchin's Demand Focuses Debate," *New York Times*, October 8, 2021, https://www .nytimes.com/2021/10/08/us/politics/manchin-democrats-means-testing .html (quoting Senator Manchin, who opposed Biden administration plans to strengthen family support, stating that his goal was to avoid "basically changing our whole society to an entitlement mentality.")

157   *Post-pandemic, a new view:* Krugman, "Good Luck to Republicans."
157   *Investment in children:* Andres S. Bustamante et al., "Adult Outcomes of Sustained High-Quality Early Child Care and Education: Do They Vary by Family Income?," *Child Development* 93 (October 2021): 502.
158   *Congress passed:* 29 U.S.C. § 218d (2022).
158   *In addition, Congress passed:* 42 U.S.C. § 2000gg-1 (2023).
158   *States have begun:* "CCSA and Its National Center Launches Map for State by State Investments in the Child Care Workforce," Child Care Services Association, report, January 31, 2022, https://www.childcareservices .org/2022/01/31/ccsa-and-its-national-center-launches-map-for-state-by -state-investments-in-the-child-care-workforce/; "How States Are Supplementing American Rescue Plan Funding," Center for American Progress, report, August 23, 2022, https://www.americanprogress.org/article/increas ing-americas-child-care-supply/.

8. Platform World: Gig Workers v. Handy

160   *Depending on how you count them:* Many of those freelancers are doing it as an income supplement. Board of Governors, "Report on the Economic Well-Being of U.S. Households in 2017," Federal Reserve System, report, May 2018, https://www.federalreserve.gov/publications/201-economic-well -being-of-us-households-in-2017-preface.htm. In a commissioned survey of 6,000 U.S. adults, conducted by independent research firm Edelman Intelligence, found that 47% of millennials were doing at least some gig work, and for 29% it was their sole source of income. "Freelancers Predicted to Become the U.S. Workforce Majority Within a Decade, with Nearly 50% of Millennial Workers Already Freelancing, Annual 'Freelancing in America' Study Finds," Upwork, press release, October 17, 2017, https://www.up work.com/press/2017/10/17/freelancing-in-america-2017/. Our figures are from 2017. Pew Research has a 2021 report, but it views gig work in a different way (as online platform work): https://www.pewresearch.org/inter net/2021/12/08/the-state-of-gig-work-in-2021/. *See also* McKinsey & Co., "Freelance, Side Hustles, and Gigs: Many More Americans Have Become Independent Workers," report, August 23, 2022, https://www.mckinsey .com/featured-insights/sustainable-inclusive-growth/future-of-america

/freelance-side-hustles-and-gigs-many-more-americans-have-become-in dependent-workers (estimating 58 million, or 36% of all who were employed are "independent workers").

160 *This number comprises around:* "Number of Freelance Workers in the United States from 2014 to 2022," *Statista*, November 3, 2023, https://www.statista .com/statistics/685468/amount-of-people-freelancing-us/.

160 *They're unlikely to have health insurance*: Emilie Jackson, Adam Looney, and Shanthi Ramnath, "The Rise of Alternative Work Arrangements: Evidence and Implications for Tax Filing and Benefit Coverage," U.S. Department of the Treasury, report, 2017, 19–22, https://www.treasury.gov/resource-center/tax -policy/tax-analysis/Documents/WP-114.pdf.

160 *They are much more concerned*: McKinsey & Co., "Freelance, Side Hustles" (54% of gig compared to 35% of "permanent").

160 *Those at the bottom*: Gretchen M. Spreitzer, Lindsey Cameron, and Lyndon Garrett, "Alternative Work Arrangements; Two Images of the New World of Work," *Annual Review of Organizational Psychology and Organizational Behavior* 4 (2017): 473, 474.

160 *And although a majority of gig workers*: Gallup, "The Gig Economy and Alternative Work Arrangements," report, 2018, 12, https://www.gallup.com /workplace/240878/gig-economy-paper-2018.aspx.

160 *All these facts are true*: Bureau of Labor Statistics, "Women in the Labor Force: A Databook," report, April 2021, Table 20, https://www.bls.gov/opub /reports/womens-databook/2020/home.htm (adding together the statistics by race, 904,000 women receive an hourly wage below the prevailing federal minimum wage compared to 459,000 men).

161 *The platform has proved*: Handy company website, [no date], https://www .handy.com/locations (last visited May 23, 2023).

161 *In fact, in 2022*: Angi Inc., "Report on Form 10-K for the Fiscal Year Ended Dec. 31, 2022," U.S. Securities and Exchange Commission website, March 1, 2023, 31, http://edgar.secdatabase.com/675/170511023000022/filing-main .htm.

161 *"I felt really violated"*: Kellen Browning and Kate Conger, "Cleaners Demand Harassment Safeguards From the Booking Service Handy," *New York Times*, September 10, 2020, https://www.nytimes.com/2020/09/10/business /handy-service-cleaners-harassment.html.

162 *At one time, most wage labor*: Naomi Cahn and June Carbone, "Uncoupling," *Arizona State Law Journal* 53 (2021): 1, 22–25.

162 *Naomi was a temporary worker*: It was known as "Kelly Girl Service, Inc." from 1957 to 1966. "You've Come a Long Way, Kelly Girl!," Kelly Services, Inc., [no date], https://www.kellyservices.us/us/about-us/company-infor mation/kelly-girl-story/ (last visited February 15, 2023).

163 *Kelly Services originated*: Kelly Services, Inc., "History," [no date], http:// www.fundinguniverse.com/company-histories/kelly-services-inc-history/ (last visited February 15, 2023); "You've Come a Long Way."

163 *The temp industry was deliberately feminized*: Erin Hatton, *The Temp*

Economy: From Kelly Girls to Permatemps in Postwar America (Philadelphia: Temple University Press, 2011), 21, 33.

163 *They did so, in part*: Jerry M. Hunter, Annual Meeting Section of Labor and Employment Law, "The National Labor Relations Board's Decision in M.B. Sturgis, Inc., and Its Impact on Employers Who Utilize Contingent Employees as Part of Their Workforce," American Bar Association, report, 2001, 3–6, http://apps.americanbar.org/labor/lel-aba-annual/papers/2001/hunter.pdf. Temporary workers were excluded from membership in the same bargaining unit with regular employees—unless the employer consented—by the National Labor Relations Board until 2000. Michael J. Hely, "The Impact of *Sturgis* on Bargaining Power for Contingent Workers in the U.S. Labor Market," *Washington University Journal of Law and Policy* 11 (2003): 295, 295–296.

163 *They emphasized that temps were less expensive*: Erin Hatton, "The Rise of the Permanent Temp Economy," *New York Times*, January 26, 2013, 3:41 p.m., https://archive.nytimes.com/opinionator.blogs.nytimes.com/2013/01/26/the-rise-of-the-permanent-temp-economy/.

163 *In 1870, the census*: Ester Bloom, "The Decline of Domestic Help," *Atlantic*, September 2015, https://www.theatlantic.com/business/archive/2015/09/decline-domestic-help-maid/406798/.

164 *and in 1880*: Tera W. Hunter, *To 'Joy My Freedom: Southern Black Women's Lives and Labors After the Civil War* (Cambridge, MA: Harvard University Press, 1997), 50 (reporting that in 1880 Atlanta, 98% of wage-earning black women were employed as domestics); Shelby Lin Erdman, "Book Details How Household Labor Unionized, Started Movement," *WABE*, August 25, 2015, https://www.wabe.org/book-details-how-household-labor-unionized-started-movement/; Daniel E. Slotnik, "Overlooked No More: Dorothy Bolden, Who Started a Movement for Domestic Workers," *New York Times*, February 20, 2019, https://www.nytimes.com/2019/02/20/obituaries/dorothy-bolden-overlooked.html. *See also* Naomi Cahn, "The Power of Caretaking," *Yale Journal of Law and Feminism* 12 (2000): 177, 223.

164 *When Congress passed the Fair Labor Standards Act*: City of Chicago, "History of Domestic Workers in the United States," Chicago.gov, [no date], https://www.chicago.gov/city/en/sites/your-home-is-my-workplace/home/history-of-domestic-workers.html (last visited June 28, 2022).

164 *At the time it was passed*: Harmony Goldberg, "The Long Journey Home: The Contested Exclusion and Inclusion of Domestic Workers from Federal Wage and Hour Protections in the United States," International Labour Organization, report, 2015, 4–7, https://www.ilo.org/wcmsp5/groups/public/---edprotect/---protrav/---travail/documents/publication/ wcms396235.pdf.

164 *Today, the approximately 2 million*: Julia Wolfe et al., "Domestic Workers Chartbook," Economic Policy Institute, report, May 14, 2020, https://www.epi.org/publication/domestic-workers-chartbook-a-comprehensive-look-at-the-demographics-wages-benefits-and-poverty-rates-of-the-professionals-who-care-for-our-family-members-and-clean-our-homes/.

164 *Since the 1970s, there has*: Louis Hyman, *Temp: How American Work,*

American Business, and the American Dream Became Temporary (New York: Viking, 2018), 84. ("Secure work for most white men began to disappear in the 1970s, but for Mexican migrants, African Americans, and even some unfortunate white men, it had happened earlier.")

164 *During the 1980s and 1990s: See* Hatton, "Rise of the Permanent."

165 *The result is a "new":* Katherine V. W. Stone, "The New Psychological Contract: Implications of the Changing Workplace for Labor and Employment Law," *UCLA Law Review* 48 (2001): 519.

165 *Employers no longer guarantee:* Hyman, *Temp*, 255; Alexandrea J. Ravenelle, *Hustle and Gig: Struggling and Surviving in the Sharing Economy* (Oakland, CA: University of California Press, 2019), 178–181.

165 *Manufacturing jobs peaked:* U.S. Bureau of Labor Statistics, "Current Employment Statistics Survey: 100 Years of Employment, Hours, and Earnings," report, August 2016, https://www.bls.gov/opub/mlr/2016/article/current-employment-statistics-survey-100-years-of-employment-hours-and-earnings.htm. *See also* Katelynn Harris, "Forty Years of Falling Manufacturing Employment," U.S. Bureau of Labor Statistics, report, November 2020, https://www.bls.gov/opub/btn/volume-9/forty-years-of-falling-manufacturing-employment.htm.

165 *with the absolute number:* Harris, "Forty Years of Falling."

165 *The largest job growth:* Bureau of Labor Statistics, "Current Employment Statistics."

165 *By 2015, retail jobs:* Bureau of Labor Statistics, "Current Employment Statistics."

165 *The demand for:* U.S. Bureau of Labor Statistics, "Occupational Outlook Handbook: Home Health and Personal Care Aides," report, September 6, 2023, https://www.bls.gov/ooh/healthcare/home-health-aides-and-personal-care-aides.htm.

165 *Starting in the 1990s, the number:* Hatton, "Rise of the Permanent."

165 *Instead, machines and temps:* Ravenelle, *Hustle and Gig*, 179.

165 *with temporary employment:* Bureau of Labor Statistics, "Current Employment Statistics."

165 *The Bureau of Labor Statistics indicates:* Bureau of Labor Statistics, "Current Employment Statistics."

166 *Still, in 2019, with the economy:* Daisuke Wakabayashi, "Google's Shadow Work Force: Temps Who Outnumber Full-Time Employees," *New York Times*, May 28, 2019, https://www.nytimes.com/2019/05/28/technology/google-temp-workers.html.

166 *LinkedIn reported:* McKenna Moore, "The Rise of Contractors in Tech," LinkedIn, 2022, https://perma.cc/RC6L-QBL8.

166 *In America, we have changed:* Gerald F. Davis, *The Vanishing American Corporation: Navigating the Hazards of a New Economy* (Oakland, CA: Berrett Koehler, 2016), 144.

166 *If this story were:* Indeed, Ford Motor Company had 300+% turnover in 1913, prompting Henry Ford to adopt the male family wage and to restrict

managers' ability to arbitrarily terminate workers. Cahn and Carbone, "Uncoupling," 16.

166 *ensuring most jobs:* Vanessa M. Oddo et al., "Changes in Precarious Employment in the United States: A Longitudinal Analysis," *Scandinavian Journal of Work and Environmental Health* 47, no. 3 (2021): 171, https:// www.ncbi.nlm.nih.gov/pmc/articles/PMC8126438/ (noting that in the United States, "[t]he number of workers in high-quality, full-time employment, with adequate wages and benefits, has decreased over the last 40 years, while the number with low-quality, precarious employment (PE) has increased.")

166 *dramatically reducing benefits*: Jordan Pfuntner, "Percent of Private Industry Workers Participating in Retirement Plans, Selected Periods, 1990–2003," U.S. Bureau of Labor Statistics, report, 2004, https://www.bls.gov/opub/mlr /cwc/percent-of-private-industry-workers-participating-in-retirement -plans-selected-periods-1990-2003.pdf; U.S. Bureau of Labor Statistics, "Retirement Plans for Workers in Private Industry and State and Local Government in 2022," report, February 1, 2023, https://www.bls.gov/opub /ted/2023/retirement-plans-for-workers-in-private-industry-and-state -and-local-government-in-2022.htm. *See also* David R. Howell and Arne L. Kalleberg, "Declining Job Quality in the United States," *Russell Sage Foundation Journal of Social Science* 5, no. 4 (September 2019): 1 (observing that "[d]eclines in nonwage benefits such as employer-paid health insurance and pensions have also been greater for lower-wage workers").

166 *The numbers are equally divided:* Jacques Buffett, "Workers on the Gig Economy, Zety (blog), August 16, 2022, https://zety.com/blog/workers-on-gig -economy.

167 *why they prefer gig work:* Tracy Brower, "What It's Really Like to Be a Gig Worker," *Forbes*, September 11, 2022, https://www.forbes.com /sites/tracybrower/2022/09/11/what-its-really-like-to-be-a-gig-work er/?sh=1776ba826507.

167 *In contrast with traditional jobs:* Brower, "What It's Really Like."

167 *her LinkedIn page:* Ana Margarita Medina, LinkedIn, [no date], https://www .linkedin.com/in/anammedina/ [https://perma.cc/KYJ6-8MRA?type=stan dard] (last visited February 16, 2023).

167 *What's going on:* Jacob S. Hacker, *The Great Risk Shift: The New Economic Insecurity and the Decline of the American Dream* (New York: Oxford University Press, updated ed. 2008).

167 *He describes it:* Jacob S. Hacker, "Average Workers Can't Bear Any More Risk," *Atlantic*, May 2020, https://www.theatlantic.com/ideas/archive/2020/05/av erage-workers-cant-bear-any-more-risk/612385/.

167 *Hacker couples:* Hacker, "Average Workers."

167 *In addition, workers are often:* Gig workers are particularly vulnerable to companies not paying them fully for their labor. This can result from embedded costs shifted onto their backs (as in the case of Uber drivers) or in even more extreme circumstances, companies that require gig workers to

pay them for training and supplies. Matthew P. Schneider, "Wage Theft in the Gig Economy," *Patheos* (blog), December 8, 2020, https://www.patheos .com/blogs/throughcatholiclenses/2020/12/wage-theft-in-the-gig-econ omy/.

167 *As secure jobs: See, e.g.,* Benjamin Halprin, "'Why Do You Want My Pass- word?': Assessing Ultimate Control of a Journalist's Twitter Account Used for Work Purposes," *Fordham Intellectual Property, Media and Entertain Law Journal* 30 (2019): 325, 391. ("[S]tudies show that millennials tend to switch jobs more often, and the 'gig economy' is increasingly prominent."); Deborah A. Widiss, "Equalizing Parental Leave," *Minnesota Law Review* 105 (2021): 2175, 2205. ("Low-skilled workers, women, and racial minorities are disproportionately likely to be excluded [from FMLA] because they are more likely to change jobs frequently, work part-time, and work for small employers.") *See also* Jeremy Pilaar, "Assessing the Gig Economy in Compar- ative Perspective: How Platform Work Challenges the French and American Legal Orders," *Journal of Law & Policy* 27 (2018): 47, 48. ("While full-time jobs were the norm in industrialized countries for much of the twentieth century, they have gradually been replaced by non-standard employment relationships that offer lower pay, less predictable hours, fewer benefits, and uncertain career prospects.")

167 *Indeed, Uber paid $20 million:* Tyler Sonnemaker, "Uber and Lyft Have Long Said They Pay Drivers Fairly, but They Haven't Shared All the Data That Could Prove It," *Business Insider*, June 17, 2021, https://www.businessin sider.com/how-much-uber-lyft-drivers-earn-mystery-company-pay-data -2021-6.

168 *Between 20 and 30 percent:* Edison Research, "Sexual Harassment in the Workplace: #Metoo, Women, Men, and the Gig Economy," report, June 2018, 3, http://www.edisonresearch.com/wp-content/uploads/2018/06/Sexual-Harass ment-in-the-Workplace-metoo-Women-Men-and-the-Gig-Economy-6.20 .18-1.pdf (reporting that "[a]lmost one-third of those working in the gig economy have experienced sexual harassment at work"); Monica Anderson et al., "The State of Gig Work in 2021," Pew Research Center, report, Decem- ber 8, 2021, https://www.pewresearch.org/internet/2021/12/08/the-state -of-gig-work-in-2021/ ("about one-in-five say they have often (7%) or some- times (12%) experienced unwanted sexual advances while completing jobs").

168 *Moreover, although platform workers:* Alexandrea Ravenelle, "The Gig Econ- omy Makes Workers Vulnerable to Sexual Harassment," *Medium: OneZero* (blog), March 27, 2019, https://onezero.medium.com/the-gig-economy -makes-workers-vulnerable-to-sexual-harassment-53208dfb5b5a.

168 *And an HR department:* Ella Glover, "Why Precarious Workers Are Facing Rife Sexual Harassment," *Huck*, May 4, 2021, https://www.huckmag.com /perspectives/activism-2/the-precarious-workers-facing-rife-sexual-ha rassment/.

168 *Gig jobs vary:* "The Freelancer Pay Gap," *ZenBusiness*, report, [no date], https://www.zenbusiness.com/freelancer-pay-gap/ (last visited May 23, 2023).

169 *A 2022 study:* "Freelancer Pay Gap."

169 *Women copywriters:* "Freelancer Pay Gap."

169 *This study is not alone:* Arianne Renan Barzilay and Anat Ben-David, "Platform Inequality: Gender in the Gig-Economy," *Seton Hall Law Review* 47 (2017): 393 ("although women work for more hours on the platform, women's average hourly rates are significantly lower than men's, averaging about 2/3 (two-thirds) of men's rates").

169 *controlled studies in the lab:* See, e.g., Christine Alksnis et al., "Workforce Segregation and the Gender Wage Gap: Is 'Women's' Work Valued as Highly as 'Men's'?," *Journal of Applied Social Psychology* 38 (2008): 1416.

169 *Women, on the other hand:* Isabel Soto and Isabella Hindley, "Women in the Gig Economy," American Action Forum, report, April 21, 2021, https://www.americanactionforum.org/insight/women-in-the-gig-economy/.

169 *or lost their job:* Erica Pandey, "The Rise of Women in the Gig Economy," *Axios*, August 26, 2021, https://www.axios.com/2021/08/26/women-gig-economy-doordash-uber-delivery-driver.

169 *These differences in motivation affect:* Sharon Goldman, "Women Make Less in the Gig Economy. A New Study Asked Why," *The Lily*, February 16, 2021, https://www.thelily.com/women-make-less-in-the-gig-economy-a-new-study-asked-why/; Naomi Cahn, June Carbone, and Nancy Levit, "Discrimination by Design?," *Arizona State Law Journal* 51 (2019): 1. ("Women may earn less on other platforms for related issues, also seen as women's 'choice.' Thus, even through a platform where the hourly rates are set by a third party, women may have different work patterns that lead them to work less, or not at all, during the better-paid surge hours in the Uber-world. Concerns about platform world thus emphasize that women tend to 'undersell themselves' by setting lower initial prices, are less likely to negotiate, are more likely to be subject to consumer biases when they do assert themselves, and are less likely to do well in platform negotiations.")

170 *The increased competition:* Michael Dunn et al., "2021 Gender Differences and Lost Flexibility in Online Freelancing During the COVID-19 Pandemic," *Frontiers in Sociology* 6 (2021), https://www.frontiersin.org/articles/10.3389/fsoc.2021.738024.

170 *The mothers of young children:* Dunn et al., "2021 Gender Differences." *See also* Carlo Pizzinelli and Ippei Shibata, "Has COVID-19 Induced Labor Market Mismatch?," International Monetary Fund, report, January 2022, https://www.imf.org/en/Publications/WP/Issues/2022/01/18/Has-COVID-19-Induced-Labor-Market-Mismatch-Evidence-from-the-US-and-the-UK-511917.

170 *Indeed, when the city:* See, e.g., "Gig-Economy Rise Prompts FTC Chief's Call to Alter Antitrust Law," *Bloomberg Law*, November 2, 2021, 4:15 a.m., https://news.bloomberglaw.com/antitrust/gig-economy-rise-prompts-ftc-chiefs-call-to-alter-antitrust-law; Hal Singer, "Uber Under the Antitrust Microscope: Is There a 'Firm Exemption' to Antitrust?," *Forbes*, February 25, 2019, 3:15 p.m., https://www.forbes.com/sites/washingtonbytes/2019/02/25

/uber-under-the-antitrust-microscope-is-there-a-firm-exemption-to-anti
trust/?sh=6b617b0c2a47.

170   *Uber workers fired back:* Kellen Browning and Noam Schieber, "Drivers'
      Lawsuit Claims Uber and Lyft Violate Antitrust Law," *New York Times*,
      June 21, 2022, https://www.nytimes.com/2022/06/21/business/uber-lyft-an
      titrust-lawsuit.html.

170   *The case against Seattle:* Monica Nickelsburg, "Uber, Seattle and U.S. Cham-
      ber End Dispute over Union Law as City Plans Minimum Wage for Drivers,"
      GeekWire, April 13, 2020, 3:00 p.m., https://www.geekwire.com/2020/uber
      -seattle-u-s-chamber-end-legal-dispute-union-law-city-plans-minimum
      -wage-drivers/.

171   *The Public Rights Project:* "PRP Reveals Handy's Misclassification of Their
      Workers Contributes to Rampant Unaddressed Sexual Harassment on
      the Platform," Public Rights Project, September 10, 2020, https://www
      .publicrightsproject.org/press-releases/prp-reveals-handys-misclassifica
      tion-of-their-workers-contributes-to-rampant-unaddressed-sexual-harass
      ment-on-the-platform; Public Rights Project, "Our Mission," 2023, https://
      www.publicrightsproject.org/what-we-do.

171   *they have to show:* Handy company website, https://www.handy.com/trust
      -and-safety (last visited May 10, 2022).

172   *Additionally, misclassified workers: See, e.g.,* Dana Rubinstein, "Demands
      Mount for New York State to Extend Benefits to Gig-Economy Workers," *Po-
      litico*, March 18, 2020, 2:18 p.m., https://www.politico.com/states/new-york
      /albany/story/2020/03/18/demands-mount-for-new-york-state-to-extend
      -benefits-to-gig-economy-workers-1267676 [https://perma.cc/7TKW-T45S].

172   *Sisters Vilma and Greta Zenelaj:* Order Granting Defendant's Motion to
      Compel Arbitration, *Zenelaj v. HandyBook Inc.*, No. 14-cv-05449-TEH, 82
      F. Supp. 3d 968 (N.D. Cal. 2015), document https://cases.justia.com/fed
      eral/district-courts/california/candce/3:2014cv05449/283005/26/0.pdf
      ?ts=1428877642.

172   *In 2015, another class action: Emmanuel v. Handy Tech., Inc.*, 992 F.3d 1 (1st
      Cir. 2021), http://media.ca1.uscourts.gov/pdf.opinions/20-1378P-01A.pdf
      (holding that the class action could not move forward because each worker
      had signed an agreement to arbitrate).

172   *And then, in 2021:* Nicholas Iovino, "California DAs Sue Gig Company for
      Misclassifying Workers," *Courthouse News Service* (March 17, 2021), https://
      www.courthousenews.com/california-das-sue-gig-company-for-misclassi
      fying-workers/.

172   *In a wide-ranging 2023:* "Handy App Pays $6 Million Dollar Labor Violation
      Settlement," *CBS News*, May 18, 2023, https://www.cbsnews.com/sanfran
      cisco/news/handy-app-pays-6-million-dollar-labor-violation-settlement/.

172   *Handy is not alone:* Rebecca Smith, "Gig Companies Are Facing Dozens of
      Lawsuits over Workplace Violations," National Empowerment Law Project,
      report, August 8, 2019, https://www.nelp.org/publication/gig-companies
      -facing-dozens-lawsuits-workplace-violations/.

173 *Not only did the Amazon strikes:* Kate Conger, "Uber and Lyft Drivers in California Will Remain Contractors," *New York Times*, November 4, 2020, https://www.nytimes.com/2020/11/04/technology/california-uber-lyft -prop-22.html.

173 *Instead of organizing labor:* Lydia DePillis, "Gig Economy Workers Need Benefits. These Companies Are Popping Up to Help," CNN, August 23, 2018, 7:41 a.m., https://money.cnn.com/2018/08/23/technology/gig-econo my-worker-benefits/index.html; Rebecca Heilweil, "California Has Rejected a Major Gig Economy Reform, Leaving Workers Without Employee Protections," *Vox*, November 4, 2020, 3:13 a.m., https://www.vox.com /recode/2020/11/4/21539335/california-proposition-22-results-gig-econo my-workers.

173 *For example, the NewsGuild:* Lydia DePillis, "Gig Economy Workers Need Benefits."

173 *Additionally, Bluecrew:* Gregory Barber, "This Company Hires Gig Workers— as Employees," *Wired*, January 13, 2020, 7:00 a.m., https://www.wired.com /story/company-hires-gig-workers-employees/.

173 *The single development:* Deanne Johnson, "Fed Economist Projects Labor Market Will Stay Tight in 2023," *Business Journal Daily*, January 11, 2023, https://businessjournaldaily.com/fed-economist-pojects-labor-market-will -stay-tight-in-2023/.

173 *As the number of workers:* Elizabeth A. Pendo, review of *Uninsured in America: Life and Death in the Land of Opportunity*, by Susan Sered and Rushika Fernandopulle, *Journal of Legal Medicine* 29 (2008): 117, 118; Peter Ubel, "Obamacare and the End of Employer-Based Health Insurance," *Forbes*, November 14, 2013, https://www.forbes.com/sites /peterubel/2013/11/14/obamacare-and-the-end-of-employer-based -health-insurance/#3f237cdc584a. A major reason for the decline in employer-provided insurance, as Pendo explains, is that an employer with a workforce in the thousands can afford to pay the health insurance premiums of a worker with cancer. An employer with a workforce of ten, like many of the cleaning services that have replaced in-house janitors, cannot afford to pay such premiums.

173 *As even traditional employers:* Indeed, even in traditional businesses, employers have been shifting more of the cost of healthcare to employees. Ryan Smith, "Employers Shifting More Health Insurance Costs to Employees— Study, *Insurance Business*, May 8, 2018, https://www.insurancebusinessmag .com/us/news/healthcare/employers-shifting-more-health-insurance-costs -to-empoyees--study-100003.aspx.

174 *And so the fight:* Li Jin et al., "A Labor Movement for the Platform Economy," *Harvard Business Review*, September 24, 2021, https://hbr.org/2021/09/a -labor-movement-for-the-platform-economy (discussing decentralized collective action as informal union activity, public media campaigns, and information dissemination to challenge working conditions in platform-based companies).

PART 4: Taming the WTA Economy

176   *Even in less toxic environments:* Patrick Ishizuka and Kelly Musick, "Occupational Inflexibility and Women's Employment During the Transition to Parenthood," *Demography* 58 (2021): 1249.

176   *Women in low-wage:* Megan Leonhardt, "Parents Who Quit Their Jobs Because They Can't Find Adequate Childcare Face a 7% Wage Penalty," *Fortune*, March 15, 2022, 8:32 a.m. CDT, https://fortune.com/2022/03/15/wage -gap-is-wider-for-moms-who-leave-the-workforce/.

176   *In the political sphere:* The first use of the term in the political arena came from Jacob S. Hacker and Paul Pierson, *Winner-Take-All Politics: How Washington Made the Rich Richer—and Turned Its Back on the Middle Class* (New York: Simon & Schuster, 2010). Pierson and Hacker, however, use the term to describe how neoliberal politicians used the political system to open the doors to the WTA economy; we are using the term in this section to describe how the political system is being gamed to entrench the power of those who undermine democracy.

177   *Women have historically:* Nora Gardner et al., "Making Government an Even Better Place for Women to Work," McKinsey & Co., report, May 25, 2023, https://www.mckinsey.com/industries/public-sector/our-insights/making -government-an-even-better-place-for-women-to-work.

177   *This clash of worldviews:* Thomas B. Edsall, "How You Feel About Gender Roles Can Tell Us How You'll Vote," *New York Times*, July 20, 2022, https://www .nytimes.com/2022/07/20/opinion/gender-gap-partisanship-politics.html.

177   *Those who identify:* Edsall, "How You Feel About Gender."

178   *Tomlinson found strength:* Jeffrey Bradbury, "Standing Up for Students: A Conversation with Melissa Tomlinson," *TeacherCast*, January 20, 2018, https://www.teachercast.net/captivate-podcast/njea20-standing-up-for-stu dents-a-conversation-with-melissa-tomlinson-badassteachersa-njea/.

179   *Unions, however:* Celine McNicholas et al., "Unlawful U.S. Employers Are Charged with Violating Federal Law in 41.5% of All Union Election Campaigns," Economic Policy Institute (blog), December 11, 2019, https:// www.epi.org/publication/unlawful-employer-opposition-to-union-elec tion-campaigns/.

179   *We also show:* "Accomplishments, State of New Jersey, Governor Phil Murphy," NewJersey.gov, [no date], https://nj.gov/governor/initiatives /accomplishments/index.shtml (last visited June 5, 2023).

179   *We nonetheless watched:* Bess Levin, "The FBI Confirms Its Brett Kavanaugh Investigation Was a Total Sham," *Vanity Fair*, August 5, 2022, https://www .vanityfair.com/news/2022/08/brett-kavanaugh-fbi-investigation.

9. Fighting Back

181   *After Christie made his stump speech:* Josh Eidelson, "'I Left Shaking': Teacher Chris Christie Yelled at Unloads to Salon," *Salon*, November 5, 2013,

9:13 p.m., https://www.salon.com/2013/11/05/i_left_shaking_teacher_chris
_christie_yelled_at_unloads_to_salon/; "Chris Christie Argues with Public
School Teacher During Somers Point Campaign Stop," *NJ.com*, November 3,
2013, https://www.nj.com/politics/2013/11/chris_christie_argues_with_public
_school_teacher_during_somers_point_campaign_stop.html.

181   *Christie poked a finger:* Charles Stile, "Chris Christie's Bully Image Endures in
the Public's Imagination," *Bergen Record*, November 17, 2017, 11:33 a.m. ET,
https://www.northjersey.com/story/news/2017/11/16/chris-christies-bully
-image-endures-publics-imagination/784701001/.

181   *For the next ten minutes:* Eidelson, "'I Left Shaking.'"

181   *Eventually Christie shut down the discussion:* David Weigel, "Behind That
Photo of Chris Christie Wagging His Finger at a Teacher," *Slate*, November 4, 2013, https://slate.com/news-and-politics/2013/11/melissa-tomlinson
-behind-that-photo-of-chris-christie-wagging-his-finger-at-a-teacher.html.

182   *Tomlinson started teaching in the early years:* Alyson Klein, "No Child Left
Behind: An Overview," *Education Week*, April 10, 2015, https://www.edweek
.org/policy-politics/no-child-left-behind-an-overview/2015/04.

183   *That loss was, according to:* Sharon Otterman, "Attacks Fly in New Jersey for
Losing Out on $400 Million Education Grant," *New York Times*, August 26,
2010, https://www.nytimes.com/2010/08/26/nyregion/26njrace.html. "Barbara Keshishian, the president of the New Jersey Education Association,
said the state's loss was a direct result of Mr. Christie's misguided decision to
reject the collaboration required by the U.S. Department of Education."

183   *She explained that:* Eidelson, "'I Left Shaking.'"

183   *She learned about the:* Badass Teachers Association, [no date], https://www
.badassteacher.org/mission (last visited June 16, 2023).

184   *And they are the single most:* Lyndsey Layton, "Chris Christie to Teachers
Union: You Deserve a Punch in the Face," *Washington Post*, August 3, 2015,
https://www.washingtonpost.com/local/education/chris-christie-to-teachers
-union-you-deserve-a-punch-in-the-face/2015/08/03/86358c2c-39de-11e5
-8e98-115a3cf7d7ae_story.html?noredirect=on&utm_term=.59294812c924.

184   *"Christie's refusal to finance":* "Governor Christie to Teacher: 'I Am Tired of
You People!'," *Jersey Jazzman* (blog), exclusive interview, November 2, 2013,
http://jerseyjazzman.blogspot.com/2013/11/exclusive-govchristie-to-teacher
-i-am.html.

184   *"whether advocating for my students":* Rebecca Klein, "Chris Christie Reportedly Lashes Out at Teacher Melissa Tomlinson," *Huffington Post*, November 4,
2013, https://www.huffingtonpost.com/2013/11/04/chris-christie-melissa
-tomlinson_n_4214652.html.

184   *The image of Chris Christie:* David Weigel, "Behind That Photo of Chris
Christie Wagging His Finger at a Teacher," *Slate*, November 4, 2013,
8:48 a.m., https://slate.com/news-and-politics/2013/11/melissa-tomlinson
-behind-that-photo-of-chris-christie-wagging-his-finger-at-a-teacher.html.

184   *Although he won reelection:* Stile, "Chris Christie's Bully Image Endures."

185   *Chris Christie's brawling tactics:* See, e.g., Nick Corasaniti and Alexandra

Berzon, "The Business of Being Chris Christie," *New York Times*, June 16, 2023, https://www.nytimes.com/2023/06/16/us/politics/chris-christie-busi ness.html; Ashley Killough, "Chris Christie Rails Against Tax Increases," CNN Politics, February 19, 2015, https://www.cnn.com/2015/02/19/politics /chris-christie-2016/index.html.

185 *When we started looking*: Sylvia Allegretto and Lawrence Mishel, "The Teacher Pay Penalty Has Hit a New High," Economic Policy Institute, report, September 5, 2018, 3, https://www.epi.org/files/pdf/153196.pdf.

185 *Since the 1960s:* Sylvia A. Allegretto et al., "The Teaching Penalty: Teacher Pay Losing Ground," Economic Policy Institute, report, 2008, 5–6, https:// www.epi.org/files/page/-/old/books/teaching_penalty/teaching-penalty -full-text.pdf.

185 *Over the course of the seventies*: Melissa C. Carr and Susan H. Fuhrman, "The Politics of School Finance in the 1990s," chapter 5 in *Equity and Ade- quacy in Education Finance: Issues and Perspectives*, ed. Helen F. Ladd et al. (Washington, D.C.: National Academies Press, 1999), 136–142, https://www .nap.edu/read/6166/chapter/5.

186 *State spending, funded:* Carr and Fuhrman, "Politics of School Finance," 147.

186 *teacher weekly wages:* Dana Goldstein, *The Teacher Wars: A History of Amer- ica's Most Embattled Profession* (New York: Doubleday, 2014), 230.

186 *Public school teachers:* Sylvia Allegretto, "The Teacher Pay Penalty Has Hit a New High," Economic Policy Institute, report, August 16, 2022, https:// www.epi.org/publication/teacher-pay-penalty-2022/.

186 *And as teachers lost ground:* "Characteristics of Public School Teachers," Na- tional Center for Education Statistics, May 2023, https://nces.ed.gov/programs /coe/indicator/clr/public-school-teachers; Alia Wong, "The U.S. Teaching Population Is Getting Bigger, and More Female," *Atlantic*, February 20, 2019, https://www.theatlantic.com/education/archive/2019/02/the-explosion-of -women-teachers/582622/ (describing teaching as 77% female).

187 *economists estimate that:* Claire Cain Miller, "As Women Take Over a Male-Dominated Field, the Pay Drops," *New York Times*, March 20, 2016, https://www.nytimes.com/2016/03/20/upshot/as-women-take-over-a -male-dominated-field-the-pay-drops.html. *See also* Center for American Progress, "Occupational Segregation in America," March 29, 2022, https:// www.americanprogress.org/article/occupational-segregation-in-america/ (citing Francine D. Blau and Lawrence M. Kahn, "The Gender Wage Gap: Extent, Trends, and Explanations," IZA Institute of Labor Economics, re- port, January 2016, IZA DP No. 9656, http://ftp.iza.org/dp9656.pdf).

187 *In the top ten most segregated jobs*: Center for American Progress, "Occupa- tional Segregation."

187 *These differences have gotten*: Blau and Kahn, "Gender Wage Gap," 8. *See also* Miller, "As Women Take Over."

187 *overt discrimination has declined:* Economists treat unexplained differences as likely the result of discrimination and those have declined over time. Blau and Kahn, "Gender Wage Gap," 23.

187   *When salaries in finance:* Claudia Goldin, *Career and Family: Women's Century-Long Journey Toward Equity* (Princeton, NJ: Princeton University Press, 2021), 4. ("[F]or the nearly five hundred occupations listed in the US census, two-thirds of the gender-based difference in earnings comes from factors within each occupation.")

187   *Gender integration:* Ariane Hegewich et al., "Separate and Not Equal? Gender Segregation in the Labor Market and the Gender Wage Gap," Institute for Women's Policy Research, report, September 2010, https://iwpr.org/iwpr-issues/employment-and-earnings/separate-and-not-equal-gender-segregation-in-the-labor-market-and-the-gender-wage-ga"/. ("Occupational gender segregation is a strong feature of the US labor market. While some occupations have become increasingly integrated over time, others remain highly dominated by either men or women. Our analysis of trends in overall gender segregation shows that, after a considerable move towards more integrated occupations in the 1970s and 1980s, *progress has completely stalled since the mid 1990s.*" [emphasis added])

188   *The U.S. Supreme Court:* San Antonio Indep. Sch. Dist. v. Rodriguez, 411 U.S. 1, 13 (1973).

188   *Starting with the California:* Serrano v. Priest, 487 P.2d 1241 (Cal. 1971).

188   *The more they see school:* Bradley W. Joondeph, "The Good, the Bad, and the Ugly: An Empirical Analysis of Litigation-Prompted School Finance Reform," *Santa Clara Law Review* 35 (1995): 763, 774 (conducting an empirical study of school finance reform and observing that although "litigation-prompted reform has reduced funding inequalities, . . . equalization may have triggered countervailing forces that undermined the states' financial commitments to public education.")

188   *In many states, increasing taxes to pay:* Carr and Fuhrman, "Politics of School Finance," 151. *See also* Christopher Berry, "The Impact of School Finance Judgments on State Fiscal Policy," in *School Money Trials: The Legal Pursuit of Educational Adequacy,* ed. Martin R. West and Paul E. Peterson, (Washington, D.C.: Brookings Institution Press, 2007), 213, 233.

188   *Grover Norquist:* "About the Pledge," Americans for Tax Reform, [no date], https://www.atr.org/about-the-pledge/ (last visited June 5, 2023).

188   *In the following years:* "Club for Growth Action," *FactCheck.Org,* August 31, 2022, https://www.factcheck.org/2022/03/club-for-growth-action-6/.

189   *Public education remains primarily:* June Carbone, Nancy Levit, and Naomi Cahn, "Failure to Shore Up State Budgets May Hit Women's Wallets Especially Hard," *The Conversation,* September 29, 2020, 8:34 a.m., https://theconversation.com/failure-to-shore-up-state-budgets-may-hit-womens-wallets-especially-hard-145524.

189   *State and local governments:* Kim S. Reuben and Megan Randall, "Balanced Budget Requirements," Urban Institute, report, November 27, 2017, https://www.urban.org/research/publication/balanced-budget-requirements.

189   *The 2009 federal stimulus package:* Justin Wolfers, "What Debate? Economists Agree the Stimulus Lifted the Economy," *New York Times,* July 30, 2014,

https://www.nytimes.com/2014/07/30/upshot/what-debate-economists
-agree-the-stimulus-lifted-the-economy.html.

189   *The budget cuts eliminated:* Michael Leachman et al., "A Punishing Decade
for School Funding," Center on Budget and Policy Priorities, report, November 29, 2017, https://www.cbpp.org/research/state-budget-and-tax/a-punish
ing-decade-for-school-funding.

189   *more than half the states:* Leachman et al., "Punishing Decade," Figure 3, 1.

190   *As of the 2017–18 school year:* Leachman et al., "Punishing Decade."

190   *Other states, like New Jersey:* Jeffery H. Keefe, "New Jersey Public School
Teachers Are Underpaid, Not Overpaid," Economic Policy Institute, report,
February 15, 2017, https://www.epi.org/publication/new-jersey-public
-school-teachers-are-underpaid-not-overpaid/.

190   *These actions meant reducing:* Valerie Strauss, "'I Am a Scavenger': The
Desperate Things Teachers Do to Get the Classroom Supplies They Need,"
Washington Post, January 3, 2020, https://www.washingtonpost.com/edu
cation/2019/11/08/i-am-scavenger-desperate-things-teachers-do-get-class
room-supplies-they-need/.

190   *Duncan commented:* Gabrielle Levy, "Rethinking Education in America,"
U.S. News & World Report, July 27, 2018, 6:00 a.m., https://www.usnews
.com/news/the-report/articles/2018-07-27/americas-schools-arent-working
-for-americas-kids.

191   *In the early 1990s: See* Amanda R. Broun and Wendy D. Puriefoy, "Public
Engagement in School Reform: Building Public Responsibility for Public
Education," *Stanford Journal of Civil Rights & Civil Liberties* 4 (2008): 217,
218.

191   *At the time Christie took office:* Susan K. Livio, "7 Reasons Why N.J.'s Property Taxes Are Highest in U.S. Again," *NJ.com*, February 18, 2017, 12:30 p.m.,
https://www.nj.com/politics/index.ssf/2017/02/7_reasons_why_njs_prop
erty_taxes_are_highest_in_us.html.

191   *An important result:* "Governor's FY 2012 Budget: Budget Summary," State
of New Jersey, February 22, 2011, https://www.nj.gov/treasury/omb/publi
cations/12bib/BIB.pdf. By 2021, New Jersey's retirement-plan exhaustion date
was the worst in the country. Jaime Lenney, Brookings Institution, "The
Sustainability of State and Local Government Pensions: A Public Finance
Approach," Brookings Institution, report, March 25, 2021, Table 2, https://
www.brookings.edu/wp-content/uploads/2021/03/BPEASP21_Lenney
-et-al_conf-draft_updated_3.24.21.pdf.

191   *Fiscally prudent states:* Max Marchitello et al., "Teacher Retirement Systems,"
Bellwether Education Partners, report, August 31, 2021, https://bellwether
education.org/sites/default/files/Teacher%20Retirement%20Systems%20
-%20A%20Ranking%20of%20the%20States%20-%20Bellwether%20Educa
tion%20Partners%20-%20FINAL.pdf.

192   *By 2013, at the time:* For Christie's version of these events, see Hillel Italie,
"Chris Christie's Book 'Republican Rescue' Coming This Fall," *Associated
Press*, June 28, 2021, https://apnews.com/article/joe-biden-chris-christie-enter

tainment-arts-and-entertainment-government-and-politics-81c17c681c
4c1caf3f827ea35a3f18db.

192   *"I love the public schools"*: Mark Weber, "Chris Christie: School Bully," *Progressive* magazine, December 17, 2014, 3:30 p.m., https://progressive.org/maga
zine/chris-christie-school-bully/.

192   *he cultivated his image:* Stile, "Chris Christie's Bully Image Endures."

192   *Christie even had an aide:* Ezra Klein, "Chris Christie's Problem Is That He's
Really, Truly a Bully," *Washington Post,* January 8, 2014, 3:06 p.m., https://
www.washingtonpost.com/news/wonk/wp/2014/01/08/chris-christies
-problem-is-that-hes-really-truly-a-bully/.

192   *"The way tween girls circulate":* Klein, "Chris Christie's Problem."

192   *One of his drubbings:* Klein, "Chris Christie's Problem."

192   *"the rhetoric we hear":* Marla Kilfoyle and Melissa Tomlinson, "Fight On,
Ladies," *L.A. Progressive,* March 3, 2015, https://www.laprogressive.com/war
-on-women-teachers/.

193   *The teachers' campaign ultimately:* John Nichols, "Chris Christie's Bully Politics: 'I Am Tired of You People,'" *Nation,* November 4, 2013, https://www
.thenation.com/article/archive/chris-christies-bully-politics-i-am-tired-you
-people/.

193   *New Jersey voters:* Klein, "Chris Christie's Problem."

193   *He succeeded in using:* Matt Arco, "N.J.'s Raging School Funding Debate:
What Your Next Governor Would Do," *NJ.com,* June 1, 2017, 12:15 p.m.,
https://www.nj.com/politics/index.ssf/2017/06/where_every_candidate
_for_nj_governor_stands_on_sc.html (describing underfunding of state
"fairness formula"); Jen Sidorova and Zachary Christensen, "We Must Overhaul Our Pension System to Keep It Solvent and to Reduce the Burden on
Taxpayers, Policy Analysts Say," *NJ.com,* opinion, June 10, 2019, 6:33 p.m.,
https://www.nj.com/opinion/2019/06/we-must-overhaul-our-pension-sys
tem-to-keep-it-solvent-and-to-reduce-the-burden-on-taxpayers-demo
cratic-leader-says.html.

193   *Teachers' unions and other associations: See, e.g.,* Matt Bai, "How Chris
Christie Did His Homework," *New York Times Magazine,* February 27, 2011,
https://www.nytimes.com/2011/02/27/magazine/27christie-t.html. *See also*
Keefe, "New Jersey Public School."

193   *the result of Christie's "reforms":* Erin Banco, "N.J. Teacher Pay Among Highest in
U.S. But Some Say That Paycheck Isn't Enough to Survive," *NJ.com,* June 21,
2018, 11:45 a.m., https://www.nj.com/news/2018/06/underpaid_and_over
worked_how_nj_teachers_are_hustl.html. ("On average, the 'Jersey Hustle'
teacher respondents are working 14-hour days. Respondents who work driving Uber and Lyft said they do not get off work until midnight or 1 a.m.")

193   *At the time Christie left office:* Mike Lilley, "N.J. Teachers Need to Be Told
the Truth: Their Pensions Are in Jeopardy," *NJ.com,* opinion, May 5, 2021,
9:37 a.m., https://www.nj.com/opinion/2021/05/nj-teachers-need-to-be-told
-the-truth-their-pensions-are-in-jeopardy-opinion.html#:~:text=The%20
state's%20latest%20pension%20report,of%20good%20money%20after%20bad.

194 *After her confrontation with Christie:* Nichols, "Chris Christie's Bully."

194 *With a profession made up:* Marla Kilfoyle and Melissa Tomlinson, "Get to Know the "Badass Teachers" Fighting Privatization," *Truthout*, opinion, April 4, 2017, https://truthout.org/articles/get-to-know-the-bats-teachers -fighting-privatization/.

194 *about 30 percent calculated nationally:* Urban Institute, State and Local Backgrounders: Elementary and Secondary Education Expenditures, [no date], https://www.urban.org/policy-centers/cross-center-initiatives/state-and -local-finance-initiative/state-and-local-backgrounders/elementary-and -secondary-education-expenditures (last visited June 16, 2023). About 9 percent goes to higher education, while less than 4 percent goes to police departments. Urban Institute, State and Local Backgrounders: Criminal Justice Expenditures: Police, Corrections, and Courts, [no date], https:// www.urban.org/policy-centers/cross-center-initiatives/state-and-local -finance-initiative/state-and-local-backgrounders/criminal-justice-police -corrections-courts-expenditures (last visited June 16, 2023).

194 *She feels that effort:* Jake Miller, "A Sit-Down with Badass Teachers," *Educator's Room*, December 18, 2015, https://theeducatorsroom.com/sit-bad-ass -teachers/.

195 *When Murphy won:* Jeff Pillets, "With Murphy Win, Teachers Union Claims Victory," *NJ Spotlight News*, November 5, 2021, https://www.njspotlight news.org/2021/11/new-jersey-education-association-njea-15-million-murphy -victory-steve-sweeney-loses/.

195 *New Jersey's 2022–23 budget:* "Murphy's 2022-2023 School Aid Budget Is a 'Positive Surprise,'" *NJ Education Report*, March 23, 2022, https://njedreport .com/2022/03/23/nj-education-aid-murphys-2022-2023-school-aid-budget -is-a-positive-surprise/#:~:text=New%20Jersey's%202022%2D23%20 state,districts%20will%20gain%20%20%24836%20million.

195 *While the controversies over public education:* Julia Wolfe and John Schmidt, "A Profile of Union Workers in State and Local Government," Economic Policy Institute, report, June 7, 2018, https://www.epi.org/publication/a -profile-of-union-workers-in-state-and-local-government-key-facts-about -the-sector-for-followers-of-janus-v-afscme-council-31/ (stating 58% of public -sector union members are women).

195 *At the state and local level:* Rose Khattar et al., "Investments in the State and Local Government Workforce Will Deliver Crucial Services and Create Economic Security, Center for American Progress," report, March 25, 2022, https://www.americanprogress.org/article/investments-in-the-state-and-local -government-workforce-will-deliver-crucial-services-and-create-economic -security/; Matthew Zane, "What Percentage of the Workforce Is Female?," Zippia, report, March 1, 2022, https://www.zippia.com/advice/what-percent age-of-the-workforce-is-female/.

195 *The starving of public-sector budgets:* Emma García and Eunice Han, "The Impact of Changes in Public-Sector Bargaining Laws on Districts' Spending on Teacher Compensation," Economic Policy Institute, report, April 29,

2021, https://www.epi.org/publication/the-impact-of-changes-in-public-sector-bargaining-laws-on-districts-spending-on-teacher-compensation/.

195 *Rather than seriously:* Lauren Camera, "Head of Powerful Teachers Union Blasts Republican Attempts to Gut Public Education," *U.S. News & World Report*, March 28, 2023, 1:20 p.m., https://www.usnews.com/news/education-news/articles/2023-03-28/head-of-powerful-teachers-union-blasts-republican-attempts-to-gut-public-education.

196 *The case Rauner inspired:* Kim Geiger et al., "U.S. Supreme Court Gives Rauner Major Victory over Labor, in Ruling That Could Undercut Public Worker Unions Nationwide," *Chicago Tribune*, June 27, 2018, 4:50 p.m., https://www.chicagotribune.com/politics/ct-met-bruce-rauner-janus-afscme-20180604-story.html (discussing how Rauner was removed as a party for lack of standing, but his orders that the state not collect union dues from union non-members helped prompt lawsuit).

196 *In 2018, the Court's 5 to 4: Janus v. Am. Fed. State, Cnty. & Municipal Employees,* Council 315, 138 S. Ct. 2448 (2018) [hereafter, *Janus*].

196 *"collective action problem": Janus,* 138 S. Ct. at 2490 (Kagan, J., dissenting).

197 *Justice Samuel Alito's majority opinion dismissed: Janus,* 138 S. Ct. at 2466.

197 *Precisely because public unions address: Janus,* 138 S. Ct. at 2475.

197 *The opinion challenged core principles: Janus,* 138 S. Ct. at 2501 (Kagan, J., dissenting) (observing that the decision involved "black-robed rulers overriding citizens' choices" and undermining democratic governance).

197 *Bruce Rauner, who sought:* Rachel M. Cohen, "How Labor Helped Bring Down Scott Walker and Bruce Rauner," *In These Times*, November 7, 2018, https://inthesetimes.com/article/labor-scott-walker-bruce-rauner-unions-2018.

197 *state restrictions on unions' collective bargaining rights:* García and Han, "Impact of Changes"; Ian Kullgren and Aaron Kessler, "Unions Fend Off Membership Exodus in 2 Years Since Janus Ruling," *Bloomberg Law*, June 26, 2020, 5:15 a.m., https://news.bloomberglaw.com/daily-labor-report/unions-fend-off-membership-exodus-in-2-years-since-janus-ruling. ("Three of the eight unions surveyed by Bloomberg Law—the Teamsters, UFCW and the United Steelworkers—suffered slight drops in membership between 2018 and 2019, all less than 5%. For the Teamsters, public-sector membership has remained around 200,000 members, out of 1.4 million members total, said Jason Rabinowitz, director of the Teamsters public services division"); "Legislation Weakening Public-Sector Unions in Five States Cut School Districts' Spending on Teaching Salaries and Benefits," Economic Policy Institute, press release, April 29, 2021, https://www.epi.org/press/legislation-weakening-public-sector-unions-in-five-states-cut-school-districts-spending-on-teacher-salaries-and-benefits/.

197 *And while the percentage:* Bureau of Labor Statistics, "Union Members—2022," report, 2023, https://www.bls.gov/news.release/pdf/union2.pdf; Dylan Matthews, "Labor Unions Aren't 'Booming,' They're Dying," *Vox*, June 10, 2023, https://www.vox.com/future-perfect/2023/6/10/23754360/labor-union-resurgence-boom-starbucks-amazon-sectoral-bargaining.

197 *Beginning in 2018:* Josh Eidelson, "For Teachers Unions, Classroom Re-openings Are the Biggest Test Yet," *Bloomberg,* October 20, 2020, 3:00 a.m., https://www.bloomberg.com/news/features/2020-10-20/covid-pandemic-classroom-reopenings-are-teachers-unions-biggest-test-yet.

198 *They won a promise:* Eidelson, "For Teachers Unions."

198 *Women constitute 58 percent:* Wolfe and Schmidt, "A Profile of Union Workers."

198 *These professions depend on state funding:* Leachman et al., "Punishing Decade" (showing the impact on education of the fiscal cliff).

198 *the underfunding of professions:* American Association of University Women, "The Simple Truth About the Gender Pay Gap," report, 2018, https://www.aauw.org/resources/research/simple-truth/.

198 *Women represented by public:* Wendy Chun-Hoon and Liz Schuler, "Want Equal Pay? Get a Union," U.S. Department of Labor (blog), February 15, 2022, https://blog.dol.gov/2022/02/15/want-equal-pay-get-a-union.

198 *Pensions have been vital:* Monique Morrissey, "Teacher Pensions—the Most Important Tool for Keeping and Retaining Good Teachers," Economic Policy Institute, Working Economics (blog), November 27, 2017, 6:14 p.m., https://www.epi.org/blog/teacher-pensions-the-most-important-tool-for-keeping-and-retaining-good-teachers/.

198 *gender wage gap among union-represented:* Chun-Hoon and Schuler, "Want Equal Pay?" ("Being represented by a union reduces women's wage gap by nearly 40 percent compared to the pay gap experienced by non-union women. For Black and Latina women, the union advantage is even greater.")

199 *According to the Bureau of Labor:* Annette Choi, "Teachers Are Calling It Quits Amid Rising School Violence, Burnout and Stagnating Salaries," CNN, May 31, 2023, https://www.cnn.com/2023/05/31/us/teachers-quitting-shortage-stress-burnout-dg/index.html.

199 *"In Washington state":* Matt Barnum, "Teacher Turnover Hits New Highs Across the U.S.," *Chalkbeat,* March 6, 2023, https://www.chalkbeat.org/2023/3/6/23624340/teacher-turnover-leaving-the-profession-quitting-higher-rate.

199 *And in Florida:* Caden DeLisa, "Is Teaching Worth It in Florida? Vacant Positions Skyrocketing Despite High Demand," *The Capitolist,* April 9, 2023, https://thecapitolist.com/is-teaching-worth-it-in-florida-vacant-positions-skyrocketing-despite-high-demand/.

199 *The attacks on teachers:* Janelle Stecklein, "Teacher Shortage: What Is It and Why Is It Happening?," *Mankato Free Press,* February 26, 2023, https://www.mankatofreepress.com/news/local_news/teacher-shortage-what-is-it-and-why-is-it-happening/article_cc432dee-b3b3-11ed-8a85-0f2415120c49.html.

199 *Politicians celebrating:* Monica Potts, "Conservatives Are Bringing an Old Policy to a New Fight over Public Schools," *FiveThirtyEight,* January 19, 2023, 11:47 a.m., https://fivethirtyeight.com/features/universal-school-vouches-education-culture-wars/.

200 *Many see the new movement:* Potts, "Conservatives Are Bringing."

200   *In this fight*: Derek Seidman, "Florida Teachers' Unions Are Front Line of Resistance Against DeSantis's Fascism," *Truthout*, April 1, 2023, https:// truthout.org/articles/florida-teachers-unions-are-front-line-of-resistance -against-desantiss-fascism/.

200   *Paul Ortiz, a Florida history professor*: Seidman, "Florida Teachers' Unions."

200   *In Florida and elsewhere*: Asha Banerjee et al., "Unions Are Not Only Good for Workers, They're Good for Communities and for Democracy," Economic Policy Institute, report, December 15, 2021, https://www.epi.org /publication/unions-and-well-being/.

10. #MeToo

201   *Marlyn Perez*: Ariel Ramchandani, "There's a Sexual-Harassment Epidemic on America's Farms," *Atlantic*, January 29, 2018, https://www.theatlantic .com/business/archive/2018/01/agriculture-sexual-harassment/550109/.

201   *Perez was earning about $35 per day*: "Modern Day Slavery in Florida," *Today's General Counsel*, February 14, 2018, https://www.todaysgeneralcounsel .com/modern-day-slavery-florida/.

201   *she had no rights*: Ramchandani, "There's a Sexual-Harassment Epidemic."

201   *When she said she would quit*: Doe v. Tapia-Ortiz, No. 2:14-cv-206-FtM- 38MRM (M.D. Fla. Apr. 10, 2014), Complaint.

202   *He threatened to kill her*: Salma Hayek, "Harvey Weinstein Is My Monster Too," *New York Times*, December 13, 2017, https://www.nytimes.com/inter active/2017/12/13/opinion/contributors/salma-hayek-harvey-weinstein .html.

202   *"in his eyes, I was not an artist"*: Hayek, "Harvey Weinstein."

202   *The* New York Times *published*: Jodi Kantor and Megan Twohey, "Harvey Weinstein Paid Off Sexual Harassment Accusers for Decades," *New York Times*, October 5, 2017, https://www.nytimes.com/2017/10/05/us/harvey -weinstein-harassment-allegations.html.

202   *Many prominent men*: Laura Bradley, "'I Was Terrified, and I Was Humiliated': #MeToo's Male Accusers, One Year Later," *Vanity Fair*, October 4, 2018, https://www.vanityfair.com/hollywood/2018/10/metoo-male-accusers -terry-crews-alex-winter-michael-gaston-interview.

202   *Hayek wrote a full account*: Hayek, "Harvey Weinstein."

202   *Her voice*: Elaina Nicolaou and Courtney E. Smith, "A #MeToo Timeline to Show How Far We've Come—& How Far We Need to Go," *Refinery29*, October 5, 2019, 11:55 a.m., https://www.refinery29.com/en-us/2018/10/212801 /me-too-movement-history-timeline-year-weinstein.

203   *In 2017,* Time *magazine*: Melissa Chan, "The Story Behind the Woman You Don't See on TIME's Person of the Year Cover," *Time* magazine, December 6, 2017, https://time.com/5052362/time-person-of-the-year-2017-arm -cover/.

203   *Latina farmworkers wrote a "letter of solidarity"*: "700,000 Female Farmworkers Say They Stand with Hollywood Actors Against Sexual Assault,"

Time magazine, November 10, 2017, https://time.com/5018813/farmworkers -solidarity-hollywood-sexual-assault/.

203 *Perez won a liquidated damage award: Doe v. Tapia-Ortiz*, No. 2:14-cv -206-FtM-38MRM (M.D. Fla. Feb. 10, 2017), https://casetext.com/case/jane -doe-v-tapia-ortiz.

203 *He received another:* Eric Levenson and Cheri Mossberb, "Harvey Weinstein Sentenced in Los Angeles to 16 Years in Prison for Sexual Assault Charges," CNN Entertainment, February 24, 2023, 12:31 a.m., ET, https://www.cnn .com/2023/02/23/entertainment/harvey-weinstein-sentencing-los-angeles /index.html.

203 *To cover his tracks:* Ronan Farrow, "Harvey Weinstein's Secret Settlements," *New Yorker*, November 21, 2017, https://www.newyorker.com/news/news -desk/harvey-weinsteins-secret-settlements.

203 *Weinstein was so successful:* Hayek, "Harvey Weinstein."

204 *the New York City District Attorney Cyrus Vance:* Eli Watkins, "Embattled DA Defends Not Prosecuting Weinstein, Trump over the Years," CNN, October 12, 2017, 11:41 a.m. EDT, https://www.cnn.com/2017/10/11/politics /cyrus-vance-harvey-weinstein-trump/index.html (original story ran in the *New Yorker*).

204 *Not only had numerous women:* "Manhattan DA Cyrus Vance on Weinstein Verdict and Why His Office Didn't Prosecute in 2015," *PBS*, February 25, 2020, 6:40 p.m. EDT, https://www.pbs.org/newshour/show/manhattan-da-cyrus -vance-on-weinstein-verdict-and-why-his-office-didnt-prosecute-in-2015.

204 *Once the dam burst:* Sarah Almukhtar et al., "After Weinstein: 71 Men Accused of Sexual Misconduct and Their Fall from Power," *New York Times*, November 10, 2017, updated February 8, 2018, https://www.nytimes.com/intera ctive/2017/11/10/us/men-accused-sexual-misconduct-weinstein.html?_r=0.

204 *The allegations included:* Almukhtar et al., "After Weinstein"; Erik Wemple, "Lawsuit Depicts Fox News as Not Just Sexist. Not Just Misogynistic. Barbaric," *Washington Post*, May 4, 2017, https://www.washingtonpost.com /blogs/erik-wemple/wp/2017/05/04/lawsuit-depicts-fox-news-as-not-just -sexist-not-just-misogynistic-barbaric/?utm_term=.8268999463a0.

204 *The #MeToo movement seemed:* "#MeToo: A Timeline of Events," *Chicago Tribune*, December 8, 2017, updated September 18, 2019, https://www.chicago tribune.com/lifestyles/ct-me-too-timeline-20171208-htmlstory.html.

204 *But it draws on centuries:* Mary Pflum, "A Year Ago, Alyssa Milano Started a Conversation About #MeToo. These Women Replied," *NBC News*, October 15, 2018, https://www.nbcnews.com/news/us-news/year-ago-alyssa-mil ano-started-conversation-about-metoo-these-women-n920246.

204 *She sought to forge connections:* Zenobia Jeffries Warfield, "Me Too Creator Tarana Burke Reminds Us This Is About Black and Brown Survivors," *Yes! Magazine*, January 4, 2018, https://www.yesmagazine.org/people-power/me -too-creator-tarana-burke-reminds-us-this-is-about-black-and-brown-sur vivors-20180104.

205 *The immediate reaction:* Stephanie Zacharek et al., "Time Person of the Year

2017," *Time* magazine, December 18, 2017, https://time.com/time-person -of-the-year-2017-silence-breakers/.

205 *Within one year*: "The #MeToo Hashtag Has Been Used Roughly 19 Million Times on Twitter in the Past Year, and Usage Often Surges Around News Events," Pew Research Center, report, October 11, 2018, https://www .pewresearch.org/fact-tank/2018/10/11/how-social-media-users-have-dis cussed-sexual-harassment-since-metoo-went-viral/ft_18-10-11_metooan niversary_hashtag-used-19m_times/.

205 *And in 2021*: Luis Ferré-Sadurni and J. David Goodman, "Cuomo Resigns Amid Scandals, Ending Decade-Long Run in Disgrace," *New York Times*, August 10, 2021, https://www.nytimes.com/2021/08/10/nyregion/andrew -cuomo-resigns.html.

206 *the* New York Times *documented*: Audrey Carlson et al., "#MeToo Brought Down 201 Powerful Men. Nearly Half of Their Replacements Are Women," *New York Times*, October 23, 2018, https://www.nytimes.com/interactive /2018/10/23/us/metoo-replacements.html.

206 *While some cynics*: Shiu-Yik Au et al., "Does Board Gender Diversity Reduce Workplace Sexual Harassment?," *Corporate Governance: An International Review* 1 (2022). ("We find that an increase of one female director is associated with a 21.81% decrease in workplace SH and that firms with high board gender diversity synchronize the reduction in SH with improved social policies [e.g., policies to better employee relations, health and safety, or diversity challenges]. Our results do not support the fem-power washing theory but rather imply that nominating female directors may have a profound impact on the firm's ethical culture.")

206 *Just the presence*: Shiu-Yik Au et al., "Times Up: Does Female Leadership Reduce Workplace Sexual Harassment?," *Academy of Management Proceedings*, report, 2020, https://journals.aom.org/doi/10.5465/AMBPP.2020.21007ab stract ("firms with a higher proportion of women on the board of directors and firms with a female CEO experience less sexual harassment").

206 *The tactic of fighting back*: See, e.g., Karla Adam and William Booth, "A Year After It Began, Has #MeToo Become a Global Movement?," *Washington Post*, October 5, 2018, https://www.washingtonpost.com/world/a-year-after-it -began-has-metoo-become-a-global-movement/2018/10/05/1fc0929e-c71 a-11e8-9c0f-2ffaf6d422aa_story.html; Indulekha Aravind, "#MeToo Movement: Women Call Out Their Past Tormentors on Social Media," *India Times*, October 13, 2018, https://economictimes.indiatimes.com/news/poli tics-and-nation/metoo-movement-women-call-out-their-past-tormentors -on-social-media/articleshow/66198396.cms.

207 *"The abuse of authority"*: Tomkins v. Pub. Serv. Elec. & Gas Co., 422 F. Supp. 553, 556 (D.N.J. 1976), rev'd, 568 F.2d 1044 (3 Cir. 1977).

207 *"[e]very single one of these kids"*: Kyle Swenson, "Who Came up with the Term 'Sexual Harassment'?," *Washington Post*, November 22, 2017, https:// www.washingtonpost.com/news/morning-mix/wp/2017/11/22/who-came -up-with-the-term-sexual-harassment/?utm_term=.8a26a170f9f3.

207   *Law professor Catharine MacKinnon:* Catharine MacKinnon, *Sexual Harassment of Working Women: A Case of Sexual Discrimination* (New Haven, CT: Yale University Press, 1979).

207   *By 1986, the Supreme Court: Meritor Sav. Bank, FSB v. Vinson,* 477 U.S. 57 (1986).

208   *the Court also quickly held: Meritor Sav. Bank,* 477 U.S. 57.

208   *The Court recognized: Harris v. Forklift Sys., Inc.,* 510 U.S. 17 (1993).

208   *Harassment flourishes: See* Vicki Schultz, "Reconceptualizing Sexual Harassment, Again," *Yale Law Journal Forum* 128 (2018): 22, 49. *See also* Marianne Cooper, "The 3 Things that Make Organizations More Prone to Sexual Harassment," *Atlantic,* November 27, 2017, https://www.theatlantic.com/business/archive/2017/11/organizations-sexual-harassment/546707/ (referring to NiCole T. Buchanan et al., "A Review of Organizational Strategies for Reducing Sexual Harassment: Insights from the U.S. Military," *Journal of Social Issues* 70 (2014): 687, 692–693).

208   *The Equal Employment Opportunity Commission:* Equal Employment Opportunity Commission, Select Task Force on the Study of Harassment in the Workplace, report, June 2016, 7–8, 16, https://www.eeoc.gov/select-task-force-study-harassment-workplace.

208   *An overwhelming number (79.5 percent) of women:* Heather McLaughlin et al., "The Economic and Career Effects of Sexual Harassment on Working Women," *Gender & Society* 31 (June 2017): 333, 344.

208   *People who have experienced harassment:* Jason N. Houle et al., "The Impact of Sexual Harassment on Depressive Symptoms During the Early Occupational Career," *Society and Mental Health* 1 (2011): 89.

208   *Women are not the only victims: Oncale v. Sundowner Offshore Servs.,* 523 U.S. 75 (1998).

208   *Each year in the past decade:* "Charges Alleging Sex-Based Harassment (Charges Filed with EEOC), FY 2010–2021," U.S. Equal Employment Opportunity Commission, [no date], https://www.eeoc.gov/data/charges-alleging-sex-based-harassment-charges-filed-eeoc-fy-2010-fy-2021 (last visited March 14, 2023).

208   *Yet claims are more likely:* Ann C. McGinley, "The Masculinity Motivation," *Stanford Law Review Online* 71 (2018): 99, 102.

209   *is especially prevalent:* Jocelyn Frye, "Not Just the Rich and Famous: The Pervasiveness of Sexual Harassment Across Industries Affects All Workers," Center for American Progress, news release, November 20, 2017, https://www.americanprogress.org/issues/women/news/2017/11/20/443139/not-just-rich-famous/.

209   *today's corporate "tournament":* "Silicon Valley's Ellen Pao Tackles Sex Discrimination, Workplace Diversity in Memoir," NPR, September 19, 2017, 5:21 a.m., ET, https://www.npr.org/transcripts/551810814.

209   *They attract and promote "toxic leaders":* Jennifer L. Berdahl et al., "How Masculinity Contests Undermine Organizations, and What to Do About It," *Harvard Business Review,* November 2018, https://hbr.org/2018/11/how-masculinity-contests-undermine-organizations-and-what-to-do-about-it.

210   *the courts simply:* Heather L. Kleinschmidt, "Reconsidering Severe or Pervasive: Aligning the Standard in Sexual Harassment and Racial Harassment Causes of Action," *Indiana Law Journal* 80 (2005): 1119, 1135.

210   *As the EEOC explains:* "Prohibited Employment Policies/Practices," U.S. Equal Employment Opportunity Commission, report, [no date], https:// www.eeoc.gov/prohibited-employment-policiespractices (last visited January 16, 2024).

210   *Of course, even if:* 42 U.S.C. § 1981a(b)(3) (2018).

211   *And the proof requirements: Meritor Sav. Bank,* 477 U.S. at 68.

211   *in short, the classic attributes:* Karen Higginbottom, "The Link Between Power and Sexual Harassment in the Workplace," *Forbes,* June 11, 2018, https://www.forbes.com/sites/karenhigginbottom/2018/06/11/the-link-be tween-power-and-sexual-harassment-in-the-workplace/#3fc26b81190f.

211   *A 2019* Investment News *survey:* Susan Antilla, "Wall Street Goes Silent on #MeToo," *The Intercept,* June 4, 2019, 10:39 a.m., https://theintercept.com /2019/06/04/wall-street-metoo-sexual-harassment/.

211   *As Catherine MacKinnon:* Catharine A. MacKinnon, "#MeToo Has Done What the Law Could Not," *New York Times,* February 4, 2018, https://www.nytimes .com/2018/02/04/opinion/metoo-law-legal-system.html?module=inline.

212   *Indeed, some men see greater sexual access:* Higginbottom, "The Link Between Power."

212   *In 2019, Carroll wrote:* E. Jean Carroll, "Donald Trump Assaulted Me, but He Is Not Alone on My List of Hideous Men," *New York* magazine, June 21, 2019, https://nymag.com/author/e.-jean-carroll/.

212   *in May 2023:* Benjamin Weiser et al., "Donald Trump Sexually Abused and Defamed E. Jean Carroll, Jury Finds," *New York Times,* May 9, 2023, https://www.nytimes.com/2023/05/09/nyregion/trump-carroll-trial-sexual -abuse-defamation.html.

213   *"I just start kissing them":* "Transcript: Donald Trump's Taped Comments About Women," *New York Times,* October 8, 2016, https://www.nytimes .com/2016/10/08/us/donald-trump-tape-transcript.html.

213   *And when Carroll's lawyer:* Dan Mangan, "Trump Says in Carroll Rape Case Deposition That Stars Have 'Historically' Grabbed Women," *CNBC,* May 5, 2023, 3:41 p.m., ET, https://www.cnbc.com/2023/05/05/trump-deposition -in-e-jean-carroll-rape-defamation-case-released-in-court.html.

213   *On the witness stand:* Shayna Jacobs et al., "E. Jean Carroll Defends Her Reputation in Trump Accusation Case," *Washington Post,* May 1, 2023, 5:17 p.m., ET, https://www.washingtonpost.com/nation/2023/05/01/e-jean -carroll-trump-trial/.

214   *All the factors:* Jessica Valenti, "It's No Accident that Sexual Harassers Rise up the Ranks," *Guardian,* November 4, 2017, https://www.theguardian.com /commentisfree/2017/nov/04/sexual-harassers-rise-ranks-red-flag("experts and research tell us that harassers and sexual abusers often adhere to traditional gender roles, that they're likely narcissists, and that they exhibit behaviors consistent with particular kinds of over-the-top masculinity").

214   *Two decades later:* Belinda Luscombe, "How Hedge Funds' Lack of Diversity Affects All of Us," *Time* magazine, January 5, 2022, 12:37 p.m. ET, https://time.com/6132594/hedged-out-book-hedge-fund-inequality/.

214   *And white men manage:* Luscombe, "How Hedge Funds' Lack."

214   *"I see things like female candidates":* Leslie Picker et al., "The Woman Suing Point72 and Steve Cohen Speaks Out About Alleged Gender and Pay Discrimination," *CNBC*, June 11, 2018, 1:26 p.m., https://www.cnbc.com/2018/06/11/the-woman-suing-point72-and-steve-cohen-for-gender-and-pay-discrimination-speaks-out.html.

215   *The* New Yorker *described Bonner's lawsuit:* Sheelah Kolhatkar, "With Lawsuit Against Steve Cohen's Firm, #MeToo Comes to Wall Street," *New Yorker*, February 16, 2018, https://www.newyorker.com/news/news-desk/with-lawsuit-against-steven-cohens-firm-metoo-comes-to-wall-street.

215   *For female employees:* Complaint, at ¶ 2, *Bonner v. Point72 Asset Mgmnt.*, No. 1:18-cv-01233 (S.D.N.Y. Feb. 12, 2018), https://www.courtlistener.com/recap/gov.uscourts.nysd.488388/gov.uscourts.nysd.488388.1.0.pdf [hereafter, Bonner Complaint].

215   *the consultant replied, "Why?":* Bonner Complaint, at ¶ 5.

215   *Overall, she alleged a "boys club":* Bonner Complaint, at ¶¶ 109–11.

216   *A* New Yorker *article :* Kolhatkar, "Lawsuit Against Steve Cohen."

216   *That prompted the Securities and Exchange Commission:* Ahiza Garcia and Evan Perez, "Insider Trading Charges Dismissed Against Michael Steinberg, 6 Others," CNN Money, October 22, 2015, https://money.cnn.com/2015/10/22/news/michael-steinberg-insider-trading-charges-dismissed/.

216   *The SEC merely banned him:* Aruna Viswanatha and Juliet Chung, "Deal Ends SEC's Pursuit of Steven Cohen," *Wall Street Journal*, January 8, 2016, 9:12 p.m., https://www.wsj.com/articles/sec-bars-steven-cohen-from-supervising-hedge-funds-for-two-years-1452278527.

216   *"This case is important":* Bonner Complaint, at ¶ 18.

216   *Continuing the not-so-veiled references:* Bonner Complaint, at ¶ 18.

216   *"I just couldn't let it go":* Picker et al., "The Woman Suing Point72."

217   *Douglas Haynes, the Point72 president:* Leslie Picker, "President of Steve Cohen's Point72 Resigns Amid Sex Discrimination Lawsuit," *CNBC*, March 19, 12:45 p.m., ET, https://www.cnbc.com/2018/03/19/douglas-haynes-of-point72-resigns-amid-sex-discrimination-lawsuit.html.

217   *Two prominent members of the Mets:* Brian Baxter, "Two New York Mets Executives Stepping Down Amid Workplace Probe," *Bloomberg Law*, June 21, 2021, 6:12 p.m., https://news.bloombergtax.com/esg/two-new-york-mets-executives-stepping-down-amid-workplace-probe?context=search&index=0.

217   *Employers also became more concerned:* See Jessica A. Clarke, "The Rules of #MeToo," *University of Chicago Legal Forum* 7 (2019), https://papers.ssrn.com/sol3/papers.cfm?abstract_id=3363875. *See also* Bobbi K. Dominick, *Preventing Workplace Harassment in a #MeToo World: A Guide to Cultivating a Harassment-Free Culture* (Alexandria, VA: Society for Human Resource Management, 2018).

218   *In a Pew Research survey:* Anna Brown, "More Than Twice as Many Americans Support Than Oppose the #MeToo Movement," Pew Research Center, report, September 29, 2022, https://www.pewresearch.org/social-trends/2022/09/29/more-than-twice-as-many-americans-support-than-oppose-the-metoo-movement/.

218   *For example, a targeted:* Anastasia Tsioulcas and Colin Dwyer, "The #Mute RKelly Movement Takes Its Protest to the Steps of His Record Label," NPR, January 16, 2019, https://www.npr.org/2019/01/16/685912752/the-muterkelly-movement-takes-its-protest-to-the-steps-of-his-record-label. *See also* Julia Jacobs and Robert Chiarito, "R. Kelly Trial in Chicago: What to Know About His Conviction," *New York Times*, September 15, 2022, https://www.nytimes.com/article/r-kelly-chicago-trial.html.

218   *Kelly was later convicted:* Robert Chiarito and Julia Jacobs, "R. Kelley Sentenced to 20 Years for Child Sex Crimes," *New York Times*, February 23, 2023, https://www.nytimes.com/2023/02/23/arts/music/r-kelly-sentenced-federal-child-sex-crimes.html.

218   *Organizers found:* Seyfarth Shaw LLP, "Been Harassed? Vote Yes. How Unions Are Leveraging #MeToo to Organize Female Workers," Seyfarth Shaw (blog), February 5, 2018, https://www.employerlaborrelations.com/2018/02/05/been-harassed-vote-yes-how-unions-are-leveraging-metoo-to-organize-female-workers/.

218   *And women organizers:* Seyfarth Shaw, "Been Harassed?"

218   *She concludes that:* Jane Mcalevey, "What #MeToo Can Teach the Labor Movement," *In These Times*, December 27, 2017, https://inthesetimes.com/article/me-too-workers-women-unions-sexual-harassment-labor-movement-lessons.

218   *In the immediate aftermath:* Equal Employment Opportunity Commission, "Sexual Harassment in Our Nation's Workplaces," report, April 2022, https://www.eeoc.gov/data/sexual-harassment-our-nations-workplaces.

218   *And the total amount recovered:* Equal Employment Opportunity Commission, "Vigorously Enforcing the Law to Combat Workplace Harassment," report, [no date], https://www.eeoc.gov/eeoc/newsroom/wysk/preventing-workplace-harassment.cfm (last visited September 26, 2019).

219   *The fact that the number:* Equal Employment Opportunity Commission, "Sexual Harassment in Our Nation's Workplaces."

219   *Sixty million workers:* Statement by Christine Owens, "NELP Welcomes Federal Legislation to Stop Forced Arbitration," National Employment Law Project, press release, February 28, 2019, https://www.nelp.org/news-releases/nelp-welcomes-federal-legislation-stop-forced-arbitration/.

219   *For more than fifteen years:* Taffy Brodesser-Akner, "The Company That Sells Love to America Had a Dark Secret," *New York Times*, April 23, 2019, https://www.nytimes.com/2019/04/23/magazine/kay-jewelry-sexual-harassment.html.

219   *The hearings were conducted:* Brodesser-Akner, "Company That Sells Love."

220   *California enacted:* Chris Marr, "States Expand Bans on Nondisclosure Pacts

Beyond #MeToo Claims," *Bloomberg*, July 7, 2022, https://news.bloomber glaw.com/daily-labor-report/states-expand-bans-on-nondisclosure -pacts-beyond-metoo-claims. *See also* Speak Out Act, Pub. L. No. 117-224 (Dec. 7, 2022).

220   *To be sure:* The Ending Forced Arbitration of Sexual Assault and Sexual Harassment Act of 2021 states that "no predispute arbitration agreement or predispute joint-action waiver shall be valid or enforceable with respect to" federal or state cases alleging sexual assault or sexual harassment. 9 U.S.C. § 402 (2022). The Act defines "predispute arbitration agreement" as "any agreement to arbitrate a dispute that had not yet arisen at the time of the making of the agreement." *See also* § 401.

220   *Congress enacted:* Sara Sirota and Austin Ahlman, "Biden Signs Law Banning Forced Arbitration—But Only Over Sexual Misconduct," *The Intercept*, March 3, 2022, 3:23 p.m., https://theintercept.com/2022/03/03/sexual-harass ment-forced-arbitration-fair-act/.

220   *Even tax law changed:* Sue Erwin Harper, "Under the Radar: Tax Rule Applies to Sexual Harassment Claim Settlements That Include a Nondisclosure Agreement," Nelson Mullins Riley & Scarborough law firm (blog), July 23, 2019, https://www.nelsonmullins.com/idea_exchange/blogs/the-hr -minute/non-disclosure/under-the-radar-tax-rule-applies-to-sexual-harass ment-claim-settlements-that-include-a-nondisclosure-agreement. ("[A]n employer may no longer simply write a check, have a sexual harassment claimant sign a nondisclosure agreement, and take a federal income tax deduction for the associated costs and attorneys' fees.")

220   *One intended consequence of #MeToo:* Anne Fisher, "Will #MeToo Spark Backlash Against Women in the Workplace?," *Fortune*, November 1, 2018, http://fortune.com/2018/11/01/me-too-backlash-women-google/ (reporting on a Society for Human Resource Management survey of 18,000 U.S. employees, across fifteen industries, in which 32% of executives stated that they have modified their behaviors to avoid risks of sexual harassment).

220   *One year after #MeToo:* "Working Relationships in the #MeToo Era: Key Findings," LeanIn.org, report, [no date], https://leanin.org/sexual-harass ment-backlash-survey-results (last visited September 22, 2019) (finding that "36% of men say they've avoided mentoring or socializing with a woman because they were nervous about how it would look").

220   *Over time, the movement:* Lesley Wexler et al., "#MeToo, Time's Up, and Theories of Justice," *University of Illinois Law Review* 2019: 45, 47, 54.

221   *McDonald's CEO, Stephen J. Easterbrook:* "McDonald's Fired CEO Returns $105 Million After Misconduct," NPR, December 16, 2021, 3:55 p.m. ET, https://www.npr.org/2021/12/16/1064943356/mcdonalds-ceo-settlement.

221   *Shareholders followed up: In re McDonald's Corporation Stockholder Derivative Litigation*, 290 A.3d 343 (Del. Ch. 2023) [hereafter, *McDonald's Litigation*].

221   *The shareholder action: McDonald's Litigation*, 289 A.3d at 352.

222   *In a precedent-setting: McDonald's Litigation*, 289 A.3d at 379–380.

222 *As the headline in a law firm:* "For the First Time, a Delaware Court Holds that Corporate Officers Have a Duty of Oversight," Covington Alert, March 6, 2023, https://perma.cc/G9E8-3UCQ.

222 *They filed more than:* American Civil Liberties Union, "Former McDonald's Workers Win $1.5 Million in Class Action Sexual Harassment Lawsuit," press release, April 4, 2022, 10:00 a.m., https://www.aclu.org/press-releases /former-mcdonalds-workers-win-15-million-class-action-sexual-harass ment-lawsuit.

222 *and in 2023:* Equal Employment Opportunity Commission, "McDonald's Franchise to Pay Nearly $2 Million to Settle EEOC Sexual Harassment Lawsuit," news report, January 6, 2023 (*EEOC v. AMTCR, Inc., et. al.*, No. 2:21-cv-01808, https://www.eeoc.gov/newsroom/mcdonalds-franchise-pay -nearly-2-million-settle-eeoc-sexual-harassment-lawsuit).

222 *The combination of the individual lawsuits:* American Civil Liberties Union, "Former McDonald's Workers."

222 *Instead, treating:* Jennifer Ann Drobac, "The Misappropriation, Embezzlement, Theft, and Waste of Corporate Human and Financial Assets: Sexual Harassment Reconceived," *ABA Journal of Labor & Employment Law* 36 (2022): 425–477, https://papers.ssrn.com/sol3/papers.cfm?abstract_id=4334547.

CONCLUSION: A Future Without WTA Excesses

224 *In the second leg:* Mark Egan et al., "When Harry Fired Sally: The Double Standard in Punishing Misconduct," National Bureau of Economic Research report, March 2017, https://www.nber.org/papers/w23242.

225 *Instead, it's his ability:* Securities and Exchange Commission, "Tesla Charged with and Resolves Securities Law Charge," press release, September 29, 2018, https://www.sec.gov/news/press-release/2018-226; Securities and Exchange Commission, "Elon Musk Charged with Securities Fraud for Misleading Tweets," press release, September 27, 2018, https://www.sec.gov/news /press-release/2018-219.

225 *as Mark Zuckerberg pointed out:* Hemant Taneja, "The Era of 'Move Fast and Break Things' Is Over," *Harvard Business Review*, January 22, 2019, https:// hbr.org/2019/01/the-era-of-move-fast-and-break-things-is-over.

225 *He fired top executives:* Kali Hays, "Elon Musk's Twitter Has Identified Thousands of Employees Who Will Be Laid Off, Representing About 50% of the Company's Workforce," *Business Insider*, November 2, 2022, https://www .businessinsider.com/elon-musks-twitter-identifies-thousands-who-will -be-laid-off-2022-11; Zoe Schiffer et al., "Extremely Hardcore," *The Verge*, January 17, 2023, 5:00 a.m. CST, https://www.theverge.com/23551060 /elon-musk-twitter-takeover-layoffs-workplace-salute-emoji.

226 *A 2022 lawsuit:* "Women Who Were Axed from Twitter After Elon Musk's Takeover File a Discrimination Lawsuit Against the Social Media Giant," *ABC*, December 8, 2022, https://www.abc.net.au/news/2022-12-09/twitter -lawsuit-elon-musk-discrimination/101755520.

226   *"Musk asked eighty"*: Hannah Getahun and Ern Snodgrass, "Elon Musk
       Asked Engineers to Boost His Tweets After Joe Biden's Super Bowl Posts
       Got More Engagement than His, Report Said," *Business Insider*, February
       14, 2023, 8:33 p.m. CST, https://www.businessinsider.com/twitter-boosted
       -elon-musk-tweets-over-biden-super-bowl-report-2023-2.

226   *In May 2023:* Daysia Tolentino and David Ingram, "Musk's Response to an
       Anti-Trans Video Sparks 24 Hours of Chaos at Twitter," *NBC News*, June
       2, 2023, 5:05 p.m. CDT, https://www.nbcnews.com/tech/social-media/musk
       -elon-twitter-ella-irwin-trans-video-what-is-a-woman-stream-rcna87429.

226   *As Paul Krugman observed*: Paul Krugman, "Why Do the Rich Have So Much
       Power," *New York Times*, July 5, 2020, https://www.nytimes.com/2020/07/01
       /opinion/sunday/inequality-america-paul-krugman.html.

226   *Today, we have a system:* Jacob Hacker and Paul Pierson, *Winner-Take-All
       Politics: How Washington Made the Rich Richer—and Turned Its Back on the
       Middle Class* (New York: Simon & Schuster, 2011).

227   *Meanwhile, economic winners: See, e.g.,* Shane Goldmacher, "How David
       Koch and His Brother Shaped American Politics," *New York Times*, Au-
       gust 23, 2019, https://www.nytimes.com/2019/08/23/us/politics/david-koch
       -republican-politics.html.

227   *over a thirty-year period: See, e.g.,* Tom C. W. Lin, "The Corporate Gover-
       nance of Iconic Executives," *Notre Dame Law Review* 87 (2011): 351, 370;
       David G. Savage, "Supreme Court Makes It *Harder* to Prosecute Officials
       for Taking Bribes," *Los Angeles Times*, June 27, 2016, https://www.latimes
       .com/nation/la-na-court-mcdonnell-corruption-20160627-snap-story.html
       [https://perma.cc/G3ZY-XFCX].

227   *No case is more symbolic: Dobbs v. Jackson Women's Health Organization*, 142
       S. Ct. 2228 (2022).

228   *Once conservative jurists:* The process illustrates everything we have described
       in winner-take-all systems: (1) Senate Leader Mitch McConnell first denying
       President Obama's candidate for the Supreme Court a hearing because it was
       supposedly too close to the election, then ramming through President Trump's
       candidate within an even closer window to the election; Russell Wheeler, "Mc-
       Connell's Fabricated History to Justify a 2020 Supreme Court Vote," Brook-
       ings Institution (blog), September 24, 2020, https://www.brookings.edu/blog
       /fixgov/2020/09/24/mcconnells-fabricated-history-to-justify-a-2020-su
       preme-court-vote/. (2) Confirming Justice Brett Kavanaugh on the basis of
       a bare 50 votes in the Senate while blocking a rigorous investigation into the
       allegations against him of sexual misconduct, and tolerating the rampant lies
       during the confirmation process from prospective justices, including Kava-
       naugh, that they would uphold long established precedents like *Roe*; Jackie
       Calmes, "New Reporting Details How FBI Limited Investigation of Kavanaugh
       Allegations," *Los Angeles Times*, September 16, 2019, 4:00 a.m. PT, https://
       www.latimes.com/politics/story/2019-09-16/fbi-investigation-brett-kava
       naugh-confirmation.

228   *Many states:* Women denied abortions, even when they face serious medical

risks, have sued and made national and international news. *See, e.g.,* Kate Zernike, "Five Women Sue Texas over the State's Abortion Ban," *New York Times,* March 6, 2023, https://www.nytimes.com/2023/03/06/us/texas-abor tion-ban-suit.html.

228 *And a number of states:* "Tracking the States Where Abortion Is Now Banned," *New York Times,* June 5, 2023, 11:00 a.m. ET, https://www.nytimes.com /interactive/2022/us/abortion-laws-roe-v-wade.html.

228 *The decision mobilized:* Alice Miranda Ollstein and Megan Messerly, "A Pre-dicted 'Red Wave' Crashed into Wall of Abortion Rights Support on Tues-day," *Politico,* November 9, 2022, 4:04 p,m., EST, https://www.politico.com /news/2022/11/09/abortion-votes-2022-election-results-00065983.

228 *A study of ten states:* Francesca Paris and Nate Cohn, "After Roe's End, Women Surged in Signing Up to Vote in Some States," *New York Times,* August 25, 2022, https://www.nytimes.com/interactive/2022/08/25/upshot /female-voters-dobbs.html.

228 *In August of 2022:* Dylan Lysen et al., "Voters in Kansas Decide to Keep Abortion Legal in the State, Rejecting an Amendment," NPR, August 3, 2022, 2:18 a.m., ET, https://www.npr.org/sections/2022-live-primary-elec tion-race-results/2022/08/02/1115317596/kansas-voters-abortion-legal-reject -constitutional-amendment.

228 *"[a]bortion transcends party lines":* Caroline Kitchener et al., "Abortion Rights Advocates Score Major Midterm Victories Across U.S.," *Washington Post,* November 9, 2022, https://www.washingtonpost.com/politics/2022/11/09 /abortion-midterms-kentucky-michigan/.

228 *In 2023, Wisconsin, voters flipped:* Reid J. Epstein, "Liberal Wins Wiscon-sin Court Race in Victory for Abortion Rights Backers," *New York Times,* April 4, 2023, https://www.nytimes.com/2023/04/04/us/politics/wisconsin -supreme-court-protasiewicz.html.

228 *Black and Latina women:* Kelly Dittmar, "Revisiting the Gender Gap in 2020: Race and the Gender Gap," Center for American Women and Politics (blog), October 8, 2020, https://cawp.rutgers.edu/blog/revisiting-gender-gap-2020 -race-and-gender-gap.

229 *Still, the gap:* Dittmar, "Revisiting the Gender Gap"; "Gender Gap: Voting Choices in Presidential Elections," Center for American Women and Politics (blog), [no date], https://cawp.rutgers.edu/gender-gap-voting-choices-pres idential-elections (last visited November 17, 2023).

229 *Women are more likely:* Indeed, today's political scientists find that the par-tisan divide on issues is much bigger than the political differences between men and women. For example, on an issue such as "Should federal spend-ing on aid to the poor be increased, decreased, or kept the same?," there was a 5-point gap between men and women, but "the gap between Demo-cratic and Republican men was 52.5 points, and between Democratic and Republican women it was 50.3 points." Women are more likely than men to support Democrats, but men and women who support stereotypically femi-nine values have substantially different preferences from those who support

masculine values. Thomas B. Edsall, "How You Feel About Gender Roles Can Tell Us How You'll Vote," *New York Times*, July 20, 2022, https://www .nytimes.com/2022/07/20/opinion/gender-gap-partisanship-politics.html.

229   *Today, voters' views:* Edsall, "How You Feel About Gender Roles." (Quote here is from an email citing the chapter by Nicholas Winter, in *Community Wealth Building and the Reconstruction of American Democracy*, ed. Melody Barnes, Corey Walker, and Thad Williamson [Cheltenham, UK: Edward Elgar, 2020].

229   *Beliefs about gender roles: See generally* Elizabeth B. Harnad and Liza Fuentes, "Abortion Out of Reach: The Exacerbation of Wealth Disparities After Dobbs v. Jackson Women's Health Organization," Guttmacher Institute, report, January 2023, https://www.guttmacher.org/article/2023/01 /abortion-out-reach-exacerbation-wealth-disparities-after-dobbs-v-jack son-womens. *See also* Mindy E. Bergman et al., "The Dobbs Decision and the Future of Occupational Health in the US," *Occupational Health Science* 7, no. 1 (February 2023): 1. ("Access to abortion care has a profound impact on women's ability to participate in the workforce.")

229   *Those who favor:* Edsall, "How You Feel About Gender Roles." *See also* Vanessa Brown Calder, "Why Conservatives Shouldn't Support Federal Paid Parental Leave," CATO Institute, commentary, December 14, 2018, https://www .cato.org/commentary/why-conservatives-shouldnt-support-federal-paid -parental-leave#; Chabeli Carrazana, "Democrats and Republicans Agree Child Care Is in Crisis. Why Can't They Get a Bill Passed?," *The 19 News*, February 14, 2023, https:/19thnews.org/2023/02/child-care-crisis-demo crats-republicans-legislation; Chabeli Carrazana, "Do Child Care Solutions Stand a Chance in Congress?" *EdSurge*, November 28, 2023, https://www .edsurge.com/news/2023-11-28-do-child-care-solutions-stand-a-chance -in-congress. *See also* Naomi Cahn and June Carbone, "Supporting Families in a Post-Dobbs World: Politics and the Winner-Take-All-Economy," *North Carolina Law Review* 101 (2023): 1549.

229   *evidence is mounting:* Risa Kaufman et al., "Global Impacts of Dobbs v. Jackson Women's Health Organization and Abortion Regression in the United States," *Sexual and Reproductive Health Matters* 30 (2022): 2135574, https:// www.ncbi.nlm.nih.gov/pmc/articles/PMC9673802/. ("The devastating impact of this decision falls hardest on people in the United States who already face discriminatory obstacles to health care, particularly Black, Indigenous, and other people of colour, people with disabilities, people in rural areas, young people, undocumented people, and people who are low-income or living in poverty.")

229   *This is likely to further:* Margot Sanger-Katz et al., "Who Gets Abortions in America?," *New York Times*, December 14, 2021, https://www.nytimes.com /interactive/2021/12/14/upshot/who-gets-abortions-in-america.html.

229   *Women generally are more:* "Gender Gap Public Opinion," Center for American Women and Politics, report, [no date], https://cawp.rutgers.edu/gender -gap-public-opinion (last visited June 20, 2022).

230 *Yet, a determined:* Hannah Hartig, "About Six-in-Ten Americans Say Abortion Should Be Legal in All or Most Cases," Pew Research Center, report, June 13, 2022, https://www.pewresearch.org/fact-tank/2022/06/13/about-six -in-ten-americans-say-abortion-should-be-legal-in-all-or-most-cases-2/.

230 *We are heartened:* Alisha Haridasani Gupta, "VC Funding Start-Ups Founded by Women Is Surging," *New York Times,* November 2, 2021, https:// www.nytimes.com/2021/11/02/business/dealbook/female-founded-star tups-vc-funding.html; Arti Raman, "Look Past Today's Metrics to Celebrate the Growth of Female Founders," *Forbes,* December 13, 2022, 6:00 a.m. ET, https://www.forbes.com/sites/forbestechcouncil/2022/12/13/look-past-to days-metrics-to-celebrate-the-growth-of-female-founders/.

230 *We found encouraging the greater recruitment:* Anna King, "The Changing Face of Finance and How to Get More Women to Top Roles," *Forbes,* February 6, 2023, 7:30 a.m., ET, https://www.forbes.com/sites/forbesfinance council/2023/02/06/the-changing-face-of-finance-and-how-to-get-more -women-to-top-roles/?sh=73feabd52ee0 ("women hold 52% of entry-level positions in financial services").

230 *and we cheered:* Andrea Sue Kramer and Alton B. Harris, "Getting Beyond Bias in the Legal Profession," *American Bar Association,* December 5, 2023, https://www.americanbar.org/groups/law_practice/resources/law-prac tice-today/2023-november/getting-beyond-bias-in-the-legal-profession/.

230 *And we were stunned:* Derek Saul, "SEC Charges Former McDonald's CEO Easterbrook for Lying About Extent of Workplace Misconduct," *Forbes,* January 9, 2023, 11:45 a.m., ET, https://www.forbes.com/sites/dereksaul /2023/01/09/sec-charges-former-mcdonalds-ceo-easterbrook-for-lying -about-extent-of-workplace-misconduct/?sh=376feb2195d5.

231 *In 2021, Nasdaq adopted:* Nasdaq, "Nasdaq's Board Diversity Rule: What Nasdaq-Listed Companies Should Know," report, August 17, 2020, 1, https://listingcenter.nasdaq.com/assets/Board%20Diversity%20Disclo sure%20Five%20Things.pdf. *See also* Securities and Exchange Commission, "Comments on the Nasdaq Rulemaking; Notice of Filing of Proposed Rule Change to Adopt Listing Rules Related to Board Diversity," commentary, [no date], https://www.sec.gov/comments/sr-nasdaq-2020-081/srnas daq2020081.htm.

231 *The Nasdaq Diversity Rule:* Securities and Exchange Commission, "Self-Regulatory Organizations; The Nasdaq Stock Market LLC; Notice of Filing of Proposed Rule Change to Adopt Listing Rules Related to Board Diversity," report, December 4, 2020, https://www.sec.gov/rules/sro/nasdaq/2020 /34-90574.pdf. *See also* Afra Afsharipour, "Investment Bankers and Inclusive Corporate Leadership," *Seattle University Law Review* 46 (2023): 1, 7–9 (describing investor pressure for greater diversity); Naomi Cahn, June Carbone, and Nancy Levit, "The Instrumental Case for Corporate Diversity," *Minnesota Journal of Law & Inequality* 40 (2022): 140–141 (observing that "[i]n short, Nasdaq reported that firms with greater diversity were less likely to be engaged in the practices most closely associated with short-termism

and competitive pay: earnings management, accounting manipulation and fraud, and the suborning of internal controls.")

231 *Debra Katz is a lawyer:* Katz Banks Kumin, attorneys, website, https://katzbanks.com/attorneys-and-staff/debra-katz (last visited January 23, 2023).

231 *She has also represented one:* Daniel Politi, "Sexual Misconduct Allegation Led to CNN Firing Chris Cuomo, Attorney Claims," *Slate*, December 5, 2021, 5:08 p.m., https://slate.com/news-and-politics/2021/12/sexual-misconduct-allegation-chris-cuomo-cnn.html.

231 *And she has represented:* "Debra S. Katz's Notable Case Successes," Katz Banks Kumin website, [no date], https://katzbanks.com/firm/successful-case-resolutions/debra-katz (last visited May 25, 2023).

232 *"Having power can make an individual feel":* Debra S. Katz and Alexandria Smith, "The Line Between a Demanding Workplace and a Demeaning One," *Bloomberg Law*, November 3, 2021, 3:01 a.m., https://www.bloomberglaw.com/bloomberglawnews/securities-law/X21MI11C000000?bna_news_filter=securities-law#jcite.

233 *Katz believes:* Luke Mullins, "Meet DC's Leading #MeToo Lawyer: Attorney Debra Katz Is a Key Advocate in the Fight against Sexual Harassment," *Washingtonian*, June 14, 2018, https://www.washingtonian.com/2018/06/14/meet-debra-katz-dc-leading-metoo-lawyer/.

233 *"That's a sea change,":* Mullins, "Meet DC's Leading #MeToo Lawyer."

233 *Carroll "took on":* Emily Peck, "#MeToo's Legacy Lives on in the E. Jean Carroll Verdict," *Axios*, May 10, 2023, https://www.axios.com/2023/05/10/trump-carroll-trial-metoo-legacy.

233 *netting a multimillion:* Benjamin Weiser et al., "Donald Trump Sexually Abused and Defamed E. Jean Carroll, Jury Finds," *New York Times*, May 9, 2023, https://www.nytimes.com/2023/05/09/nyregion/trump-carroll-trial-sexual-abuse-defamation.html.

233 *Katz faced anti-Semitic:* "How Debra Katz Became One of the Nation's Top #MeToo Lawyers," *Jewish Journal*, May 22, 2019, https://jewishjournal.com/online/299017/how-debra-katz-became-one-of-the-nations-top-metoo-lawyers/.

235 *Indeed, public reports indicate:* Ben Protess et al., "Trump Administration Spares Corporate Wrongdoers Billions in Penalties," *New York Times*, November 3, 2018, https://www.nytimes.com/2018/11/03/us/trump-sec-doj-corporate-penalties.html.

235 *Revelation of their:* Michael Perino, *The Hellhound of Wall Street: How Ferdinand Pecora's Investigation of the Great Crash Forever Changed American Finance* (New York: Penguin Random House, 2010), 147.

236 *Even the head of General Motors:* Jonathan Berr, "Thousands of Workers Take Buyouts at GM—Good News, Sort Of," *Yahoo! News*, March 26, 2009, https://news.yahoo.com/2009-03-26-whats-good-for-gm-is-good-for-america.html (stating the head of General Motors said what was good for the company was good for the U.S. at a time "when GE's dominance of the automotive world was unquestioned").

236   *While some economists today:* Paul Krugman, "The Economics of Soaking the Rich: What does Alexandria Ocasio-Cortez Know About Tax Policy? A Lot," opinion, *New York Times*, January 5, 2019, https://www.nytimes.com /2019/01/05/opinion/alexandria-ocasio-cortez-tax-policy-dance.html.

236   *The average CEO of the 1950s:* Diana Hembree, "CEO Pay Skyrockets to 361 Times That of the Average Worker," *Forbes*, May 22, 2018, 4:28 p.m., https:// www.forbes.com/sites/dianahembree/2018/05/22/ceo-pay-skyrockets-to -361-times-that-of-the-average-worker/?sh=f32ab36776dd; Josh Bivens and Jori Kandra, "CEO Pay Has Skyrocketed 1,460% Since 1978," Economic Policy Institute, report, October 4, 2022, https://www.epi.org/publication/ceo -pay-in-2021/. ("In 2021, the ratio of CEO-to-typical-worker compensation was 399-to-1 under the realized measure of CEO pay.")

236   *Limiting the wealth: See* Nick Hanauer and David M. Rolf, "The Top 1% of Americans Have Taken $50 Trillion from the Bottom 90%—and That's Made the U.S. Less Secure," *Time* magazine, September 14, 2020, https:// time.com/5888024/50-trillion-income-inequality-america/ (citing Carter C. Price and Kathryn A. Edwards, "Trends in Income From 1975 to 2018," Rand Corporation, working paper, 2020, https://www.rand.org/pubs/work ing_papers/WRA516-1.html).

237   *Yet the single biggest:* Elise Gould and Katherine deCourcy, "Low-wage Workers Have Seen Historically Fast Real Wage Growth in the Pandemic Business Cycle," Economic Policy Institute, report, March 23, 2023, https:// www.epi.org/publication/swa-wages-2022/. *See also* "The State of Women in the Labor Market in 2023," Center for American Progress, fact sheet, February 6, 2023, https://www.americanprogress.org/article/fact-sheet-the-state -of-women-in-the-labor-market-in-2023/#.

237   *And if companies have to:* Eric Garton, "The Case for Investing More in People," *Harvard Business Review*, September 4, 2017, https://hbr.org/2017/09 /the-case-for-investing-more-in-people; Pedro S. Martins, "The Economic Implications of Training for Firm Performance," Global Labor Organization, paper, February 2022, file://C:/Users/levitn/Downloads/GLO-DP-1046.pdf; Ian Thomas, "Raising Wages Isn't Enough to Attract and Keep Workers, Experts Say," *CNBC*, September 1, 2021, 9:23 a.m. ET, https://www.cnbc .com/2021/09/01/raising-wages-isnt-enough-to-attract-and-keep-workers -experts-say-.html.

237   *If companies were then forced:* John Van Reenan et al., "Improving Productivity Through Better Management Practices," *LSE Business Review* (blog), May 20, 2022, https://blogs.lse.ac.uk/businessreview/2022/05/20/improving -productivity-through-better-management-practices/.

237   *Today, diverse groups:* David Rock and Heidi Grant, "Why Diverse Teams Are Better," *Harvard Business Review*, November 4, 2016, https://hbr.org /2016/11/why-diverse-teams-are-smarter.

238   *It can also lead to:* The Federal Glass Ceiling Commission examined data about workforces among the top 500 Standard and Poor companies that were diverse along race and gender dimensions: "The researchers found that

the stock performance . . . of the 100 companies making the strongest efforts toward equal employment opportunity was 2.5 times greater than that of 100 companies that rated lowest in EEO effort." Kenneth L. Karst, "Equal Citizenship at Ground Level: The Consequences of Nonstate Action," *Duke Law Journal* 54 (2005): 1591, 1615n102.

238   *Increasing wages has ripple effects:* Lily Roberts and Ben Olinsky, "Raising the Minimum Wage Would Boost an Economic Recovery—and Reduce Taxpayer Subsidization of Low-Wage Work," *Center for American Progress*, January 27, 2021, https://www.americanprogress.org/article/raising-minimum-wage -boost-economic-recovery-reduce-taxpayer-subsidization-low-wage-work/.

238   *While some economists argue:* Compare Roberts and Olinsky, "Raising the Minimum Wage," and Scott Nueman, "States That Raised Minimum Wage See Faster Job Growth, Report Says," NPR, July 19, 2014, 12:25 p.m., https:// www.npr.org/sections/thetwo-way/2014/07/19/332879409/states-that -raised-minimum-wage-see-faster-job-growth-report-says, with Doruk Cengiz et al., "The Effect of Minimum Wages on Low-Wage Jobs," *Quarterly Journal of Economics* 134 (2019): 1405, https://academic.oup.com/qje/article /134/3/1405/5484905. ("Moreover, we find that the level of the minimum wages that we study—which range between 37% and 59% of the median wage—have yet to reach a point where the job losses become sizable.")

238   *As the famed Stockton:* Nueman, "States That Raised"; Annie Lowrey, "Stockton's Basic-Income Experiment Pays Off," *Atlantic*, March. 3, 2021, https:// www.theatlantic.com/ideas/archive/2021/03/stocktons-basic-income-ex periment-pays-off/618174/.

238   *Participants spent their money:* Lowrey, "Stockton's Basic Income."

239   *Providing economic security resulted in:* Jason DeParle, "Cash Aid to Poor Mothers Increases Brain Activity in Babies, Study Finds," *New York Times*, January 24, 2022, https://www.nytimes.com/2022/01/24/us/politics/child -tax-credit-brain-function.html?referringSource=articleShare.

239   *More than thirty:* "Guaranteed Income Pilots Dashboard," Stanford Basic Income Lab, report, [no date], https://basicincome.stanford.edu/research /guaranteed-income-dashboard/ (last visited September 12, 2023).

239   *Investment in children:* Maxine Eichner, *The Free Market Family: How the Market Crushed the American Dream (and How It Can Be Restored)* (New York: Oxford University Press, 2019), 202–203.

239   *The child tax credit:* Kalee Burns, "Expansions to Child Tax Credit Contributed to 46% Decline in Child Poverty Since 2020," U.S. Census Bureau, news release, September 13, 2022, https://www.census.gov/library /stories /2022/09/record-drop-in-child-poverty.html; Catherine Rampell, "We Let Child Poverty Soar Last Year," Washington Post, opinion, September 12, 2023, https://www.washingtonpost.com/opinions/2023/09/12/biden -child-tax-credit-poverty-doubled/. See also Greg Iacurci, "Child Tax Credit Lifted 3 Million Kids from Poverty in July," CNBC, August 25, 2021, 3:23 p.m., https://www.cnbc.com/2021/08/25/child-tax-credit-lifted-3-million -kids-from-poverty-in-july.html.

239 *After the child tax credits:* Rampell, "We Let Child Poverty."

240 *If just the child tax credit:* "Record Rise in Poverty Highlights Importance of Child Tax Credit," Center on Budget and Policy Priorities, press release, September 12, 2023, https://www.cbpp.org/press/statements/record-rise-in-poverty-highlights-importance-of-child-tax-credit-health-coverage.

240 *Numerous other countries:* Steven Jessen-Howard, "Fighting Child Poverty in the United States: The Universal Child Benefit," *Georgetown Journal on Poverty Law and Policy* 30 (2023): 589, 602. ("It is thus unsurprising that the U.S. has the thirty-fourth highest child poverty rate out of thirty-nine OECD countries, sandwiched in the rankings between Bulgaria and Chile.")

240 *Parents spend the money:* See, e.g., Lauren E. Jones et al., "Child Cash Benefits and Family Expenditures: Evidence from the National Child Benefit," *Canadian Journal of Economics* 52 (2019): 1433, https://onlinelibrary.wiley.com/doi/full/10.1111/caje.12409; Jake Schild et al., "Effects of the Expanded Child Tax Credit on Household Spending: Estimates Based on U.S. Consumer Expenditure Survey Data," National Bureau of Economic Research, working paper, June 2023, 14, https://www.nber.org/system/files/working_papers/w31412/w31412.pdf.

240 *Economists calculate:* Irwin Garfinkel et al., "The Benefits and Costs of a U.S. Child Allowance," National Bureau of Economic Research, working paper, March 2022, https://www.nber.org/system/files/working_papers/w29854/w29854.pdf.

240 *In addition, giving cash transfers:* Jason DeParle, "Cash Aid to Poor Mothers Increases Brain Activity in Babies, Study Finds," *New York Times*, January 24, 2022, https://www.nytimes.com/2022/01/24/us/politics/child-tax-credit-brain-function.html.

240 *Investing in prekindergarten:* Eichner, "Free Market Family," 205; Andres S. Bustamente et al., "High-quality Early Child Care and Education: The Gift That Lasts a Lifetime," Brookings Institute (blog), November 4, 2021, https://www.brookings.edu/blog/education-plus-development/2021/11/04/high-quality-early-child-care-and-education-the-gift-that-lasts-a-lifetime/.

240 *better educational outcomes:* Bustamente et al., "High-Quality Early Child Care"; Beth Meloy et al., "Untangling the Evidence on Preschool Effectiveness: Insights for Policymakers, Learning Policy Institute, report, January 31, 2019, https://learningpolicyinstitute.org/product/untangling-evidence-preschool-effectiveness-report (providing a meta-analysis of studies).

240 *Offering high-quality preschool:* Bryce Covert, "How Universal Free Preschool in DC Helped Bring Moms Back to Work," *Vox*, September 26, 2018, 9:50 a.m., https://www.vox.com/identities/2018/9/26/17902864/preschool-benefits-working-mothers-parents.

Index

About the Authors

Naomi Cahn is the Justice Anthony M. Kennedy Distinguished Professor of Law, Nancy L. Buc '69 Research Professor in Democracy and Equity, and director of the Family Law Center at the University of Virginia School of Law.

June Carbone is the Robina Chair in Law, Science, and Technology at University of Minnesota Law School.

Nancy Levit is an associate dean for faculty and the Curators' and Edward D. Ellison Professor of Law at the University of Missouri–Kansas City School of Law.